D0793882

The Road from Runnymede
*Magna Carta and
Constitutionalism in America*

VIRGINIA LEGAL STUDIES

Sponsored and supported by the School of
Law of the University of Virginia for the
publication of meritorious original works
and reprints in law and related fields.

The Road from Runnymede

Magna Carta and

Constitutionalism in America

A. E. Dick Howard
Professor of Law, University of Virginia

The University Press of Virginia   *Charlottesville*

The University Press of Virginia

Copyright © 1968 by the Rector and Visitors
of the University of Virginia

First published 1968

Library of Congress Catalog Card Number: 68–15941
Printed in the United States of America

Lines from NOW WE ARE SIX by A. A.
Milne are reprinted by permission of the
publishers, E. P. Dutton & Co., Inc. Copyright,
1927, by E. P. Dutton & Co., Inc. Renewal,
©, 1955 by A. A. Milne. Acknowledgment
is also made to Methuen & Company, Ltd.,
London, for permission to reprint these
lines from NOW WE ARE SIX by A. A.
Milne.
The lines from Alice Duer Miller's THE
WHITE CLIFFS (Copyright, 1940, by Alice
Duer Miller) are reprinted by permission
of the publishers, Coward-McCann, Inc.,
New York.

For Lois and Jennifer

King John was not a good man —
   He had his little ways.
And sometimes no one spoke to him
   For days and days and days.

—A. A. Milne

Foreword

A FEW months after Britain and the United States had fought side by side to the successful conclusion of the Second World War, Winston Churchill gave a speech to the General Assembly of Virginia, the oldest representative assembly in the New World. In that speech he recalled the way in which the Founders of the American Republic had drawn upon the "title deeds of freedom": trial by jury, habeas corpus, Magna Carta, the English common law. In so saying, Churchill, who himself truly belonged to both England and America, was reminding his Virginia listeners of the fact that the story of English liberties, beginning in some respects with Magna Carta, is the story of American liberties.

The Great Charter of English Liberties was given by King John at Runnymede in June 1215. Ten of its provisions still remain on the statute books of England. Bishop Stubbs perhaps exaggerated when he said that "the whole of the constitutional history of England is little more than a commentary on Magna Carta," but the part which the Charter has played in inspiring English-speaking peoples in defense of their liberties is undeniable. Seventeenth-century parliamentarians in England and eighteenth-century colonists in America both looked to the Charter in their respective fights.

Magna Carta is in many ways the spiritual and legal ancestor of what we today call the "rule of law." This ideal is summed up most precisely in the most famous provision of the Charter, chapter 39: "No free man shall be taken, imprisoned, disseised, outlawed, banished, or in any way destroyed, nor will We proceed against or prosecute him, except by the lawful judgment of his peers and by the law of the land." Chapter 39 has an echo in the Fifth Amendment to the Constitution of the United States: "No person shall be . . . deprived of life, liberty, or property, without due process of law. . . ."

Magna Carta, as forced upon King John, embodied the principle, in Maitland's words, "that the king is and shall be below the law." Moreover, the Charter specified much of what that law was. Confirmed and reissued by John's successor, Henry III, Magna Carta passed eventually onto the statute books of the realm. As the most comprehensive written statement of law which England yet possessed, Magna Carta was cited in the courts of law, actions were founded upon it, and decisions were based upon it. Through this process in the courts, the Charter ceased to be a political program for the barons of England and became absorbed into the common law.

In the fourteenth century particularly, the terms of the Charter came to have widened meaning and application, the phrase *per legem terrae,* for example, coming to mean "by due process of law." If Magna Carta in its origins was a charter of barons' liberties, it was well on its way to becoming a charter of the Englishman's liberties. Not only was the Charter repeatedly used in the law courts; it was confirmed over and over by the Crown—nearly fifty times in the fourteenth and fifteenth centuries—so that Magna Carta took on a significance and symbolism clearly not enjoyed by the ordinary statute.

The great commentators, notably Bracton and Fortescue, paid great homage to the concept of the rule of law, Bracton laying it down that the King is under God and the law. It was the effort of the Stuart kings to proclaim themselves as being above the law which led to the struggles between Parliament and the Crown in the seventeenth century. In some ways the issues which had been joined between barons and king in the thirteenth century were rejoined by parliamentarians and king in the seventeenth. The common lawyers rested their case against the Crown on their notion of an English constitution of immemorial antiquity, binding on king and subject alike. In this ancient constitution they claimed to discover the rights and privileges of Parliament.

The cornerstone of this ancient constitution was Magna Carta. "The Great Charter of the Liberties of England" was, as Sir Edward Coke described it, "for the most part declaratory of the fundamental lawes of England." It took a civil war and a bloodless revolution to settle the larger question of which should be supreme, the rule of law or the will of a ruler. In 1689, with the revolution settlement, the rule of law became firmly established in England. The revival of Magna Carta had played a central part in the events leading to that outcome.

Events in England had echoes in America. During the turbulent years of Stuart and Commonwealth rule in England, English colonies were being planted in the New World, and English emigrants to America carried with them English laws. Magna Carta went, too, and was woven into the fabric of the laws of the colonies. Lawbooks arrived from England, and Americans in the eighteenth century began to study in numbers at the Inns of Court. By the eve of the American Revolution a great body of legal and political ideals had been drawn from the colonists' English heritage and shaped into a force to be turned against what the colonists saw as abuses on the part of the mother country. As Alice Duer Miller put it in "The White Cliffs," written during the Second World War:

> Never more English than when they dared to be
>   Rebels against her—that stern intractable sense
> Of that which no man can stomach and still be free,
>   Writing, "when, in the course of human events . . ."
> Writing it out so all the world could see
>   Whence came the powers of all just governments,
> The tree of Liberty grew and changed and spread,
>   But the seed was English.[1]

[1] Alice Duer Miller, *The White Cliffs* (New York: Coward-McCann, 1940), p. 70.

And so it was when the Americans wrote their own constitution. Like Magna Carta, the Constitution of the United States limits the power of government to deal with persons and their property to actions that comport with due process of law. And like Magna Carta, the Constitution stands as one of the great written embodiments of the rule of law.

From the time of the American Revolution to the present day, Great Britain and the United States have shared the ideal of the rule of law. In both countries Magna Carta has played its part. It was fitting that during the Second World War the United States should have received the Lincoln Cathedral copy of the Great Charter and that fifteen million Americans should have made a pilgrimage to see it.

Today, as in the reign of King John, as in the days of the Stuarts, as in the time of the American Revolution, Magna Carta serves as a constant reminder of the dangers of arbitrary government. It remains an example of those countries, Britain and the United States foremost among them, in whose constitutional development it has been so influential. It serves, too, as a signpost to the nations of the world, a reminder of what can be when rulers and ruled are able to live under a rule of law.

Accordingly, I have no hesitation in recommending this book by Professor Howard to all who have the liberty of the subject or the citizen at heart. It is a scholarly contribution to the study of American constitutional law and of the lasting significance of Magna Carta in the world today.

PARKER OF WADDINGTON
Lord Chief Justice of England

Royal Courts of Justice
London, January 1968

Contents

Illustrations

Cover and frontispiece: Colophon from title page of *Journal of the Continental Congress* (1774). Colophon is supported by Magna Carta. (Courtesy, Library of Congress.)

The Road from Runnymede
Magna Carta and
Constitutionalism in America

Prologue

Tнis is a book about an idea—more precisely, about a document and the ideas associated with it. The story of Magna Carta is the story of a number of concepts central to Anglo-American jurisprudence, most notably due process of law. But the story is more than one of specific concepts associated with Magna Carta; it is also an account of the growth of an attitude that government is or ought to be, at its base, constitutional government. This attitude was not without competitors; the notion of rule by magisterial discretion and the idea of subjective rule according to one's idea of natural law have been, and still are, among them. That competitors can be allies is also part of the story, as the history of the love-hate relationship between constitutionalism and natural law may suggest.

The proper place which should be given to the force of ideas in the study of American history and institutions is a major intellectual battle. At times the worship of texts like Magna Carta and the American Constitution has approached a cult. At other times we are treated to debunking and demythologizing expeditions which would have us understand that it is economics, or self-interest, or class interest, or some other earthier consideration which, after all, explains the origin of documents which our forefathers mistakenly assumed to be statements of idealism.

Magna Carta has seen its fortunes fluctuate from near-idolatry to debunking to revival. In 1895 F. W. Maitland wrote that "this document becomes and rightly becomes a sacred text, the nearest approach to an irrepealable 'fundamental statute' that England has ever had."[1] Such were the sentiments oft voiced in the nineteenth century. But the debunkers were close at hand. In 1904 Edward Jenks wrote a piece entitled "The Myth of Magna Carta" in which he treated the Charter as essentially the selfish program of some barons who could not have been less interested in the liberties of other men.[2] Morris R. Cohen leaped into the fray in 1933 when he wrote that "very few" of the provisions of Magna Carta could have been of any use to the "great mass" of people; Cohen found justice in Jenks's conclusion that the Charter was a "reactionary document and a great nuisance and stumbling block to the generation which came after it."[3] And more recently Edmond Cahn dismissed Magna Carta as "a parasol but no umbrella, good on sunny days when few needed it, but useless in a storm."[4]

Recent scholarship, especially the thorough and balanced study by J. C. Holt,[5] has brought a better sense of perspective about Magna Carta. If we are now informed enough not to read twentieth-century ideas into a thirteenth-century document, we can at the same time appreciate the remarkable forces in English and American history which carry in them some of the imprint of Magna Carta. As Professor Holt has put it:

> The history of Magna Carta is the history not only of a document but also of an argument. The history of the document is a history of repeated reinterpretation. But the history of the argument is a history of a continuous element of political thinking. In this light there is no inherent reason why an assertion of law originally conceived in aristocratic interests should not be applied on a wider scale. . . . Approached as political theory it [Magna Carta] sought to establish the rights

[1] F. Pollock and F. W. Maitland, *History of English Law* (Cambridge, 1898), I, 173.

[2] 4 *Independent Review* 260 (1904).

[3] "The Conservative Lawyer's Legend of Magna Carta," in Cohen, *Law and the Social Order* (New York, 1933), p. 19, at pp. 20–21.

[4] *The Great Rights* (New York, 1963), p. 4.

[5] *Magna Carta* (Cambridge, 1965).

of the subjects against authority and maintained the principle that authority was subject to law. If the matter is left in broad terms of sovereign authority on the one hand and the subject's rights on the other, this was the legal issue at stake in the fight against John, against Charles I and in the resistance of the American colonists to George III.[6]

Thus we can study Magna Carta not simply as the political program of thirteenth-century barons, but also as a milestone in the evolution of constitutional concepts—concepts which clearly are a long way today from what they were in 1215 but which owe something to the agreement hammered out at Runnymede.

We live in an age increasingly familiar with behavioral studies, with economic determinism, and with other approaches of a generation which has read Darwin and Marx and Freud. But, as with Magna Carta, we are learning that the significance of legal documents, especially statements of constitutional doctrine, is not exhausted when one has studied the behavior patterns, or economic interests, or social class of those who gave the document birth. The determinism of Charles A. Beard's *An Economic Interpretation of the Constitution of the United States*[7] is counterbalanced by Forrest McDonald's 1958 study in which he is bold enough to put to Beard the blunt reply: "economic interpretation of the Constitution does not work."[8]

Likewise we have found that the giants of American Legal Realism—men like Jerome Frank—for all their enormous contribution to the science of the law, told but part of the story when they tried to reduce the study of the law essentially to what courts *did,* rather than what they *said.*[9] Their realism was an effective antidote to the notion of the law as a "brooding omnipresence" in the sky, but we have suffered since from an overdose of realism. Happily, as the behaviorists attempt to

[6] *Ibid.,* p. 16.   [7] (New York, 1913).

[8] *We the People: The Economic Origins of the Constitution* (Chicago, 1958), p. ix. See Daniel J. Boorstin, "Paperbacks: History and the Constitution," *New York Times Book Review,* Nov. 28, 1965.

[9] See, e.g., Frank, *Law and the Modern Mind* (New York, 1930).

reduce the jurisprudence of the Supreme Court to scalograms and game theories and to predict the Court's opinions "independently of what the Court said by way of reasoning in its decisions," [10] others step in to remind us that rationality does play a part in judicial decisions and that the judicial process does, after all, have an integrity and a legalistic quality not capable of expression in behavioristic terms.[11] Benjamin Cardozo well expressed this tradition when he said that the judge, even when most free to innovate, "is not to innovate at pleasure. He is not a knight-errant roaming at will in pursuit of his own ideal of beauty or of goodness." [12]

In the study of American history, as in the study of law, there is a renewed interest in the significance of ideas, in the perhaps rationalistic assumption that doctrines and ideals can move men as readily as can their appetites. Gordon S. Wood, in his stimulating piece on "Rhetoric and Reality in the American Revolution," has observed that it seems at the present day that "the thought of the Revolutionaries, rather than their social and economic interests, has become the major focus of research and analysis." [13] Some of the most important works of recent years bear out Wood's statement. Bernard Bailyn, for example, has said that there is "undeniable evidence of the seriousness with which colonial and revolutionary leaders took ideas. . . ." [14] On another occasion Bailyn has characterized the American Revolution as an "ideological, constitutional,

[10] Fred Kort, "Predicting Supreme Court Decisions Mathematically: A Quantitative Analysis of the 'Right to Counsel' Cases," 51 *American Political Science Review* 1 (1957). See, among other articles, Glendon A. Schubert, "The Study of Judicial Decision-Making as an Aspect of Political Behavior," 52 *ibid.* 1007 (1958); S. Sidney Ulmer, "Supreme Court Behavior and Civil Rights," 13 *Western Political Quarterly* 288 (1960).

[11] See Wallace Mendelson, "The Neo-Behavioral Approach to the Judicial Process: A Critique," 57 *Am. Pol. Sci. Rev.* 593 (1963). Contrary to some observers, I have taken the position that the jurisprudence of Mr. Justice Black is faithful to this concept of the judicial process. A. E. Dick Howard, "Mr. Justice Black: The Negro Protest Movement and the Rule of Law," 53 *Va. L. Rev.* 1030 (1967).

[12] *The Nature of the Judicial Process* (New Haven, 1921), p. 141.

[13] 23 *William and Mary Quarterly* (3d ser.) 3 (1966). See also Richard B. Morris, *The American Revolution Reconsidered* (New York, 1967), p. 35.

[14] "Political Experience and Enlightenment Ideas in Eighteenth-Century America," 67 *American Historical Review* 339, 343 (1962).

political struggle and not primarily a controversy between social groups." [15]

For our present purposes it is significant to note that along with the primacy of ideas during the revolutionary period went consistency of ideas. Whereas Carl Becker in 1922 wrote that "step by step, from 1764 to 1776, the colonists modified their theory to suit their needs," [16] Edmund S. Morgan, writing thirty years after Becker, has stressed the consistency of the colonists' statements of constitutional doctrine. The significance of the Stamp Act crisis, Morgan submits, "lies in the emergence, not of leaders and methods and organizations, but of well-defined constitutional principles. The resolutions of the colonial and intercolonial assemblies in 1765 laid down the line on which the Americans stood until they cut their connection with England." [17] Similarly, Jack P. Greene, in an article on "The Flight from Determinism," cites the consistency of the American position on most questions as "an indication of American devotion to principle." The Revolution, he concludes, was more "political, legalistic, and constitutional than social or economic." [18]

Such statements point the way for the present study. Whether the object of our attention be the complaints of eighteenth-century colonists or the decisions of the modern Supreme Court, we can, without feeling sadly out of step with the times, once again be interested in ideas as ideas. Behaviorists, economic determinists, and others have given us new insights into American history and institutions. We would be foolish to suppose that we can discard the lessons of psychology, to name but one modern discipline. Yet we can, without apology, study the resolutions of colonial assemblies, the opinions of American

[15] *The Ideological Origins of the American Revolution* (Cambridge, Mass., 1967), p. vi.

[16] *The Declaration of Independence* (New York, 1922), p. 133.

[17] Edmund S. Morgan and Helen M. Morgan, *The Stamp Act Crisis: Prologue to Revolution* (Chapel Hill, N.C., 1953), p. 295.

[18] 61 *South Atlantic Quarterly* 235, 257 (1962). The tradition of legalism has been prominent in American history. That this has been so may be better understood when one considers that "even a cursory examination of the lives and activities of the most influential public figures in American history immediately reveals a marked preponderance of lawyers, completely out of proportion to their actual number." Anton-Hermann Chroust, *The Rise of the Legal Profession in America* (Norman, Okla., 1965), I, viii [hereinafter Chroust, *Legal Profession*].

courts, and other legal and constitutional documents on the assumption that, at least a good part of the time, those who wrote the documents both knew what they were saying and meant it.

This book, therefore, is not a study of the behavior of Americans—save in the very real sense that ideas themselves can take on an autonomy and thus become one of the factors determining the behavior of men. In this sense determinism and idealism meet. The burden of the present book is to present one theme, but an important one, in American history. The aim here is to write a kind of biography of a document and the ideas it set loose—the document being Magna Carta, and the most significant idea being constitutionalism.

Before Englishmen Came to America

Before speaking of Magna Carta in America, a few words should be said about Magna Carta in England. Since this book is primarily concerned with what happened from the time of the first settlements in English America, only the barest highlights of the Charter's history to the seventeenth century can be given here. It is essential, however, to say that but for what Magna Carta had become in England by the end of the seventeenth century it could have played no important part in later constitutional developments in the New World.

Magna Carta was thrust upon an unwilling king by rebellious barons. The grievances which fed the unrest were manifold—the heavy financial burdens imposed upon the realm by King John's unsuccessful wars on the Continent, abuses perpetrated upon all ranks of men by royal officials, the spoliation of church property, John's harsh use of debts and other devices to secure political discipline among his subjects. Paradoxically, John hastened the crisis by paying more attention to his royal duties than had his predecessor, Richard the Lion-hearted, who had spent most of his reign fighting Saladin in the Holy Land or Philip Augustus in France. John, by contrast, gave his personal stamp to the administration of affairs in England. But his serious flaws of character, his military failures (he earned the hardly flattering nickname of "Softsword"), and his ability to provoke enmity among barons, churchmen, and commoner folk alike brought him in 1215 to Runnymede, where he gave his assent to Magna Carta.[19]

The barons were rebelling against the accumulation and abuse of royal power. But this is not to say that they were seeking to remake the fabric of feudal society. Quite the contrary, they sought to restore customary limits on the power of the Crown, limits which drew a distinction, already understood in medieval political theory, between rule according to law and rule by the imposition of arbitrary will. It would be unrealistic to suppose that the barons had no selfish interests at stake in the quarrel, that they were disinterested protectors of the common good. Yet because the ills occasioned by the rule of King John touched so many elements of English society, the leaders in the opposition to him were able to formulate a kind of constitutional program with implications beyond simply the barons' own interests.

The face of the document suggests the Charter's generality. Chapter 60, for example, says that all the customs and liberties which the King promised to observe on behalf of his subjects were in turn to be secured by these subjects to their inferiors in the feudal hierarchy. And there is every reason to think that a number of the Charter's specific provisions—for example, those concerning scutages, debts, amercements, the place of trials, the frequency of assizes, granting of writs, and others—would have been of widespread interest to Englishmen of humbler status than the barons.[20]

[19] For accounts of the events leading up to the issuance of Magna Carta, see J. C. Holt, *The Making of Magna Carta* (Charlottesville, Va., 1965); Holt, *Magna Carta;* William F. Swindler, *Magna Carta: Legend and Legacy* (Indianapolis, 1965) [hereinafter Swindler, *Magna Carta*].

[20] Until recently the classic account of the provisions of Magna Carta has been William Sharp McKechnie's *Magna Carta: A Commentary on the Great Charter of King John* (2d ed.; Glasgow, 1914) [hereinafter McKechnie, *Magna Carta*]. In 1965 there appeared J. C. Holt's *Magna Carta,* a notable study which promises to become the modern-day classic on the subject. For a briefer treatment of the Charter's provisions, see A. E. Dick Howard, *Magna Carta: Text and Commentary* (Charlottesville, Va., 1964). The full text of the Charter in English can be found in all these sources, as well as in Professor Swindler's book.

Runnymede was only the beginning. The Charter had to survive, among other things, the implacable opposition of John, who was successful in having Pope Innocent III declare the Charter to be null and void as having been agreed to by the King only under duress. Everything that had been gained in the Charter might have seemed lost, but John died in 1216. His successor, Henry III, was only nine years old, and his guardians seized upon a reissuance of the Charter (less some of the provisions of 1215) as a means of rallying support to the young King. In 1217 there was another reissue, and in 1225 yet a third. These reiterations of the terms of Magna Carta, and the public readings of the Charter which were ordered on these occasions, served to secure the document and its chief provisions in the minds of Englishmen of all classes. Already Magna Carta was becoming to many an expression of the Englishman's security against the excessives of arbitrary government. The Charter was as yet but a hint of what it would become in the hands of seventeenth-century polemicists like Sir Edward Coke, but the germ was there all the same. In 1297, in the reign of Edward I, Magna Carta was put on the Statute Books of England, where nine of the provisions of the 1225 charter (twelve of the provisions of the 1215 charter), as modified, remain today.

Magna Carta survived because of its potential for growth. After the Charter had, in 1225, taken its more or less permanent shape, the process of interpretation and evolution so familiar to the law began.[21] In the fourteenth century, for example, Acts of Parliament interpreted, and in doing so enlarged, the meaning of some of the most important of the Charter's provisions—including those relating to "judgment of peers" (which, unlike its meaning in 1215, now came to mean trial by jury) and "law of the land" (which now became "due process of law").[22] Repeatedly through the Middle Ages Magna Carta

[21] For the history of the Charter in the centuries after 1215, see Doris M. Stenton, *After Runnymede: Magna Carta in the Middle Ages* (Charlottesville, Va., 1965); Faith Thompson, *Magna Carta: Its Role in the Making of the English Constitution, 1300–1629* (Minneapolis, 1948) [hereinafter Thompson, *Magna Carta*].

[22] See Holt, *Magna Carta*, p. 9.

was reconfirmed. Already it was taking on the character (implicit in the circumstances of its origin) of fundamental law. The Charter came to be a standard by which the legality of new measures could be tested; one of the more famous instances of this attitude to the Charter was the statute of 42 Edward III which said that the Great Charter should be "holden and kept in all Points; and if any Statute be made to the contrary that shall be holden for none." [23]

During the Middle Ages the Charter was absorbed into the law of England. But, while "actions on the Great Charter" were common in the law reports, Magna Carta was not in Tudor times surrounded by the drama which had been its lot in the thirteenth century. The most dramatic days lay ahead: the revival of Magna Carta by the opponents of the Stuart kings in the seventeenth century.[24] With the accession to the throne of James I in 1603, grievances began to accumulate— grievances over purveyances (the King's right to requisition supplies and horses at a fixed price), import duties, monopolies, the jurisdiction of ecclesiastical courts. Under Charles I, James' successor, the antagonisms grew, especially with Charles' imposition of a forced loan on his subjects to support his wars abroad (echoes of the days of King John) and his arbitrary imprisonment of a number of subjects who refused to pay the loan. Parliamentarians invoked Magna Carta against the Crown. Sir Benjamin Rudyerd declared: "For my own part, I shall be very glad to see that good, old decrepit Law of Magna Charta which hath been so long kept in and lain bed-rid as it were; I shall be glad I say to see it walk abroad again, with new Vigour and Lustre. . . ." [25]

The political turmoil of the seventeenth century brought civil war, a king's execution, the Cromwellian regime, restoration, and a bloodless revolution. It also brought three new "liberty documents" to stand along with Magna Carta as guar-

[23] See Thompson, *Magna Carta*, p. 16; Holt, *Magna Carta*, p. 12.
[24] For this period, see Maurice Ashley, *Magna Carta in the Seventeenth Century* (Charlottesville, Va., 1965).
[25] Cobbett, *Parliamentary History of England* (London, 1807), II, 335–36.

antees of the liberties of the subject—the Petition of Right (1628), the Habeas Corpus Act (1679), and the Bill of Rights (1689). These documents established a number of rights not found as such in Magna Carta—rights such as the right to petition for redress of grievances, free speech in Parliament, and the outlawing of cruel and unusual punishments.

It is significant that at the same time the rights which through centuries of interpretation (including the commentaries of Sir Edward Coke) had come to be associated with Magna Carta received widespread assent, notably the principle of no taxation without the consent of Parliament and that of freedom from imprisonment or trial without due process of law. These rights of Magna Carta remained the foundation. When the Stuarts withheld them, Parliament looked to the Great Charter. Significantly, when Parliament breached those rights, as many claimed after the defeat of Charles I, Magna Carta was invoked against Parliament. Arrested for slandering the Speaker of the House of Commons, the Leveller leader John Lilburne ("Free-born John") claimed the privileges of the Charter; committed to prison, he wrote *England's Birth-Right Justified,* in which he looked to Magna Carta as the charter of English liberties.[26] Whether in the hands of parliamentarians like Sir Edward Coke or Leveller pamphleteers like John Lilburne, nothing was more basic to the constitutional discourse of England than Magna Carta. And as this discourse took place, English colonies were being planted in America, colonies which could not help but be aware of the principles being aired and acted upon in the mother country.[27]

Magna Carta in America

F INALLY, something should be said about the arrangement of this book. The reader will find that in the first chapter Magna Carta is mentioned only occasionally. The aim of this chapter is

[26] See Pauline Gregg, *Free-born John* (London, 1961), pp. 120–22; Ashley, *Magna Carta in the Seventeenth Century,* pp. 38–40.

[27] For the role of Coke in the constitutional developments in Stuart England, see pp. 119–21 *infra.*

to set the stage for what follows, to delve into the charters of the early English colonies in America, as well as into events in seventeenth-century Virginia, to understand something of the process whereby the "rights of Englishmen"—of which Magna Carta was the chief embodiment—and the laws of England first came to America.[28]

In the next three chapters (II, III, and IV) Magna Carta figures more specifically. In the chapter on the New England colonies, there appears one of the leitmotivs of constitutional history in this country (especially as concerns Magna Carta), the interplay between government according to known laws and discretionary government—a quarrel not without overtones of the time of King John and that of Charles I. In Chapter III one finds that people living in the proprietary colonies were as ready to invoke the principles of Magna Carta against their proprietary governments as were those living in any other colony. And in Chapter IV there appears in the London trial of William Penn and his later constitutional efforts in America one of the most notable and palpable links between lessons taught in the Old World and those learned in the New.

In Chapters V and VI several general topics are explored with the object of throwing additional light on the meaning of the colonial uses of Magna Carta: the arguments over the extension of English laws to America, the influence of the "Whig" view of history, and the state of legal learning in the colonies—what kind of lawbooks the colonists read (with special reference to Coke) and what manner of legal education lawyers received (notably at the Inns of Court).

With Chapter VII there begins more of a narrative—the events leading up to the break with England and the significance of Magna Carta in the colonial case. Here the reader should be on reasonably familiar ground: James Otis and the writs of assistance, the Stamp Act, the Boston Port Bill, the Continental Congress, Independence. No effort is made in these chapters to plough new ground in the telling of the story of the

---

[28] See Appendix A, *infra,* for relevant chapters of Magna Carta.

American Revolution or the interpretation of what that event signified. Rather the attempt is to set Magna Carta, as understood and used by the colonists, into the pattern of colonial thought and action. In addition to tracing the uses of the Charter in such documents as the resolutions against the Stamp Act and the resolves of the Continental Congress, special attention is paid to one of the great recurring themes of American constitutionalism, before and after the Revolution: the reliance on natural law as opposed to (or as allied with) more legalistic traditions—the dialogue, in a sense, between philosopher and lawyer.

In Chapters XI and XII we speak of the drafting of constitutions, state and federal. Hitherto, the account has been largely one of veneration for Magna Carta; now the attitudes become more mixed. To what extent Americans drafting their own constitutions still looked to Magna Carta, and to what extent they now felt they must look beyond it, is the burden of these chapters.

At this point, the narrative in a sense broadens. We remain concerned with Magna Carta, but the reader will sense that its influence is now less direct. It appears in the context of debates over the adoption of British statutes and over the merits of the English common law as a system adapted to the needs of the United States. It appears in the development of legal education and legal commentaries in this country. That these chapters should speak in a more general way of Magna Carta is an indication of the fortunes of the Charter. In the eighteenth century, the Charter was at the very core of colonial arguments and documents. It was invoked in the way lawyers would have used it, as precedent and authority. After Independence, its force was at one step removed. Americans now had their own fundamental laws—state and federal constitutions; Magna Carta, for all its unquestioned influence, could not be what it had been in the eighteenth century.

But to demonstrate that the force of Magna Carta was not spent, the last several chapters, save the conclusion, deal with the great jurisprudential contributions of the Charter to American constitutional law—justice freely available to all on a

basis of equality and, the contribution most obviously associated with Magna Carta, the concept of due process of law.
With due process of law the story reaches its broadest, and
Magna Carta becomes an ancestor on the family tree of American constitutionalism—an ancestor who might be surprised to
see what his progeny have become.

Chapter I

Colonial Charters and

First Settlement

The "Liberties of Englishmen"

HAVE you heard the news of Virginia?" As eyes in England turned toward the New World, men of adventure sought their fortunes in chartered companies. The spirit of the age was breathed into the language of these charters; that of Virginia of 1606, for example, was granted by the Crown to Sir Thomas Gates and others styled as "adventurers." These men were expected to carry the Christian religion to the savages living "in darkenesse and miserable ignorance," as well as to do a bit of "traffique and bargaining" among them.[1]

Charters like that of Virginia were in many ways very practical documents. The enterprises they represented were expected to make money; hence the charter of 1606 took care to speak of rights to "landes, woods, soile, groundes, havens, ports, rivers, mines, mineralls, marshes, waters, fishinges, commodities and hereditamentes." The Crown, of course, took care that it would share in the anticipated wealth of the new lands; of the "Gold, Silver, and Copper" the adventurers should find, "the fifth Part" of the gold and silver and "the fifteenth Part" of the

---

[1] *Three Charters of the Virginia Company of London*, ed. Samuel M. Bemiss (Williamsburg, Va., 1957), pp. 1, 2, 6. See also Francis Newton Thorpe, ed., *Federal and State Constitutions, Colonial Charters, and Other Organic Laws* (Washington, D.C., 1909), VII, 3784, 3786 [hereinafter cited as Thorpe].

copper were to be yielded up to the Crown.[2] In 1632, when Charles I granted the Charter of Maryland to Cecil Calvert, a nominal annual rent of "Two Indian Arrows of these Parts" was to be delivered on Tuesday of Easter Week, but the King also prudently claimed one-fifth of all gold and silver ore.[3]

Government, too, was provided for. The charter of 1606 ordained that "each of the said Colonies shall have a Council, which shall govern and order all Matters and Causes" and that such councils should have governmental powers as enumerated in the charter. Then followed this significant language:

Alsoe wee doe, for us, our heires and successors, declare by theise presentes that all and everie the parsons being our subjects which shall dwell and inhabit within everie or anie of the said severall Colonies and plantacions and everie of theire children which shall happen to be borne within the limitts and precincts of the said severall Colonies and plantacions shall have and enjoy all liberties, franchises and immunites within anie of our other dominions to all intents and purposes as if they had been abiding and borne within this our realme of Englande or anie other of our saide dominions.[4]

The "liberties, franchises, and immunities" of Englishmen: historic words that would roll and echo down through the

---

[2] *Three Charters of the Virginia Company,* p. 2; Thorpe, VII, 3786. By the time of the chartering of the Virginia Company, charters to companies of Englishmen trading abroad were well known. As early as 1391 Richard II had empowered English merchants in Prussia to elect a governor, who should have certain powers of government. *Select Charters of Trading Companies,* ed. Cecil T. Carr (Selden Society Pubs., vol. xxviii; London, 1913), p. xi. Of special interest are the letters patent of 1578 to Sir Humfrey Gilbert and the charter of 1584 to Sir Walter Raleigh, both of which contained features later appearing in the Virginia Company's charters. *Ibid.,* p. lxxxiii; the texts of these two documents appear in Thorpe, I, 49, 53. Precedents for some of the provisions of the Virginia charters appear also in the 1600 charter of the East India Company. See *Select Statutes and Other Constitutional Documents Illustrative of the Reigns of Elizabeth and James I,* ed. G. W. Prothero (4th ed.; Oxford, 1913), p. 448. Sir Thomas Smythe, the first Governor of the East India Company, was influential in the chartering of the Virginia Company and was for a time that company's Treasurer. Howard Robinson, *The Development of the British Empire* (rev. ed.; Boston, 1936), p. 62.

[3] Thorpe, III, 1679.

[4] *Three Charters of the Virginia Company,* p. 9; Thorpe, VII, 3788. For like provisions in the letters patent of 1578 to Sir Humfrey Gilbert and the charter of 1584 to Sir Walter Raleigh, see Thorpe, I, 51, 55.

decades of colonial history. They would appear, in one form or another, again and again—in the charters of the other American colonies, in the statute law of colonial assemblies, in petitions against tyrannical royal governors, in the declarations of the Stamp Act Congress, in the pamphlets and writings of John Adams and John Dickinson and scores of others, in the resolutions of the Continental Congress, and finally in the Declaration of Independence.

That Americans, in invoking their rights within the British Empire and ultimately in asserting a claim to be free of it, should have, throughout and with consistency, looked to the "liberties, franchises, and immunities" of Englishmen invites us to consider the character and significance of these early charters. The colonial charters were, as much as anything else, contracts—contracts between the Crown and the "adventurers." They stated, like many a private commercial contract, the rights and duties of the parties—what territory the adventurers could exploit, the manner in which land should be held, what profits were to go to the King, what tariffs might be levied upon traders and vessels, even the inscription on the colony's seal.

But the charters were more than a contract; they were an advertisement, an inducement to those who might want to settle in the New World. Stephen Vincent Benét, in *Western Star*,[5] captured the spirit of the spell that news of the new lands across the Atlantic cast over men of all walks of life in England—coopers and cordwainers, glovers and mercers, soldiers of fortune and younger sons.[6] It was such men as these, men eager for the opportunity which life in England seemed to deny them, men moved by piety or greed or some other motive, who found appeal in inducements to pull up stakes and cross the ocean. In an age which lacked travel posters, the colonial charter could, at least to a man of some education, serve a like purpose. If that was so, then the insertion of language guaranteeing to colonists the same rights as they would have enjoyed in England was not

[5] (New York, 1943).

[6] Among the "adventurers" listed in the Virginia Charter of 1609 were 56 of the livery companies of London, including the Companies of Mercers, Cordwaynes, and Coopers. *Three Charters of the Virginia Company*, pp. 40–41; Thorpe, VII, 3794–95.

a meaningless gesture. Whatever such language meant to the drafters of colonial charters, it meant something to the colonists who relied on it, as King and Parliament were to discover in the eighteenth century.

One evidence that the charters were meant as inducements to settlement is found in the provisions for landholding. The Virginia Charter of 1606, for instance, stated that land in Virginia should be held of the King "as of our Manor at *East-Greenwich, in the County of Kent,* in free and common Soccage only, and not in Capite." This language, which falls so strangely on modern ears, was a step away from the complex and frequently burdensome incidents of feudal land tenures. In the Middle Ages, and even for some time afterward, land was not deemed to be owned outright but was held of the Crown or some other lord. This system of property carried with it a variety of feudal tenures and services, including such things as knight service, wardship, and aids (to ransom the lord's person, knight his eldest son, and marry his eldest daughter). Relics like these obviously had no allure for the prospective emigrant to the New World. Socage tenures carried the lightest burdens, especially as compared with holding by knight service; indeed, use of a more burdensome tenure than socage might well have discouraged colonization.[7] Hence the colonial charters of the eighteenth century typically provided for landholding in free and common socage, as of East Greenwich (or "as of our Castle of Windsor, in our County of Berks," which had the same effect),[8] and American landholding developed free of the intri-

---

[7] See J. Hurstfield, "The Greenwich Tenures of the Reign of Edward VI," 65 *L.Q. Rev.* 72 (1949). Among the least burdensome services must have been the requirement in the Charter of Maine (1664) that James, Duke of York, pay his brother, Charles II, "forty Beaver skins" as annual rental. Thorpe, III, 1638.

[8] The reference to East Greenwich was the most common. For examples of the reference to Windsor, see the charters of Maryland (1632) and Pennsylvania (1681). Thorpe, III, 1679, V, 3037. The charter of Georgia (1732) provided for landholding as of "our honour of Hampton-court, in our county of Middlesex." *Ibid.,* II, 771.

The charters of proprietary colonies were in one respect *more* feudal than contemporary English land law. They had a provision that the statute of *Quia Emptores* (1290), which forbade the practice of "subinfeudation" of land-holdings (creating a hierarchy in which each tenant in turn had a tenant), should not apply in those colonies. See *ibid.,* III, 1684–85 (Maryland, 1632); V, 2750 (Carolina, 1663); V, 3043 (Pennsylvania, 1681).

cacies of feudal relationships (most of which even in England were abolished before the end of the seventeenth century).

Edward Channing has suggested that the Virginia Charter of 1606 "is a landmark in the history of territorial boundaries and of the constitutional rights of English colonists in America." The charter is notable for its territorial claims; it is "even more memorable for its constitutional declarations." [9] The guarantee of the liberties, franchises, and immunities that the colonists would have had in England was in effect a declaration that the settler in an English colony was to enjoy a status not accorded hitherto to colonists of Spain or France or other countries. A Spaniard who settled in a colony of Spain, for example, did not enjoy the benefits of the laws and privileges he might have had in his homeland. But, according to the charter of 1606, the English colonist was to carry with him the protections and privileges of the common law which were his in England.

The Virginia Charter of 1606 takes on even greater significance when one considers that the text of the charter may well have been scrutinized by the sometime English Attorney General Edward Coke and by the then Solicitor General, Sir John Dodderidge, and had the Great Seal affixed by Lord Chancellor Ellesmere, three of the greatest English lawyers of their time.[10] The guarantee of the rights of Englishmen would have had special significance to Coke, who was to become the great seventeenth-century expositor of the common law. It was Coke who in 1610 decided *Dr. Bonham's Case,* in which he said that an Act of Parliament "against common right and reason" would be voided by the common law,[11] and who later wrote the famous *Institutes* on the laws of England, in which he said that any statute passed by Parliament contrary to Magna Carta, the cornerstone of the rights of Englishmen, should be "holden for none." [12] And it was Coke who was to have such dramatic

[9] Edward Channing, *A History of the United States* (New York, 1932), I, 157, 161.

[10] See Charles M. Andrews, *The Colonial Period of American History* (New Haven, 1934–37), I, 85 [hereinafter Andrews, *Colonial Period*].

[11] 8 Coke Rep. 113b, 118a, 77 Eng. Rep. 646, 652 (1610).

[12] *Second Institute* (London, 1797), Proeme.

influence on the course of American legal and constitutional thought, an influence which will be developed in the pages which follow.[13]

The pattern established with the charter supporting the first permanent settlement, that at Jamestown in 1607, was followed in later charters. The guarantee in the 1606 charter of the Englishman's "liberties, franchises, and immunities" (or like phraseology) became standard language in the charters which were granted for later colonies. The Charter of Massachusetts Bay of 1629, for example, declared that all who should settle in that colony should "have and enjoy all liberties and Immunities of free and naturall Subiects . . . to all Intents, Constructions, and Purposes whatsoever, as yf they and everie of them were borne within the Realme of England." [14] Similar language appears in the charters of colonies that followed, including Maryland (1632), Maine (1639), Connecticut (1662), Carolina (1663), Rhode Island (1663), Carolina (1665), and Massachusetts Bay (1691).[15] Indeed it is instructive to note that the last American charter, that of Georgia in 1732, has almost word for word the language of the Massachusetts Bay Charter granted over a century before: that the colonists should "have and enjoy all liberties, franchises and immunities of free denizens and natural born subjects . . . to all intents and purposes, as if abiding and born within this our kingdom of Great-Britain. . . ." [16]

At first, life in the new settlements was harsh. The winter of 1609–10, aptly called the "starving time," reduced the population of Jamestown from five hundred to about sixty. But the Virginia settlement survived, and others, beginning with the landing at Plymouth in 1620, followed. As these tiny and struggling societies secured a hold on the American continent, laws,

---

[13] See especially pp. 118–24, *infra.*

[14] Thorpe, III, 1856–57. A similar provision had already appeared in the Charter of New England of 1620. *Ibid.,* III, 1839.

[15] *Ibid.,* III, 1681 (Maryland, 1632); III, 1635 (Maine, 1639); III, 533 (Connecticut, 1662); V, 2747 (Carolina, 1663); VI, 3220 (Rhode Island, 1663); V, 2765 (Carolina, 1665); III, 1880–81 (Massachusetts Bay, 1691).

[16] *Ibid.,* II, 773.

simple at first, more complex with time, became a necessity. As one would expect, the settlers looked to their homeland for a model: for English colonies, English laws.

The language of the charters encouraged this natural tendency to model the colonies' laws after those of England. The typical recurrence in the charter of the guarantee of the "rights of Englishmen" is but one instance. Another standard provision, carefully inserted in charter after charter, required that laws and ordinances passed in the colonies be agreeable to the laws of England. Typical was the language of the second Charter of Virginia, that of 1609, which, in giving governmental authority to the Treasurer and Company of Adventurers and Planters of the City of London, required that all "statuts, ordinannces and proceedinges as neere as convenientlie maie be, be agreable to the lawes, statutes, government and pollicie of this oure realme of England." [17] A similar proviso may be found in other colonial charters.[18] The element of flexibility for adaptation to local conditions was more explicit in the Rhode Island Charter of 1663, which said that the duty to conform to the laws of England should take into account the "nature and constitutione of the place and people" in the colony.[19]

Later charters tended to include a device for ensuring that colonial laws should be in accord with those of England: the transmission of enacted statutes to England for approval or disapproval. For example, the commission of Sir Edmund Andros for the Dominion of New England (1688),[20] in giving

[17] *Three Charters of the Virginia Company*, p. 52; Thorpe, VII, 3801. For similar provisions in the letters patent of 1578 of Sir Humfrey Gilbert and the charter of 1584 to Sir Walter Raleigh, see Thorpe, I, 51, 55; for such a provision in the charter of the East India Company (1600), see *Select Statutes and Other Constitutional Documents Illustrative of the Reigns of Elizabeth and James I*, p. 451.

[18] *Three Charters of the Virginia Company*, pp. 86–87, and Thorpe, VII, 3806 (Virginia, 1611–12); Thorpe, III, 1833 (New England, 1620); III, 1853 (Massachusetts Bay, 1629); III, 1680 (Maryland, 1632); III, 1628 (Maine, 1639); I, 533 (Connecticut, 1662); V, 2746 (Carolina, 1663); VI, 3215 (Rhode Island, 1663); III, 1638, 1639 (Maine, 1664); V, 2764 (Carolina, 1665); III, 1642 (Maine, 1674); V, 3038 (Pennsylvania, 1681); III, 1882 (Massachusetts Bay, 1691).

[19] Thorpe, VI, 3215.

[20] Andros was appointed Captain General and Governor of the Dominion of New England (Massachusetts Bay, New Plymouth, New Hampshire, Maine, and the Narragansett Country), to which the King had annexed Rhode Island, Connecticut, New York, and East and West Jersey.

Andros "full power and authority," with the advice and consent of the Council, to make laws for the territory, had the usual language requiring that such laws be agreeable to the laws and statutes of England. But the commission also required that all laws "of what nature or duration soever" be transmitted within three months of their making to England for the Crown's "allowance or disapprobation of them." For safety's sake, the requirement was added that duplicates of all such laws be sent "by the next conveyance." [21] Such a provision was, of course, primarily for the benefit of the King. As the Charter of Pennsylvania of 1681 put it, transcripts of the colony's laws had to be transmitted to the Privy Council for review so that the colonists might not "through inadvertencie or designe depart from that Faith and due allegiance" which they owed the Crown and so that any laws "inconsistent with the Sovereigntey or lawful Prerogative" of the Crown could be declared void.[22]

The concern that colonial laws accord with the English model was not limited to substantive law. The commission to Andros in 1688 ordained the Council of the territory to be a

constant and setled Court of Record . . . in all causes as well civill as Criminall . . . and therein after due and orderly proceeding and deliberate hearing of both sides, to give judgement and to award execution . . . so as always that the forms of proceedings in such cases and the judgment thereupon to be given, be as consonant and agreeable to the lawes and statutes of this our realm of England as the present state and condition of our subjects inhabiting within our said Territory and Dominion and the circumstances of the place will admit.[23]

Sometimes a charter, such as that of Connecticut of 1662, would provide that punishments in criminal cases should be "according to the Course of other Corporations within this our Kingdom of *England*." [24] The concern for procedure found in these charter provisions reflects the theme, often recurring in Anglo-

---

[21] Thorpe, III, 1864.

[22] *Ibid.*, V, 3039. The effectiveness of such provisions for review, as the King's advisors were to observe in the eighteenth century, might be questioned, in light of the Pennsylvania charter's allowing five years for the transmission of colonial laws.

[23] *Ibid.*, III, 1865.   [24] *Ibid.*, I, 534.

American jurisprudence, that (to quote Mr. Justice Frankfurter) "the history of liberty has largely been the history of observance of procedural safeguards." [25]

Two other ties between the laws of the colonies and those of the mother country were provided in a few charters: appeals to England of certain judgments of colonial courts and the form of oaths. An example of the former is the Charter of Massachusetts Bay of 1691, which ordained that in actions in which the amount in controversy exceeded £300 parties who should "not rest satisfied" with the judgment of the provincial court might appeal within fourteen days to the Privy Council in England, provided security be given.[26] An example of a provision for the form of oath is the Connecticut Charter of 1662, requiring that oaths should be administered to those holding public office, "such Oaths not being contrary to the Laws and Statutes of this Our Realm of *England.*" [27]

So much for the textual language of the colonies' charters. But to set out charter provisions, as has been done here, is hardly conclusive. While charter provisions like those requiring Privy Council approval of colonial laws were doubtless meant to be used, a cynic might well wonder how much reliance to place upon some generality about the "liberties, franchises, and immunities" of Englishmen. History is replete with examples of parchment guarantees breached at the first opportunity, of noble promises made with great ceremony only to be dishonored. Magna Carta, after all, might have perished soon after its proclamation—and would have, if King John had had his way.[28] Those who read or heard of the charter provisions quoted above, especially as the seventeenth century progressed, might well have wondered if the Stuart kings meant to keep their word when they promised settlers the "liberties, franchises, and immunities" of Englishmen. The Englishman of the time,

---

[25] McNabb v. United States, 318 U.S. 332, 347 (1943). In a similar vein, Arthur L. Goodhart has commented that "a fair trial is the essence of justice." *"Law of the Land"* (Charlottesville, Va., 1966), p. 62.

[26] Thorpe, III, 1881–82.   [27] *Ibid.,* I, 534.

[28] See J. C. Holt, *Magna Carta* (Cambridge, 1965), pp. 242–68; A. E. Dick Howard, *Magna Carta: Text and Commentary* (Charlottesville, Va., 1964), pp. 23–24.

after all, had the spectacle, unknown to England since the time of King John himself, of the monarch's being brought to book in a formal document, the Petition of Right of 1628, for his sins against those very rights of Englishmen. And, in a clash of ruler and ruled which excelled even the civil war between John and his barons, England in 1649 was treated to the even more remarkable scene of a King's being taken to the scaffold.

Small wonder if an Englishman-turned-settler, or perhaps the modern-day reader, might ask what, if anything, those words in charters meant to those who lived under them. It remains, then, to turn the pages of seventeenth- and eighteenth-century American history, to re-create some of the legal quarrels and constitutional crises of the time, and to place in perspective the empirical evidence of colonial America's reliance on, and invocation of, the traditions and guarantees of the English Constitution, and especially, since it is the focus of our attention, Magna Carta.

First Settlement: the Virginia Colony

At JAMESTOWN there stands a plaque erected by the Virginia State Bar Association in 1959 to memorialize the advent of the common law in Virginia. The inscription reads:

THE COMMON LAW

Here the Common Law of England was established on this continent with the arrival of the first settlers on May 13, 1607. The first charter granted by James I to the Virginia Company in 1606 declared that the inhabitants of the colony "shall have and enjoy all liberties, franchises and immunities . . . as if they had been abiding and borne within this our realme of Englande. . . ." Since Magna Carta the Common Law has been the cornerstone of individual liberties, even as against the Crown. Summarized later in the Bill of Rights its principles have inspired the development of our system of freedom under law, which is at once our dearest possession and proudest achievement.

Statements such as this have been the subject of a good deal of academic scrutiny, much of it not very helpful. Charles M.

Andrews, for example, in his *Colonial Period of American History*, takes earlier writers to task (quite rightly) for finding in a phrase like "liberties, franchises, and immunities" something akin to "universal human rights." Yet Andrews would have us understand that the words "have nothing to do with civil liberty, self-government, or democracy." They were, he says, strictly "legal, tenurial, and financial" in their application.[29] But if (to take only one example) one of the "liberties" of Englishmen was—as Coke maintained and the colonists argued repeatedly—the right to be taxed only with their consent, this surely has to do with civil liberty and self-government. And it takes not only imagination, but a disregard for a good deal of constitutional development, to suppose that such things as due process of law and trial by jury—among the most ancient "liberties" of Englishmen—are unrelated to civil liberty. One need only to recall, for example, the historic interrelationship between the role of the jury and freedom of the press to have grave doubts about Andrews' thesis.[30]

The sentiments expressed on the Jamestown plaque itself have been questioned as implying too much. Wilcomb E. Washburn has said that the inscription is "more confusing than enlightening and reflects the assumptions and heritage of a later age rather than the experience of an earlier age." [31] This seems an odd criticism, since the inscription, by its own terms, obviously *intends* to reflect the "assumptions and heritage of a later age"; it speaks, not of a set of principles frozen at some point in time, but rather of a *developing* system of "freedom under law, which is [today] at once our dearest possession and proudest achievement." Viewed on its own terms, the statement appears both defensible and fair.

Yet Washburn does make a useful point. In reading words such as those of the Virginia State Bar Association, one should

[29] Andrews, *Colonial Period,* I, 86 note.

[30] For the interplay between trial by jury and freedom of the press, see Helen Hill Miller, *The Case for Liberty* (Chapel Hill, N.C., 1965), pp. 29 ff.

[31] See Wilcomb E. Washburn, "Law and Authority in Colonial Virginia," in George Athan Billias, ed., *Law and Authority in Colonial America* (Barre, Mass., 1965), pp. 116 ff.

not imagine some sort of instant and wholesale passage of the English common law to Virginia in the hip pocket of Captain John Smith. The phrase was, as suggested elsewhere, an inducement meant to arouse certain expectations in the minds of seventeenth-century Englishmen who might understand perhaps a little about seventeenth-century English law. The words were certainly sufficient to express the intention that English rights and liberties could in some general sense be the inheritance of Englishmen who emigrated to the colonies. But, looking toward the future from 1607, what the words "liberties, franchises, and immunities" would mean, and what shape the English law would take in Virginia, would depend on the events and experience of the years to come.

The settlers of Virginia, like those of other colonies, might well have been expected to look to England for laws and customs to govern their own public and private lives. As Henry St. George Tucker, the son of St. George Tucker (the great American commentator on Blackstone), later asked, what would have been more natural to the seventeenth-century Virginian than a "tacit acquiescence by every individual in the authority of the laws to which they had always been accustomed?" [32] In fact in probably no other colony were there more instances in the seventeenth century of a natural inclination to adopt English legal practices.

One of the earliest legal events in Virginia's history, aside from the charters from the King, was the appearance of the so-called "Great Charter" of 1618, sometimes called the Instructions to Governor Yeardley, ordained by the Virginia Company. This charter has been described in the most fulsome language. At the end of the last century, Alexander Brown referred to it as "our first executed Magna Charta" and recounted the story of the appearance, at the time of the charter of 1618, of a "blazing star" in the sky, which the superstitious took to be a "sign in the heavens." [33] No copy of the charter of 1618 as a whole survives; the part which remains to us deals

[32] *Commentaries on the Laws of Virginia* (Winchester, Va., 1831), I, 6.
[33] *The First Republic in America* (Boston, 1898), p. 293.

with land tenure (itself a matter of no mean importance to the colonists).[34] But we know that among the charges to Virginia's Governor, Sir George Yeardley, was that, soon after his arrival in Virginia, he should summon a general assembly to participate in the colony's governance.

Later observers have not agreed on the motives which led the Virginia Company to introduce representative government into the colony. Some writers, such as Thomas J. Wertenbaker, have seen in the instructions of 1618 the idealism and liberalism of Sir Edward Sandys.[35] Others have treated the establishment of the first assembly as a "straight commercial proposition"—an effort on the part of the Company to shore up its investment in times of financial difficulties.[36] But whatever the backers' motives, Yeardley did convene the Assembly in 1619—the first representative legislative assembly in the New World. And, whether the men in London were moved by ideals or profits, Virginians might not unreasonably have looked upon this event as the realization of at least one of the "liberties, franchises, and immunities" to which the colony's charter entitled them.

There was, interestingly enough, at least one palpable link to the English Parliament (which by this event in 1619 would begin earning its name as "mother of Parliaments"): one of those who sat in the first Virginia legislature was John Pory, who, having previously sat in the English Parliament, thus earned the distinction of being the first Englishman to sit in legislative bodies on both sides of the Atlantic.

Hard times lay ahead for the colony—hundreds were to die of disease or at the hands of the Indians in the massacre of 1622— but the idea of representative government survived. The durability of the idea is attested by the personal plea of Yeardley, who

[34] See Andrews, *Colonial Period*, I, 180–84. For the text of the extant portion, see *Three Charters of the Virginia Company*, pp. 95–108; *Records of the Virginia Company of London*, ed. Susan Myra Kingsbury (Washington, D.C., 1933), III, 98; and 2 *Virginia Magazine of History and Biography* 154–65 (1894).

[35] *Virginia under the Stuarts: 1607–1688* (Princeton, N.J., 1914), pp. 32–36.

[36] Perry Miller, "Religion and Society in the Early Literature: The Religious Impulse in the Founding of Virginia," 6 *William and Mary Quarterly* (3d ser.) 24, 25 (1949). For the fullest statement of this thesis, see W. F. Craven, *Dissolution of the Virginia Company* (New York, 1932).

on the death of James I crossed the Atlantic in 1625 to plead on behalf of Virginia that King Charles "avoid the oppression of Governors there, that their liberty of Generall Assemblyes may be continued and confirmed, and that they may have a voice in the election of officers, as in other Corporations." [37]

The laws and customs of England came to Virginia in many ways and forms, of which a representative assembly was but one. In 1631 the Governor and Council, together with the Assembly, agreed that there should be courts, meeting monthly or more often, in some of the "remote plantations," that is, Charles City and Henrico (both upriver from Jamestown). Commissioners in the courts were instructed to do justice "as neere as may be after the lawes of the realme of England and statutes thereof made." The same oath, in language recalling chapter 40 of Magna Carta, required that commissioners "doe equall right, to the poore and to the rich," and, laying down a rule which Sir Edward Coke had proclaimed twenty years before in *Dr. Bonham's Case*,[38] admonished commissioners: "you shall not be of counsell in any case or quarrell hanginge before you. . . ." [39]

Even today Virginia is called the "Old Dominion." It earned that name by its loyalty to the Crown during the period of Cromwellian rule in England. That loyalty was a sure reflection of a feeling that Virginia had enjoyed benefits from its relations with England to that time (it was not to be so fortunate after the Restoration) ; that feeling of good fortune would, of course, have been a factor reinforcing the natural disposition to the adoption of English laws and legal practices in Virginia.

So strong was Virginia's loyalty to the monarchy that, on hearing of the execution of Charles I in 1649, the Virginia Assembly took note that, whether out of ignorance or out of

---

[37] Wertenbaker, *Virginia under the Stuarts*, p. 62.

[38] 8 Coke Rep. 113b, 77 Eng. Rep. 646 (1610). In that case, a fine imposed by the Royal College of Physicians was held invalid, partly on the ground that the College was to receive half the fine. For a modern application of the principle that it offends due process for a judge to have a direct interest in a case before him, see Tumey v. Ohio, 273 U.S. 510 (1927). For chapter 40 of Magna Carta and other relevant chapters, see Appendix A, *infra*.

[39] 1 *Hening's Statutes at Large* 168–69 (1823) [hereinafter *Hening*].

malice, some people were "casting blemishes of dishonour upon the late most excellent and now undoubtedly sainted king" and passed an act declaring that if any person in the colony should "defend or maintain the late traiterous proceedings" by words or speeches, such person should be judged an accessory *post factum* to the King's death and be dealt with as such. Moreover, anyone expressing any doubt about the right of Charles II to succeed his father as King of England and his right to dominion of the colony of Virginia should be adjudged guilty of high treason.[40]

Soon Virginia had to face the problem of its relation to the Cromwellian Commonwealth in England. When the Puritan Parliament began, by punitive trade regulations, to try to make Virginia suffer for its continued allegiance to the monarchy, the Virginia Assembly convened to consider how best to meet this threat. The Governor, Sir William Berkeley, calling for resistance to Parliament, pointed to the benefits which Virginia had enjoyed from its traditional society:

[W]hat is it can be hoped for in a change, which we have not already? Is it liberty? The sun looks not on a people more free then we are from all oppression. Is it wealth? Hundreds of examples shew us that Industry & Thrift in a short time may bring us to as high a degree of it, as the Country and our Conditions are yet capable of: Is it securety to enjoy this wealth when gotten? With out blushing I will speake it, I am confident theare lives not that person can accuse me of attempting the least act against any mans property. . . . But Gentlemen by the Grace of God we will not so tamely part with our King, and all these blessings we enjoy under him; and if they oppose us, do but follow me, I will either lead you to victory, or loose a life which I cannot more gloriously sacrifice then for my loyalty, and your security.[41]

On the conclusion of Berkeley's speech, the House of Burgesses, together with the Governor and Council, unanimously resolved to resist the Cromwell regime. The resolution is interesting for the homage which it paid to the laws of England. The colonists were, it was resolved, sworn to govern and be governed

---

[40] 1 *ibid.* 359–61.   [41] 1 *Va. Mag. Hist. & Biog.* 77 (1893).

by these laws, a pledge which the colonists had "inviolably and sacredly" kept as far as their abilities permitted. Only the laws of England "in such times of tumults, stormes, and tempests, can humanely prevent our ruines. . . . These lawes we professe are our guides and do beleeve we deserve punishment and infamy if we willingly, or willfuly deviate from them." Therefore the Virginians resolved to continue in their allegiance to Charles II, to trade with all nations having amicable relations with the King, and to pray for Charles' restoration to the throne.[42]

This direct challenge having been flung at the feet of Parliament, the Puritan Commonwealth determined that it must subdue Virginia by force of arms. A fleet and parliamentary commissioners arrived in Virginia in January 1652, and Governor Berkeley called upon the people to resist. Finally, after some jockeying for position on both sides—Berkeley even summoned Indian allies to join the expected fray—negotiations were undertaken. Both sides ultimately agreed upon articles of submission which, probably because of the commissioners' relief at being able to reduce the colony without bloodshed, were rather favorable to the colony. In the articles Virginia agreed to submit to the Commonwealth of England and to its laws, but the submission was to be treated as voluntary, not one forced upon the colony by force or conquest, a distinction which was of no small significance in view of the developing English legal view that colonists in conquered countries did not enjoy the same legal status as those in other colonies.[43] To be sure that the point was made, the agreement explicitly guaranteed that Virginians should "have and enjoy such freedoms and priviledges as belong to the free borne people of England"—a reenunciation of the like guarantee of the royal charters to Virginia.

Representative government, which had been in existence since 1619, was to continue: "the Grand Assembly as formerly shall convene and transact the affairs of Virginia, wherein nothing is to be acted or done contrarie to the government of the common wealth of England and the lawes there established."

[42] *Ibid.*, pp. 78–81.   [43] See pp. 99–108, *infra*.

The right to consent to taxes, a right traced by Englishmen to Magna Carta, was assured by the articles, as were rights of free trade.[44]

The Assembly and the parliamentary commissioners agreed that Richard Bennett, one of the commissioners, should serve as governor for the ensuing year. A Council was named and admonished to "do right and equall justice" to the people of the colony "according to the knowne lawe of England"—in other words, according to the "law of the land."[45]

The evidence is rather clear in these early years of the Virginia Colony of Virginians' concern for the benefits of the English law and for the "rights of Englishmen," including the rights which had originated in or by evolution been adduced from Magna Carta—due process of law, no taxation without consent, and others. It is worth noting the other natural paths which the laws and customs of England took to become part of the accepted pattern of life in Virginia: the introduction of lawbooks and the development of a bar.

From the earliest times Virginia courts had been admonished by the General Assembly to do justice according to the laws of England, as, for example, by the statute of 1631. The officials of government were expected to do the same, as the resolution creating the Bennett government illustrates. But neither judges nor other officials could be expected to do right and justice according to English law unless they had English lawbooks. In 1666 the General Assembly recognized the need for "the better conformity of the proceedings of the courts of this country to the lawes of England" and accordingly directed the importation from England of the English Statutes-at-Large, Dalton's *Justice of the Peace* and *Office of a Sheriff*, and Swinburne's *Book of Wills and Testaments*, all of these books to be kept at James City for the use of the courts and legislature. Moreover, the several county courts were instructed to send for the same books.[46] Records of books of various Virginia counties for the 1660's and 1670's have entries recording orders placed for lawbooks through local persons who were traveling to England.[47]

[44] 1 *Hening* 363–64. [45] 1 *ibid.* 371–72. [46] 2 *ibid.* 246.
[47] See p. 117, *infra*.

Individuals, especially those who served as county clerks or in other public capacities, also built respectable legal libraries.[48]

If lawbooks were much sought after, lawyers were not so welcome. The General Assembly could not decide whether the colony would be better off to regulate lawyers or to do without them altogether. Initially the Assembly took the course of regulation; in 1643 it required attorneys to have the leave of a court before arguing a case before it, restricted the number of courts before which an attorney could practice, imposed heavy fines upon lawyers who exceeded a minimum fee schedule set out in the act, and forbade an attorney to refuse a case unless he was already employed by the adverse party.[49] Before three years were out, the Assembly apparently was fed up with lawyers. Complaining that "many troublesom suits are multiplied by the unskillfulness and coveteousness of attorneys, who have more intended their own profit and their inordinate lucre then the good and benefit of their clients," the Assembly decreed that all attorneys for hire be expelled from the courts, save in pending cases.[50] A number of other acts were passed in the years that followed. In 1656 the Assembly, finding "many inconveniences" had resulted, repealed its ouster of attorneys and authorized the Governor and Council to license them.[51]

Two years later, however, another stature was enacted prohibiting any attorney from pleading cases for a fee, under penalty of a fine of 5,000 pounds of tobacco.[52] The legislation of 1658 was submitted to the Governor and Council for their action, and they replied, "The Governor and Council will consent to this proposition so far as it shall be agreeable to Magna Charta." This communication was in turn referred to a committee, who reported, "We have considered Magna Charta, and do not discover any prohibition contained therein." [53]

It was well into the eighteenth century before the law as a profession enjoyed any considerable reputation in the colony. But the long tradition of admiration for the laws of England which had flourished over the years in Virginia was to serve as a

[48] See pp. 118–19, 122–23, *infra.*   [49] 1 *Hening* 275.   [50] 1 *ibid.* 302.
[51] 1 *ibid.* 419.   [52] 1 *ibid.* 482–83.
[53] Edward D. Neill, *Virginia Carolorum* (Albany, 1886) , p. 264.

firm footing for Virginia lawyers when they took their place with other colonial leaders in invoking against England the rights of Englishmen in the 1760's and 1770's.

In the late seventeenth century justice continued, as before, to be done along English lines. A proclamation of the Governor and Council in 1686 followed earlier tradition and statute by enjoining courts to proceed "as reasonably near as our present condition will admit to ye practice of ye courts in England." [54] In fact, in some ways law as administered in colonial Virginia may have been an improvement upon that of the mother country, especially in the meting out of punishments in criminal cases. The criminal law was harsh in seventeenth-century England; the trend there was to a definite increase in the number of capital offenses. Virginia, by contrast, had few offenses for which the death sentence was provided. The charter of 1606 had made only the most serious offenses, such as murder and mutiny, punishable by death, and in general the criminal system of the colony was probably closer to Magna Carta's philosophy of punishments to fit the crime (chapter 20) than was that of England at the time. Indeed, there was a spectacular rise in the number of capital offenses in England during the eighteenth century (63 were created in the first fifty years of the reign of George III alone) so that by the early nineteenth century, before the reforms spurred by Jeremy Bentham and his utilitarian philosophy, England had over two hundred capital crimes. In 1810 Sir Samuel Romilly declared that "there is probably no other country in the world in which so many and so great a variety of human actions are punishable with loss of life as in England." [55]

As the influence of English law continued to grow, the General Assembly often had occasion to adopt English statutes outright. In 1631–32, for example, the Assembly adopted the statute of James I for artificers and workmen, the laws of England against drunkards, and the English laws against fore-

[54] Philip Alexander Bruce, *Institutional History of Virginia in the Seventeenth Century* (New York, 1910) , I, 554.

[55] Leon Radzinowicz, *A History of English Criminal Law: The Movement for Reform, 1750–1833* (New York, 1948) , pp. 3–5.

stallers and engrossers. In 1646 the legislature decreed that no merchant or trader, whether English or Dutch, should use in trade "any other weights and measures than are used and made according to the statute of parliament in such cases provided"; one result of this act was to make chapter 35 of Magna Carta in force in Virginia. English statutes on a variety of subjects—distress for quit-rents, crimes at sea, attendance at parish church, fraudulent devises, vexatious appeals—were at various times adopted by the Virginia Assembly. The Assembly even adopted in 1646 England's "laudable custom" of binding out the children of poor families to be brought up in some trade or calling, in this case, two children from each county to be employed in the public flax houses in James City.[56]

During this time Magna Carta had observable influence. It was used, as in the case of the ban on mercenary attorneys, as a measure of the validity of legislation—a reminder of the special status accorded to the Great Charter in the laws of England and of the precedent that was being set for the doctrine of judicial review in the United States. The Charter was also pleaded in judicial proceedings. In 1682 malcontents in Gloucester, New Kent, and Middlesex counties cut up tobacco plants, and their ringleaders were arrested. Robert Beverley (father of the author of the famed *History of Virginia*) was arrested and made a prisoner aboard the *Duke of York,* lying at anchor in the Rappahannock River. Transferred to the ship *Concord,* Beverley escaped but was retaken at his home. Some months later, through his attorney, William Fitzhugh, Beverley applied for a writ of habeas corpus. Interestingly enough, Fitzhugh did not rely on the Habeas Corpus Act of 1679 (about which there might be dispute as to whether it applied in the colonies), but on chapters 36 and 39 of Magna Carta, the chapters concerning writs of inquisition upon life or limb and guaranteeing proceedings according to the law of the land.[57]

Later the ties which bound Virginia to the mother country

[56] 1 *Hening* 167, 172, 331, 336, 351; 3 *ibid.* 171, 178, 360; 4 *ibid.* 164; 6 *ibid.* 339.
[57] See Robert Beverley, *History of Virginia* (Richmond, 1855), pp. 1–2; J. A. C. Chandler, *Genesis and Birth of the Federal Constitution* (New York, 1924), p. 99.

were to weaken. The loyalty to the Crown which had been so evident at the time of Governor Berkeley was sorely tested by the actions of the English Government taken to deal with Bacon's Rebellion (1676), and those who had backed Berkeley in earlier days tended to be at odds with his successors. This period marked the decline of the custom of looking to the Crown for leadership and the beginning of a greater interest in the colony's own welfare, without reference to that of England.[58] But this turn of events by no means altered the already strongly ingrained habit of looking to the laws of England for the standards of legislation and justice in Virginia. If anything, the growing disenchantment with England as a master only highlighted the need to look for something other than sentiment or loyalty as a foundation for the colonists' rights and interests. That something was the "rights of Englishmen," as expressed in Magna Carta and the later English statutes and as carried to Virginia in its charters.

[58] See Wilcomb E. Washburn, *The Governor and the Rebel* (Chapel Hill, N.C., 1957), pp. 150–52.

Chapter II

The New England Colonies

The "Word of God" and

the "Laws of England"

Law in the early years of the Massachusetts Colony was in good part judge-made law. Given the theocratic flavor of the government of Massachusetts and the elements of judicial discretion usually associated with judge-made law, this brand of lawmaking was not welcome to all who lived under its rule. The primary sources of laws in the early years in Massachusetts were in orders and decisions of the magistrates in the Court of Assistants, although after the enlargement of the General Court, the legislative body, in 1634, legislation in the proper sense became an increasingly important source of law in the colony.

But discretionary justice, as administered by the magistrates, continued, and therein lay the seeds of one of the most illuminating legal controversies of seventeenth-century America, a controversy which produced two of the notable documents of that time, the Body of Liberties of 1641 and the *Lawes and Liberties of Massachusetts* of 1648. The rumblings began as early as 1635. The discontent took the form of demands for written laws, to restrain the discretion of the magistrates, and it is interesting that the first such demand of which we have record suggested that such laws should resemble "a Magna Charta." Governor Winthrop noted in his journal that when the General Court met in May 1635 at Newton, "The deputies having conceived great danger to our state, in regard that our magistrates, for want of positive laws, in many cases, might proceed according to their discretions, it was agreed that some men should be appointed to frame a body of laws, in resemblance to a Magna Charta, which . . . should be received for fundamental laws."[1]

At this juncture, one might wonder whether it would be Magna Carta and the common law of England or a celestial law which would form the model for a written code for Massachusetts. In May 1636 the General Court, meeting at Boston, appointed a committee to "make a draught of lawes agreeable to the word of God," which should serve as the fundamentals of the colony, and to present their proposals to the next General Court. In the meantime, the General Court had a weather eye cocked to the offending magistrates, to whom it was "ordered, that in the meane tyme the magistrates & their associates shall p'ceede in the courts to heare & determine all causes according to the lawes nowe established, & where there is noe law, then as neere the lawe of God as they can. . . ."[2]

In effect, the judgment of the General Court as expressed in the resolutions of 1635 and 1636 set forth two frames of reference from which standards for written laws for the colony could be drawn: the traditional rights of Englishmen, especially as embodied in Magna Carta, and the word of God. These were not necessarily—and ultimately proved not to be— incompatible sources of standards. In fact, there is an interesting parallel between the invocation in seventeenth-century Massachusetts of both streams of legal thought and a similar duality of legal and constitutional expression in the pamphlets and writings leading up to the American Revolution a century and a half later.

[1] *Winthrop's Journal,* ed. James Kendall Hosmer (New York, 1908), I, 151. Massachusetts magistrates were "judge, prosecutor, and attorney." Chroust, *Legal Profession,* I, 69.

[2] *Records of the Governor and Company of the Massachusetts Bay in New England,* ed. Nathaniel B. Shurtleff (Boston, 1853), I, 174–75 [hereinafter *Records of Massachusetts Bay*].

The result of the resolutions of 1635 and 1636 was the Body of Liberties of 1641. This compilation was not a detailed code of existing positive law in the sense that we think of a code today; rather it was more in the nature of a statement of constitutional principles. In fact, the document notes that its provisions "are expressed onely under the name and title of Liberties, and not in the exact form of Laws or Statutes." [3] Thus the Body of Liberties deals with such things as due process of law, general application of laws, the relationship of church and state, judicial procedures, and (in separate sections) "liberties" of freemen, women, children, servants, and foreigners. It resembled, to look backwards, the kinds of principles stated in Magna Carta, and, to look forward, it foreshadowed the bills of rights which were in the next century to become standard features of the American federal and state constitutions. Its resemblance to Magna Carta is striking. The Body of Liberties begins with the declaration that no man's life, person, family, or property should be proceeded against or in "any way indammaged under coulor of law or Countenance of Authoritie, unlesse it be by vertue or equitie of some expresse law of the Country waranting the same, established by a generall Court and sufficiently published, or in case of the defect of a law in any parteculer case by the word of god." [4] Except for the proviso allowing proceedings to be rested on the "word of god" (an invitation to an exercise of discretion by a judge), this language is the obvious descendant of chapter 39 of Magna Carta: "No free man shall be taken, imprisoned, disseised, outlawed, banished, or in any way destroyed, nor will We proceed against or prosecute him, except by the lawful judgment of his peers and by the law of the land." And it marks a link in one of the longest of jurisprudential chains, the concept of "due process," or "law of the land," which stretches at least from Magna Carta's chapter 39 to the mandate of the Fifth Amendment of the United States Constitution that no

[3] *The Colonial Laws of Massachusetts,* ed. William H. Whitmore (Boston, 1889), p. 61 [hereinafter *Colonial Laws of Massachusetts*].
[4] *Ibid.,* p. 33.

person shall be deprived of "life, liberty, or property, without due process of law," and the like provisions of the state constitutions.

The next provision of the Body of Liberties sounds another of the most fundamental notes of Anglo-American jurisprudence, equality in the application of the laws: "Every person within this Jurisdiction, whether Inhabitant or forreiner shall enjoy the same justice and law, that is generall for the plantation, which we constitute and execute one towards another without partialitie or delay." [5] Again the debt is to Magna Carta, this time to chapter 40: "To no one will We sell, to none will We deny or delay, right or justice." And in both we find the idea now expressed in the equal protection clause of the Fourteenth Amendment to the United States Constitution.

Other provisions of the Body of Liberties state principles drawn from Magna Carta. "No mans Cattel or goods," says the 1641 document, shall be taken for public use "without such reasonable prices and hire as the ordinarie rates of the Countrie do afford"; if the cattle or goods suffer damage, "the owner shall be suffitiently recompenced." [6] Compare chapter 28 of Magna Carta, which forbids the King's officers to take "the corn or other chattels of any man without immediate payment, unless the seller voluntarily consents to postponement of payment." [7] Again, both provisions, that of 1215 and that of 1641, lie in a tradition culminating in provisions of the federal and state constitutions, the requirement of just compensation for property taken for public use.

While, as already noted, the Body of Liberties was not set out "in the exact form of Laws or Statutes," nevertheless all who were in authority were admonished "to consider them as laws" and in executing them to mete out "proportionable punishments upon every man impartiallie" who should violate them. [8] In this emphasis on proportion, on the idea that the punishment should fit the crime, there is an echo of the provision of

[5] *Ibid.*   [6] *Ibid.*, p. 35.
[7] See also Magna Carta, chapters 30 and 31, dealing with the taking of horses and wood.
[8] *Colonial Laws of Massachusetts*, p. 61.

Magna Carta (chapter 20) which declared that a "free man shall be amerced [fined] for a small fault only according to the measure thereof, and for a great crime according to its magnitude. . . ." [9]

Among other chapters of the Body of Liberties harking back to Magna Carta was one giving rights of "free fishing" in the great ponds, bays, coves, and rivers,[10] a provision whose distant ancestor is Magna Carta's chapter 33, requiring removal of fishweirs from the Thames and Medway.

Finally it is of special interest to note that great care was taken that the Body of Liberties be carefully and fully publicized, to both the citizens and their rulers. In addition to the guarantee, quoted above, that no man should be proceeded against save under general laws "sufficiently published," the Body of Liberties, at the very end of the document, decreed: "Lastly because our dutie and desire is to do nothing suddainlie which fundamentally concerne us, we decree that these rites and liberties, shall be Audably read and deliberately weighed at every Generall Court that shall be held, within three yeares next insueing." [11] One purpose of this latter provision was to allow the General Court to make such alterations as they felt the Body of Liberties required, but the emphasis (symbolically, in the first and last chapters of the document) on "sufficiently published" laws and on liberties "Audably read" parallels the royal command of four hundred years earlier that Magna Carta "be publicly read and firmly held." Lady Stenton has emphasized the importance, in the case of Magna Carta, of these public readings all over England, of the awe which must have been felt by the people who heard the King's officer read the terms of the Great Charter from the actual document sealed with the King's Great Seal.[12] The effect of the public reading of a polity's fundamental laws must have been as forceful in seventeenth-century Massachusetts as in thirteenth-century England. Indeed, the numbers of people who peer through the

---

[9] See also chapters 21 and 22, giving the same right to barons and to clergymen.
[10] *Colonial Laws of Massachusetts*, p. 37.   [11] *Ibid.*, p. 61.
[12] Doris M. Stenton, *After Runnymede: Magna Carta in the Middle Ages* (Charlottesville, Va., 1965), pp. 9–10.

glass at venerable documents in the National Archives in Washington are a testimonial that this awe is not a spent force today.

The Body of Liberties, in the substantive provisions cited above, was demonstrably a restatement of the fundamental rights of Englishmen as understood by the colonists in Massachusetts. As the Supreme Court of Massachusetts was to suggest two hundred years later, the Body of Liberties, even in its use of the term "liberty" in the sense of right, franchise, and privilege, was drawing directly on Magna Carta.[13] In some respects the Body of Liberties went even beyond the guarantees then known to English law; for example, the Body of Liberties granted (with certain exceptions) a privilege against self-incrimination, banned cruel and inhuman punishments, forbade that a man be twice punished for the same offense, and gave every man (whether an inhabitant or not) the liberty to speak to any question in town meetings or other public assemblies. Some of these liberties—such as a ban on cruel and unusual punishment—were to become part of the fundamental law of England only with the Bill of Rights in 1689; others not even then. Still others—such as the privilege against self-incrimination—have never become part of the English Constitution.

The Body of Liberties was not, certainly by modern lights, perfect; while it forbade "Tirrany or Crueltie towards any bruite Creature" and decreed that a wife should be "free from bodilie correction or stripes by her husband," its list of capital offenses—including the worship of false gods, witchcraft, blasphemy, and bestiality—are hardly candidates for a model penal code. Yet its provisions for due process of law, for equal application of the laws, for procedural rights to an accused, and other enlightened features make the Body of Liberties a notable milestone in the evolution of America's constitutional principles.

Enlightened or not, the Body of Liberties did not end the

[13] Commonwealth v. Alger, 7 Cush. (61 Mass.) 53, 71 (1851). The court also suggested that a statement of liberties in this form might seem more compatible with a regard for the authority of the mother country than would the enactment in terms of a body of laws.

disquiet among various citizens of Massachusetts. In 1646 a number of freemen of the colony, led by Robert Child, submitted to the Governor and General Court a Remonstrance and Petition asking, as English subjects, for the rights of Englishmen. The petition averred that, notwithstanding that Massachusetts had been settled under a charter from the Crown containing a guarantee of privileges and immunities, the petitioners could not,

according to our judgments, discerne a setled forme of government according to the lawes of England, which may seem strange to our countrymen, yea to the whole world, especially considering we are all English. Neither do we so understand and perceive our owne lawes or libertyes, or any body of lawes here so established, as that thereby there may be a sure and comfortable enjoyment of our lives, libertyes, and estates, according to our due and naturall rights, as freeborne subjects of the English nation.[14]

If the Body of Liberties of 1641 had guaranteed due process of law and equality before the law, the petitioners of 1646 failed to find that they were enjoying either of these rights. The petition complained of an "overgreedy spirit of arbitrary power" and said, "Further, it gives cause to many to think themselves hardly dealt with, others too much favored, and the scale of justice too much bowed and unequally ballanced. . . ." Nor did the petitioners find that they were living under a genuine rule of law, since oaths were "subject to exposition, according to the will of him or them that gives them, and not according to a due and unbowed rule of law, which is the true interpreter of all oathes to all men, whether judge or judged." [15]

In short, what the petitioners wanted were the traditional and fundamental rights of Englishmen, the establishment of "the fundamentall and wholesome lawes of our native country, and such others as are no wayes repugnant to them. . . ." As with the complaints leading up to the Body of Liberties of 1641, the petitioners of 1646 asked in particular for relief from

[14] Prince Society, *The Hutchinson Papers* (Albany, 1865), I, 216 [hereinafter *Hutchinson Papers*].
[15] *Ibid.*, p. 217.

the arbitrariness of the magistrates: "And for the more strict and due observation and execution of the said lawes by all the ministers of justice, That there may be a setled rule for them to walke by in all cases in judicature. . . ." [16]

Child and his copetitioners were, to put it mildly, considered troublemakers. As Governor Thomas Hutchinson put it in his *History of the Colony of Massachusetts-Bay*, "The court, and great part of the country, were much offended at this petition." [17] But the authorities felt they could not ignore the petition; hence the General Court, at a session in October 1646, appointed the Governor and others to draw up an answer. As the petitioners were planning also to carry their case to London, the committee was also to meet with Edward Winslow, the colony's agent in London, and to agree with him "to answer to what shalbe obiected against us in England." [18]

The answer of the General Court to the Child petition fairly exuded confidence in the righteousness of the government's case—perhaps a bit too much confidence. The Court marveled at the effrontry of the petitioners; their petition was "without presedent in any plantation or established commonwealth." (This was, as of 1646, probably true.) But, instead of throwing the petition out (as, the answer implied, the petition deserved), the General Court would "examine their particular grievances" and give "account of our government and administrations." [19]

The principal argument of the Court was that the laws and government of Massachusetts, contrary to the petition's claim, were based on the laws of England: "For our government itself, it is framed according to our charter, and the fundamental and common lawes of England, and carried on according to the same . . . with as bare allowance for the disproportion between an ancient, populous, wealthy kingdome, and so poore an in-

---

[16] *Ibid.*, pp. 217–18.

[17] (2d ed., London, 1760), I, 146 [hereinafter Hutchinson, *History of Massachusetts Bay*]. Puritan leaders were "zealous in their efforts to prevent and suppress any manifestation of independence in religious or political matters." Chroust, *Legal Profession*, I, 56.

[18] *Records of Massachusetts Bay*, II, 162.

[19] *Hutchinson Papers*, I, 223, 226.

fant thinne colonie, as common reason can afford." In particular the General Court claimed that the inhabitants of Massachusetts enjoyed the liberties guaranteed by Magna Carta, and the Court intended to demonstrate this: "And because this will better appeare by compareing particulars, we shall drawe them into a parallel. In the one columne we will sett downe the fundamental and common lawes and customes of England, beginning with Magna Charta. . . . In the other columne we will sett downe the summe of such lawes and customes as are in force and use in this jurisdiction. . . ." [20]

Then followed the "parallels": one column titled "Magna Charta," the other titled "Fundamentalls of the Massachusetts." While the attempt to show that Magna Carta and the English common law ruled in all their glory in Massachusetts has rightly been called "ingenious," [21] one is entitled to wonder to what extent this bit of advocacy was an honest and accurate account (advocacy, after all, is rarely dispassionate). But it is not necessary to answer that question here; for present purposes there lies enough significance in the fact that the General Court of a theocratic commonwealth thought it necessary, in answer to a troublemaking petition, to assure its own people and the government at Whitehall that the rights given by Magna Carta and the common law were not denied to the people of Massachusetts.

The provisions of Magna Carta which, according to the "parallels," were preserved by the laws of Massachusetts included the guarantee that the Church should enjoy all of her liberties (Magna Carta, chapter 1), that all towns and cities should have their liberties and free customs (chapter 13), that there should be one measure of corn and wine throughout the kingdom (chapter 35), that courts of judicature should be kept in a certain place (chapter 17), that amercements should be proportionate to the offense and should be assessed only by the oath of honest men of the neighborhood (chapter 20), that there should be no wager of law without witnesses (chapter

---

[20] *Ibid.,* I, 226–27.
[21] Richard B. Morris, *Studies in the History of American Law* (New York, 1930), p. 14.

38),[22] and that merchants should have safe conduct to go and come out of and into the country (chapter 41). Opposite each statement of a provision of Magna Carta (sometimes rather loosely stated), the "parallels" summarized the comparable provisions of Massachusetts law, usually some chapter of the Body of Liberties, sometimes a session law of the General Court, occasionally a "custom," where there was no comparable provision on the statute books. Having thus covered the relevant chapters of Magna Carta, the "parallels" went on to make other similar matches between "The Common Lawes of England" and the "Fundamentalls of the Massachusetts." [23]

The chief concern of the General Court's Declaration of 1646, as of the Body of Liberties of 1641, was constitutional or public law. Nearly all the provisions of Magna Carta and of the English common law set out in the "parallels" were propositions of public law. The tenor of Child's petition, and the form of the Court's reply—even to the use of the phrase "Fundamentalls of the Massachusetts"—suggest that the argument was not about the common law in the sense that we think of it today (that is, judge-made law in private areas such as contracts, torts, etc.) nor indeed about private law whatever its source, but rather about the fundamental principles of constitutional law. Not only was the English common law as a regulator of private interests still relatively undeveloped at this time, but also the colonists were not concerned, indeed probably viewed it as natural, if private law in Massachusetts varied from that of England.[24] But a charge that the authorities were not faithful to Magna Carta and other basic guarantees of the rights of Englishmen was another matter; in 1727 in North Carolina Edmond Porter was indicted for libel and other "high Misdemeanors" for charging that the Governor had by his arbitrary conduct violated Magna Carta, a "most high heinous and Scan-

[22] By the "wager of law" an accused person swore to his innocence and was required to find "oath-helpers" to swear that the accused's oath was reliable.

[23] For the full text of the "parallels" of 1646, see Appendix C, *infra*.

[24] See Mark DeWolfe Howe, "The Sources and Nature of Law in Colonial Massachusetts," in George Athan Billias, ed., *Law and Authority in Colonial America* (Barre, Mass., 1965), p. 1, at pp. 9–11.

dalous & false Aspersion & in great contempt of the Sayd Governor." [25] Similarly, in Massachusetts in 1646 it was a serious thing to urge publicly that those in power were disregarding the Great Charter and the rights of Englishmen. To do this, as Child and the others did, was to call for an energetic rebuttal of the kind which formed the General Court's Declaration of 1646.[26]

Apparently the General Court was not content to let the argument rest solely on the plane of disputation and persuasion, for Child and his fellow petitioners were accused by the Court of contemptuous and seditious statements and were fined. The petitioners claimed an appeal to the Commissioners for Plantations in England, but it was not allowed. The petitioners did, however, make complaint to England praying that the laws of England might be established in Massachusetts and that freeholders there might enjoy such privileges as were enjoyed in England and the other plantations. The General Court's Declaration of 1646 also went to England, to the Long Parliament, and Governor Hutchinson (writing in the eighteenth century) recorded that Winslow, as agent for the colony, answered the petitioner's complaint, "and by his prudent management, and the credit and esteem he was in with many of the members of parliament and principal persons then in power, he prevented any prejudice to the colony" from the petitioners' applications.[27]

The charges and rebuttals of 1646 were not the end of the struggle. The field of argument was now pretty well marked out: there appears to have been, on all sides, the shared, if unspoken, assumption that the guarantees of liberty found in Magna Carta and the common law marked the boundaries of permissible governmental conduct, rather in the way (if less formalized) that the United States Constitution sets limits to the power of both federal and state governments today. In

[25] *Colonial Records of North Carolina,* ed. William L. Saunders and Walter Clark (Raleigh, N.C., 1886–1914) , II, 689.
[26] Hutchinson, *History of Massachusetts-Bay,* I, 148.
[27] *Ibid.,* I, 147–49.

particular it was becoming increasingly clear that colonial Americans were looking to fundamental documents, the archetype being Magna Carta, and to written laws as guarantees against arbitrary power of rulers and the uncontrolled discretion of magistrates. Hence soon after the exchanges of 1646 committees were appointed to proceed with a comprehensive compilation of the laws of Massachusetts. In 1647, as the work of compilation proceeded, the General Court ordered two copies each of six legal texts then in wide current use in England: *Coke upon Littleton, Coke on Magna Carta,* Coke's *Reports, New Terms of the Law, Book of Entries,* and Dalton's *Country Justice.*[28] It is significant that three of the six works came from the pen of Sir Edward Coke, the great exponent of Magna Carta and the common law, and a key figure in the parliamentarian struggles against the Stuart kings. This heavy infusion of Coke, especially Coke on Magna Carta, is in line with the care taken by the General Court in its Declaration of 1646 to align the laws of the colony with the guarantees of Magna Carta and to demonstrate that the liberties of Englishmen were protected in Massachusetts. Further, the reliance on Coke is part of a tradition which began taking shape in the American colonies soon after Coke's writings began appearing and grew stronger with time: the adoption of Coke's legal and constitutional views, and his interpretations of Magna Carta, as a basic feature of colonial jurisprudence.[29]

The drafting of a code for Massachusetts was not a simple matter. It has been suggested that, contrary to the view that the law of the time was "rude, untechnical popular law," the courts of Massachusetts were, within fifty years of the colony's settlement, concerning themselves with "difficult and complex questions of law."[30] Hence, while Massachusetts has often been referred to as a "Bible Commonwealth," increasingly complex legal problems naturally impelled the colonists to look to a

[28] *Records of Massachusetts Bay,* II, 212.

[29] Coke's doctrines and their influence in the American colonies are more fully developed below at pp. 118–24.

[30] George L. Haskins, "Reception of the Common Law in Seventeenth-Century Massachusetts: A Case Study," in Billias, ed., *Law and Authority in Colonial America,* p. 17, at p. 18.

1. Contemporary copy of the Virginia Charter of 1606. (Courtesy, Library of Congress.)

2. Sir Edward Coke. Portrait attributed to Cornelius Jansen. (Courtesy, *Country Life*.)

3. John Locke, by Sir Godfrey Kneller. (Courtesy, Christ Church, Oxford.)

THE COMMON LAW

HERE THE COMMON LAW OF ENGLAND WAS ESTABLISHED ON THIS CONTINENT WITH THE ARRIVAL OF THE FIRST SETTLERS ON MAY 13,1607. THE FIRST CHARTER GRANTED BY JAMES I TO THE VIRGINIA COMPANY IN 1606 DECLARED THAT THE INHABITANTS OF THE COLONY"...SHALL HAVE AND ENJOY ALL LIBERTIES, FRANCHISES AND IMMUNITIES... AS IF THEY HAD BEEN ABIDING AND BORNE WITHIN THIS OUR REALME OF ENGLANDE...". SINCE MAGNA CARTA THE COMMON LAW HAS BEEN THE CORNERSTONE OF INDIVIDUAL LIBERTIES, EVEN AS AGAINST THE CROWN. SUMMARIZED LATER IN THE BILL OF RIGHTS ITS PRINCIPLES HAVE INSPIRED THE DEVELOPMENT OF OUR SYSTEM OF FREEDOM UNDER LAW, WHICH IS AT ONCE OUR DEAREST POSSESSION AND PROUDEST ACHIEVEMENT.

PRESENTED BY THE VIRGINIA STATE BAR MAY 17, 1959

4. Plaque at Jamestown commemorating the introduction of the common law into America. (Courtesy, Jamestown Foundation.)

fully developed legal system as a model. The Old Testament and the laws of Moses, while prominent in the shaping of rules for moral and religious conduct and as a basis for capital offenses, offered little guidance in the drafting of most of the public and private law for the colony. But a ready model lay at hand, the common law of England; moreover, popular pressure from the freemen and their deputies, and the possibility of intervention by a parliamentary commission from England, added impetus to the reliance on the laws of England as the guide.

The result of the drafting was the famous *Lawes and Liberties of Massachusetts* of 1648. This document has been called "the first modern code of the Western world," antedating Colbert's project in France by twenty years.[31] In fact, rather than a code, it might be more accurate to call it an abridgment of the laws, of the kind already popular among lawyers in England. In any event it was a boon to the colonists, for now the laws in force were available in accessible form, and should a magistrate wield his authority with untoward severity or in disregard of the liberties of the subject, the printed word could be invoked in the subject's defense.

A number of the provisions of the *Lawes and Liberties* draw their substance from Magna Carta. In two notable respects the *Lawes and Liberties* restate the central themes of the Charter: proceedings according to known and general laws, and impartiality in the rendering of justice. The first theme appears at the very outset of the *Lawes and Liberties* in the requirement, like that of the Body of Liberties of 1641, that no punishments were to be meted out "unless it be by the vertue or equity of some expresse law of the Country warranting the same established by a General Court & sufficiently published"—a guarantee made less sure by the proviso, as in 1641, that were a specific law lacking a case might be governed by the "word of God." The other theme, that of impartial justice, is sounded by the repetition in the 1648 document of the 1641 assurance that "every person within this Jurisdiction, whether Inhabitant or

[31] George L. Haskins, *Law and Authority in Early Massachusetts* (New York, 1960), p. 120.

other shall enjoy the same justice and law that is general for this Jurisdiction . . . without partialitie or delay." [32]

Other New England Colonies

THE tension in Massachusetts between those who wanted the laws of England and those who wanted to rule by the word of God had its echo in other parts of New England. Fundamental documents drawn up in several of the New England colonies reflected a marked religious orientation. In Connecticut, a provisional government had been instituted under a 1635 commission of the General Court of Massachusetts to some persons who wished to settle in the Connecticut River Valley. Three towns—Hartford, Windsor, and Wethersfield—in January 1638/39 formed a voluntary compact or constitution called the Fundamental Orders of Connecticut. The settlers pledged themselves to maintain "an orderly and decent Gouerment established according to God"; the Governor was to take an oath to "further the execution of Justice according to the rule of Gods word. . . ." While the Governor was to execute "all wholsome lawes that are or shall be made by lawfull authority here established," the form of the oath is singularly silent on the maintenance of the laws of England.[33]

The theological grounding of the Colony of New Haven was even more evident in its Fundamental Agreement, drawn up in June 1639. The free planters of the colony gathered in a general meeting to establish a civil government in such form as "might be most pleasing unto God." John Davenport put a series of queries to the meeting and asked them to give such answers as "they would be willing should stand upon record for posterity." The first query was "whether the scriptures do hold forth a perfect rule for the direction and government of all men in all duties which they are to perform to GOD and men, as well in families and commonwealth, as in matters of the church?"

[32] *Lawes and Liberties of Massachusetts* (1648) , pp. 1, 32.
[33] Thorpe, I, 519, 522.

This was agreed to unanimously, by show of hands. In answer to another query, the company unanimously voted its reaffirmation of the colony's "plantation covenant" (so called to distinguish it from a church covenant, but the appellation "covenant" having significant theological overtones) and agreed that in all affairs of civil government, such as "choice of magistrates and officers, making and repealing laws, dividing allotments of inheritance, and all things of like nature, we would all of us be ordered by those rules which the scripture holds forth to us. . . ."[34]

These actions taken, Davenport declared that the scriptures gave guidance for the choice of the sort of persons who might best be trusted with the affairs of government and read from Exodus, Deuteronomy, and First Corinthians to prove his point.[35] The company then considered whether their burgesses should be chosen from among church members only. There was some discussion, and a certain amount of wavering on this question, but the meeting finally agreed that only church members should be burgesses and be chosen as magistrates and officers of government.[36]

Theocracy was likewise the form of government provided for in the Government of New Haven, adopted by the General Court held at New Haven in October 1643. The first words of that document stated, "It was agreed and concluded as a fondamentall order nott to be disputed or questioned hereafter, thatt none shall be admitted to be free burgesses . . . butt such planters as are members of some or other of the approved churches of New England, nor shall any butt such free burgesses have any vote in any election . . . nor shall any power or trust in the ordering of any civill affayres, be att any time putt into the hands of any other than such church members. . . ." Only church members could be judges in the trial courts, and

---

[34] *Ibid.*, I, 523–24.

[35] Exod. 18:2; Deut. 1:13; Deut. 17:15; I Cor. 6:1, 6:7. All of these chapters seem relevant to affairs of state, save the verse from Exodus: "Now Jethro, Moses' father in law, took Zipporah, Moses' wife, after he had sent her back." The relevance of this verse is somewhat less than obvious.

[36] Thorpe, I, 524–25.

punishments in criminal cases were to be "according to the minde of God, revealed in his word." [37]

The people of New Haven, like those of Massachusetts, were to discover that government "according to the minde of God" did not furnish especially precise guidelines for the conduct of their offices by magistrates and other officials. About 1653–54 some of the inhabitants of Stamford, Southold, and Milford voiced discontent with the form of government of the New Haven Colony and asked for the admission of English law and for the right of appeal of cases to England. In the Stamford town meeting, Robert Basset declared that he would accept no authority except such as came out of England.

The complaints of Basset and men of like mind in New Haven were about as cordially received as the petition of Robert Child in Massachusetts. The malcontents were haled before the General Court and charged with "words and carriage" against the colony. The leaders were accused of breaking their oath of fidelity by attempting to undermine the authority of the colony's government. Punishment took the form of severe reprimands, heavy fines, and the posting of bond for good behavior.[38]

The dissenting voices were stilled for the time being, but with the Restoration of Charles II (1660) the call for the laws of England was heard once again in New Haven. Francis Browne declared that now that Charles was on the throne the magistrates were acting without authority; he refused to obey laws unless they had come from England. The controversy was in a sense absorbed when the Colony of New Haven was absorbed into Connecticut. In 1662 Charles II granted a charter to John Winthrop and others for the Colony of Connecticut, a charter which followed the traditional pattern of royal charters to the other colonies, including the guarantee that all of the King's subjects who lived in the colony should enjoy "all Liberties and Immunities of free and natural Subjects" as if they lived in England. The charter also contained the standard language requiring that laws of the colony be "not Contrary to the Laws of this Realm of *England*" and a requirement that

[37] *Ibid.*, I, 526–27.   [38] Andrews, *Colonial Period*, II, 183.

fines, imprisonments, and other punishments should be governed by English practices.[39] Connecticut claimed the territory of New Haven under the 1662 charter and demanded New Haven submit to incorporation. New Haven at length yielded, and in January 1665 its towns became part of the Connecticut Colony, bringing at last the laws of England to New Haven.

Some of the New England settlers, in drawing up frames of government, were more anxious to have the laws of England than had been the church fathers of New Haven. The settlers at Exeter, in New Hampshire, drafted an agreement in 1639, in which they combined to set up a government "professing ourselves Subjects to our Sovereign Lord King Charles according to the Libertyes of our English Colony of Massachusetts. . . ." On the laws of England the men of Exeter took what appears to be a middle ground; they bound themselves "to submit to such Godly and Christian Lawes as are established in the realm of England. . . ." An agreement of settlers in the same region in 1641 adopted a more positive stance toward the English law. That agreement said that the settlers had formed a body politic "that wee may the more comfortably enjoy the Benefit of his Majesties Laws" together with such of their own laws as were "not repugnant to the laws of England." [40]

The early days of Rhode Island furnish an interesting contrast to those of its older, larger, and more theocratic neighbor, Massachusetts. It was founded in 1636 by Roger Williams and other refugees from Massachusetts seeking religious and political freedom. English law was from the outset a major factor in the colony's government, and, unlike the laws of the Puritan colonies, Rhode Island's laws, especially the acts and orders of 1647, were founded, not on the word of God, but on the laws of England. The acts and orders of 1647 comprise one of the earliest American codes of laws and, as Charles M. Andrews has observed, the "first to embody in all its parts the precedents set by the laws and statutes of England." [41]

Not only the 1647 acts but also the acts of other years typically were accompanied by a reference to the English statute

[39] Thorpe, I, 533–34.   [40] *Ibid.*, IV, 2445.
[41] Andrews, *Colonial Period*, II, 26.

books. For example, an act of 1673, concerning forceable entries and forceable detainers, listed a series of English statutes
beginning with 5 Richard II, chapter 7, and adopted "every
clause in them or any of them (soe far as the nature and
constitution of this place and people can admitt) ." [42] The concern to be governed by the laws of England appears, too, in the
charter of incorporation granted by the colony's government to
the freemen of Providence in 1648, in which there is the proviso
that the laws of Providence Plantation must be "conformable
to the lawes of England, so neare as the nature and constitution
of the place will admit. . . ." [43]

In the disputes and events in seventeenth-century New England we see emerge one of the recurring themes of American
legal and constitutional history: the interplay between the tradition of looking to fundamental documents for guarantees of
men's liberties and the vision of a "higher" law from which
those liberties spring. Of all the American colonies of the seventeenth century none were so likely as those in New England to
display theocratic tendencies. The early years of Massachusetts
Bay and of New Haven are apt examples. But equally early in
these colonies appeared the tendencies of constitutionalism, the
appeal to fundamental laws made by men. In the decades and
centuries that followed, natural law and the laws of England
were sometimes to be the catchwords of opposing forces, and
other times to be arrayed on the same side of a struggle. In
Massachusetts in the 1640's they were opposed; in the Continental Congress in 1774 they were merged. But whether in
conflict or in unison, the two traditions of natural law and
constitutional law so evident in seventeenth-century New England were becoming part and parcel of life and law in America.

[42] *Records of the Colony of Rhode Island and Providence Plantations*, ed. John
Russell Bartlett (Providence, 1856–65) , II, 513.
[43] *Ibid.*, I, 214. In Maine Sir Ferdinando Gorges was creating what he expected
to be a society on the English model. In 1642 he issued a charter for the City of
Georgeana providing that the city should have such privileges, liberties, and
freedoms "as far as in me lieth" as the City of Bristol, England, had under its
charter. Andrews, *Colonial Period*, I, 424–25. The King's charter of 1639 to
Gorges for the "Mayne Land of New England" contained the customary guarantees of the rights of Englishmen. Thorpe, III, 1631.

Chapter III

The Proprietary Colonies

Maryland

MARYLAND owes its original existence to George Calvert, first Lord Baltimore. A convert to Roman Catholicism and a man of high place in England, Calvert sought to establish a haven for Roman Catholics in America. Calvert died before a charter could be granted, and the first Charter of Maryland was issued to Calvert's son, Cecil, second Lord Baltimore, in 1632. Charles I's regard for his "well beloved and right trusty" subject, the late George Calvert, was evident in the preamble to the Maryland Charter, and the charter, observing that Cecil was "treading in the steps of his Father," granted broad powers to the proprietor of the new colony.[1]

The Colony of Maryland, which was launched without the hardships and suffering that had attended the earlier settlement at Jamestown, was to be, for over a century, the scene of notable struggles between the proprietary government and popular movements over the rights of the colonists. The charter of 1632, like the charters of the other colonies, guaranteed to Marylanders "all Privileges, Franchises and Liberties of this our Kingdom of England . . . without Impediment, Molestation, Vexation, Impeachment, or Grievance of Us, or any of our

[1] Thorpe, III, 1677.

Heirs or Successors; any Statute, Act, Ordinance, or Provision to the contrary thereof, notwithstanding."[2] In the years that followed, this guarantee was to become the rallying cry for inhabitants seeking the benefits of Magna Carta and the laws of England.[3]

Within the first ten years of the colony's life at least four attempts were made to put on the statute books of Maryland statements of the rights of Englishmen, specifically the guarantees of Magna Carta. In 1637 the Maryland Assembly passed a bill "for the liberties of the people," and in the following year another "Act for the liberties of the people" was introduced, providing that Marylanders should enjoy "all such rights liberties immunities priviledges and free customs within this Province as any naturall born subject of England hath or ought to have" by virtue of the common or statute law of England, save as such law might be altered by the laws of Maryland. The bill of 1638 went on to guarantee proceedings according to the "law of the land"; in a paraphrase of chapter 39 of Magna Carta, the bill said that no one should be "imprisoned nor disseised or dispossessed of their freehold goods or Chattels or be out Lawed Exiled or otherwise destroyed fore judged or punished then according to the Laws of this province," saving the prerogatives of the proprietor.[4]

The Marylanders were bound to have Magna Carta. In March 1639 an "Act ordeining certain Laws for the Goverment of this Province" provided that the "Inhabitants of this Province shall have all their rights and liberties according to the great Charter of England." And in 1640 another act for the "Peoples liberties" was adopted.[5]

An interesting incident in 1661 shows that the Governor was willing to concede Magna Carta's effect in Maryland or at least to signify his intention to abide by its guarantees. In that year

---

[2] *Ibid.*, III, 1681.

[3] See Joseph H. Smith, "The Foundations of Law in Maryland: 1634–1715," in George Athan Billias, *Law and Authority in Colonial America* (Barre, Mass., 1965), p. 92.

[4] *Archives of Maryland,* ed. William Hand Browne (Baltimore, 1883———), I, 20, 41 [hereinafter *Archives of Maryland*]. A note records that the 1638 bill was engrossed to be read the third time but was never read or passed. *Ibid.*, I, 39.

[5] *Ibid.*, I, 82, 83, 94.

the lower house of the Maryland Assembly asked the upper house to consent to an act assuring assemblymen free speech and debate, without fear of prejudice for having given their opinions on pending bills. The Governor invited both houses to meet together and said that such an act was unnecessary since he would assure them that they would have as much liberty as "Magna Charta did afforde them in England. . . ." This satisfied the popular house, and they withdrew their request for an act. The next year, in providing that abuse by members of this right of free debate should be punishable only by the Assembly itself, the lower house took note that they had not forgotten the Governor's promise that they should enjoy "liberty of speeche as being free borne children of England according to Magna charta." [6]

The first chapter of Magna Carta had declared that "the English Church shall be free and enjoy her rights in their integrity and her liberties untouched." As early as 1639 the Assembly of Maryland enacted that "Holy Churches within this province shall have all her rights and liberties." In 1640 another "Act for Church liberties" restated chapter 1 of Magna Carta in the words, "Holy Church within this Province shall haue and enjoy all her Rights liberties and Franchises wholy and without Blemish." [7]

Chapter 1 of Magna Carta was not a statement of the separation of church and state as we understand it today, nor was it a guarantee of freedom of conscience; rather, it was a grant of clerical privilege, especially in regard to church elections.[8] But the language of chapter 1 was general and elastic, and in 1661 Maryland's restatement of this language was to be invoked in a Maryland court as guaranteeing freedom of religion. To an indictment charging unlawful teaching of religious doctrines, a defendant named Francis Fitzherbert demurred on the ground that "by the very first Lawe of this Country Holy Church within this Province shall haue & Enjoye all her Rights libertyes and Franchises wholy and without Blemish, amongst which that of preacheing and teacheing is not the least. . . ."

[6] *Ibid.*, I, 398, 429–30.   [7] *Ibid.*, I, 83, 96.
[8] See McKechnie, *Magna Carta*, pp. 191–94.

Fitzherbert argued that "every Church professing to believe in God the father Sonne and holy Ghoste is accounted Holy Church" in Maryland. Fitzherbert also cited an act providing that no one professing belief in Jesus Christ should be "molested for or in Respect of his or her Religion or the free Exercise thereof"; undoubtedly, preaching and teaching "is the free Exercise of every Churchmans Religion. . . ." Fitzherbert's demurrer was sustained.[9]

Marylanders showed a special concern that the laws of England govern criminal proceedings in the colony. In 1674 the upper house of the Maryland Assembly voted to send a message to the lower house to ask if they would concur with the upper house in drawing up a "List of such Lawes of England" as might be necessary to govern criminal cases in the province. The lower house agreed that such a list ought to be compiled and asked if a joint committee might be appointed for that purpose. But the lower house, while ready to remedy deficiencies in the laws, wanted it made clear that "the Lawes of England ought to be esteemed & Adjudged of full force and Power within this Province. . . ." The upper house was hesitant to take this step, arguing that because the laws of England were so voluminous and sometimes uncertain it would be better if the Assembly simply drew up a specific list.[10]

In 1684 the two houses again had occasion to debate the application of English laws to Maryland. The issue was the right of the Speaker to issue warrants for elections to vacant seats, and the Proprietor argued that "the King had power to dispose of his conquests as he pleased." The lower house, irate over this suggestion, insisted on the rights of its members as being those of Englishmen, "their birthright by the words of the Charter." The upper house explained that it had not meant to liken the freemen of the province to a conquered people.[11] But it had touched a sore nerve on a subject which through the eighteenth century was to occupy legal minds on both sides of

[9] Attorney General v. Fitzherbert (1661), in *Archives of Maryland*, XLI, 566.

[10] *Archives of Maryland*, II, 347–48, 368–69, 374–75.

[11] St. George Leakin Sioussat, "The Theory of the Extension of English Statutes to the Plantations," in *Select Essays in Anglo-American Legal History* (Boston, 1907–09), I, 416, at p. 424.

the Atlantic, namely, whether the American countries were conquered territory and therefore not automatically entitled to have English laws extended to them, or whether the colonies were settlements in uninhabited country and entitled as a matter of course to the benefits of English laws.[12]

Even the Indians in Maryland were to live under the English law. To the Articles of Peace concluded with the Nanticoke Indians in 1687 there was added an article "that if any Indian commits an offence against the English he should be tried by the English law. . . ."[13]

To look to the laws of England for guidance meant to look, above all, to Magna Carta. Perhaps the most explicit acknowledgment of the connection between the Maryland Charter's guarantee of the "liberties of Englishmen" and Magna Carta was made by a number of Marylanders in a statement in 1682 in which they defended the Lord Proprietor against charges that he had favored Roman Catholics over Protestants in the colony. The signers of the statement agreed on the Proprietor's impartiality in the distribution of public offices and published "to the world" the freedoms Marylanders enjoyed "according to the grand priviledges of Magna Charta, as effectually and in as full & ample manner to all intents & purposes as any of His Majestie's Subjects within any part of His Majestie's dominions whatsoever. . . ."[14]

With this connection made explicit, it is not surprising that Magna Carta was pleaded in lawsuits in the Maryland courts. In 1670 Henry Hooper filed suit in a provincial court, alleging that he was administrator of a decedent's estate and as such in lawful possession of the deceased's property. Hooper complained that the defendants had by force taken a number of cattle belonging to the estate. The complaint quoted in full the 29th chapter of Henry III's issue of Magna Carta (chapters 39 and 40 of the charter of 1215) and alleged that for the defendants to take the cattle without a trial or other lawful authority

---

[12] See pp. 99–108, *infra*.

[13] The Articles of Peace were confirmed at a Council of Maryland at St. Mary's on Sept. 19, 1687. *Archives of Maryland*, V, 558.

[14] *Ibid.*, V, 354.

was "Contrary to the form and effect of the said Act of Magna Charta." The court agreed that the defendants had acted "Contrary to the Act of Parliam' of Magna Charta" and awarded Hooper damages of 45,950 pounds of tobacco.[15] It is interesting that Magna Carta should thus have been invoked against private citizens, but the complaint alleged that the defendants had acted "by Pretence and Colour of an order of Court" empowering them to require an accounting of the estate. In this respect Hooper's complaint resembles modern pleadings in which, in order to invoke the Fourteenth Amendment to the United States Constitution (which of its own force operates on States, not individuals), a party may seek to show that there is "state action" present in the actions of individuals, for example, when an individual seeks to have a state court enforce discriminatory private conduct.[16]

Following the Glorious Revolution in England, the Anglican Church was established in Maryland. The Maryland act of 1692 providing for the establishment is interesting on two points. Like earlier Maryland statutes it drew on the language of Magna Carta's first chapter in assuring to the Anglican Church "all her Rights Liberties and Franchises wholly inviolable." Moreover, the Assembly used the occasion of establishment to reaffirm the people's demand for the rights of Magna Carta; the 1692 act commanded that "the Great Charter of England be kept and observed in all points"—a mirror image of the language of the statute of Edward III of 1368 which had provided that Magna Carta "be holden and kept in all points." [17] The act of 1692 was, however, disallowed by the

[15] Hooper v. Burgess (1670), in *ibid.*, XXXIV, 676–77, LVII, 571–74. Similarly, see the petition of Thomas Toney, Thomas Frost, and Thomas Smyth alleging that another, acting under letters of administration, had put them out of a tract of land "whence by Magna Carta they ought not to be removed but by legall Judgm' of theire Peares." *Ibid.*, LVII, 75.

[16] For example, the judicial enforcement of a private agreement barring Negroes from owning certain real estate. See Shelley v. Kraemer, 334 U.S. 1 (1948). Compare the respective opinions of Justices Douglas and Black in Bell v. Maryland, 378 U.S. 226, 242, 255–60, 318, 326–35 (1964).

[17] *Archives of Maryland,* XIII, 425–26. The act of 1692 also had a prohibition on "bodily Labour or Occupation" on Sunday. That act was, as the United States Supreme Court put it, the "obvious precursor" of the Maryland Sunday Closing Laws upheld by the Court against claims that such laws constituted an "establishment of religion." McGowan v. Maryland, 366 U.S. 420, 446 (1961).

Privy Council on the insistence of the Solicitor General that "he knew not how far the enacting thereof will be agreeable to the constitution of this colony or consistent with the royal prerogative." [18] (Maryland was a royal colony from 1692 until 1715.) Maryland's establishment act, as finally passed in 1702, made no reference to the rights of the people.[19]

The eighteenth century saw repeated arguments over the extent to which English statutes had application in Maryland. In 1722 the upper and lower houses clashed over the "tobacco question"—the issue whether, as the lower house insisted, there should be repeal of the so-called trash act (an act which, by forbidding the export of inferior tobacco, bore heavily on smaller planters). After the upper house voted against repeal of the "trash act," the lower house passed a set of resolutions which, directed at the form of judges' oaths, were destined to provoke unsettling constitutional questions. The oath strikingly recalled Magna Carta, for a judge was to swear to do "equall Law and right to all the Kings Subjects rich and poor" and to disregard any instructions of the King, the Lord Proprietor, or any other. Where the law of Maryland furnished no rule of decision, a judge was to render judgment "According to the Laws Statutes Ordinances and reasonable Customs of England and of this province." [20] Such a resolution, by introducing English law in gross into Maryland and by freeing judges from royal or proprietary commands, posed a direct challenge to proprietary prerogative, and the councilors of the upper house postponed consideration of the resolution until the next session.[21]

The Lord Proprietor soon made it clear that he was opposed to the wholesale importation into Maryland of English statutes and vetoed an act of the lower house (to which the upper house and the Governor had consented) which by implication had introduced the English statutes.[22] When the Assembly reconvened in 1723 a committee was appointed to inspect the province's ancient records and to determine to what extent the

---

[18] George Chalmers, *Introduction to the History of the Revolt* (Boston, 1845), I, 259.

[19] See *Archives of Maryland*, XXIV, 265–73.   [20] *Ibid.*, XXXIV, 440–42.

[21] *Ibid.*, XXXIV, 469.   [22] *Ibid.*, XXXIV, 493.

laws and statutes of England had been received into the courts of Maryland. The committee found four kinds of evidence bearing on this question: the royal charter of the colony, acts of assembly, instructions to magistrates and other officers, and judicial proceedings in civil and criminal cases. The Charter of Maryland, the committee observed, contained "remarkable Clauses" assuring emigrants to Maryland all the liberties and immunities they would have enjoyed in England. Tracing in considerable detail the various acts of assembly, commissions to magistrates, and proceedings in the colony's courts, the committee concluded that governors and governed alike had acted on the assumption that the English statutes had effect in Maryland. It could hardly be otherwise, thought the committee, for their ancestors had been promised the liberties of Englishmen as an inducement to settle in the New World. It would, they believed,

be very Strange and unreasonable, and most Miserable Would our Case be, if freemen by Runing such Risques and becomeing beneficiall to their Mother Country, Should be in Worse Circumstances than their fellow Subjects and denied to participate with them in those things that are equally their birth Rights and be in a State of Slavery (as the Case must undoubtedly be of any People that have not the means of Preserving their Liberties) and it would be a great Absurdity to advance that we are intituled to all the Rights and Liberties of British Subjects and that we Can't have the Benefite of the Laws by which those Rights and Liberties are Reserved.[23]

But when the Assembly passed an act declaring the general extension to Maryland of the English statutes, the Proprietor vetoed the act and instructed the Governor not to allow passage of any act for the wholesale introduction of English statutes.[24]

In 1727 the question again involved the form of the oaths of judges. The Assembly passed an act setting out the form of the judges' oath. Those who drafted the oath clearly had Magna Carta in mind for not only was a judge to swear to do "equal

[23] *Ibid.*, XXXIV, 661–79.
[24] St. George Leakin Sioussat, *The English Statutes in Maryland* (Baltimore, 1903), pp. 32–33.

Law and Right to all the King's Subjects, rich and poor," but also he was not to "take any Gift, Bribe, or Fee, for delaying, or rendering judgment"—the very abuse which had led, in 1215, to Magna Carta's promise (chapter 40) that justice would not be sold, denied, or delayed. Again, where the laws of Maryland gave no rule of decision, a judge was required to render judgment "according to the Laws, Statutes, and reasonable Customs of England, agreeable to the Usage and Constitution of this Province." This act was disallowed by the proprietary.[25]

Steps and countersteps followed; bills and resolutions were introduced in the Assembly only to be vetoed by the Governor. In 1728 the Assembly's case was stated in one of the great pamphlets of the period, Daniel Dulany the Elder's *The Right of the Inhabitants of Maryland to the Benefit of the English Laws.*[26] Dulany, who had studied law at Gray's Inn in London, was a leader of the Maryland bar. In those days before the separation of powers, Dulany was the Governor's Attorney General and at the same time a member of the Maryland Lower House, sitting for Annapolis. He had taken his seat in 1722, the session in which the upper and lower houses had parted company over the "tobacco question." After the upper house had voted against repeal of the "trash act," Dulany had had a hand in drafting the resolutions governing the form of judges' oaths. As the dispute deepened in the next few years, Dulany took to his study to pore over works of history, philosophy, and law. The result, in 1728, was his tract, *The Right of the Inhabitants of Maryland to the Benefit of the English Laws.*[27]

Dulany's pamphlet was addressed to the "pretty warm Contest" then going on over the right of Marylanders to the benefits of English laws. He was persuaded that "it is of the utmost Consequence to be at a Certainty about it; It behoves every

---

[25] *Archives of Maryland,* XXXVI, 81–82.

[26] *The Right of the Inhabitants of Maryland to the Benefit of the English Laws* (Annapolis, 1728), in Sioussat, *The English Statutes in Maryland* [hereinafter *Benefit of the English Laws*]. Page references which follow are those of the Dulany appendix in Sioussat.

[27] For an account of Dulany's role in the events of the 1720's, see Aubrey C. Land, *The Dulanys of Maryland* (Baltimore, 1955), pp. 62–85.

Man, that has any regard to, or Interest in the Country, to use his utmost Endeavor to put it in a true Light. . . ." [28]

English laws, proved by the mother country to be "beneficial to Society, and adapted to the Genius, and Constitution of their Ancestors," Dulany thought preferable to composing new sets of laws, an expensive undertaking for a new country, and certainly to be preferred to being governed "by the Discretion (as some People softly term the *Caprice,* and *Arbitrary Pleasure,*) of any Set of Men." [29] Dulany, in contrasting government according to the laws of England with discretionary and arbitrary rule, would have felt at home with the Massachusetts folk who petitioned in 1646 for the laws of England and an end to government by magistrates' discretion.[30]

Quoting Sir Edward Coke, Dulany linked the common law and the liberty of the subject:

This Law, of England, is the Subject's Birth-Right, and best Inheritance; and to it, may be justly applied, what the great Oracle of the Law, the Lord Coke, saith of the Common Law. "Of Common Right, that is, by the Common Law; so called, because this Common Law, is the best and most Common Birth-Right, that the Subject hath, for the Safeguard and Defence, not only of his Goods, Lands, and Revenues; but of his Wife, and Children, his Body, Fame, and Life, also." [31]

In fact, Dulany began to sound rather like Coke challenging the Stuart kings from the floor of Parliament. It was the law of England which, said Dulany, allowed the Englishman to stand up to the most powerful of rulers:

'Tis this Law, that will effectually secure every Honest Man, who has the benefit of it, in his Life, the Enjoyment of his Liberty, and the Fruits of his Industry. 'Tis by Virtue of this Law, that a British Subject, may with Courage, and Freedom, tell the most daring, and powerful Oppressor, that He must not injure him, with Impunity. This Law, uprightly and honestly applied, and administered, will secure Men from all Degrees of Oppression, Violence, and Injustice; it tells the Magistrate what he has to do, and leaves him little Room, to gratify his own Passion, and Resentment, at the Experience of his Fellow-Subject.[32]

[28] *Benefit of the English Laws,* p. 1.   [29] *Ibid.,* pp. 1–2.
[30] See pp. 35–48, *supra.*   [31] *Benefit of the English Laws,* p. 4.   [32] *Ibid.*

The first settlers came to Maryland with the consent of the Crown. The colony prospered, and the colonists remained throughout loyal subjects. As such, they had a right to enjoy their liberty and property. Dulany noted the argument of some who had suggested that it was English liberties, not English laws, to which the colonists were entitled. To this Dulany gave the answer that "Right, and Remedy, are inseparable," and that it was the English law which gave security to English liberties. And the colonists must have *all* of the English law. If they could be deprived of any part of it, they might "by the same Reason, and Authority, be deprived of some other Part; and this, will naturally render the Whole, uncertain; and our Lives, Liberties, and Properties, Precarious." [33]

Dulany showed that he shared Coke's reverence for Magna Carta, especially for its guarantee of justice according to the "law of the land." Dulany would make Magna Carta a textbook: "The 29th chapter [chapters 39 and 40 of the charter of 1215] is not long, and ought to be read by every Body, and (in my humble Opinion,) taught to Children, with their first Rudiments. . . ." [34]

If the rights of Englishman, in statutory form, had begun with a charter, Magna Carta, it was through another charter, that of Maryland, that Dulany traced the colonists' present claim to English laws. Dulany quoted the language of the royal charter to Cecil Calvert assuring the colony's inhabitants the "Liberties, Franchises, and Privileges" that they would have enjoyed in England. How, asked Dulany, could Marylanders enjoy the benefit of the rights their charter had given them unless they also had the English laws necessary to secure those rights? [35] In thus tying together the prototype English charter, Magna Carta, as a declaration of substantive rights, and the colonial charter as the vehicle for those rights, Dulany was putting his argument in a form which would reappear in the pamphlets written two score years later, when, with Independence approaching, the stakes were far higher.[36]

Finally, in 1732 all parties agreed on a bill, which became

---

[33] *Ibid.,* pp. 6–13. [34] *Ibid.,* p. 14. [35] *Ibid.,* pp. 24, 27.
[36] See pp. 188–202, *infra.*

law, requiring a judge to swear, among other things, to "do equal Law and Right to all the King's Subjects, Rich and Poor, according to the Laws, Customs, and Directions, of the Acts of Assembly of this Province, so far forth as they provide, and where they are silent, according to the Laws, Statutes, and reasonable Customs of England, as used and practised within this Province. . . ." [37]

From this time to the eve of the Revolution resolutions regarding the laws of England were introduced and unanimously passed in session after session of the Maryland Assembly. These resolutions not only instructed judges to observe the laws of England; they also explicitly rejected the argument that the province was a conquered country and as such not necessarily entitled to the benefits of the English laws. The assemblymen resolved that anyone who should argue that Marylanders had forfeited "any part of their English Liberties" mistook the country's "happy Constitution." Thus Maryland held itself always to have had the common law and such English statutes as secured the "Rights and Liberties of the Subject." The texts of these resolutions, passed in successive sessions of the Assembly, bear a striking resemblance to each other, varying for the most part only in the smallest points of punctuation and style. Each set of resolutions obviously was copied from, and was in the tradition of, those which had gone before. [38] They were passed with such regularity over a thirty-year period that their proposal became a kind of ritual, a periodic renewing of faith, rather like the annual proclamation by the President of the United States of sympathy for the plight of the "captive nations" behind the Iron Curtain. [39]

So deeply imbedded in colonial Maryland's consciousness was the belief in the values of the English laws that after

[37] *Archives of Maryland,* XXXVII, 519.

[38] See *ibid.,* XLII, 320–21 (1742), XLIV, 69–70, 256–58 (1745, 1746), XLVI, 235–37, 651–53 (1749, 1751), L, 596–98 (1754), LV, 207–8 (1757), LVI, 16–18 (1758), LVIII, 72–74 (1762), LIX, 133–35 (1765), LXI 330–31 (1768), LXIII, 80–81 (1771).

[39] The presidential proclamations of "Captive Nations Week" were first requested by joint resolution of Congress in 1959. It remains a subject of intense concern to many inside and outside Congress. See, e.g., the remarks of Congressman Derwinski in 111 Cong. Rec. 15279–83 (June 30, 1965).

Independence, when the new State of Maryland drafted its first constitution, the Maryland Declaration of Rights of 1776 said that the inhabitants of Maryland were entitled to "the common law of England," including trial by jury, and to "the benefit of such of the English statutes, as existed at the time of their first emigration, and which, by experience, have been found applicable to their local and other circumstances," and of such later English statutes as had been introduced and used in the Maryland courts.[40] Paradoxically, it took separation from the British Crown finally to settle Marylanders' rights as proclaimed in statute and pamphlet since the first years of the colony.

The Carolinas

THE political history of the Carolinas, South and North, in the colonial era is essentially one of a contest between the interests of the people and those of the Proprietors. In 1629 Charles granted to his Attorney General, Sir Robert Heath, all the land from sea to sea lying between the 31st and 36th parallels, but no settlements were made under this charter. In 1663 the same lands were granted by Charles II to the Earl of Clarendon and seven other favorites of the Crown. This charter contained the usual requirement that in making laws and ordinances the grantees should take care to see that they were, as near as circumstances permitted, agreeable to the laws of England.[41]

A popular voice in the government was provided for at the outset. By the 1663 charter there was to be an assembly of the freemen of the province, and, while the Proprietors were given the power to make "ordinances" when the Assembly was not sitting, laws as such were required to have the "advice, assent and approbation of the freemen of the said province." Property rights received special protection. The charter said that ordinances might not extend "to the binding, charging, or taking away of the right or interest of any person or persons, in their freehold, goods or chattels whatsoever." [42] In this provision

[40] Thorpe, III, 1686–87.   [41] *Ibid.,* V, 2745–46.   [42] *Ibid.,* V, 2746.

there is an interesting parallel both to Magna Carta's chapters 28, 30, and 31, which placed limits on the taking of property by the Crown, and (since the Carolina Charter allowed only laws, to which the freemen had to assent, to affect property interests) to the Great Charter's mandate that no scutage or aid should be imposed save by "common counsel" of the kingdom. In 1665 another charter from the King enlarged the area which comprised Carolina and repeated the terms of the 1663 grant as to how laws and ordinances should be made for the province.[43]

The Proprietors were anxious to encourage settlement in the colony and circulated prospectuses offering quite liberal terms to those who might emigrate to Carolina. In 1665 the Concessions and Agreements of the Lords Proprietors put lawmaking powers into the hands of assemblies in the respective counties (three were proposed), with the proviso that such laws must conform, as near as convenience would permit, to those of England. Moreover, the Proprietors declared that in these counties there should be no tax, custom, subsidy, tallage, assessment, or other duty "upon any Culler or pretence" other than such as were imposed by the authority and consent of the assemblies.[44]

Notwithstanding this seemingly auspicious start, there was in the seventeenth century growing discontent among the settlers with the Proprietors' rule. The colonists resisted the adoption of the Fundamental Constitutions of 1669, which were principally the work of John Locke and which were feudal even by European standards.[45] By the turn of the century the principal causes of unrest were the Proprietors' methods of managing land grants and the pressures for the payment of quit-rents. An idea of what bothered the Carolinians may be had from an address and remonstrance sent in 1698 to the Lords Proprietors by the Commons House of South Carolina (North and South Carolina having been governed as separate provinces though theoretically a single province).

In their address the Commons listed grievances which they hoped the proprietors would remedy, among them the complaint that there was not in the colony an exemplified copy of

[43] *Ibid.,* V, 2761.   [44] *Ibid.,* V, 2758, 2761.   [45] See *ibid.,* V, 2772.

the King's charter. Other complaints were lodged against the same person's holding both the offices of high sheriff and judge of the Court of Pleas, want of power in the colony's government to repeal objectionable laws, excessive land grants, and restrictions on trade.[46] The Commons sought and found a basis for their interests in the laws of England. In 1702 they protested the threat of the Governor and Council to use martial law to force their will on the Commons. This, said the Commons' address, might be appropriate to a French king, "who Rules by a Will that hath no Law or bounds Sett to it," but not to English colonies, where "English Kings & Governo*: make us happy in Ruleing by those Laws the People forme. . . ." [47]

In 1703 the South Carolinians made explicit their demand for the rights of Englishmen. In an address to the Lords Proprietors, they referred to the "miserable Estate" of the colony and submitted that "it cannot stand with the Duty we owe to our selves as *Englishmen,* or to our Posterity, to sit down contented with less than that which every Liege and Freeborn Subject of the Crown of *England* may, and of right ought to have." Naming free elections to be among the "fundamental rights & unquestionable Privileges belonging to *English-men,*" the petitioners complained of abuse of members of the Assembly, irregularities in elections, and other things.[48]

North Carolinians were no less concerned with the liberties of Englishmen. In 1715 North Carolina's Assembly voted that the common law should be in force as in England. Further it was agreed that all English statute law "providing for the privileges of the people" should be in force in North Carolina even though the province might not be named in those statutes.[49] Events in North Carolina within the next few years were to prove how seriously North Carolinians—governor and governed alike—took Magna Carta and the rights of Englishmen.

[46] *Journals of the Commons House of Assembly of South Carolina* (1698), ed. A. S. Salley, Jr. (Columbia, S.C., 1914), pp. 34–36.

[47] *Ibid.,* (1702), pp. 76–78.

[48] William James Rivers, *A Sketch of the History of South Carolina to the Close of the Proprietary Government by the Revolution of 1719* (Charleston, S.C., 1856), pp. 453–60.

[49] *Public Acts of the General Assembly of North Carolina,* ed. James Iredell, rev. Francois-Xavier Martin (New Bern, N.C., 1804), pp. 14–15.

North Carolinians never got on especially well with their colonial governors; indeed North Carolina at any period in its history has had something of a reputation for an independent spirit. In 1724 Sir Richard Everard became governor of the province; within two years he had so alienated the popular house of the provincial government that they felt obliged to draw up a memorial which they styled "The Exclamations of the Injured & Oppress'd." The assemblymen complained in particular of the arbitrary and illegal imprisonment, without cause, of members of the House and the refusal to give such prisoners the grounds for their committal. "This," declared the Assembly, "we take to be a great Infringement of our Libertys as we are Freemen Brittains, to be Contrary to the Great Charter & to that Invaluable Act of Parliament commonly called the Habeas Corpus Act." [50]

To charge a governor with violating Magna Carta was a serious matter, as a member of the Council, Edmond Porter, discovered in 1727. A grand jury impaneled at a General Court of Oyer and Terminer at Edenton indicted Porter upon a number of charges. Porter, the grand jury said, had been "instigated & moved by the Devill and his own wicked heart and Seditious Spirit" to sow dissension among the people, to bring the Governor into contempt, and to raise faction and rebellion against the government. Porter was charged with having "doubled his Fist & shaking it" at the Governor and having called the Governor a "worthless fellow."

Moreover, the indictment continued, when a Negro claiming his freedom had applied to the Governor, who had ordered the Negro kept safe until a trial of the question could be had, Porter had written a libelous letter to the Chief Justice, Cristopher Gale, saying that the Governor, by the rule he had laid down, might take "my Bed my horse or my Oxe." Porter was charged with having said that, if the Governor thought himself "invested with an absolute power of Acting as he thinks fitt," the people would have to disabuse him of that notion and "make him Sensible that English born Subjects will never

[50] *Colonial Records of North Carolina,* ed. William L. Saunders and Walter Clark (Raleigh, N.C., 1886–1914), II, 613–14.

tamely give up their undoubted right while so inestimable a Book as Magna Charta is. . . ." Thus to insinuate that the Governor had "acted in an Arbitrary manner against Magna Charta," was, the indictment concluded, "a most heinous and Scandalous & false Aspersion & in great Contempt of the Sayd Governo^r." [51] (One thinks of the legal aphorism, "The greater the truth, the greater the libel.")

Porter obviously was a burr under the Governor's saddle. In 1729 North Carolina became a royal colony. The new royal Governor, George Burrington, wrote the Lords of Trade in 1731 that he had managed to keep the people of the colony "in perfect Peace and Quietness" and had put an end to the tumults which had been frequent when he had first arrived. The disorders, Burrington reported, had been stirred up by Porter, whose character was so "infamous" that Burrington thought it best if he were to be removed from his positions as admiralty judge and as member of the Council. [52]

Ironically, Porter, who had charged Governor Everard with violating Magna Carta, was, as judge, alleged by others to have infringed the Great Charter himself. William Little, on behalf of himself and "divers other persons Late sufferers of the Court of Admiralty here" asked leave of the Governor in 1731 to lay before him evidence of the manner in which Porter had, by his arbitrary conduct on the bench, "divested the Subjects of the Benifit of the common law which is Every Englishmans birth right. . . ." Further, in a charge sounding of the guarantees of chapters 39 and 40 of Magna Carta, Little said that Porter had threatened parties with contempt citations in disregard of the principle that "every man without fear dread ought to have free Liberty to make his Defence. . . ."

Little described a suit in admiralty brought in the name of the King against Little for the King's share of a seizure made at Bath when Little had been appointed agent and the condemnation money had come into his hands. Little had offered the judge, Porter, a full discharge from the collector for the King's share, but even though no prosecutor appeared Porter retained

---

[51] *Ibid.,* II, 687–89. [52] *Ibid.,* III, 202–3.

the suit and compelled Little to give £600 bail. Little complained that "such Excessive Bail was against Magna Charta and the Laws and Liberties of an English Subject. . . ." Little concluded his petition by alleging that in every case that had been before Porter he had apparently proceeded in an "arbitrary and unlawfull manner." [53]

Porter's charges against Governor Everard and William Little's allegations against Porter have one striking characteristic in common: the invocation of Magna Carta as the subject's safeguard against arbitrary government. In the one instance a governor, in the other a judge, were held obliged to discharge their offices in accordance with the limits laid down by the Great Charter. This antithesis between the Charter and arbitrary rule is an interesting historical antecedent of the like antithesis drawn by American courts of a later time between due process of law (itself a concept derived from Magna Carta) and arbitrariness. As modern Americans invoke due process of law, so Carolinians of the eighteenth century looked to Magna Carta.

New York

In 1664 the Dutch colony of New Amsterdam, which had begun about four years before with a small settlement planted by the Dutch West India Company, came to an end. Surrendered without a fight to an English fleet, the territory became part of the domain granted by King Charles II to his brother James, Duke of York. The charter to James carried unusual significance, for it was the only charter in the history of colonial America issued to a member of the royal family. The document itself, drawn in great haste, is the shortest of all the colonial charters and gives sweeping powers to the grantee. Among other things, the Duke received sole power, unhampered by any popular assembly, to make laws, regulate trade, make land grants, and fix taxes. It is interesting, however, that short as the charter was and few as the restrictions were, there was the

[53] *Ibid.*, III, 224, 231–32.

requirement that laws and ordinances of the province "be not contrary to the lawes and statutes of this our Realme of England." Moreover, the King reserved to himself the right to hear appeals "touching any judgment or sentence" meted out in the colony.[54]

Richard Nicolls became governor of the province and proceeded to ascertain the boundaries of the Duke's grant. He obtained the somewhat unwilling assent of Connecticut to that colony's southern boundary being fixed as the sea; Long Island, the eastern end of which Connecticut had laid claim to, thus became part of the Duke's domain. Nicolls sent out letters in which he said that, when the weather permitted (it then being winter of 1664), he would have the inhabitants of Long Island send deputies "to meete in relation to ye affaires of the Island." Nicolls assured the people of Long Island that they would have "equall (if not greater freedomes & Imumityes) than any of his Majesties Colonyes in New England." [55]

The adoption of English laws for the Duke's colony was an acknowledged need. Nicolls, in a circular letter to the Long Island towns and Westchester, observed that because of unsettled times "few or no Lawes could be putt in due Execution," with the result that land titles were in doubt, civil liberties unprotected, and private disputes unresolved. He would, therefore, in accordance with his commission from the Duke, undertake "to Settle good and knowne Laws" on the colony and, to that end, was calling a "General Meeting" of deputies elected by the freemen (Dutch and English) of the several towns.[56]

The code of laws promulgated for Long Island (and later extended to the rest of the province) gave the freeholders a voice in the government and included guarantees of jury trial and religious freedom. But there was considerable unrest and opposition to the enforcement of the Duke's laws, especially those imposing taxes. Opposition centered in towns on Long Island, towns whose population was English in origin. In 1672

[54] Thorpe, III, 1638–39.
[55] Morton Pennypacker, *The Duke's Laws: Their Antecedents, Implications and Importance* (N.Y.U. Anglo-American Legal History Series No. 9; New York, 1944), pp. 14–15.
[56] *Ibid.*, pp. 16–17.

towns in the far eastern end of Long Island asked the Privy Council in England to allow them to be annexed to Connecticut or to be made into a separate colony, complaining that they were being denied the "rights of English subjects." In East Hampton the people refused to accept the Duke, acknowledging instead the King as their sovereign.[57]

In 1680 a dispute over the collection of customs duties by the Duke's officers led to the indictment of a customs collector for violating Magna Carta and ultimately to the establishment of a representative assembly in New York. The customs duties in question expired by limitation in 1680, and the merchants of New York accordingly refused to pay the duties. The collector of the port, William Dyre, detained goods on which customs duties had not been paid. Upon this, a grand jury was impaneled and returned a true bill against Dyre, in which he stood accused of having imposed "Unlawfull Customes and Imposicons on the Goods and Merchandizes, of his Majtis Leige People trading in this Place . . . Contrary to the Greate Charter of Liberties" and statutes of England.[58]

When the grand jury made their return on the true bill against Dyre, they took the occasion to air their grievances against the way they were being governed by the Duke and his officials. They presented a paper, signed by all of them, in which they expressed their sense of the "Great Manifold and Insupportable Greevances under the which this Collony hath a Long time and still Doth Groan Praying to bee Delivered. . . ." The remedy? The grand jury looked to the rights of Englishmen. They implored that they "bee made Equall sharers of that Imparalled Governmt of the Realme of England" by having the colony's government elected by the freeholders so that the colonists might "Enjoy the benefitt of the Good and wholsome Laws of the Realme of England. . . ." Accordingly, the Aldermen of the City of New York and the Justices of the Peace, assembled at a special court of assize, received the grand jury's message and, on a motion for a concurrence with the grand

[57] See Andrews, *Colonial Period,* III, 109–10.
[58] New-York Historical Society, *Collections,* 45 (1912), 11.

jury's proposal, had a petition drawn up asking for an elected assembly.[59]

Dyre was discharged, but the colonists had won a moral victory, for in 1683 the Duke sent out Governor Thomas Dongan with instructions to call the representative assembly which the colonists wanted. The new legislative body passed a number of laws, among which was the Charter of Liberties and Privileges (1684). In large part the charter, which bears the stamp of a familiarity with the English constitution, was the work of Matthias Nicolls, a lawyer by profession and Speaker of the Assembly.[60] Probably the most notable feature of the charter was its basing the right of the colonists to tax themselves directly on Magna Carta, a vindication of the reliance they had placed on the Great Charter in indicting William Dyre. The charter was signed and sealed by the Duke but never sent back to England; in 1685 James became King and disallowed the charter.[61]

New Jersey

NEW JERSEY was also the scene of some spirited clashes between inhabitants and rulers. The grant from Charles II to his brother James, Duke of York, in 1664 included the territory which later became New Jersey, but the Duke soon transferred the land between the Hudson and Delaware Rivers to Lord Berkeley and Sir George Carteret, thereby bringing into being the colony of New Jersey or New Caesarea. To attract settlers the proprietors issued their "Concessions and Agreement." A significant provision of this document was the assurance that there would be imposed no "tax, custom, subsidy, tallage, assessment, or any other duty whatsoever upon any colour or pretence, upon the said Province and inhabitants thereof, other than what shall be imposed by the authority and consent of the General Assembly. . . ."[62]

[59] *Ibid.*, pp. 14–17.   [60] Andrews, *Colonial Period*, III, 115–17.
[61] *Documents Relative to the Colonial History of the State of New York*, ed. John Romeyn Brodhead (Albany, 1853), III, 357.
[62] Thorpe, V, 2540.

There was a brief period of Dutch control, and after the province was restored to English hands it was divided into East and West New Jersey, the latter being settled by Quakers for whom William Penn and Edward Byllinge drew up the *Fundamental Laws of West New Jersey*. The "General Free Assembly" of the western province met in 1681 and agreed upon a set of basic laws for their government, "to be as fundamentals to us and our posterity, to be held inviolable. . . ." These fundamentals provided for an annual assembly and said that the Governor should not make laws, levy taxes, or take other action without the consent of the Assembly.[63]

East New Jersey also passed into Quaker hands when in 1682 Penn and eleven associates purchased the province from trustees who had been administering the province for the benefit of the creditors of Carteret. The new proprietors declared a fundamental constitution for East New Jersey, among the provisions of which there was this restatement of chapters 39 and 40 of Magna Carta (chapter 29 of the charter of 1225) :

> That no person or persons within the said Province shall be taken and imprisoned, or be devised of his freehold, free custom or liberty, or be outlawed or exiled, or any other way destroyed; nor shall they be condemn'd or judgment pass'd upon them, but by lawful judgment of their peers; neither shall justice nor right be bought or sold, defered or delayed, to any person whatsoever: in order to which by the laws of the land, all tryals shall be by twelve men, and as near as it may be, peers and equals, and of the neighborhood. . . .[64]

In 1702 East and West New Jersey were united and were governed as a royal colony. The new Governor, Viscount Cornbury, carried instructions from Queen Anne requiring that the Governor get the Assembly's assent to any act for raising revenues to defray the costs of government, including the salary of the Governor himself. The Governor, with the advice and consent of the Council, was to regulate fees, which should be within the bounds of moderation and be well publicized. Government according to Magna Carta's assurance of "law of the land" was required by the Queen's admonition to the Gover-

[63] *Ibid.,* V, 2565–66.   [64] *Ibid.,* V, 2580.

nor, "You are to take care that no man's life, member, freehold, or goods be taken away or harmed in our said province, otherwise than by established and known laws, nor repugnant to, but as much as may be, agreeable to the laws of England." [65]

The new Governor and the people of New Jersey soon found they had dissimilar philosophies of government. The Governor sought to impose taxes without the consent of the lower house of the legislature, a move rankling to a colony which remembered the assurances in the earlier charters and fundamental laws against taxation without consent. Discontent stirred the colonists to prepare a remonstrance covering a number of subjects—unexecuted murderers, court costs, probate of wills, monopolies, records, etc.—one of them being the establishment of fees without the Assembly's assent. This, they protested, was against Magna Carta:

6thly. Establishing Fees by any other Power or Authority then by the Governour, Councill, and Representatives met in General Assembly, we take it to be a great grievance, directly repugnant to Magna Charta, and contrary to the Queens express directions in the Governours Instructions which says, you are to take care, that no Man's Life, Member, Free-hold or Goods, be taken away or harmed in our Province under your Government, otherwise than by established and known Laws, not repugnant to, but as much as may be agreeable to the Laws of England. We therefore pray that the Governour will assent to an Act to be passed to settle Fees, without which we think no more can be legally demanded, than the Persons concerned by agreement oblige themselves to pay.[66]

Lord Cornbury answered the Assembly's remonstrance in a document characterized by hauteur worthy of a Viscount, sprinkling his reply with references to "the Enormities contained in this Remonstrance" and to the remonstrance as having been "contriv'd on purpose to amuse poor ignorant People with a notion of Grievances, when, in truth, there is not the least colour of Cause of Complaint." Cornbury did, however, deign to make answer to the points raised by the Assembly. The

[65] *Documents Relating to the Colonial History of the State of New Jersey,* ed. William A. Whitehead (Newark, N.J., 1881), II, 513, 521.

[66] *Ibid.,* III, 176.

complaint against his fees Cornbury characterized as of an "Extravagant Nature," for the Assembly had presumed "to call that a great Grievance, and affirm it to be directly repugnant to Magna Charta, and contrary to the Queens express Directions in the Governours Instructions" when in fact Cornbury had followed the Queen's instructions to him. For this the Assembly deserved to be scolded; to make the accusation it did was the same as "accusing her most sacred Majesty, the best of Queens, of commanding her Governour to do things which in themselves are great Grievances." Cornbury referred to the clause of the instructions directing the Governor to fix fees, so long as they were moderate. In sum Cornbury challenged the Assembly to show how "any Mans Life, member, Free-hold or Goods" had been taken in New Jersey since the royal government had begun "otherwise than by established and known Laws . . . agreeable to the Laws of England." [67]

Cornbury transmitted the Assembly's remonstrances to the Lords of Trade in England. They referred the question of fees to the Attorney General, who gave his opinion that "no fee is lawful, unless it be Warranted by Prescription, or Erected by the Legislature, as was adjudged in parliament in the 13th Hen 4th in the Case of the Office then Erected, for measurage of Cloths and Canvass." In support of this opinion the Attorney General also cited to Coke's *Second Institute*. Replying to Cornbury, the Lords of Trade included with their communication the Attorney General's opinion, so that the Governor might know the limits which the laws of England placed upon his power to set fees without consulting the Assembly.[68]

The events detailed in this chapter, drawn from proprietary colonies—Maryland, the Carolinas, New York, and New Jersey —should serve to illustrate the extent to which the ancient statute of Magna Carta had by the end of the seventeenth century become embedded in the legal and constitutional ethos of the American colonies. Magna Carta was being absorbed into the lifeblood of English America much in the way in which it had become an accepted feature of private and public

[67] *Ibid.*, III, 188–89.　　[68] *Ibid.*, III, 323–27.

law in England in the Middle Ages. In Maryland colonists attempted again and again to put the guarantees of the Great Charter on the colony's statute books, they pleaded the Charter in private actions in court, they sought to have judges swear to administer the brand of justice underwritten by Magna Carta. In the Carolinas a governor was charged with violating Magna Carta by an opponent who, as a judge, later found himself likewise accused of disregarding the Charter. In New York a customs collector was indicted by a grand jury for having abridged the rights of Magna Carta, and in New Jersey colonists, having received assurances from their proprietors of the Great Charter's protection, invoked that instrument against their governor when theirs became a royal colony.

Clearly a tradition was being established. Faith Thompson has told us how in England the use by Sir Edward Coke and others in the early seventeenth century of Magna Carta as a rallying cry against the tyrannies of the Stuarts was not "an abrupt and novel phenomenon." [69] Rather those statesmen who had invoked the Charter on behalf of the liberty of the subject were relying on an instrument with a considerable history in the plea rolls and Year Books, parliament and statute rolls, legal treatises, and chronicles. History was, in a sense, repeating itself in the American colonies. Through repeated, almost reflexive, use—against proprietors, against governors, against judges, against lesser officials—England's liberty document was becoming America's liberty document.

[69] *Magna Carta: Its Role in the Making of the English Constitution, 1300–1629* (Minneapolis, 1948), p. 3.

Chapter IV

William Penn and Pennsylvania

The Trial of William Penn

Few trials in England or America have left more of a mark on American history than has the trial of William Penn at Old Bailey in London, in 1670, for "tumultuous assembly." The occasion of the "assembly" was the preaching of Quaker beliefs by Penn and others, and it is fair to say that Penn was more on trial for these beliefs than for what the indictment termed "disturbance of the peace of the said Lord the King" (which we today would call breach of the peace). Penn published his own version of the trial, entitled *The People's Ancient and Just Liberties, asserted, in the Trial of William Penn and William Mead.* In a preface Penn admonished his readers, "How much thou art concerned in this ensuing Trial, where not only the Prisoners, but the Fundamental Laws of England, have been most arbitrarily arraigned, read, and thou mayest plainly judge." In particular, said Penn, Magna Carta itself was on trial: "Magna Charta is Magna f____ with the Recorder of London [the judge in the trial]; and to demand right an affront to the court. Will and Power are their great charter, but to call for England's, is a crime, incurring the penalty of their Baledock, and Nasty-hole, nay, the menace of a Gag, and Iron Shackles too." [1]

[1] 6 Howell's State Trials 951, 953 (1670). Sir John Keeling, Lord Chief Justice of the King's Bench, was summoned to the bar of the House of Commons to

5. William Penn in armor. (Courtesy, Christ Church, Oxford.)

The Excellent Priviledge of

LIBERTY & PROPERTY

BEING THE #16

BIRTH - RIGHT

Of the Free-born Subjects of *England*

CONTAINING

I. *Magna Charta*, with a learned Comment upon it.

II. The Confirmation of the Charters of the Liberties of *England* and of the Forreſt, made in the 35th year of *Edward* the Firſt.

III. A Statute made the 34 *Edw.* 1. commonly called *De Tallageo non Concedendo*; wherein all Fundamental Laws, Liberties and Cuſtoms are confirmed. With a Comment upon it.

IV. An abſtract of the Pattent granted by the King to *VVilliam Penn* and his Heirs and Aſſigns for the Province of *Pennſilvania*.

V. And *Laſtly*, The Charter of Liberties granted by the said *VVilliam Penn* to the Free-men and Inhabitants of the Province of *Pennſilvania* and Territories thereunto annexed, in *America*.

Major Hæreditas venit unicunq; noſtrum a Jure & Legibus, quam a Parentibus.

---

6. Title page, William Penn's *The Most Excellent Priviledge of Liberty & Property* (1687). (Courtesy, Haverford College.)

7. St. George Tucker. (Courtesy, College of William and Mary.)

BLACKSTONE'S COMMENTARIES:

WITH

NOTES of REFERENCE

TO THE

CONSTITUTIONS, AND LAWS,

OF THE

FEDERAL GOVERNMENT

OF THE

UNITED STATES;

AND OF THE

COMMONWEALTH of VIRGINIA.

With an APPENDIX to each volume, containing short tracts upon such subjects as appeared necessary to form a connected view of the LAWS of VIRGINIA as a MEMBER of the FEDERAL UNION.

BY S: GEORGE TUCKER, PROFESSOR OF LAW IN THE UNIVERSITY OF WILLIAM AND MARY, AND ONE OF THE JUDGES OF THE GENERAL COURT, IN VIRGINIA.

8. Title page, St. George Tucker's edition of *Blackstone's Commentaries* (1803).
(Courtesy, College of William and Mary.)

The indictment charged that Penn, Mead, and others did "unlawfully and tumultuously" gather in Gracechurch Street, London, where Penn did "take upon himself to preach and speak" to Mead and others "against the peace" of the King.[2] Presented with this indictment, Penn insisted on knowing its basis, and there followed this colloquy on the common law:

Penn. I affirm I have broken no law, nor am I Guilty of the indictment that is laid to my charge; and to the end the bench, the jury, and myself, with these that hear us, may have a more direct understanding of this procedure, I desire you would let me know by what law it is you prosecute me, and upon what law you ground my indictment.

Rec. [Recorder, Thomas Howell] Upon the common-law.

Penn. Where is that common-law?

Rec. You must not think that I am able to run up so many years, and over so many adjudged cases, which we call common-law, to answer your curiosity.

Penn. This answer I am sure is very short of my question, for if it be common, it should not be so hard to produce.

Rec. Sir, will you plead to your indictment?

Penn. Shall I plead to an Indictment that hath no foundation in law? If it contain that law you say I have broken, why should you decline to produce that law, since it will be impossible for the jury to determine, or agree to bring in their verdict, who have not the law produced, by which they should measure the truth of this indictment, and the guilt, or contrary of my fact? . . .

Rec. You are an impertinent fellow, will you teach the court what law is? It is "Lex non scripta," that which many have studied 30 or 40 years to know, and would you have me to tell you in a moment?

Penn. Certainly, if the common law be so hard to be understood, it is far from being very common; but if the lord Coke in his Institutes be of any consideration, he tells us, That Common-Law is common right, and that Common Right is the Great Charter-Privileges: confirmed 9 Hen. 3, 29, 25 Edw. 1, 12 Ed. 3, 8 Coke Instit. 2 p. 56.

Rec. Sir, you are a troublesome fellow, and it is not for the honour of the court to suffer you to go on.

---

answer the charge that, when a defendant had invoked Magna Carta, Sir John had called it "Magna Farta" (a phrase attributed to Cromwell) . See Maurice Ashley, *Magna Carta in the Seventeenth Century* (Charlotteville, Va., 1965) , pp. 48–49.

[2] 6 Howell's State Trials 954–55.

Penn. I have asked but one question, and you have not answered me; though the rights and privileges of every English-man be concerned in it.[3]

The prisoners were put out of the court into the Bale-dock, and the jury charged in their absence, at which Penn in a raised voice (being at some distance from the bench) said that to charge the jury in the defendants' absence violated Magna Carta:

I appeal to the jury who are my Judges, and this great assembly, whether the proceedings of this court are not most arbitrary, and void of all law, in offering to give the jury their charge in the absence of the prisoners; I say it is directly opposite to, and destructive of the undoubted right of every English prisoner, as Coke, in the 2 Instit. 29. on the chap. of Magna Charta.[4]

The jury's sympathies in this trial were evident, and it was with great reluctance and only after considerable abuse and threats from the bench that the jury finally came in with any verdict at all. The clerk called for the verdict as to Penn. The foreman spoke for the jury:

Foreman. Guilty of speaking in Grace-churchstreet.
Court. Is that all?
Foreman. That is all I have in commission.
Rec. You had as good say nothing.
May. [Mayor, Samuel Starling] Was it not an unlawful assembly? You mean he was speaking to a tumult of people there?
Foreman. My Lord, This is all I had in commission.[5]

The court questioned the jury. Some of the jurors seemed to waver under the court's questions, but others, notably Edward Bushel, said that they allowed of "no such word as an unlawful Assembly in their Verdict." For this they were vilified by the Recorder, the Mayor, and the Aldermen. The Recorder warned the jury that they would not be allowed to go home until they had given their verdict, but the jury persisted in their answer that they had given in the only verdict they could. The jury was sent out again, but upon their return their answer was the same. The Recorder's wrath mounted, and he made his threats more explicit: "Gentlemen, you shall not be dismissed till we

---

[3] *Ibid.,* pp. 958–59.   [4] *Ibid.,* p. 961.   [5] *Ibid.,* p. 962.

have a verdict that the court will accept; and you shall be locked up, without meat, drink, fire, and tobacco; you shall not think thus to abuse the court; we will have a verdict, by the help of God, or you shall starve for it." [6]

Penn lent moral support to the jury: "You are Englishmen, mind your privilege, give not away your right." To which, Bushel and others, like a Greek chorus, responded: "Nor will we ever do it." Enraged, the court swore several persons to keep the jury all night, without meat, drink, or fire, "not so much as a chamber pot," and adjourned the court until the next morning. At that time the clerk called again for the verdict, to which Bushel said that "we give no other verdict than what we gave last night; we have no other verdict to give." The court's utter exasperation was evident in the Recorder's threat to Bushel: "I will set a mark upon you," to which the Mayor, not to be outdone, added, "I will cut his nose." [7]

Penn objected to all these threats with the statement: "It is intolerable that my jury should be thus menaced: Is this according to the fundamental laws? Are they not my proper judges by the Great Charter of England?" The court's wrath turned once again to Penn; the Mayor called for fetters to restrain Penn, and the Recorder exploded: "Till now I never understood the reason of the policy and prudence of the Spaniards, in suffering the inquisition among them: And certainly it will never be well with us, till something like unto the Spanish inquisition be in England." And he told the jury to "bring in another Verdict, or you shall starve; and I will have you carted about the city, as in Edward 3rd's time." [8]

Finally the jury returned a verdict of not guilty as to Penn and Mead, and for this "contempt" of the court they were fined forty marks apiece and were ordered to be imprisoned until the fine was paid. Penn demanded his freedom, having been acquitted by the jury, but the Mayor replied that Penn was in for his "fines." At this, Penn asked, "Fines, for what?" and the Mayor answered, "For contempt of the Court." Penn objected that this contravened Magna Carta: "I ask, if it be according to the

[6] *Ibid.*, pp. 962–63.   [7] *Ibid.*, pp. 964–65.   [8] *Ibid.*, pp. 965–66.

fundamental laws of England, that any Englishman should be fined or amerced, but by the judgment of his peers or jury; since it expressly contradicts the 14th and 29th chapters of the Great Charter of England, which say, 'No freeman ought to be amerced but by the oath of good and lawful men of the vicinage.' " [9]

The jury were sent to Newgate prison, but their punishment was unquestionably illegal. Three years before, in 1667, the House of Commons, on hearing reports of harassment of juries, had resolved that Sir John Keeling, Lord Chief Justice of the King's Bench, had "under-valued, vilified, and condemned Magna Charta, the great preserver of our lives, freedom, and property," and that he should be brought to trial. The Chief Justice was heard in his own defense, and, while the House concluded not to proceed further against him, it resolved that "the precedents and practice of fining or imprisoning jurors, for verdicts, is illegal." [10] In line with this authority, a writ of habeas corpus issued in November 1670 (two months after the Penn's trial) to the Sheriff of London to produce Bushel, and he and the other jurors in Penn's case were discharged.[11] Thus was reinforced the rule, as stated by Blackstone, that the practice of "fining, imprisoning, or otherwise punishing jurors . . . for finding their verdict contrary to the direction of the judge, was arbitrary, unconstitutional, and illegal. . . ." [12]

Penn and Magna Carta

I f the trial of William Penn was significant in the development of an unfettered right to jury trial in England, it was probably even more important for the effect it had on the thinking of Penn himself and, through him, upon the jurisprudence of the American colonies. To his account of his trial, Penn attached an appendix by way of what "might have been

[9] *Ibid.*, pp. 967–69.
[10] Judge Keeling's Case, 6 Howell's State Trials 992, 995 (1667).
[11] Case of the Imprisonment of Edward Bushell, for alleged Misconduct as a Juryman, 6 Howell's State Trials 999 (1670).
[12] *Blackstone's Commentaries* (Oxford, 1765–69), IV, 354.

offered against the Indictment and illegal Proceedings of the Court thereon, had they not violently overruled and stopped them." [13] Penn's appendix was in effect a commentary on Magna Carta. It set out a "REHEARSAL of the MATERIAL PARTS of the GREAT CHARTER of ENGLAND," in which Penn quoted the preamble to the Charter as granted by Henry III, the Charter's grant of liberties to all men (chapter 1 of the 1225 charter), the provision that amercements should be assessed only by oath of good and honest men of the vicinage (chapter 14), the guarantee of judgment of peers (chapter 29), and the King's promise to uphold the Charter. Penn, being of a theological bent, took care to include the sentence of curse given by the Bishops against those who should break the Great Charter.[14]

Then Penn discussed "some of those maxims of law, dearer to our ancestors than life; because they are the defense of the lives and liberties of the people of England. . . ." In this discussion, Coke's *Institutes* are the source cited for virtually all the propositions enunciated by Penn, and most of the propositions are drawn from Magna Carta, as interpreted in the *Institutes*. Finally, Penn listed the ways in which the fundamental laws of England, principally Magna Carta, were disregarded in his trial: (1) taking and imprisonment "contrary to the Grand Charter," (2) the refusal to produce the law on which the court was proceeding, (3) the refusal to allow the prisoners to plead "the Great Charter, and other good laws," (4) charging the jury in the prisoners' absence, (5) rejecting the jury's verdict, (6) fining the prisoners for contempt, and (7) fining and imprisoning the jury instead of accepting their verdict "according to the Great Charter." [15]

It was to Magna Carta that Penn looked as the touchstone of individual liberties: [16]

But we have lived to an age, so debauched from all humanity and reason, as well as faith and religion, that some stick not to turn butchers to their own privileges, and conspirators against their own liberties. For however Magna Charta had once the reputation of a sacred unalterable law, and few hardened

---

[13] 6 Howell's State Trials 970 *et. seq.*   [14] *Ibid.*, pp. 977–79.
[15] *Ibid.*, pp. 982–84.   [16] *Ibid.*, p. 984.

enough, to incur and bear the long curse, that attends the violators of it, yet it is frequently objected now, that the benefits there designed are but temporary, and therefore liable to alteration, as other statutes are. . . .

But that the privileges due to Englishmen, by the Great Charter of England, have their foundation in reason and law: and that those new Cassandrian ways, to introduce will and power, deserve to be detested by all persons professing sense and honesty, and the least allegiance to our English Government; we shall make appear from a sober consideration of the nature of those privileges contained in that Charter.

Clearly, Penn concluded, Magna Carta had the status of a supreme law, and "no person may legally attempt the subversion, or extenuation of the force of the Great Charter." Penn cited the statutes of 25 Edward I, chapter 2, to the effect that any judgment given contrary to Magna Carta "is to be undone, and holden for nought," 25 Edward I, chapter 4, declaring that all who should "by word, deed, or counsel go contrary to the said Charter" should be excommunicated, and 42 Edward III, chapter 1, that the Great Charter "be holden and kept in all points" and that statutes made contrary to Magna Carta "shall be holden for nought." [17]

A more complete demonstration of Penn's thorough grounding in the traditions of Magna Carta and the writings of Coke could hardly be asked. Penn's trial, and the thinking which it forced Penn to do about the rights of Englishmen, came at a crucial time for constitutional development in the American colonies. In the years that followed his trial, Penn was to develop his ideas of law and government in a pamphlet entitled *England's Present Interest* (1675), was to be responsible for the first publication in the American colonies of a commentary on Magna Carta (1687), and finally was to have the chance so often denied political philosophers, the drafting of fundamental laws—in Penn's case, the Fundamentals of West New Jersey (1676) and the Frame of Government for Pennsylvania (1682). Jean-Jacques Rousseau, a far more creative thinker than Penn, had his chance at constitution-drafting in his *Constitution of Corsica;* John Locke, that great empiricist and

[17] *Ibid.,* pp. 986–87.

synthesizer of seventeenth-century English thought, had his in the *Fundamental Constitutions for the Government of Carolina.* Yet neither of these ventures at putting political philosophy into practice had the lasting effect of Penn's instruments for West New Jersey and for Pennsylvania.

In his objections lodged before the court in 1670, and in his commentary written as an appendix to the account of the trial, Penn had already mapped out the path his thinking would take. In *England's Present Interest,* in 1675, again drawing heavily on Coke's commentaries on Magna Carta in the *Institutes,* Penn proposed three fundamental rights of the Englishman: ownership of property, a voice in making the laws, and a share in the judicial power.[18]

Penn's Interest in New Jersey

P ENN, who up until this time had devoted his activities largely to affairs in England (including an active role in politics), soon was to be drawn into events on the other side of the Atlantic. Two Quakers, Edward Byllinge and John Fenwick, had proprietary rights in New Jersey. When a dispute arose between them, they asked Penn to arbitrate. Once involved in the affairs of New Jersey, Penn was instrumental in obtaining a formal division between East and West New Jersey, and soon thereafter Penn and Byllinge drew up the *Fundamental Laws of West New Jersey* (1676).[19] This remarkable document was the embodiment in constitutional form of the lessons drawn by Penn from his bitter experience in the English courtroom six years before. It is a document which spans the centuries, for on the one hand it draws inspiration (as did Penn himself in

[18] *The Select Works of William Penn* (3d ed.; London, 1782), III, 218–19. Chroust, *Legal Profession,* I, 207, comments on the Quakers' "basic aversion to the laws of England" and implies that Penn shared this aversion. The evidence points the other way. Penn had good reason to be suspicious of English courts and English judges, but throughout his writings—in his account of his trial, in his pamphlets, in his Frame of Government of Pennsylvania, and elsewhere— Penn makes unmistakably clear his belief in the guarantees and protections of the English law.

[19] See Joseph E. Illick, *William Penn the Politician* (Ithaca, N.Y., 1965), pp. 13–14.

pleading his own cause in 1670) from Magna Carta, and on the other it is in some ways a century ahead of its time.

Obviously having in mind Coke's discussion of the statute of Edward III decreeing acts contrary to Magna Carta to be void, Penn began the Fundamentals by a declaration that they were to be "the foundation of the government, which is not to be altered by the Legislative authority" and that the legislature was "to make no laws that in the least contradict, differ or vary from the said fundamentals, under what pretence or alligation soever." [20] Here was a forecast of the way in which the precedent set by the statute of Edward III, and so revered by Coke, was to be embodied a century later in the United States Constitution's provision that the Constitution should be "the supreme Law of the Land" and that the judges of the States should be bound thereby, "any Thing in the Constitution or Laws of any State to the Contrary notwithstanding."

If Caligula saw fit, in the first century A.D., to put the laws of Rome in a place so high that the populace could not read them, Penn, like Englishmen before him, insisted that the laws of West Jersey have the widest publicity possible. Just as in 1215 the King's sheriffs, foresters, bailiffs, and other officials were commanded that Magna Carta "should be publicly read," the Fundamentals of West New Jersey were to be recorded in a "fair table" in the Assembly House and were to be read at the opening and adjournment of every session. Moreover, the Fundamentals were to be written on tables "in every common hall of justice within this Province" and were to be "read in solemn manner four times every year, in the presence of the people, by the chief magistrate of those places." [21]

Then came the substantive provisions of the Fundamentals. Due process of law was guaranteed; Coke's understanding of Magna Carta's chapter 39 was duplicated in the Fundamentals' provision that no person should be deprived of life, limb, liberty, or property, or his privileges, freedoms, or franchises in any way hurt, "without a due tryal, and judgment passed by twelve good and lawful men of his neighborhood first had. . . ." Summons in person or at a defendant's last dwelling place

[20] Thorpe, V, 2548.   [21] *Ibid.*, V, 2548–49.

was required, the summons to give a "full and plain account of the cause or thing in demand," and the defendant was to have sufficient time to appear and answer, the time being extended proportionately to the distance of his home from the court.[22]

Trials, whether civil or criminal, were to be open to the public, "that justice may not be done in a corner nor in any covert manner. . . ." No person was to be required to hire counsel but was to have "free liberty to plead his own cause, if he please. . . ." Not only was trial by jury guaranteed (in two places in the document), but the trial of 1670 echoed most clearly in the provision that judges "shall pronounce such judgment as they shall receive from, and be directed by the said twelve men in whom only the judgment resides, and not otherwise." [23] No juror in West New Jersey would have to spend the night without meat, drink, fire, or chamber pot!

The Founding of Pennsylvania

PENN's ambitions went far beyond his interests in New Jersey. In 1680 he petitioned Charles I for the grant of a tract of land bounded on the south by Maryland and on the east by the Delaware River. Though the tide of the time was running against the creation of proprietary colonies, Penn, who had close connections in court circles, received the grant he sought. As early as 1668 Penn had begun the prolific writing and pamphleteering which produced during his lifetime over a hundred works, ranging in length from broadsheets to long books. Now he had a colony in which he could put his ideas on religious and civil liberties to work. Disillusioned with what he saw happening in England, he conceived of Pennsylvania (named for his father, a noted admiral) as a refuge for Quakers and other persecuted peoples. "There may be room there, though not here," he wrote a friend in America, *"for such an holy experiment."* [24]

The King's charter to Penn placed a number of limits on the

---

[22] *Ibid.*, V, 2549.   [23] *Ibid.*, V, 2550.
[24] Quoted in Illick, *William Penn the Politician,* p. 40.

88 *The Road from Runnymede*

proprietorship to protect the interests of the Crown. One such restriction was the requirement, the first of its kind in the charter of any proprietary and corporate colony, that any laws passed in Pennsylvania must be transmitted to England for approval by the Privy Council. Another proviso was the right retained by the King to hear and determine all appeals from the courts of the province; though there had been a right of appeal in royal colonies, hitherto none had existed in a proprietary colony.[25] Still, there was ample scope for Penn the proprietor to create the experiment in liberties which he had in mind.

He set sail for America in August 1682. With him he carried his blueprint for Pennsylvania, the Frame of Government of Pennsylvania. In drafting this instrument, Penn drew deeply on the traditions of Magna Carta, especially in the administration of justice in the courts. Chapter 40 of the Great Charter was duplicated in the Frame of Government's requirement "that all courts shall be open, and justice shall neither be sold, denied nor delayed." All judicial pleadings, processes, and records, were to be short, in English, and of a "plain character" to the end that they might be readily understood and justice speedily administered. Penn's document decreed that "all fines shall be moderate, and saving men's contenements, merchandize, or wainage," a clause obviously derived from chapter 20 of Magna Carta, which promised that amercements should be proportionate to a man's fault, saving to a freeman his position, to a merchant his merchandise, and to a villein his tillage. Laws were to be well publicized; the Frame of Government itself was to be hung up in the assembly chamber and in the provincial courts and was to be read annually at the opening of every provincial Council, General Assembly, and court of justice.[26]

The First American Publication of Magna Carta

Penn carried Magna Carta to Pennsylvania in more ways than one. Not only did he draw on its contents for some of the provisions of his Frame of Government, he had an exact copy of

[25] Thorpe, V, 3038–39.   [26] *Ibid.*, V, 3060–63.

the Charter made, "certified by the Keeper and other officers of the Cottonian Library, illuminated and ornamented as the original," and had it deposited in the archives of the colony.[27] Moreover, to ensure wide public knowledge of the Charter's contents, he was responsible for the first publication in America of a commentary on Magna Carta. This appeared in 1687 under the title *The Excellent Priviledge of Liberty & Property Being the Birth-Right of Free-Born Subjects of England,* published at Philadelphia by William Bradford. The pamphlet was in five parts: Magna Carta, with a commentary upon it; Edward I's confirmation of Magna Carta; the statute *De Tallageo non Concedendo;* an abstract of the King's patent to Penn for Pennsylvania; and the Charter of Liberties granted by Penn to the colonists.

A preface to the reader noted the dearth of lawbooks in Pennsylvania and thought it likely that there were many in the province who were strangers to an understanding of the liberty which was the "inestimable Inheritance that every Free-born Subject of England is Heir unto by Birthright." It was hoped that the publication of Magna Carta and the other fundamental documents might "raise up Noble Resolutions in all the Freeholders in these new Colonies, not to give away any thing of Liberty and Property that at present they do, (or of right as Loyal English Subjects, ought to) enjoy, but take up the good Example of our Ancestors, and understand, that it is easie to part with or give away great Priviledges, but hard to be gained, if once lost." [28]

The commentary on Magna Carta as it appeared in the *Excellent Priviledge* was not original with Penn. It was lifted word for word from Henry Care's *English Liberties,* which enjoyed immense popularity in England (and later in America) and ran to many editions. Care in turn had drawn heavily

---

[27] *The Excellent Priviledge of Liberty and Property Being a Reprint and Fac-simile of the First American Edition of Magna Charta* (Philadelphia, 1897), p. xiii. The "Cottonian library" refers to the collection of Sir Robert Cotton. Of the four exemplifications of the Charter of 1215 which survive today, the two presently in the British Museum were both at one time in the Cottonian library.

[28] "To the Reader." The quotations conform with the only known perfect copy of the original book, which is in the Quaker Collection at Haverford College, Haverford, Pa.

upon what Sir Edward Coke had said in his *Second Institute*. In presenting Magna Carta to the American reader, the *Excellent Priviledge* was presenting, above all, chapter 29, as commented on by Coke. And the *Excellent Priviledge* matched Coke's praise of chapter 29. Where Coke had admonished his reader to study the chapter with the same care that a goldsmith took to save every grain of his gold, the *Excellent Priviledge* (drawing from Care) said: "The 29th Chapter, NO FREE-MAN SHALL BE TAKEN, &c. Deserves to be written in Letters of Gold; and I have often wondred the Words thereof are not Inscribed in Capitals on all our Courts of Judicature, Town-Halls, and most publick Edifices; they are the *Elixer* of our *English Freedoms,* the Store-house of all our Liberties." [29]

The commentary on Magna Carta was followed with the text of the Confirmation of the Charters, to which was appended the sentence or curse of the Bishops of England (1253) against those who should break the Great Charter. The *Excellent Priviledge* commented: "And I declare ingeniously, I would not for the world incur this Curse, as every man deservedly doth, that offers violence to the fundamental Freedoms thereby repeated and confirmed." [30]

Pennsylvania Follows Penn's Lead

The seeds planted by Penn bore fruit. Within two years of the proprietary grant from the Crown to Penn the Assembly of Pennsylvania was passing laws reaffirming the rights of Englishmen. In 1682 and 1683 the Assembly drew heavily on Magna Carta, on Sir Edward Coke's writings, and on the examples of Penn in spelling out a number of the fundamental liberties of the people of Pennsylvania. The laws of the province were ordered to be published and printed so "that every person may have the knowledge thereof"; moreover, the laws as published were to be "one of the Books taught in the Schooles of this

[29] P. 23.
[30] P. 40. For the text of the Introduction and the commentary on Magna Carta, see Appendix D, *infra*.

Province." Due process of law was guaranteed in language which was the virtual carbon copy of chapter 39 of Magna Carta; the Pennsylvania statute declared that no freeman "shall be taken or imprisoned, or Dispossessed of his freeholds, or liberties, or be Outlawed, or Exiled, or any other wise hurt, Damnified or Destroyed, nor shall hee be tryed or Condemned but by the lawful Judgement of his equalls, or by the Laws of this Province and territories thereof." [31]

Trial by jury—a right which Coke had read into Magna Carta—was guaranteed by the Pennsylvania Assembly, which took care to provide such procedural safeguards as the right of "all persons of all persuasions" freely to appear "in their own way, and according to their own manner, and there personally plead their own Caus themselves, or if unable, by their friends. . . ." A defendant was to have ten days' notice of a proceeding, and a copy of the complaint was to be served on him.[32]

Taxation by consent of those taxed—another right which Coke had traced to Magna Carta (which had provided for the calling of the "common counsel of the kingdom" for the fixing of feudal aids)—was secured by a statute requiring that taxes could be raised only "by a law for that purpose made by the Governour and freemen of the said Province." And, lest would-be tax gatherers be in any doubt, the statute declared that any one assessing taxes in violation of this law should be "punished as a publick enemy to the Province, and a Betrayer of the Liberty of the people" (a fate the modern taxpayer might decree even for tax officials operating under the authority of statute).[33]

With these statutes on the books, the Assembly saw fit to give them a status above that of the usual law. Just as Coke had observed that Magna Carta was a kind of superstatute, so that acts violating it should be "holden for none," the Assembly of Pennsylvania observed that "in all Governments, there are some laws more essentially requisite to the Well being thereof";

[31] *Charter to William Penn and Laws of the Province of Pennsylvania,* ed. John Blair Linn (Harrisburg, Pa., 1879), pp. 123, 127.
[32] *Ibid.,* pp. 117, 128.   [33] *Ibid.,* p. 123.

accordingly, upon a "Serious Consideration of those laws which have been made in this Province" certain named chapters were declared to be fundamental and were not to be "Altered, Diminished or Repealed in whole or part" without consent of the Governor and six-sevenths of the province's freemen met in Council and Assembly.[34] (What would have been the legal effect of the vote of a majority, but less than six-sevenths, of the legislators to repeal the act requiring a six-sevenths vote to repeal the other acts we will leave for speculation by those who enjoy the conceptual puzzles of the law.)

This code of laws was abrogated by William and Mary in 1693. Benjamin Fletcher, the newly appointed royal governor of Pennsylvania, had in November 1692 been issued a commission giving him in Pennsylvania the same governing powers as he had in New York. Upon the abrogation of the statutes passed in 1682 and 1683, the Pennsylvania Assembly addressed a "Petition of Right" to the Governor, asking the recognition of certain named laws as being in force in the province.[35] The use of the style "petition," rather than "bill," was a deliberate one; as with the English Petition of Right of 1628, this designation suggested that the document was a petition for the acknowledgment of rights and liberties which the petitioners held themselves already entitled to, not a bill for the enactment of new law.

In the years that followed, the Pennsylvania Assembly showed a continuing concern that the people of the province enjoy the privileges and liberties of Englishmen, a concern shared and actively supported by Penn. In 1700 Pennsylvania enacted "An Act of Privileges to a Freeman." Phrased, like the act of 1683, in the language of chapter 39 of Magna Carta, this statute declared that no freeman should be "taken, or imprisoned, or disseized of his freehold or liberties, or be outlawed or exiled, or any otherwise hurt, damnified or destroyed, nor be tried or condemned but by the lawful judgment of his twelve equals, or by the laws of this province and territories thereof." [36]

[34] *Ibid.*, p. 154.   [35] *Ibid.*, p. 188.
[36] *Statutes at Large of Pennsylvania from 1682 to 1801*, ed. James T. Mitchell and Henry Flanders (Harrisburg, Pa., 1896–1915) , II, 18 [hereinafter *Pennsylvania Statutes at Large*].

This statute ran into objections interposed by the Commissioners for Trade and Plantations in London. The Commissioners feared that the Act of Privileges to a Freeman would interfere with the jurisdiction of the admiralty courts in the colonies.[37] This concern arose from the fact that cases in admiralty were (and are today) tried by a judge sitting without a jury. Expansion of the right to a jury trial would correspondingly limit the jurisdiction of admiralty courts, at least in so far as they sat without a jury. (Equally, one might add at this point, expansion of the jurisdiction of the admiralty courts would curtail the right to a jury trial, a fact which was to be, in 1765, one of the chief rallying cries of the American colonists against the Stamp Act.) [38]

William Penn, appearing before the board in August 1705, defended the Pennsylvania statute as being something the colonists were entitled to by virtue of Magna Carta: "I cannot help it; 'tis the great charter that all Englishmen are entitled to, and we went not so far to loose a little of it." [39] But the Lords Commissioners for Trade recommended that Queen Anne repeal a number of Pennsylvania statutes, including that on the privileges of a freeman, and in February 1706 the Queen, with the advice of the Privy Council, did so.[40]

In 1711 the Pennsylvania Assembly returned to the fray and passed another "Act of Privileges to a Freeman," in language virtually identical to that of the act of 1700. This time the Assembly added a proviso that "nothing herein contained shall extend to obstruct the power of the court of admiralty concerning any matter properly cognizable in the said court." The English Solicitor General, Robert Raymond, in an opinion on various Pennsylvania laws, nevertheless recommended repeal of the new Act of Privileges to a Freeman. He acknowledged the presence of the saving clause, but said he was still apprehensive that it might interfere with the admiralty courts. "Besides," he added, "I can't well see what occasion there is for this act, since by the laws already in being, the freeman are already entitled to all the priviledges therein." [41] (One is reminded of the not

---

[37] *Ibid.*, II, 464–65. [38] See pp. 141–46, *infra*.
[39] *Pennsylvania Statutes at Large*, II, 467.
[40] *Ibid.*, II, 479, 449. [41] *Ibid.*, II, 359, 550.

very reassuring answer of Charles I, when asked to agree to the Petition of Right, that he would see that "right was done according to the laws and customs of the realm.") [42] The Board of Trade submitted to the Queen a list of Pennsylvania laws, along with the Solicitor General's objections thereto (objections flowed readily from Raymond's pen), and in February 1714 the Queen in Council disallowed, among other laws, the Act of Privileges to a Freeman.[43]

In 1715 Pennsylvania tried again. (Since the colony had, under its charter, five years within which to submit to England any new laws, these repeated reenactments were not entirely futile.) The Assembly passed a third Act of Privileges to a Freeman, in the same language as before, and as with the act of 1711 containing a proviso saving the jurisdiction of the courts of admiralty. Penn again appeared in defense of the Pennsylvania laws. In a memorial to the Lords of Trade and Plantations in 1718, Penn laid recent Pennsylvania laws before the Lords of Trade and gave the reasons underlying their passage. As with its predecessor, Penn said that the Act of Privileges to a Freeman gave Pennsylvanians simply what they were entitled to under Magna Carta: "In this act nothing more is contained than what every Englishman enjoys by Magna Charta. Therefore, it is presumed the people of Pennsylvania (having done nothing to forfeit that) may have this act confirmed, more especially because it has been held by some that acts of parliament extend not to America unless it be expressly named in them." [44]

The Lords of Trade referred the Pennsylvania acts to Richard West, one of King George I's counsels at law, and West submitted an opinion (in March 1719) in which, of the Act of Privileges to a Freeman, he said that if the colonists did not intend to interfere with the admiralty courts then "it is very difficult to imagine what other intention they can possibly have; since by the laws already in being the freemen are entitled to all privileges mentioned therein so far as is consistent with [the statute of William III], or any other laws of this

[42] See Maurice Ashley, *Magna Carta in the Seventeenth Century*, p. 24.
[43] *Pennsylvania Statutes at Large*, II, 554, 543.   [44] *Ibid.*, III, 31, 445, 447.

kingdom." The Lords of Trade agreed with West. In their recommendation to the Crown they referred to Pennsylvania's "two former acts with the same title and contents" which had been repealed. Despite the saving clause, the Lords of Trade were apprehensive lest the new act interfere with the admiralty courts, and they concluded that "we cannot well see what occasion there is for this act, since by the laws already in being freemen are entitled to all the privileges intended by this act." In July 1719 the Lords Justices in Council, acting under the powers reserved to the Crown in Penn's charter, disallowed the third Act of Privileges to a Freeman.[45]

Toward Central Control

IT IS interesting that the first of the three acts sought to be passed by Pennsylvania should have been passed as the eighteenth century opened, for the volleying which took place between the colony and the authorities in London is indicative of the way in which the fairly easy and decentralized relationships between mother country and colonies in the seventeenth century were giving way to greater centralization in London. In their representation to the Lords Justices in 1719, the Lords of Trade had taken the occasion to observe on the "ill effects of a proprietary government" and said that "we are of opinion the plantations will never be upon a right foot till the dominion of all the proprietary colonies shall be resumed to the crown. . . ." They recommended "that all fair opportunities shuld be laid hold on for that purpose." [46] This recommendation reflected the Lords of Trade's growing feeling, increasingly evident from the 1670's, that the existence of proprietary colonies was impeding the enforcement of laws of trade and efforts to provide adequate defense against the French (the latter was especially true in the colonies, such as Pennsylvania, where Quakers predominated) .[47] Actually England was late in taking steps toward a mercantilist policy; it is fair to say that England's colonial policy began to

[45] *Ibid.*, III, 457, 458, 463, 439.   [46] *Ibid.*, III, 468.
[47] See Andrews, *Colonial Period,* III, 279.

take a definite shape only after 1660. Following the Restoration, the mother country began to look at the colonies with greedier eyes and to see in their growing numbers and commerce an opportunity for greater returns to England.

As the seventeenth century wore on, the bodies in England most concerned with colonial affairs—the Privy Council and the Lords of Trade—realized that a stumbling block to an enforceable and effective colonial trade policy lay in the existence of so many colonies independent of the Crown. Gradually a policy against proprietary and other independent colonies began to take form, and quo warrantos were issued against the Charters of Connecticut, Rhode Island, the Jerseys, Pennsylvania, Maryland, the Carolinas, the Bahamas, and Bermuda.[48] New York had automatically become a royal colony when its proprietor, the Duke of York, had become James II.

The stage was set for a new venture in English colonial policy, the creation of the Dominion of New England.[49] The Charter of Massachusetts, a colony which had proved especially unmanageable, had been voided in 1684 and a provisional government established. There was no provision for a representative assembly, a sore point with the people of Massachusetts for, even though their charter had not had any express provision for a house of representatives, "they supposed the natural rights of Englishmen, reserved to them, implied it."[50] Edward Randolph, who had been appointed secretary and register of the province, arrived in 1686, but the old General Court resisted surrender to the new authority, contending that since the new government did not provide for a representative assembly the people of Massachusetts were "abridged of their liberty as Englishmen, both in the matter of legislation and in the laying of taxes."[51] The new Council of Massachusetts met in May 1686. Four of those nominated in the commission declined to serve, Dudley Bradstreet and Simon Bradstreet on the

[48] See *ibid.*

[49] The definitive study is that of Viola Florence Barnes, *The Dominion of New England* (New Haven, 1923) [hereinafter Barnes, *Dominion*], to which this author is much indebted.

[50] Hutchinson, *History of Massachusetts-Bay*, I, 37.

[51] *Records of Massachusetts Bay*, V, 516.

ground that the commission was "a thing contrived to abridge them of their libertye and indeed against Magna Charta." [52]

In December 1686 Sir Edmund Andros arrived in New England to combine under one government all of the colonies of New England save Connecticut and Rhode Island. His new government was a highly centralized instrument, the Council being legislature, executive, and judiciary in one. When Andros took over the reins of government, there were no revenue laws in existence in Massachusetts, the General Court having repealed them in 1683 in anticipation of the demise of the colony's charter. The laws passed by the Andros administration made drastic changes, among other things, in the system of revenue and aroused bitter opposition.

When the first county taxes came due in 1688, they were widely opposed. Most towns in fact refused to obey the law. In Ipswich the warrant for the taxes was condemned at a meeting of the local selectmen on the ground that it "did abridge them of their liberty as Englishmen." [53] The selectmen agreed to a paper in which they gave as their basis for refusing to pay the taxes the illegality under Magna Carta of a tax levied without the consent of an assembly. The leaders of the resistance were brought before the Governor and Council for examination, but the Reverend John Wise, who had spoken against the taxes in the Ipswich meeting, boldly "asserted the priviledges of Englishmen according to Magna Charta." [54]

Six Ipswich "insurrectioners" were tried at a special court of oyer and terminer in Boston in October 1688. In their defense the prisoners pleaded the right of Englishmen, secured to them by Magna Carta, not to be taxed without their consent.[55] The Governor's patronizing answer was, "We must not think the laws of England follow us to the ends of the earth or whither we went." [56] The defendants were convicted and fined.

Ultimately the Dominion of New England proved a failure

---

[52] Robert Noxon Toppan and Alfred Thompson Scrope Goodrick, *Edward Randolph* (Boston, 1898–1909), VI, 171–72.
[53] Barnes, *Dominion*, p. 87.   [54] *Ibid.*, p. 88.
[55] Toppan and Goodrick, *Edward Randolph*, pp. 171–83.
[56] See Charles Warren, *A History of the American Bar* (Boston, 1911), p. 11 [hereinafter Warren, *American Bar*]; Barnes, *Dominion*, p. 89.

and was dissolved. To some extent its demise can be traced to the lack of a representative assembly. Paradoxically, when the Puritan theocrats had been in power before the Dominion was established, they had not hesitated to tax non-Puritans, who were unrepresented in the government.[57] Out of power, Puritans and non-Puritans had a common cause against the Andros government, and their resistance played a part in bringing it to an end. Magna Carta as a rallying cry had served them well.

The transition which ultimately took place to royal colonies (where colonies were not already royal) went hand in hand with increased regulation by Great Britain of colonial trade.[58] The transatlantic volleys between 1700 and 1719 over Pennsylvania's successive Acts of Privileges to a Freeman were a kind of dress rehearsal of the positions which would be taken on the two sides of the Atlantic between 1765 and 1776: the colonies claiming the guarantees of Magna Carta and the rights of Englishmen, the British Government jealous of its prerogatives and suspicious that any attempt by the colonists to restate English liberties was a covert attack on those prerogatives.

[57] Barnes, *Dominion,* p. 97.

[58] For a study of the enforcement of British commercial regulations from the Restoration to the American Revolution, see Thomas C. Barrow, *Trade and Empire: The British Customs Service in Colonial America, 1660–1776* (Cambridge, Mass., 1967).

Chapter V

English Laws and

English History

The Extension of English Laws to America

WILLIAM BLACKSTONE, in the first volume of his *Commentaries on the Laws of England* (1765), held English plantations or colonies to be of two kinds: those which, being found uninhabited and uncultivated, were claimed by right of occupancy, and those which, being found already inhabited, were taken by conquest or ceded by treaty. This distinction Blackstone thought important in terms of the laws which would be in force in the two kinds of colonies. Blackstone laid down the rule that, in the case of uninhabited lands discovered and settled by the English, "all the English laws then in being, which are the birthright of every subject, are immediately there in force." This rule was subject to the significant qualification that the colonists carried with them "only so much of the English law, as is applicable to their own situation and the conditions of an infant colony." Thus the "artificial refinements and distinctions" incident to a highly developed commercial nation and a number of other laws would not be appropriate to a new colony. The decision as to what laws should be admitted, and what rejected, was a matter for case-by-case adjudication in the provincial courts, subject to the revision and control of the King in Council.[1]

But these rules did not, in Blackstone's view, apply in the case of "conquered or ceded countries, that have already laws of

[1] *Blackstone's Commentaries* (Oxford, 1765–69), I, 106–7.

their own." In those countries the King was free to alter the existing laws, but until he actually did so, the "antient laws of the country" remained in force, unless they were such as to be against the "law of God." [2] The reader may, at this juncture, picture, on the one hand, a Pacific island, where the foot of man has never fallen, as an illustration of Blackstone's "uncultivated" country, and, on the other hand, a French or Spanish colony in the New World, taken by siege or ceded by treaty, as an example of Blackstone's "conquered or ceded" country. Except for such rare cases as New Amsterdam, the reader might well assume most of the American continent to have been of the former kind, that is, countries acquired by settlement, rather than by conquest or treaty.

This is not the view which Blackstone took. He held that "our American plantations are principally of this latter sort, being obtained in the last century either by right of conquest and driving out the natives (with what natural justice I shall not at present enquire) or by treaties." It followed then, by Blackstone's classification, that "the common law of England, as such, has no allowance or authority there. . . ." The American colonies would, of course, be subject to the authority of Parliament, though (like Ireland) not subject to a given Act of Parliament unless specifically named in the act.[3]

If the reader finds this classification of the American colonies dubious, so did St. George Tucker, who, as George Wythe's successor in the chair of law at the College of William and Mary, produced the greatest American commentary on Blackstone. Tucker emphatically disagreed with Blackstone. The English emigrants to America were not, he pointed out, a conquered or a ceded people. Tucker quoted the language of the several charters of Virginia, in which the emigrants were guaranteed the liberties and privileges of Englishmen. From this Tucker inferred the probability that the charters of the other colonies had the like guarantee.[4] (He was, of course, right; they did contain the assurance of the rights of Englishmen.) [5]

[2] *Ibid.*, I, 107.   [3] *Ibid.*, I, 107–8.
[4] *Tucker's Blackstone* (Philadelphia, 1803), Appendix, I, 382–83.
[5] See p. 19, *supra*.

To Tucker the colonial charters were compacts, in the Lockean sense. Thus whatever other arguments there might be for or against saying that English law followed the English emigrants to America, Tucker was able to conclude "upon the ground of compact alone, that the English emigrants who came out to settle in America, did bring with them all the rights and privileges of free natives of England; and, consequently, did bring with them that portion of the laws of the mother country, which was necessary to the conservation and protection of those rights." [6]

A face-to-face debate between the holder of the first chair of law in England and the incumbent, after Wythe, of the first such chair in America would have been a stimulating intellectual event. The name of Blackstone is much the better known, but it is far from clear that the talented Tucker—whose accomplishments ranged from being president of the Virginia Supreme Court of Appeals to coaching young French officers in the art of courting in the English language [7]—would not have battled him to a standstill. But the issue was not one of concern solely to legal scholars. To the American settlers who claimed the benefit of the laws of England it was far from an academic question.

It is fair to say that there was never an articulate colonial theory of what it meant to say that the colonists were entitled to the laws of England. A writer who called himself "An American" wrote *An Essay on the Government of the English Plantations,* published at the beginning of the eighteenth century, and made this complaint:

No one can tell what is law and what is not in the plantations. Some hold that the law of England is chiefly to be respected, and, where that is deficient, the laws of the several colonies are to take place. Others are of the opinion that the laws of the Colonies are to take the first place and that the laws of England are in force only where they are silent. Others there are who contend for the laws of the colonies, in conjunction with those that were in force in England at the first settlement of the colony, and lay down that as the measure of our obedience,

[6] *Tucker's Blackstone,* Appendix, I, 384.
[7] See *A Williamsburg Scrap Book* (Richmond, 1932), pp. 26–27.

alleging that we are not bound to observe any late acts of parliament in England except such only where the reason of the law is the same here that it is in England.[8]

It is doubtful if the colonists had any precise idea what was meant by the "common law" or similar phrases. It is, in fact, doubtful that a clear definition could have been had in England. William Penn, after all, was thought impertinent when in his trial he asked to know the common law on which his indictment was based, the Recorder snorting, "You must not think I am able to run up so many years, and over so many adjudged cases, which we call common-law, to answer your curiosity." [9] The truth of the matter is that English law in the seventeenth century was a house with many separate entrances and exits. In England these legal doorways had many names: Court of Chancery, the Church's ecclesiastical tribunals, Court of Admiralty, the King's courts of common law, and so on. The law itself was also diverse and pluralistic in character; Coke, in his *Commentaries upon Littleton,* said that "there be divers lawes within the realme of England" and listed fifteen kinds of English law.[10] It has been well said by Mark DeWolfe Howe that "it did take a subtle mind and an ingenious form of learning to find virtue in a legal system—all the King's—in which one court took pleasure in undoing the work of its rival. . . ." [11]

It should not be surprising then that the colonists were not very clear about what they were claiming when they said they were entitled to the "laws of England" or when they undertook to put those laws into operation in the colonies. But whether they could define the "laws of England" with any precision or not, the colonists knew they wanted them. Their claim gave rise over a period of time to various legal opinions on what part of the laws of England did have force in the colonies.

As early as *Calvin's Case* (1608), the English courts had been

---

[8] Quoted in St. George Leakin Sioussat, "The Theory of the Extension of English Statutes to the Plantations," in *Select Essays in Anglo-American Legal History* (Boston, 1907–09), I, 416, at 429–30.

[9] 6 Howell's State Trials 951, 958 (1670).   [10] (1628), p. 116.

[11] "The Sources and Nature of Law in Colonial Massachusetts," in George Athan Billias, ed., *Law and Authority in Colonial America* (Barre, Mass., 1965), p. 1, at p. 5.

concerned with problems of the extent to which the English law "followed the flag." In that case the court held that a Scot born after the accession of James VI of Scotland to the English throne could bring an action of novel dissesein (a land action) in England. In its opinion the court discussed the distinction between the ways in which a country might come under the dominion of the Crown.[12]

Much of the argument in the seventeenth and eighteenth centuries over the extension of English law to America was over statutes, in particular statutes passed by Parliament after the settlement of the colonies. For example, in 1681 the King's Attorney General, Sir William Jones, delivered an opinion on the effect in Virginia of a British statute enacted in 1677 in which Virginia was not specifically mentioned. Sir William was of the opinion that "a new Law or Statute made in England, not naming Virginia or any other Plantation, shall not take Effect in Virginia or the other Plantation" unless received by the colonial assembly. As his reasons the Attorney General stated that (1) it would not be presumed that Parliament, in passing a statute, had in mind the peculiar conditions in the colonies unless it named the colonies, and (2) because of the time required to get word to the colonies of new laws, they would be bound by laws of which they were ignorant.[13]

A 1720 opinion of Richard West, counsel to the Board of Trade, drew a distinction between those statutes (such as Magna Carta) passed before a colony's settlement and those passed afterward:

The Common Law of England is the Common Law of the Plantations, and all statutes in affirmance of the Common Law, passed in England antecedent to the settlement of a colony, are in force in that colony, unless there is some private Act to the contrary; though no statutes, made since those settlements, are there in force unless the colonies are particularly mentioned. Let an Englishman go where he will, he carries as much of law and liberty with him, as the nature of things will bear.[14]

[12] 7 Coke Rep. 1a, at 17b–18a, 77 Eng. Rep. 377, at 397–98.
[13] Barradall's Reports, in *Virginia Colonial Decisions* (Boston, 1909), II, B1–B2.
[14] George Chalmers, *Opinions of Eminent Lawyers on Various Points of English Jurisprudence* (London, 1814), I, 194.

An opinion of the English Attorney General Philip Yorke (later the first Earl of Hardwicke), written in 1729 in relation to Maryland, agreed that a statute passed by the British Parliament after the colony's settlement and not by its language referring to the colonies (individually or collectively) would not be in force in the colonies. Yorke did add, however, that it might become law in a colony by the action of that colony's assembly or might "have been received there by a long uninterrupted usage or practice" such as to give it the force of law.[15]

The Blackstonian distinction between the settlement of an uninhabited country and a country acquired by conquest appeared in a Privy Council memorandum of the same period. In an uninhabited country the English law is the "birthright of every subject, so, wherever they go, they carry their laws with them. . . ." However, Acts of Parliament passed after the country's settlement apply only if the country is named. But where the King conquers a country, there "he may impose upon them what laws he pleases."[16] Certain English decisions drew a like distinction between settlement and conquest.[17]

It is apparent from the opinions quoted above that claims to the benefit of, and disputes over the extension of, English law to the American colonies could have taken more than one form. It mattered whether statutes or common, non-statutory law was being discussed. It mattered whether, if statutes were involved, the statutes had been passed before the emigration or after. It might matter whether the law was public (such as those touching the liberties of the subject) or private (such as the law of wills and estates). And it mattered whether the claim was that English laws automatically crossed the ocean or that a colonial assembly had the power or right to adopt such laws as it might choose.

One thing should be understood: the colonists at no time wanted the laws of England *en masse*. Many English laws would have been at best irrelevant to, at worst destructive of,

---

15 *Ibid.*, I, 206.
16 Quoted in Elizabeth Gaspar Brown, *British Statutes in American Law 1776–1836* (Ann Arbor, Mich., 1964), p. 11 [hereinafter Brown, *British Statutes*].
17 See the decisions of Holt, C. J., in Blankard v. Galdy, 2 Salk. 411, 91 Eng. Rep. 356, and Smith v. Brown, 2 Salk. 666, 91 Eng. Rep. 566.

colonial values. The colonies in the early seventeenth century had no use for the developing commercial law of Britain; it is hardly surprising then to find no record of the colonists' numbering it among their "rights." The colonists certainly did not want feudal land laws or laws giving privileges to the Church, established or not. What they wanted from the English law was its best traditions—due process of law, trial by jury, procedural fairness in courts of law, punishments in tune with the growth of civilized standards, a say in the imposition of taxes. They wanted to pick what appealed to them, and reject the rest.

The colonial charters invited this kind of selectivity. The standard language requiring that laws and ordinances passed in the colonies conform to the laws of England always added the qualification "as near as conveniently may be." [18] English opinions such as that of Sir William Jones in 1681, quoted above, showed an awareness that different conditions in the colonies called for comparable differences in the applicable laws. The colonists knew better than anybody that even the English laws which they did use to guide decisions in the colonies often required adaptation. Chief Justice Peter Oliver of Massachusetts gave examples one evening in 1773 while having dinner with Ezra Stiles, the president of Yale College. One such example was that in England and Massachusetts, a Quaker's evidence, given by affirmation rather than oath, would not support a capital conviction; yet when an English judge tried to invoke this rule in the Jerseys the local people said it was their usage to admit Quaker testimony in capital cases, and the judge was obliged to give way, though it was a departure from the laws of England. [19]

In general, when the colonists wanted the laws of England, or some part of them, they had two courses open to them. They could point to their colonial charters as giving them the automatic benefit of English laws, or they could, by act of a colonial

[18] Some charters were even more explicit; for example, the patent for Providence Plantations of 1643 said that local laws should conform to the laws of England "so far as the Nature and Constitution of the place will admit." Thorpe, VI, 3210–11.

[19] *Literary Diary of Ezra Stiles*, ed. Franklin Bowditch Dexter (New York, 1901), I, 331.

assembly, make specific introduction of given English laws. There are a number of instances of a colonial assembly's adopting the latter course, notably in the southern colonies, where the pull of English law seems to have been stronger than in New England. North Carolina, for example, sought a wholesale adoption of both the common and statute law of England. Its assembly ordained that "the common law is, and shall be, in force, in this government. . . ." And it decreed that "all statute laws of England . . . providing for the privileges of the people . . . are and shall be in force here, altho' this province, or the plantations in general, are not therein named." [20] South Carolina in 1712 declared the common law and an enumerated list of English statutes to be in force.[21]

Such efforts, where they had to pass muster in England, were often overturned. Maryland, from soon after its chartering in 1632 until well into the seventeenth century, was the scene of repeated efforts to legislate into the law of Maryland the benefits of the laws of England. The upper and lower houses of the Maryland legislature exchanged views over whether the laws of England ought to be declared of force in Maryland. The Maryland Assembly passed a series of acts over the years, attempting to secure for Marylanders the rights of the English laws in general or the guarantees of Magna Carta in particular. Such efforts often ran into the veto, and one of the by-products of these maneuverings in Maryland was Daniel Dulany the Elder's authorship of his *Rights of the Inhabitants of Maryland to the Benefit of the English Laws* (1728).[22]

Of all the demands for the benefits of English law, one claim stands out clearly from the rest: the insistence on the rights of Magna Carta. Whatever value the colonists thought there was in the English common law in general, whatever benefit they thought they might get from individual Acts of Parliament passed after the emigration, they were determined they should have Magna Carta. Even when life in the colonies was at its

[20] *Public Acts of the General Assembly of North Carolina,* ed. James Iredell, rev. Francois-Xavier Martin (New Bern, N.C., 1804) , pp. 14–15.

[21] *Statutes at Large of South Carolina,* ed. Thomas Cooper (Columbia, S.C., 1836–41) , II, 401.

[22] For the events in Maryland, see pp. 53–65, *supra.*

rudest, and the need for law was only for the law's simplest aspects, Magna Carta was thought indispensable. Indictments were founded on Magna Carta, demurrers were rested on Magna Carta, acts of proprietors and governors and the British Government were assailed as contravening Magna Carta. To the colonists this was both the symbol and the statement of their rights, their best heritage as subjects of the British Crown.

With all respect for Blackstone, one must cast his lot with the judgment of St. George Tucker. Only a lawyer with a biologist's love for neat categories could draw a deceptively simple line between the settlement of uninhabited territories, where settlers carried with them the laws of England, and conquered or ceded countries, where the existing laws continued, and assign the American colonies to the latter category. This is to treat Virginia or Massachusetts—where the settlements were carved out of wilderness and, through force or treaty, were made secure against the Indians—like the acquisition of an already civilized country, with its own advanced culture and laws. When the American colonies were planted (with fairly unimportant exceptions such as New Amsterdam), there was no native legal system which could be used to govern the colonists' affairs. If England conquered a Spanish colony, complete with Spanish settlers, then of course Spanish laws, left undisturbed, could continue to serve local legal needs. But realistically the American colonists could look to only one source for their laws: England.

Moreover, they had every expectation that it was their right and privilege to look to those laws. Their charters said so. There might have been some doubt as to whether they might automatically have the benefit of later laws—and this was to be of special importance when they wanted the significant advances in individual liberty made possible by the Bill of Rights of 1689 or the Habeas Corpus Act of 1679—but as to the documents of liberty which formed the foundation of English law at the time of the emigration, there can be little doubt. It would stagger reason to suppose that what Englishmen had won at Runnymede almost four hundred years before Virginia was settled would no longer be available to Englishmen who settled under charters carrying the Crown's assurances of the liberties, franchises, and immunities of Englishmen.

The "Whig View" of History

I t would be misleading to speak of attitudes in the American colonies toward the English common law without also speaking of their attitudes toward English history.[23] The eighteenth century was the time of the Enlightenment, an age of rationalism. A characteristic assumption indulged by many eighteenth-century men in England or Europe was that human nature was everywhere the same, with some allowance (as in Montesquieu) for climate and geography. Given these variables, what one learned about man in one country or time was instructive about mankind in general.[24]

In thinking of history and historians in the eighteenth century, one is likely to think of those sweeping national and world histories turned out by an age of men confident, often overly so, of their capacity to deal with the great themes of the centuries. Greatest of these efforts and, for all the advances in historical method since that time, a landmark work was Edward Gibbon's *The History of the Decline and Fall of the Roman Empire,* in which Gibbon advanced the thesis of an Empire's declining with the decline in moral and intellectual values. Gibbon thought by his *Decline and Fall* to make a point of relevance to his own age. In so doing he was writing not only as historian, but as philosopher.

[23] The brief section which follows is meant only to give enough of the flavor of the "Whig view" of history and its influence on the American colonists to add perspective to the main narrative, which is concerned with legal and constitutional thought. The discussion in these several pages leans heavily on the excellent study by H. Trevor Colbourn, *The Lamp of Experience: Whig History and the Intellectual Origins of the American Revolution* (Chapel Hill, N.C., 1965) [hereinafter Colbourn, *Lamp of Experience*]. For a fuller discussion, the reader should turn to Colbourn, from whose insights he would unquestionably profit.

[24] This idea was already under heavy attack in the eighteenth century by such thinkers as Giambattista Vico, who substituted the relativistic notion of an evolving human nature for the prevailing view that all rational men must see things the same way, and J. G. von Herder, who said that the only meaningful study was of particular times and places.

Given the eighteenth-century view of the nature of man, history became a teacher of special value. The Englishman of that time (Whig or Tory) was especially likely to subscribe to this view of the usefulness of the study of history.[25] Henry St. John, Viscount Bolingbroke, in his *Letters on the Study and Use of History* written in 1735, said that "history is philosophy teaching by examples." To learn from history, he believed, was better than to learn the hard way, by experience alone: "If experience alone can make us perfect in our parts, experience cannot begin to teach them till we are actually on the stage: whereas, by a previous application to this study . . . we are not quite unprepared, we learn our parts sooner, and we learn them better." [26]

James Burgh, in his *Political Disquisitions,* placed a like premium on the value of history. Pointing to the use of history by Plato, Aristotle, Montesquieu, Montaigne, Saint-Pierre, and Rollin, Burgh told his reader: "I considered, that history is the inexhaustible mine, out of which political knowledge is to be brought up." [27] Burgh's book enjoyed immense popularity on both sides of the Atlantic; no sooner had it appeared in London in 1774 than, the following year, it was brought out in Philadelphia.

The American colonist of the eighteenth century was likely to feel the same way about history. Benjamin Franklin, who had something to say about virtually every subject of human knowledge, had something to say about history. In his *Proposals Relating to the Education of Youth in Pennsylvania* (1749), Franklin discussed the advantages of studying history and concluded, "As nothing *teaches* (saith Mr. Locke) so nothing *delights* more than history." [28]

The significance of this attachment to history as mentor lies in the contrast between the so-called "Whig" and "Tory" views

---

[25] See R. N. Stromberg, "History in the Eighteenth Century," 12 *Journal of the History of Ideas* 295 (1952).

[26] Henry St. John, 1st Viscount Bolingbroke, *Works* (Dublin, 1793), II, 245, 252.

[27] James Burgh, *Political Disquisitions* (London, 1774), I, vi.

[28] *Papers of Benjamin Franklin,* ed. Leonard W. Labaree (New Haven, 1959———), III, 397, 410–15.

of history, for if (as noted above) Whigs and Tories alike made use of history, it was by and large the "Whig" view of history which had the greater impact on thinking in the American colonies.[29] Whig history tended to be a kind of polemic, though of a very high order. Born of political controversies, Whig history sought to support parliamentary opposition to royal prerogative by exalting the antiquity of Parliament and tracing Parliament's claims to ancient custom.

Research into the ancient customs of the realm had begun in Tudor times. The first Society of Antiquaries was found in 1572; that scholarship at that time had political overtones is suggested by the fact that the Society was suppressed in 1604.[30] The research and writing of the Whig historians produced an idealized picture of England before the Norman invasion. 1066 became a watershed. Before that time, English liberties went hand-in-hand with Anglo-Saxon democracy; after that time, democracy and liberties alike went under the Norman yoke.

The enthroning of Anglo-Saxon virtues carried with it the idealization of Magna Carta. If English liberties had been submerged by the Conquest, then they must have been revived by the submission of that bad Norman King, John, to the barons of England. Algernon Sidney (who in 1683, after a partisan trial, was executed upon a sentence of high treason) typified this view of Magna Carta in his principal work, the *Discourses Concerning Government*. English liberties, he said, did not originate with Magna Carta; that document declared them. It was "the great charter that recapitulates and acknowledges our

[29] "Whig" and "Tory" are not susceptible of easy definition. G. H. Guttridge has observed that the difference between Whiggism and Toryism lay less in specific program than in temperament and interpretation of society. The essence of the division, according to Guttridge, "lay in antithesis. In the seventeenth and eighteenth centuries the basis of controversy over the nature of government might be religious, political, or legal. It might emphasize the law of God, the law of nature, or the English Constitution. In any event, the tory would find reason to justify unity and authority, the whig to assert particular rights. The law of God might ordain a king; it might also restrain the exercise of his power. The law of nature might presuppose monarchical government; it might also sanction revolution. The laws and customs of England could confer a broad prerogative; they provided also the precedents of Magna Carta and the Bill of Rights." *English Whiggism and the American Revolution* (Berkeley, Calif., 1963), p. 1.

[30] See Helen M. Cam, *Magna Carta—Event or Document?* (London, 1965), p. 20.

antient inherent liberties, obliges [the King] to swear, that he will neither sell, delay, nor deny justice to any man, according to the laws of the land. . . ." Magna Carta, not the King, is supreme: "Fortescue says plainly, the king cannot change any law: Magna Charta casts all upon the laws of the land and customs of England. . . . [The King] must therefore take the laws and customs as he finds them, and can neither detract from, nor add any thing to them." [31]

Sidney's *Discourses* were much read and admired in America. So were the works of Paul de Rapin, Sieur de Thoyras, whose *History of England* and *Dissertation on the Whigs and Tories* were best sellers in the American colonies. In his *History*, Rapin described the sealing of Magna Carta and said, "From that time these two charters [Magna Carta and the Charter of the Forest] have been the foundation of the English liberties, notwithstanding the endeavours of John himself and some of his successors, to annul them." [32]

Burgh's *Political Disquisitions* put the American colonists' resistance to British policies squarely in the mainstream of the Whig historical tradition. Comparing the "greatly oppressed" colonies' resistance to British taxing measures to Hampden's resisting payment of ship money, Burgh agreed with the colonial position that Magna Carta gave them the right not to be taxed without their consent:

> *Magna Charta,* and the Bill of Rights, prohibit the taxing of the mother-country by prerogative, and without consent of those who are to be taxed. If the people of *Britain* are not to be taxed, but by parliament; because otherwise they might be taxed without their own consent; does it not directly follow, that the colonists cannot, according to *Magna Charta,* and the bill of rights, be taxed by parliament, so long as they continue unrepresented; because otherwise they may be taxed without their own consent? [33]

The colonial charters ensured the emigrants and their posterity all liberties enjoyed by Englishmen in England. Surely, to

---

[31] Algernon Sidney, *Discourses Concerning Government* (Edinburgh, 1750), II, 113, 122.

[32] *History of England* (4th ed.; London, 1757), II, 469.

[33] *Political Disquisitions*, II, 310.

tax the colonists without giving them representation was to deny them the privileges of Englishmen. Moreover, Burgh submitted, "to raise the price of justice so high," by the passage of the Stamp Act, "that the people shall not be able to obtain it, is much the same as flatly denying them justice; while *Magna Charta* says, *Nulli negabimus, nulli vendemus justitiam. . . .*"[34]

Whig history had great influence in America[35] and the works of the Whig historians were commonly found in colonial libraries. John Adams, for example, had the second edition of Rapin's *History of England* and a copy of the London edition of Burgh's *Political Disquisitions*—a presentation copy to Adams from the author himself.[36] As the colonies moved nearer to Independence, they sought legal counsel in Coke and historical precedent in the Whig view of history. If, after all, Magna Carta had not been a revolutionary document, but simply a restatement of the ancient liberties of Englishmen, for the colonists to insist on those same rights was not revolutionary either. So history was on the colonists' side. As the *Newport Mercury* put it on September 7, 1772, "Provoke us not too far! *Runymede* is still to be found, as we may there assert our rights."[37]

And it is one of those curious footnotes of history that the first publication in book form of the Declaration of Independence took place in 1776 as part of a volume entitled *The Genuine Principles of the Ancient Saxon, or English Constitution.*[38]

[34] *Ibid.*, II, 312.   [35] See Colbourn, *Lamp of Experience.*
[36] Boston Public Library, *Catalogue of the John Adams Library* (Boston, 1917), p. 38.
[37] Quoted in Colbourn, *Lamp of Experience,* p. 187.   [38] *Ibid.*, pp. 190–91.

Chapter VI

Lawyers and Lawbooks

Lawyers were not popular figures in either England or America in the seventeenth century. One can only surmise what the seventeenth-century playgoer in England, seeing Part II of Shakespeare's *King Henry VI*, thought on hearing Dick the butcher implore the rebel leader, Jack Cade of Ashford, "The first thing we do, let's kill all the lawyers." Lawyers were the targets of pamphlets of the time, with such suggestive titles as *Doomsday Drawing Near with Thunder and Lightning for Lawyers* and *A Rod for Lawyers Who are Hereby declared Robbers and Deceivers of the Nation.*[1]

This unpopularity was true in the American colonies as well. Charles Warren, the historian of the American bar, has observed that nothing in the early legal history of the colonies is more striking than the "uniformly low position held in the community by the members of the legal profession. . . . In every one of the Colonies, practically throughout the Seventeenth Century, a lawyer or attorney was a character of disrepute and of suspicion. . . ."[2] This attitude is reflected in a late seventeenth-century account of the province of Pennsylvania: "Of *Lawyers* and *Physicians* I shall say nothing because this

---

[1] See Warren, *American Bar*, p. 7.
[2] *Ibid.*, p. 4. See Chroust, *Legal Profession*, I, 27–28.

countrey is very Peaceable and Healthy: long may it so continue and never have occasion for the Tongue of the one nor the Pen of the other—both equally destructive of Men's Estates and Lives. . . ."[3]

The low regard for lawyers in the colonies was not surprising, for many people who held themselves out as attorneys had no legal training whatever. Clever and unscrupulous laymen often appeared in legal causes, and the resulting disrepute of the practice of law resulted in the passage of restrictive laws in nearly all the colonies, some banning any fees for arguing another's case in court. Fundamental law often contained such restrictions. John Locke, in drafting the *Fundamental Constitutions of Carolina* (1669), included the provision: "It shall be a base and vile thing to plead for money or reward; nor shall any one (except he be a near kinsman, not farther off than cousin-german to the party concerned) be permitted to plead another man's cause, till, before the judge in open court, he hath taken an oath that he doth not plead for money or reward. . . ."[4] Similarly, Massachusetts' Body of Liberties of 1641 allowed attorneys to plead causes other than their own but disallowed all fees or rewards.[5]

If the fundamental law of a colony did not contain such restrictions on lawyers, typically it was forthcoming by act or ordinance. The minutes of the Council of New York City for May 16, 1677, contain the following entry:

Query? Whether attorneys are thought to be useful to plead in courts or not. Answer. It is thought not. Whereupon resolved and ordered, That pleading attorneys be no longer allowed to practise in ye Government, but for ye pending cases.[6]

As we have seen above, the General Assembly of Virginia in the seventeenth century passed a number of statutes attempting to deal with attorneys, at one point simply banning them from the colony's courts altogether because of their "unskillfulness and coveteousness."[7]

---

[3] Gabriel Thomas, *An Historical and Geographical Account of the Province and Country of Pensilvania; and of West New Jersey in America* (London, 1698), p. 37.
[4] Thorpe, V, 2781.   [5] *Colonial Laws of Massachusetts*, pp. 38–39.
[6] Quoted in Warren, *American Bar*, p. 94.   [7] See p. 31, *supra*.

Lawyers, in the proper sense, were rare in the early years of colonial America. The legal profession in New England in the seventeenth century was inconsequential. Even in judicial posts, lawyers were not common. Among the Chief Justices of Massachusetts, many were nonlawyers, even down to the time of the American Revolution; most of the associate justices were laymen. In New York few judges other than the Chief Justice had had legal training; the first Chief Justice, in fact, had been educated as a clergyman and had been in politics but had no legal education. Similarly, in Pennsylvania, with a few exceptions, laymen (frequently merchants) filled judgeships even in the eighteenth century.[8] As a consequence the courts were often as unpopular as the lawyers; a popular Maryland poem attacked the unjust treatment meted out to strangers in the courts of that colony, noting that twice a year the bench did

> gravely meet
> Some to get drink, and some to eat
> A swinging Share of Country Treat.[9]

The low state of the legal profession in seventeenth-century America tended to retard the introduction into the colonies of the principles of the English common law. Moreover, in the early years especially, life in the colonies was rude as compared to that in England, and it took time before trade, commerce, and other aspects of colonial life developed to the point where the relatively technical and sophisticated law of England was suited to colonial needs. Frequently, too, there were vested interests which found it expedient to oppose the growth of a professional bar; this was true, for example, of the merchants and planters, especially in the middle colonies. Opposition also came from certain religious elements, for example, some of the theocratically minded Puritans of New England, who preferred discretionary government based on the "word of God" or the "law of Moses," rather than a system of more exact limitations

---

[8] See Richard B. Morris, *Studies in the History of American Law* (New York, 1930), pp. 41–42; Warren, *American Bar*, pp. 75–105.

[9] Ebenezer Cooke, *The Maryland Muse Containing . . . The Sotweed Factor, or Voiage to Maryland* (3d ed.; Annapolis, 1731).

116   *The Road from Runnymede*

based on the common law of England. Illustrative is the instance in Massachusetts, already noted, when a defendant pleaded that Magna Carta and other English statutes "secure the subjects' properties and estates," and a judge replied, "We must not think the laws of England follow us to the ends of the earth or whither we went." [10]

By the eighteenth century, a genuine bar was taking shape in the colonies and bringing into being a group of professional men, tending to positions of leadership, who were well placed to appreciate the potential for individual liberty which was one of the best traditions of the common law. If the colonies did not need or want the burdensome incidents of feudal land law or the more intricate features of English commercial law, they could still have the features they found most appealing, in particular, Magna Carta and other guarantees of their rights.

Several factors played their part in the growth of an American bar—among them the growth of commerce, bringing with it legal disputes over contracts and commercial paper; the making of individual fortunes, calling for such services as the drafting of wills and the administration of estates; creation of large landholdings, requiring men who were skilled at land law; and, most significant for the habit of looking to Magna Carta and like sources for a statement of the rights of Englishmen, in the colonies as at home, an increasingly active political climate.

The study of law became both useful and fashionable. Although the foundation of the education of a planter's son in Virginia was the classics, typically he went on from there to study law. Even if the planter did not make law his profession, he would use the law while serving as justice of the peace. Even more would he use the law if he served in the House of Burgesses. And in any event there would be land disputes or claims by merchants in London or the like. As Thomas Wertenbaker has said, every planter, "especially the large planter, was supposed to know his Coke and his Blackstone." [11]

[10] *Supra,* p. 97.
[11] Thomas J. Wertenbaker, *The Golden Age of Colonial Culture* (New York, 1942), p. 108. Wertenbaker's statement is more apt as to Coke, since Blackstone's *Commentaries* were not published until 1765–69.

Lawbooks and the Writings of Coke

O NE of the limiting factors in the implanting in colonial legal thought of ideas drawn from Magna Carta and the English common law was the lack, a severe one at first, of English lawbooks. The need for basic treatises on English law was sorely felt. For want of a copy of the statutes-at-large for the court to consult, a prisoner in Lower Norfolk County, Virginia, was bailed in 1690.[12] In 1666 the General Assembly of Virginia directed that the English statutes-at-large and several other lawbooks be ordered for the use of the Assembly and of the courts at James City. The legislature also directed the several county courts to obtain the same books for their use.[13] County justices began to order needed books from England. In 1671, Major Adam Thoroughgood (whose house in Norfolk stands today as one of the best examples of seventeenth-century domestic architecture in America) was about to set sail for England, and the justices of Lower Norfolk County requested him, while in England, to purchase certain lawbooks for the county's use. The resolution of the justices indicated that they were acting in obedience to the wish of the General Assembly of Virginia.[14] Similar requests were made by the justices of other Virginia counties; the justices of Lancaster County put such a request to Captain James of the ship *Duke of York*,[15] and the justices of York County asked Colonel John Page to buy lawbooks for their use.[16] In 1690 Nicholas Spencer secured in England for the use of the court of Westmoreland County, Virginia, perhaps the most complete set of lawbooks owned by any county court in the colony, its value being estimated at £8 or 4,000 pounds of tobacco.[17]

[12] Lower Norfolk County Records, Orders, vol. 1686–95 (order of Aug. 15, 1690).
[13] 2 *Hening* 246.
[14] Lower Norfolk County Records, vol. 1666–75, p. 94 (resolution of April 18, 1671).
[15] Lancaster County Records, Orders, vol. 1666–80, p. 133 (order of Nov. 26, 1689).
[16] York County Records, vol. 1665–72, p. 516 (order of Oct. 25, 1671).
[17] Westmoreland County Records, Orders, vol. 1690–98 (order of Jan. 28, 1690).

By the end of the seventeenth century, quite respectable law libraries, either in public or private hands, had come into being in the colonies. The contents of these libraries are especially revealing. The cost of importing books into the colonies was high, and it was the rare colonist who could collect books simply for ostentation. Louis B. Wright has suggested that books brought to Virginia by the planters, or imported later, "were chosen with a definite notion of their value, and they were often literally read to pieces. It is this fact that gives seventeenth- and early-eighteenth-century book lists unusual significance, for the choice of books provides a clue to the settlers' conception of intellectual and social values." [18]

Lawbooks were a conspicuous and meaningful feature of private libraries in seventeenth-century America. If they were outstripped in absolute numbers by books of devotion (which, typically, they were), legal treatises were, as much as any part of the colonist's library, there to be used in the colonist's daily affairs. Many colonists had to be their own lawyers, and to have the right lawbook at hand might well mean a man's land or fortune. But if the books were bought and used with practical ends in mind, it is unquestionable that these books also planted in the colonists' minds the traditions of the English common law and the rights of Englishmen.

Foremost among the titles to be found in private libraries of the time were the works of Coke, the great expounder of Magna Carta, and similar books on English liberties. The inventory of the library of Arthur Spicer, who died in Richmond County, Virginia, in 1699, included Coke's *Institutes*, another work on Magna Carta, and a "Table to Cooks Reports." [19] The library of Colonel Daniel McCarty, a wealthy planter and member of the Virginia House of Burgesses who died in Westmoreland County in 1724, included Coke's *Reports,* an abridgment of Coke's *Reports, Coke on Littleton,* and "Rights of the Comons of England." [20] Captain Charles Colston, who died in Rich-

[18] Louis B. Wright, *The First Gentlemen of Virginia: Intellectual Qualities of the Early Colonial Ruling Class* (San Marino, Calif., 1940) , p. 117.
[19] 3 *Wm. & Mary Qtly.* (1st ser.) 133–34 (1894) .
[20] 8 *ibid.* (1st ser.) 19–20 (1899) .

mond County, Virginia, in 1724, and Captain Christopher Cocke, who died in Princess Anne County, Virginia, in 1716, each had copies of Coke's *Institutes*.[21] That these libraries were typical is suggested by a study of the contents of approximately one hundred private libraries in colonial Virginia, which revealed that the most common law title found in these libraries was Coke's *Reports*.[22] They were typical of other colonies, too. Another study, of the inventories of forty-seven libraries throughout the colonies between 1652 and 1791, found that of all the books on either law or politics in these libraries the most common was Coke's *Institutes* (found in 27 of the 47 libraries). The second most common title was a poor second; it was Grotius' *War and Peace,* found in 16 of the libraries (even Locke's *Two Treatises on Government* appeared in only 13 of the libraries).[23]

The popularity of Coke in the colonies is of no small significance. Coke himself had been at the eye of the storm in the clashes between King and Parliament in the early seventeenth century which did so much to shape the English Constitution. He rose to high office at the instance of the Crown—he was Speaker of the House of Commons and Attorney General under Queen Elizabeth, and James I made Coke first his Chief Justice of Common Pleas and then his Chief Justice of King's Bench. During this time Coke gained an unchallenged position as the greatest authority of his time on the laws of England, frequently burying an opponent with learned citations from early Year Books. Having been a champion of the Crown's interests, Coke (in a change of role that recalls the metamorphosis of Thomas à Becket) became instead the defender of the common law. Making effective use of common law writs, notably the writ of prohibition and the writ of habeas corpus, Coke opposed the King's will until, at length, having defied the King to his face (when Coke's fellow judges submitted), he was dismissed from office.

[21] 3 *ibid.* (1st ser.) 132–33 (1894) ; 4 *ibid.* (1st ser.) 94 (1895) .
[22] George K. Smart, "Private Libraries in Colonial Virginia," 10 *American Literature* 24 (1938) .
[23] Rodney L. Mott, *Due Process of Law* (Indianapolis, 1926) , p. 89 n. 9.

Soon thereafter, Coke entered a new stage in his public career with his election to Parliament in 1620 as a member for a Cornish borough. King James had sought, in emulation of the Lancastrian kings, to rule without calling a Parliament, but his need for funds obliged him to convene the Parliament to which Coke was elected. Crown and Parliament crossed swords over a number of issues, including grants by the King of trade and industrial patents, which, among other abuses, led to arbitrary imprisonment of those thought to be infringing such patents. Coke took a conspicuous part in the debates over the patent issue and urged the Commons to reassert Magna Carta's guarantee against arbitrary confinement. The public debate over the prerogatives of King and the rights of Commons became yet more strident when Charles I succeeded James I on the throne. Charles in 1626 imposed a forced loan after he had failed to get funds he had sought from Parliament. Many refused to pay, and the result was the *cause célèbre* of the *Five Knights Case,* a test of the legality of the imprisonment of five who had been imprisoned. Parliament took up the challenge posed by the King's authoritarian acts, and there followed a great debate on the liberties of the subject. Many were the invocations of Magna Carta by members of the House, but perhaps the most memorable was Coke's declaration:

I know that prerogative is part of the law, but sovereign power is no Parliamentary word; in my opinion, it weakens Magna Carta and all our statutes; for they are absolute without any saving of sovereign power. And shall we now add to it, we shall weaken the foundation of Law, and then the building must needs fall; take we heed what we yield unto—Magna Carta is such a Fellow, he will have no Sovereign.

The House then agreed upon the great Petition of Right, a landmark in English constitutional history and in effect a ratification of Coke's own interpretation of Magna Carta, not as written down in 1215, but as the basis of liberties in seventeenth-century England.[24]

What Coke thought Magna Carta to mean, and what the

[24] For a fuller account of Coke's role in the events of the early seventeenth century, see Swindler, *Magna Carta*, pp. 166–207.

Commons took it to stand for when they voted the Petition of Right of 1628, was fundamental to what the Great Charter came to mean in the American colonies. Ever since his dismissal from the bench in 1616, Coke had been working on his monumental commentaries on the laws of England. So dangerous were they to the claims of the Crown that the *Second Institute,* which restated the rights of the subject drawn from Magna Carta, was not published until the outbreak of the Civil War in England, years after Coke's death. But once they appeared they quickly became (and remained at least until the publication of Blackstone's *Commentaries* over a century later) the authoritative statement of the laws of England. As such, their influence, and that of Coke's *Reports,* in the American colonies was immense.

In *Dr. Bonham's Case,* decided in 1610 when he was on the bench, Coke had stated that the "common law will controul Acts of Parliament, and sometimes adjudge them to be utterly void: for when an Act of Parliament is against common right and reason, or repugnant, or impossible to be performed, the common law will controul it, and adjudge such Act to be void. . . ." [25] There is some argument whether this proposition simply stated a canon of statutory construction or set forth a constitutional mandate.[26] But whether or not Coke was stating a doctrine of judicial review, Americans took him to mean that, and his pronouncements came to have great historical importance as a factor in the later development in the United States of the doctrine of the power of a court to declare legislative acts unconstitutional.

Of special significance to events in the American colonies, notably in its use as a source for arguments made by the colonists against British policies before the American Revolution, was Coke's discussion of Magna Carta. In the proeme to the

[25] 8 Coke Rep. 113b, 118a, 77 Eng. Rep. 646, 652 (1610).

[26] For the view that *Dr. Bonham's Case* states a theory of fundamental law, see Theodore F. T. Plucknett, "Bonham's Case and Judicial Review," 40 *Harv. L. Rev.* 30 (1926), and his *Concise History of the Common Law* (5th ed.; Boston, 1956), p. 337. For the view that *Dr. Bonham's Case* simply states a theory of strict statutory construction, see S. E. Thorne, "Dr. Bonham's Case," 54 *L.Q. Rev* 543, 548–52 (1938); J. W. Gough, *Fundamental Law in English Constitutional History* (Oxford, 1955), pp. 31–40.

Second Institute, Coke observed that by virtue of statutes of 25 Edward I and 42 Edward III "it is enacted (only to shew their tender care of *Magna Charta,* and *Charta de Foresta*) that if any statute be made contrary to the great charter, or the charter of the forest, that shall be holden for none. . . ." [27] Magna Carta likewise worked to void unlawful acts of the King's judges or ministers. Referring to a statute of 25 Edward I, Coke said, "And albeit judgements in the kings courts are of high regard in law . . . yet it is provided by act of parliament, that if any judgment be given contrary to any of the points of the great charter, or *Charta de Foresta,* by the justices, or by any other of the kings ministers, &c. it shall be undone, and holden for nought." [28] Coke was speaking of statutes which had thus enshrined Magna Carta, but his commentaries helped lay the way for the view, subscribed to in the American colonies, of the Charter as a kind of superstatute, a constitution placing fundamental liberties beyond the reach of Parliament as well as the King and his ministers.

So Coke's writings found their way into American libraries and, as we have already seen, were the most frequent legal title to be found among lawbooks in the hands of the colonists. The proportion of the books in some of the colonial libraries represented by lawbooks is also revealing. To take as illustrations the libraries already mentioned above, of 120 titles in Arthur Spicer's library 53 were lawbooks (an unusually large collection for his time). Of Colonel McCarty's 110 titles, about half were lawbooks. In smaller libraries, similar proportions often obtained. Captain Colston had 22 listed books, of which nine were lawbooks. Captain Cocke had 24 titles, of which nine were on the law. Those who held public office were especially apt to have strong collections in the law; Godfrey Pole, a clerk in the Virginia House of Burgesses and also clerk of Northampton County, had a library of 111 titles, of which 56 were lawbooks.[29]

Some of the colonial libraries were truly notable. The library

---

[27] *Second Institute,* Proeme.   [28] *Ibid.*

[29] 3 *Wm. & Mary Qtly.* (1st ser.) 133–34 (1894); 8 *ibid.* (1st ser.) 19–20 (1899); 3 *ibid.* (1st ser.) 132–33 (1894); 4 *ibid.* (1st ser.) 94 (1895); 17 *Va. Mag. Hist. & Biog.* 147–50 (1909).

of the Carters, one of the influential families of seventeenth- and eighteenth-century Virginia, is an instance. The Carters, a prolific family, had wealth and power, and a special knack for good alliances with other important families. Robert Carter—better known to us as "King" Carter—represented the peak of the family's wealth and influence. A member of the Council of Virginia from 1699 to 1732 and its president from 1726 to 1732 (the year of his death), "King" Carter built a library which at his death numbered over 260 titles. It included what has been called "the best law library in the American colonies at that time—with perhaps the exception of the one then being gathered by William Byrd II at Westover" (Byrd's great plantation house on the James River below Richmond). Over one-third, or approximately one hundred titles, of "King" Carter's library at his house, Corotoman, consisted of lawbooks. Sir Edward Coke was represented with his *Institutes* and with an abridgment of his *Reports*.[30]

These libraries of colonial Virginia—county courts, planters, and others—and the presence of Coke and other sources on Magna Carta are not atypical of what one would find in libraries in other colonies, especially in the eighteenth century. New England libraries tended to vary in one significant respect; lawbooks, of whatever title, usually formed a far smaller proportion of a given library, public or private, than they did in most southern colonies. But if a New England library had any legal treatises at all, they were apt to include the works of Coke or some book on the liberties of the Englishman. When the Philogrammatican Society of Connecticut bought 94 works for its library in 1735, five of these books were on the law, and two of the five were of Coke—Coke's *Institutes* and Coke's *Reports*. Likewise, when the Rev. Thomas Prince of Boston died in 1758, his large library (mostly theology) had only five books on the common law, but one was Henry Care's *English Liberties,* from which the colonial reader could, as from Coke, drink deep of the lore of Magna Carta.[31]

[30] Wright, *The First Gentlemen of Virginia: Intellectual Qualities of the Early Ruling Class,* pp. 235–64.
[31] Warren, *American Bar,* pp. 162–63.

The Boston Public Library's catalogue of John Adams' library shows that Adams had ready access to the jurisprudence of Coke. In Adams' library are to be found such works of Coke as *A Book of Entries* (2d ed.; London, 1671), *Certain Select Cases in Law* (2d ed.; London, 1677), the *First and Fourth Institutes* (London, 1628), the *Second and Third Institutes* (6th ed.; London 1680–81), and the twelfth part of the *Reports* (2d ed.; London, 1677).[32] As will be related below, Adams put his knowledge of Coke and Magna Carta to good use in the years leading up to the American Revolution.[33]

The importation of lawbooks into the American colonies was supplemented in time with books turned out from colonial presses. Penn's commentary on Magna Carta, *The Excellent Priviledge of Liberty and Property,* appeared under the imprint of William Bradford in Philadelphia in 1687. Gradually American presses increased in number until in 1755 there were 24 presses in 15 towns (in ten of the colonies) ; as of that year these presses had produced perhaps 1200 titles.[34] Magna Carta became available in a number of books published in the colonies; in addition to Penn's commentary of 1687, Henry Care's *English Liberties,* in which Magna Carta could be found, was reprinted in Boston in 1721. Even almanacs could be consulted to learn of Magna Carta. *Bickerstaff's Boston Almanac* for 1768 contained an account of "remarkable Events since the Deluge," including "an Account of Magna Charta, which is our most antient written law," as well as the "New Magna Charta" (the Bill of Rights of 1689).[35]

Care's *English Liberties* was an especially influential work on both sides of the Atlantic. The Boston printing of 1721 simply duplicated the book as it had already appeared in England. The preface invited the reader to consider the "many Struggles which the People of this Nation have had to rescue their almost oppress'd Liberties" and urged him to impress in his mind the

[32] Boston Public Library, *Catalogue of the John Adams Library* (Boston, 1917), p. 54.
[33] See pp. 156–64, *infra.*
[34] Lawrence C. Wroth, *An American Bookshelf, 1755* (Philadelphia, 1934), pp. 3–4.
[35] Mott, *Due Process of Law,* p. 92 n. 24.

"Laws and Rights that from Age to Age have been deliver'd down to us" and to let those rights "never perish in our hands." Care's book began with the "excellent Law" of Magna Carta, the text of which was set out in full and supplemented with a commentary on most of the chapters.[36]

Among the lawbooks to appear from colonial presses was a subscription reprint of William Blackstone's *Commentaries.* The original volumes had been published individually between 1765 and 1769 in Oxford; only two years later, in 1771–72, the subscription reprint was published in Philadelphia. Heading the list of subscribers was "John Adams, Esq. barrister at law, Boston, Massachusetts Bay." [37]

Study at the Inns of Court

By the middle of the eighteenth century the formal study of law on the English model was producing a prestigious bar throughout the American colonies. As law studies became more rigorous and formalized, they increasingly were based on the traditional English commentators, notably Coke. Some lawyers went to England to study at the Inns of Court; some read law in the colonies. In either case, as Roscoe Pound has observed, colonial lawyers "were brought up on ideas of 'the law of the land,' of the immemorial rights of Englishmen guaranteed by Magna Carta." [38]

No one factor was to have more influence in inculcating in American lawyers a sense of the traditions of Magna Carta than the great numbers of colonials who went to London to read law at the Inns of Court. Before 1700 only seven Americans—four from Massachusetts, three from Virginia—had been admitted to the Inns of Court.[39] By contrast, from 1760 to the Revolution, 115 Americans were admitted to study at the Inns of Court, the representation from the southern colonies being

---

[36] Henry Care, *English Liberties* (Boston, 1721), pp. 1–32.
[37] Roscoe Pound, *The Development of Constitutional Guarantees of Liberty* (New Haven, 1957), p. 61.
[38] *Ibid.*   [39] Chroust, *Legal Profession,* I, 33.

especially great—47 from South Carolina, 21 from Virginia, 16 from Maryland.[40]

Studying at the Inns of Court had its perils. Blackstone, near the beginning of the first volume of his *Commentaries* (1765), paints a vivid picture:

We may appeal to the experience of every sensible lawyer, whether any thing can be more hazardous or discouraging than the usual entrance on the study of the law. A raw and unexperienced youth, in the most dangerous season of life, is transplanted on a sudden into the midst of allurements to pleasure, without any restraint or check but what his own prudence can suggest. . . . In this situation he is expected to sequester himself from the world, and by a tedious lonely process to extract the theory of law from a mass of undigested learning. . . . How little therefore is it to be wondered at, that we hear of so frequent miscarriages; that so many gentlemen of bright imaginations grow weary of so unpromising a search, and addict themselves wholly to amusements, or other less innocent pursuits; and that so many persons of moderate capacity confuse themselves at first setting out, and continue ever dark and puzzled during the remainder of their lives! [41]

Americans studying at the Inns were apt to agree with Blackstone's verdict. Charles Carroll of Carrollton, later to sign the Declaration of Independence for Maryland, heaped scorn on English legal education:

Nothing can be more absurd than the usual manner of young gentlemen's studying the law. They come from the University, take chambers in the Temple, read Coke Little: whom they cannot possibly understand, frequent the courts whose practice they are ignorant of; they are soon disgusted with the difficulties and dryness of the study, the law books are thrown aside, dissipation succeeds to study, immorality to virtue, one night plunges them into ruin, misery, and disease.[42]

The truth is that, despite their reputation as sharing the prestige of Oxford and Cambridge, the Inns of Court in the

[40] Warren, *American Bar*, p. 188. See C. E. A. Bedwell, "American Middle Templars," 25 *Am. Hist. Rev.* 680 (1920). Of the fifty-eight lawyers admitted to practice in South Carolina before the Revolution, at least forty-seven had been educated at the Inns of Court. Chroust, *Legal Profession*, I, 303–4.

[41] *Blackstone's Commentaries*, I, 31.

[42] Kate Mason Rowland, *Life of Charles Carroll of Carrollton, 1737–1832, with His Correspondence and Public Papers* (New York, 1898), I, 53–54.

eighteenth century, like Oxford and Cambridge themselves, were in a state of decadence. Yet the student who did not succumb to the fleshpots and other temptations of London, and who did not yield to the no doubt frequent moods of despair that he would ever master the law, could find his sojourn at one of the Inns a time of great value. Whatever their demerits, the Inns did have matchless law libraries (assuming that the student had the self-discipline to use them; the use of an English college library even in the twentieth century can tax the most patient and resourceful student). Moreover, the student found himself in the company of eminent barristers and legal scholars. And, if nothing else, the student at the Inns could hear important cases argued at the nearby courts of law in London—a considerable advantage in a day when reports of cases were not the commonplace they are today.

The Americans who went to study at the Inns of Court usually sought out these advantages and profited from them. John Dickinson of Pennsylvania spent three years at the Inns of Court (1753–56) and soon after his arrival there caught the spirit of the English law. In a letter to his father, Dickinson described his feelings: "I tread the walks frequented by the antient sages of the law; perhaps I study in the chambers where a Coke or Plowden has meditated." The modern reader, seeing these lines, will probably dismiss them as an eighteenth-century flourish, especially in a letter in which the dutiful son assures his father, who is footing the bill for those years in London, "I fly to books, to retirement, to labour & every moment is an age till I am immersed in study." [43] But Dickinson does seem to have made good use of his time, especially in taking notes in court. In another letter to his father, Dickinson said that, on his return to America, he hoped to present his father with two or three volumes of reports he himself had compiled at the courts of Westminster. The usefulness of these notes, Dickinson felt, was "inconceivable," as he would "be often oblidgd to quote them in court. . . . I have a great many points resolvd which I

[43] H. Trevor Colbourn, "A Pennsylvania Farmer at the Court of King George: John Dickinson's London Letters, 1754–1756," 86 *Pennsylvania Magazine of History and Biography* 241, 257 (1962).

have not met with elsewhere, & a great many I have met with are in these contradicted & denied." [44]

The proof of what Dickinson absorbed at the Inns of Court was to come with his writings on constitutional problems and the rights of Englishmen during the troubled times in the 1760's and 1770's. As author of the notable *Letters from a Pennsylvania Farmer* and as a key figure in the work of the Stamp Act Congress, Dickinson was to earn the name of "Penman of the American Revolution." In this penmanship Dickinson's years at the Inns of Court were a forceful shaping factor.

Another American, John Rutledge of South Carolina, in 1769 wrote his brother Edward, then a student in London, of the benefits which could be his from his law studies there. Rutledge's letter is a compendium of brotherly advice (much of which he had already given Edward orally in Charleston) on learning shorthand (to take down cases in court), on going to church regularly, on hearing oratory in the House of Commons and the House of Lords, on reading the classics and English history, on keeping a book of the "remarkable expressions and sayings of wise and great men . . . not to serve as Joe Miller's jests or a collection of bon-mots, to make one pass for a merry fellow, or rather a maker of fun at table for a pack of fools; but rather to embellish your arguments or writings." In recommending what Edward should read, John is especially anxious that he be immersed in Coke: "Coke's Institutes seem to be almost the foundation of our law. These you must read over and over with the greatest attention, and not quit him till you understand him *thoroughly,* and have made your own every thing in him which is worth taking out." [45]

These Americans who studied at the Inns of Court returned to their homes to become leaders, not only at the bar, but in the public life of their colonies. Later they were to take the lead in the transatlantic debates over the British Constitution and the rights of the colonies, and in the formation of the new Republic. Virginians at the Inns of Court, for example, included Peyton Randolph (Inner Temple), who became Attorney

[44] *Ibid.,* p. 426.
[45] Letter of July 30, 1769, in 14 *American Jurist* 480, 484 (1835).

General of Virginia and later was president of the First Continental Congress in 1774, and John Blair (Middle Temple),
Chief Justice of the Virginia Court of Appeals and afterwards
an Associate Justice of the United States Supreme Court.[46] Both
Daniel Dulanys, father and son of Maryland, read law at the
Inns of Court; the former, as we have noted, wrote *The Right
of the Inhabitants of Maryland to the Benefit of English Laws*
(1728) in the course of the Maryland Assembly's running battle with the proprietor, and the son, Daniel Dulany, Jr., wrote
in 1765, on the occasion of the Stamp Act, *Considerations on
the Propriety of Imposing Taxes on the British Colonies for the
Purpose of Raising a Revenue by Act of Parliament.*[47]

The signatures on the Declaration of Independence and on
the United States Constitution included the names of many
who had studied at the Inns of Court. All four of the South
Carolinians who signed the Declaration of Independence, for
example, had read law at the Middle Temple. And among the
signers of the Federal Constitution were, to name only some
Middle Templars, William Livingston (first Governor of New
Jersey), Jared Ingersoll (twice Attorney General of Pennsylvania), John Blair, John Rutledge (later George Washington's
nominee to be the second Chief Justice of the United States),
Charles Cotesworth Pinckney (later U.S. minister to France),
and Charles Pinckney (later U.S. minister to Spain).[48]

Study at Home

O F COURSE a great many would-be American lawyers were
not in a position to travel to England to study at the Inns of
Court. Many of the greatest lawyers of the time read law in the
colonies, typically under the direction of some established member of the bar. But to study in the colonies rather than in
London did not mean that the student of the law found himself
in a different legal tradition. In the colonies, as at the Inns of

[46] Roscoe Pound, *The Lawyer from Antiquity to Modern Times* (St. Paul,
1953), p. 162–63.
[47] See pp. 147–48, *infra*.   [48] Bedwell, *op. cit. supra* note 40, pp. 681–82.

Court, the cornerstone of a legal education, however acquired, was Sir Edward Coke's works. It is easy for the twentieth-century American to suppose that the backbone of colonial legal studies was Blackstone, as that has been since the early nineteenth century a source to which American lawyers and judges have so often turned for a classic statement of a point of English law. But we should recall that Blackstone's *Commentaries,* an outgrowth of Blackstone's Vinerian lectures at Oxford, did not begin appearing until 1765, were not complete until 1769, and were not published in the colonies until 1771–72. Thus the legal education of the colonial lawyers who stated the Americans' constitutional case against English policy from the Stamp Act to the Revolution had been acquired before Blackstone's *Commentaries* were ever heard of. Where did they turn? To Coke. As Randolph G. Adams has pointed out, in tracing the intellectual roots of the American Revolution, the colonial lawyers "got what they knew from the writings of that celebrated Sir Edward Coke, who did not scruple to inform James, of Divine Right fame, that even the King was under the law, from Coke's Reports, Coke's Institutes, Coke on Littleton." [49]

In fact Thomas Jefferson lamented the seductive effect of Blackstone. There had been a time, he said in a letter to James Madison, when *Coke upon Littleton* "was the universal elementary book of law students, and a sounder whig never wrote, nor of profounder learning in the orthodox doctrines of the British constitution, or in what were called English liberties." But when the "honied Mansfieldism of Blackstone became the student's hornbook, from that moment, that profession (the nursery of our Congress) began to slide into toryism. . . ." [50] But if indeed Jefferson was right in his distrust of Blackstone,

[49] Randolph G. Adams, *Political Ideas of the American Revolution* (3d ed.; New York, 1958), p. 141.

[50] *Writings of Thomas Jefferson,* ed. Paul Leicester Ford (New York, 1892–99), X, 376. (Probably Jefferson had in mind not Coke on Littleton, but Coke on Magna Carta—Coke's *Second Institute.*) Jefferson, in his student days, had not always spoken so kindly of Coke. In a letter to his friend John Page in 1762, Jefferson lamented, "Well, Page, I do wish the Devil had old Cooke, for I am sure I never was so tired of an old dull scoundrel in my life." *Papers of Thomas Jefferson,* ed. Julian P. Boyd (Princeton, 1950———), I, 5.

this is a development which belongs to the history of postrevolutionary America. To the extent that the American case in the 1760's and 1770's was a constitutional one (and, as we shall see below, to an amazing degree it was), that case was erected on the jurisprudence of Coke, above all, of Coke on Magna Carta.

The leading lawyers of eighteenth-century America would, as one Oxford don has said, be "giants in any age." Samuel Tyler, a member of the Maryland bar and the chosen biographer of Chief Justice Roger B. Taney, said of Daniel Dulany the Younger, "The opinions of this great Maryland lawyer had almost as much weight in courts in Maryland, and hardly less with the crown lawyers of England, than the opinions of the great Roman jurists. . . ." [51] (In fact, in the first volume of Harris and McHenry's reports of the provincial cases in Maryland from 1700 to the American Revolution, there is an appendix containing the texts of ten legal opinions of Dulany.) [52]

In short, American lawyers had come a long way since they were thought to be "base and vile." Instead of being outlawed as exploiters of the unwary, the American lawyer by the latter half of the eighteenth century was a figure of prestige and a leader—in colonial assemblies, in court contests, in pamphlets and speeches—in the fight to preserve to Americans the guarantees of Magna Carta and the rights of Englishmen. Along with the rising influence of the lawyer came a higher place for the common law itself. Edmund Burke, in his 1775 speech on *Conciliation with America,* argued that one of the circumstances contributing to the colonists' "untractable spirit" of liberty was the Americans' study of the law:

In no country perhaps in the world is the law so general a study. The profession itself is numerous and powerful; and in most provinces it takes the lead. The greater number of the deputies sent to the Congress were lawyers. But all who read, and most do read, endeavour to obtain some smattering in that science. I have been told by an eminent bookseller, that in no branch of his business, after tracts of popular devotion, were so many books as those on the law exported to the Plantations.

[51] Samuel Tyler, *Memoir of Roger Brooke Taney* (Baltimore, 1872), pp. 132–33.
[52] 1 H. & McH. 551 *et seq.* (Md. 1809).

The colonists have now fallen into the way of printing them for their own use. I hear that they have sold nearly as many of Blackstone's *Commentaries* in America as in England." [53]

Burke's assessment was a fair one. John Adams, in a statement in 1763 which would prove prophetic of the star by which the colonists would steer in framing their arguments against Great Britain from then until the Revolution, eulogized the common law of England as the best statement of Americans' rights. Adams maintained that "the liberty, the unalienable and indefeasible rights of man, the honor and dignity of human nature . . . and the universal happiness of individuals, were never so skillfully and successfully consulted as in that most excellent monument of human art, the Common Law of England." [54]

The colonial lawyer's education in Magna Carta and the rights of Englishmen, his belief in the principles laid down by Coke, his English commitment to English values, were to be tested when, after 1760, the English nation seemed to him to be unfaithful to those values. Like most lawyers, he would tend to use, if he could, in one legal arena the authorities which had served him well in another. It was Coke which the colonial lawyer cited, and which the colonial courts relied on, far more than any other authority.[55] It was natural that the colonial lawyer should put this same tradition to work in defense of his rights in the years before the Revolution. It was because he had learned the lessons of the common law so well that the American was able to use Magna Carta and Coke and the other precedents so effectively in arguing the colonial case against England.

[53] *Burke's Speech, On Conciliation with America,* ed. Charles R. Morris (New York, 1945) , p. 31.
[54] "On Private Revenge," *Boston-Gazette,* Sept. 5, 1763, quoted in Colbourn, *Lamp of Experience,* p. 25.
[55] In 228 colonial cases decided before 1776, the most cited authority was Coke's *Institutes,* including his *Commentaries on Littleton.* These were cited 294 times; the next most common citation, 172 times, was to Bacon's *Abridgement.* Mott, *Due Process of Law,* p. 89 n. 10.

Chapter VII

The Stirrings of Colonial Discontent

IN HIS old age John Adams wrote a letter to William Tudor (a onetime clerk in Adams' law office) in which Adams vividly recreated the scene in the Superior Court in Boston when, in February 1761, he had been present to hear James Otis argue against the issuance of writs of assistance. These writs, hated by the American colonists, were search warrants allowing entry and search of premises for contraband. They required no oath by the person seeking the writ as to what he expected to find; they were not limited to any particular premises or goods but were general in nature. The 1761 argument, which had such a profound influence on Adams, was to take its place alongside Patrick Henry's "Liberty or Death" speech as one of the most memorable moments of the years leading up to the Revolution.[1]

Adams' letters, written nearly sixty years after the event, portrayed a scene characterized by the pageantry of the law and the expectancy of the occasion:

In this chamber, round a great fire, were seated five Judges, with Lieutenant-Governor Hutchinson at their head, as Chief

---

[1] Indeed, Adams insisted in a letter to Henry's biographer, William Wirt, that Otis had electrified the continent "more than Patrick Henry ever did in the whole course of his life." Letter of Jan. 5, 1818, in *Works of John Adams*, ed. Charles Francis Adams (Boston, 1850–56), X, 272 [hereinafter *Works of John Adams*].

Justice, all arrayed in their new, fresh, rich robes of scarlet English broadcloth; in their large cambric bands, and immense judicial wigs. In this chamber were seated at a long table all the barristers at law of Boston, and of the neighbouring county of Middlesex, in gowns, bands, and tie wigs. They were not seated on ivory chairs, but their dress was more solemn and more pompous than that of the Roman Senate, when the Gauls broke in upon them.[2]

Among the assembled barristers sat Adams, whom one should picture, according to his letter to Tudor, as looking like "a short thick archbishop of Canterbury, seated at the table with a pen in his hand, lost in admiration," now and then taking down notes.[3]

The occasion had every reason to excite the attention of the Boston bar, for the controversy over the writs of assistance was a furious one. Not enjoying the rich agricultural abundance of the southern colonies, the New Englanders looked to the sea and to trade for their livelihood. Since the British Navigation Acts by taxing their commerce made it less profitable, the New Englanders were not reluctant in the least to smuggle cargo ashore on some lonely shore, or, which was often less trouble, to line the pockets of a customs official to overlook the importation. So effective were the colonists at evading customs duties that revenues to the Crown, which ought to have been handsome, failed even to equal the cost of collection. To do something about this loss of revenue, the surveyor of rates and duties for Boston, Charles Paxton, in 1755 sought and obtained a writ of assistance from the Superior Court of Massachusetts.

In England, where the writ had been used since 1662 to enforce the Crown's customs laws, its issuance was supervised by the Exchequer.[4] In Massachusetts the power to issue the writ was vested in the Superior Court, which granted the writ to Paxton in 1755. The use of the writ was received with particular bad grace by the New Englanders because of their fondness for smuggling, and in 1760 they had a chance to say something about the detested writ. That year, the death of King George II required the issuance of new writs, the old writs surviving the

---

[2] Letter of March 29, 1817, in *ibid.*, X, 245.   [3] *Ibid.*, X, 245–46.
[4] 13 & 14 Car. 2, c. 11 (1662).

sovereign's death by only six months. Officers of the Crown therefore petitioned the Superior Court for issuance of the writ, and the result was the argument which Adams recorded in February 1761.

Jeremiah Gridley spoke for the Crown; Oxenbridge Thatcher and James Otis, representing the merchants of Boston, opposed issuance of the writs. Gridley and Thatcher seem to have addressed themselves to fairly specific questions, Gridley maintaining that there was ample statutory authority for the writs to issue, Thatcher arguing that the powers of the Superior Court were narrower than those of the English Court of Exchequer. It was James Otis who raised broader questions and who so excited Adams.

Otis was an unusual figure. Adams had described Otis in his diary as "fiery and fev'rous. His Imagination flames, his Passions blaze. He is liable to great Inequalities of Temper—sometimes in Despondency, sometimes in a Rage." [5] Otis, a graduate of Harvard, studied law with the same Jeremiah Gridley against whom he argued in the writs of assistance case. As a lawyer, Otis read deeply, especially in Coke, pursuing the avid reading habits which he had developed young. He owned a copy of the sixth edition of Coke on Magna Carta, in which the mark ☞ is frequently found written in the margin of chapter 29 ("law of the land") and Coke's commentary thereon. [6]

Adams gave this picture of Otis during the argument in Superior Court: "Otis was a flame of fire!—with a promptitude of classical allusions, a depth of research, a rapid summary of historical events and dates, a profusion of legal authorities, a prophetic glance of his eye into futurity, and a torrent of impetuous eloquence, he hurried away every thing before him." [7] Otis noted as he opened his remarks that he had been asked to argue the case for the Crown, but he took a greater pleasure in arguing the side of "British liberty." He conceded that some kinds of writs were legal, namely, special writs, di-

[5] *Diary and Autobiography of John Adams,* ed. L. H. Butterfield (Cambridge, Mass., 1961), I, 271 [hereinafter *Adams Diary and Autobiography*].
[6] Quincy (Mass.) Reports, 484–85.   [7] *Works of John Adams,* X, 247.

rected to specific officers, giving leave to search certain named houses, issued upon oath that the person seeking the writ had reason to believe certain goods were in the house. But general warrants were another case: these placed "the liberty of every man in the hands of every petty officer." Otis objected to general warrants on the grounds that, because of their sweep, they would annihilate "one of the most essential branches of English liberty," the principle that "a man's house is his castle." [8]

Otis disputed the authorities which Gridley had cited but went further. Even if there was precedent—and Otis could find only one, at the time of Star Chamber—the courts did not have to follow a precedent which was against "reason and the constitution." Citing the decision of Coke in *Dr. Bonham's Case,* Otis put the argument on the level of fundamental law: "An Act against the Constitution is void: an Act against natural Equity is void: and if an Act of Parliament should be made, in the very Words of this Petition, it would be void. The executive Courts must pass such Acts into disuse." [9]

The argument concluded, the court seemed to have some doubt about the extent of the Exchequer practice in England. Judge Hutchinson inquired into that practice, the Superior Court heard reargument of the case in November 1761, and the final decision was a unanimous one in favor of the writs. Otis had lost his case. But he had sounded a constitutional note which was to make its influence felt in the years that followed.

Of Otis' argument, John Adams later said, "Then and there the child Independence was born." [10] If this seems too bold a judgment, certainly it is not easy to dismiss the later influence of the ideas Otis had expounded. A summary of his arguments appeared in the *Boston-Gazette* for January 4, 1762,[11] and the colonies continued to resist the use of general search warrants. Otis went into politics and at the next general election was overwhelmingly elected to the Massachusetts Assembly, where in 1762 he promoted a bill to restrain the Superior Court from

[8] *The Legal Papers of John Adams,* ed. L. Kinvin Wroth and Hiller B. Zobel (Cambridge, Mass., 1965) , II, 140–42 [hereinafter *Adams Legal Papers*].
[9] *Ibid.,* II, 127–28.   [10] *Works of John Adams,* X, 248.
[11] Reprinted in Quincy (Mass.) Reports, 488–94.

issuing any but special search warrants, a measure vetoed by Governor Sir Francis Bernard. His true victory was to come after Independence, when Massachusetts in 1780 wrote into its constitution the guarantee that "every subject has a right to be secure from all unreasonable searches, and seizures, of his person, his houses, his papers, and all his possessions" and the requirement that all warrants must be supported by oath or affirmation and describe with particularity the place to be searched, the person to be arrested, or the property to be seized.[12] In 1789 the protection against unreasonable searches and seizures and the requirement that warrants issue only upon probable cause, supported by oath or affirmation and particularly describing the objects of search or seizure, was submitted to the States for ratification as the Fourth Amendment to the Federal Constitution.

Otis' 1761 argument spurred another trend in American constitutional thinking: the doctrine that legislatures should be bound by the fundamental law. Coke in *Dr. Bonham's Case* had said that when an Act of Parliament "is against Common Right and Reason . . . the Common Law will controll it, and adjudge such Act to be Void." It was this proposition that Otis cited against the writs of assistance. Whatever the merits of the scholarly debate over whether Coke's proposition, in its context, was in fact a constitutional theory or simply a common law canon of construction,[13] there is no doubt that Otis meant the argument as a constitutional one, a statement of constitutional limits on the power of Parliament and the right or duty of courts to police those limits.

Otis was no more able to persuade the court to accept this constitutional theory than he was to convince them that general search warrants could not issue. If the issue of fundamental law versus the supremacy of Parliament was an open question in the day of Coke, by the time the Massachusetts court heard argument on the writs of assistance the question had been resolved in favor of parliamentary supremacy. As Blackstone said four years later in the first volume of his *Commentaries,* if

[12] Thorpe, III, 1891. [13] See p. 121 n. 26, *supra.*

Parliament "will positively enact a thing to be done which is unreasonable, I know of no power that can control it." [14]

Although Otis failed to win the court on this point, he had had a significant opportunity to research the problem of limits to legislative authority and to articulate his conclusions in a court of law. Three years later, in an appendix to his pamphlet *The Rights of the British Colonies Asserted and Proved,* Otis once again drew on Coke and *Dr. Bonham's Case* for the argument that the powers of Parliament were limited by natural equity and the British Constitution:

'Tis hoped it will not be considered as a new doctrine that even the authority of the Parliament of *Great Britain* is circumscribed by certain bounds which if exceeded their acts become those of mere *power* without *right,* and consequently void. The judges of England have declared in favor of these sentiments when they expressly declare that *acts of Parliament against natural equity are void.* That *acts against the fundamental principles of the British constitution are void.* This doctrine is agreeable to the law of nature and nations, and to the divine dictates of natural and revealed religion.[15]

Apparently, as his pamphlet of the following year, *A Vindication of the British Colonies,* suggests, Otis would concede the supremacy of Parliament in the sense that, if a court ruled against a statute, Parliament was not bound to yield to that ruling, even though in natural justice it ought to.

Whatever limits Otis might draw on his argument for Parliament's being bound by the fundamental law, there is no question that he pointed the way in 1761 for later statements of the colonial position against British acts in the 1760's and 1770's. Nor is there any question that by his arguments against the writs of assistance and his development of his thesis in his later pamphlets, Otis gave momentum to the habits of thinking which evolved, after independence, into the American constitutional doctrine of judicial review of legislation to the end that it may be measured against the limits of the Constitution.

---

[14] *Blackstone's Commentaries* (Oxford, 1765), I, 91.
[15] Bernard Bailyn, ed., *Pamphlets of the American Revolution, 1750–1776* (Cambridge, Mass., 1965——), I, 476–77 [hereinafter cited as Bailyn, *Pamphlets*].

The Stamp Act

THE Seven Years' War (1756–63) is notable in the history of Europe for the manner in which Prussia, under the leadership of Frederick the Great, stood almost single-handed against a coalition of European powers—Austria, France, Russia, Saxony, and Sweden. Its great battles—Rossbach, Zorndorf, and others—have a significant place in military history. The Seven Years' War is important, too, for the momentous effects it had on France's colonial empire. England had taken Prussia's side, adding to the war a maritime and colonial struggle between England and France around the globe. By the time of the signing of the Treaty of Paris, such French defeats as those she suffered at the hands of Wolfe at Quebec and Clive at Plassey had deprived her of her dominions in America and her influence in India.

But England paid a price for her victories. And that price she sought to share with her American colonies. At the close of the Seven Years' War, England's national debt had nearly doubled. An English army of 10,000 men was stationed in America to secure the territory wrested from France. Not unnaturally, England looked to the colonies to pay part of the bill. The first step was the enactment of the Revenue Act of 1764, the avowed purpose of which was to raise revenue in the American colonies "for defraying the Expences of defending, protecting and securing the same." [16] The act levied customs duties on sugar and other commodities. Perhaps the unkindest cut of all to many colonists was the provision withdrawing the existing exemption allowing free importation of Madeira wine, a favorite among well-to-do Americans.

The colonies were quick to protest. A movement to boycott commodities taxed by the Revenue Act was spear-headed by the "young Gentlemen of Yale College," who unanimously agreed to spurn "foreign spirituous Liquors." A New York newspaper commended the students, not only for "setting so laudable an

[16] 4 Geo. III, c. 15, *Statutes at Large,* IX (London, 1765), 152.

Example" to others in the colonies, but also for taking a step which presumably would be "very favourable to the Health and Improvement of the Students." [17]

Formal petitions of protest were passed by colonial assemblies in Massachusetts, Rhode Island, Connecticut, New York, Pennsylvania, Virginia, North Carolina, and South Carolina. The colonial case was a constitutional one: no taxation without consent. Virginia's petition to the King, passed in December 1764, asked the monarch "to protect your People of this Colony in the Enjoyment of their ancient and inestimable Right of being governed by such Laws respecting their internal Polity and Taxation as are derived from their own Consent . . . A Right which as Men, and as Descendents of *Britons,* they have ever quietly possessed since first by Royal Permission and Encouragement they left the Mother Kingdom to extend its Commerce and Dominion." [18] Virginia, in a companion memorial addressed to the House of Lords, explicitly rested her claim on the grant in the colonial charters of the "rights of Englishmen": "As our Ancestors brought with them every Right and Privilege they could with Justice claim in their Mother Kingdom, their Descendents may conclude they cannot be deprived of those Rights without Injustice." [19] The same argument was put in a third petition, a remonstrance addressed to the House of Commons and passed the same day as the petition to the Crown and the memorial to the Lords.[20]

A more severe test of the British Constitution was in the making. George Grenville had proposed in Parliament a stamp tax, which, if laid, would do what even the Revenue Act had not done. Hitherto, British revenue measures in the colonies, such as the Sugar Act of 1733 and the Revenue Act of 1764, had been external taxes, such as customs duties. The stamp tax would be the first direct, internal tax ever laid by Parliament in the American colonies. On March 22, 1765, the

[17] Samuel Eliot Morison, *Oxford History of the American People* (New York, 1965) , p. 185.
[18] *Journals of the House of Burgesses of Virginia, 1761–1765,* ed. John Pendleton Kennedy (Richmond, 1907) , p. 302 [hereafter cited as *Journals of the Burgesses*].
[19] *Ibid.*   [20] *Ibid.,* pp. 303–4.

Stamp Act became law.[21] It was a heavy tax, bearing in some way on virtually every sort and condition of American. Legal pleadings, college diplomas, liquor licenses, licenses to practice law, deeds to land, almanacs, playing cards—these and many other items were to bear taxes ranging from 4*d.* to £10, the tax to be paid in sterling, not in colonial currencies. Each separate copy (not merely each issue) of a newspaper was to be taxed at one shilling a sheet. Offenses against the act were to be tried in admiralty courts, where a defendant had no right to trial by jury.

The Colonists React

COLONIAL reaction to the Stamp Act was often ugly. "Sons of Liberty" sprang up in seaports up and down the Atlantic coast. A New York mob forced the Lieutenant Governor to flee to a British warship for his own safety. In Boston a riotous assembly sacked the private homes of customs collectors and of provincial officials, including those of the Governor, the Lieutenant Governor, and the Chief Justice. Everywhere stamped paper was burned, effigies of customs officers were hanged, and unpopular officials were threatened.

The colonial leaders were quick to state their legal and constitutional case. Virginia set the pattern. In fact, Virginia had already had a kind of dress rehearsal of the question of colonial legislative independence. In 1758 the Virginia General Assembly had passed the Two-Penny Act, allowing rents, salaries, and other sums usually payable in tobacco to be paid at the rate of 2*d.* a pound (since tobacco had risen to a price of 6*d.* a pound). For the clergy, whose salaries had been payable in tobacco, this had meant a two-thirds cut in salary, and they had been successful in obtaining Privy Council disallowance of the Two-Penny Act. In response to this disallowance, Richard

---

[21] 5 Geo. III, c. 12, in *Statutes at Large,* X (London, 1771), 18. The Stamp Act may also be found in Edmund S. Morgan, *Prologue to Revolution: Sources and Documents on the Stamp Act Crisis, 1764–1766* (Chapel Hill, N.C., 1959), pp. 35–43 [hereafter cited as Morgan, *Prologue to Revolution*].

Bland had published *The Colonel Dismounted* (1764), a statement of the right of the Virginia legislature to enact any law
they pleased for their internal government.[22]

In 1765, with the passage of the Stamp Act, Virginians took a
like stand for self-government as to internal matters. In the
Virginia Assembly, in May, after older members of the House
had been inclined to temporize, Patrick Henry, then twenty-
nine, electrified the body with his famous words, "Tarquin and
Caesar each had his Brutus, Charles the First his Cromwell and
George the Third"—at which there were cries of "Treason"
from the Speaker and others—"may profit by their example. If
this be treason, make the most of it."[23]

The House adopted four resolutions. The first declared that
the original settlers of Virginia brought with them and transmitted to their posterity the right to all the "Liberties, Privileges, Franchises, and Immunities" enjoyed by the people of
Great Britain. The second recalled that James I, by royal charter, had formally declared this right. The third resolution
called the right not to be taxed without consent "the distinguishing Characteristick of *British* Freedom, without which the
ancient Constitution cannot exist." The final resolution urged
that this right of internal self-government and self-taxation had
been regularly recognized in Great Britain.[24]

The first reaction to the Henry resolutions was one of astonishment; some thought them treasonable. But astonishment
soon gave way to approbation. Newspapers in other colonies
applauded Virginia's example and urged its imitation. Hutchinson, who suffered so at the hands of the Boston mob, credited
the reports of the Virginia resolutions as having had a "tendency to bring on those acts of violence which soon after were
committed in Boston."[25] Whether or not the Virginia declarations stirred the mob, they certainly brought widespread imita-

[22] For the text of *The Colonel Dismounted*, see Bailyn, *Pamphlets*, I, 292. The
controversy over the Two-Penny Act also occasioned the famous "Parsons' Cause,"
a suit by the clergy to recover unpaid salaries. In that case, Patrick Henry argued
against the clergy, and the jury awarded damages of one penny.

[23] William Wirt Henry, *Patrick Henry* (New York, 1891), I, 86.

[24] *Journals of the Burgesses*, p. 360. The full text of the Virginia resolutions is
set out in Appendix F, *infra*.

[25] Hutchinson, *History of Massachusetts-Bay*, III, 119.

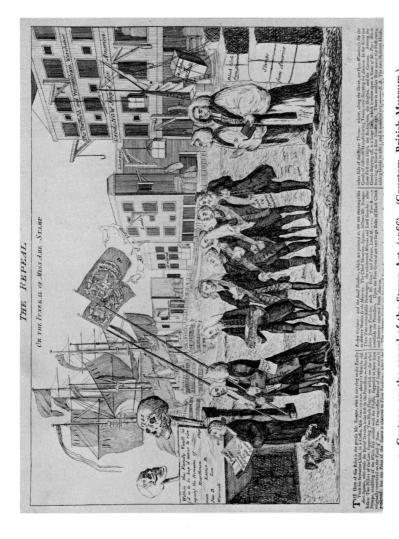

9. Cartoon on the repeal of the Stamp Act (1766). (Courtesy, British Museum.)

10. Frontispiece, third edition, John Dickinson's *Letters from a Farmer in Pennsylvania* (1768). Magna Carta appears under the right elbow, and *Coke upon Littleton* on the shelf. (Courtesy, John Carter Brown Library, Brown University.)

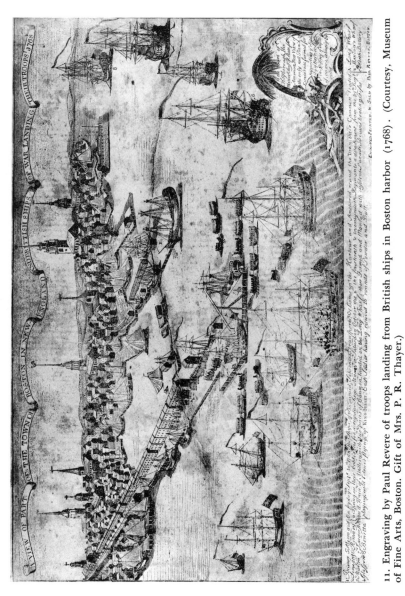

11. Engraving by Paul Revere of troops landing from British ships in Boston harbor (1768). (Courtesy, Museum of Fine Arts, Boston. Gift of Mrs. P. R. Thayer.)

JOURNAL

OF THE

PROCEEDINGS

OF THE

CONGRESS,

Held at PHILADELPHIA,

September 5, 1774.

PHILADELPHIA:

Printed by WILLIAM and THOMAS BRADFORD,
at the *London Coffee House.*

M,DC C,LXXI V.

12. Title page, *Journal of the Continental Congress* (1774). Colophon is supported by Magna Carta. (Courtesy, Library of Congress.)

tion in other colonial assemblies. The Virginia resolutions had been passed only two months after the enactment of the Stamp Act; the resolutions of the other colonies were adopted mainly between September and December of 1765. More time having been available for their drafting, these later resolutions spelled out in greater detail the colonists' legal arguments against the Stamp Act.

The resolutions placed a notable reliance on Magna Carta. The assemblies had two chief complaints against the Stamp Act; first, that it imposed taxes without the consent of those taxed; second, that it impaired the right to trial by jury. Both steps, thought the American assemblymen, contravened Magna Carta. The Maryland Assembly, for example, unanimously resolved in September "that it was Granted by Magna Charta and other the Good Laws and Statutes of England and Confirmed by the Petition and Bill of Rights that the Subject should not be Compelled to Contribute to any Tax Tallage Aid or other like Charge not set by common Consent of Parliament." [26] Similarly, Massachusetts in October resolved that "no Man can justly take the Property of another without his Consent" and that "this *inherent* Right, together with all other, essential Rights, Liberties, Privileges and Immunities of the People of *Great Britain,* have been fully confirmed to them by *Magna Charta. . . .*" [27]

Trial by jury was likewise guaranteed by Magna Carta. Pennsylvania in September resolved, no member dissenting, that the vesting of jurisdiction in the courts of admiralty to hear cases arising under the Stamp Act "is highly dangerous to the Liberties of his Majesty's *American* Subjects, contrary to *Magna Charta,* the great Charter and Fountain of *English* Liberty, and destructive of one of their most darling and acknowledged Rights, that of Trials by Juries." [28] In almost identical language, Connecticut, the next month, attacked the vesting of jurisdiction in the admiralty courts as "contrary to the great Charter of English Liberty, and destructive of one of their most darling Rights, that of Tryal by Juries. . . ." [29]

[26] Morgan, *Prologue to Revolution,* p. 52.   [27] *Ibid.,* p. 56.
[28] *Ibid.,* p. 52.   [29] *Ibid.,* p. 55.

The Stamp Act Congress

Thus had Virginia rung an "alarum bell to the disaffected." Not only did the individual colonies pass resolutions, they responded to a call from Massachusetts to send delegates to a congress in New York. This was a momentous move, for it was the first spontaneous colonial effort at united action, and it foreshadowed the Continental Congresses which were to meet in the years just before the Revolution. The Stamp Act Congress was a distinguished gathering. It brought together some of the leading thinkers of the colonies—among them, James Otis of Massachusetts, John Dickinson of Pennsylvania, Daniel Dulany the Younger of Maryland, and Christopher Gadsden of South Carolina.

The Congress resolved itself into a committee of the whole to prepare a declaration of the colonies' rights and privileges. John Dickinson played a leading role. He had spent three years at the Inns of Court, where he drank deep of the lore of Coke, took notes in the courts of Westminster, and wrote home of the value of his time there.[30] After his return to Pennsylvania, he enjoyed a successful and profitable practice. In 1774 Dickinson was to write that things had become so bad in England that only Englishmen in America were likely to preserve the ancient rights secured from King John in the thirteenth century and from the Stuarts in the seventeenth, saying *"England* must be saved in *America.* Hereafter, she will *rejoice* that we have *resisted*—and *thank* us for having *offended* her." [31] Now, in 1765, at the Stamp Act Congress, he was to have the opportunity to resolve, in written form, his high regard for the British Constitution as an ideal with the distaste for the system as he had seen it operating while he was in London.

Dickinson made three drafts of a list of resolves, the language of which tends to support his later claim to having been the

[30] See pp. 127–28, *supra.*
[31] *An Essay on the Constitutional Power of Great Britain over the Colonies in America* (Philadelphia, 1774) , p. 62.

principal author of the resolves of the Congress.[32] The care which the delegates took in framing their final resolutions is suggested by a letter written in October by Caesar Rodney, a delegate from Delaware, to his brother Thomas:

You, and many others, perhaps are Surprised to think We Should Set So long When the business of our Meeting Seemed only to be the Petitioning the King, and Remonstrating to both houses of Parliament—But When you Consider That We are Petitioning & addressing That august Body the great Legislative of the Empire for Redress of Grievances; That in order to point out Those Grievances it Was likewise Necessary to Set forth the Liberty We have, and ought to Enjoy, (as freeborn Englishmen) according to the British Constitution. This We Set about To Do by way of Declaration, in the Nature of Resolves, as a foundation to the Petition, and Addresses; and was one of the most Difficult Tasks I have ever yet seen Undertaken, as We had Carefully to avoid any Infringement of the prerogative of the Crown, and the Power of Parliament, and Yet in Duty bound fully to Assert the Rights & Privileges of the Colonies.[33]

The declarations of the Stamp Act Congress were similar in content to those of the individual colonial assemblies. The Congress held that his Majesty's subjects in the colonies were entitled to "all the inherent Right and Liberties" enjoyed by his subjects in Great Britain, specifically, the right not to be taxed without their consent and the right to trial by jury. In their petition to the King, the Congress rested both of these rights on Magna Carta: "The invaluable Rights of Taxing ourselves, and Trial by our Peers, of which we implore your Majesty's Protection, are not, we most humbly conceive Unconstitutional; but confirmed by the Great CHARTER of *English* Liberty." [34]

Opposition to the Stamp Act took yet other forms. In October 1765 the justices of Stafford County, Virginia, resigned in a body rather than enforce the act. They sent an address to

---

[32] See David L. Jacobson, *John Dickinson and the Revolution in Pennsylvania, 1764–1776* (Berkeley, Calif., 1965), p. 32.

[33] *Letters to and from Caesar Rodney, 1756–1784,* ed. George Herbert Ryden (Philadelphia, 1933), pp. 25–26.

[34] Morgan, *Prologue to Revolution,* pp. 62–65.

Governor Fauquier, written by John Mercer of Marlborough. In the address the justices quoted the motto of the county seal, taken from Magna Carta—"We will deny or delay no man justice"; this, they said, "we are firmly persuaded is inconsistent with the Stamp Act." [35] The county court of Northampton County, Virginia, showed their disagreement with the act in another way; they "unanimously declared it to be their opinion that the said act did not bind, affect, or concern the inhabitants of this colony, in as much as they conceive the same to be unconstitutional . . . ." [36] An echo of Coke's opinion in *Dr. Bonham's Case* and a prophecy of judicial review as it later was enunciated by Chief Justice Marshall in *Marbury v. Madison,* this decision of the Northampton County court was probably the first in America to declare a legislative act void because of unconstitutionality.

Pamphlets and Tracts

THE constitutional crisis of 1764–65 brought forth a number of individual pamphlets by some of the brightest legal lights of the colonies—among them, James Otis, Daniel Dulany, and John Adams—delving into the constitutional basis for the colonists' resistance to Parliament's legislation. Otis in 1764 produced *The Rights of The British Colonies Asserted and Proved.* This was a pamphlet squarely in the Whig tradition of historiography, for Otis maintained that it was not the colonial charters or even Magna Carta which was the proper starting point for tracing the colonists' rights, it was the golden age of Anglo-Saxon England. For "liberty was better understood and more fully enjoyed by our ancestors before the coming in of the first Norman tyrants than ever after, till it was found necessary for the salvation of the kingdom to combat the arbitrary and wicked proceedings of the Stuarts." [37]

[35] Kate Mason Rowland, *Life of George Mason, 1725–1792* (New York, 1892) , I, 124–25.
[36] *Virginia Gazette,* March 21, 1766. The text of the court's order is reprinted in Henry Steele Commager, *Documents of American History* (3d ed.; New York, 1943) , p. 59.
[37] Bailyn, *Pamphlets,* I, 441.

Otis then interwove natural law, the common law, and acts of Parliament as the basis for the colonial claim to the rights of Englishmen, even without reliance on the colonial charters. Among these "natural, essential, inherent and inseparable rights" Otis listed no arbitrary legislation, no taxation without consent, no delegation of legislative power, and justice according to known settled rules by independent judges (this last claim in effect combining several principles from Magna Carta —chapter 39's guarantee of proceedings according to the "law of the land"; chapter 40's promise not to sell, deny, or delay justice; and the promise of chapter 45 to appoint as judges "only such men as know the law of the land and will keep it well").[38]

The right not to be taxed without consent, the nub of the controversy, Otis traced to Magna Carta. This right Otis proclaimed to be "part of the common law, part of a British subject's birthright"; the American colonists "are, by Magna Carta, as well entitled to have a voice in their taxes as the subjects within the realm." [39]

In the following year, 1765, there flowed from Otis' pen *A Vindication of the British Colonies*. A pro-British writer, Martin Howard, Jr., had written a pamphlet called the *Halifax Letter*, in which Howard had submitted that the colonists could have no rights independent of their charters. Otis disagreed, saying that the relation between England and the colonies was rooted in nature and natural law as well as in the particulars of charters and statute law. If, as Otis conceded, Parliament had supreme power over the colonies, it did not follow that Parliament could do what it pleased. "Now Magna Carta is but a law of their [Parliament's] making, and they may alter it at pleasure; but does it thence follow that it would be expedient to repeal every statute from William the Conqueror to this time?" In particular, Otis urged that while Parliament might have the power to tax the colonies it would be a matter of "wonder and astonishment" if it in fact did so when the colonies were not actually represented.[40]

Daniel Dulany the Younger, probably the most eminent lawyer at the Maryland bar, contributed his thoughts to the Stamp

[38] *Ibid.*, I, 444–46.   [39] *Ibid.*, I, 466.   [40] *Ibid.*, I, 547, 560.

Act dispute in *Considerations on the Propriety of Imposing Taxes on the British Colonies,* published at Annapolis in 1765. Writing in rebuttal to pamphlets which had appeared in England defending the Stamp Act, Dulany undertook to refute the English theorists' claim that parliamentary taxation of the colonies was justified by the colonies' "virtual" representation in the House of Commons. Dulany's argument brought into play the guarantees of two orders of charters: the colonial charters and Magna Carta, the first ensuring the colonists the rights protected by the other. Combining constitutional law with a kind of Lockean compact theory, Dulany said that, following the spirit of the English Constitution, the original settlers "entered into a compact with the Crown." By these compacts, that is, by the colonial charters, the colonists claim the rights of Englishmen, including the exemption from taxes not imposed with their consent.[41]

Central to Dulany's argument was Magna Carta. One of the English apologists, William Knox, in *The Claim of the Colonies to an Exemption from Internal Taxes . . . Examined* (1765), had submitted that the "common law, the Great Charter, the Bill of Rights" declared "with one voice" that the inhabitants of the colonies should be taxed by no other authority than that of the British Parliament. Not so, said Dulany. He stated the principle of the common law to be that no property might be taken from a British subject without his consent as given by his representatives, a principle "enforced by the declaration of the GREAT CHARTER and *the Bill of Rights,* neither the one nor the other introducing any *new* privilege." [42]

The year of the Stamp Act saw the emergence of John Adams into the arena of public controversy.[43] In February of that year, Adams, then a member of an informed circle of Boston lawyers, wrote a rather scholarly and thoughtful essay, *Dissertation on the Canon and Feudal Law.* His thesis might well be called the "conspiratorial" theory of British policy, for Adams seemed to see something like the Norman submersion of Saxon liberties, or like the Stuart encroachments on English freedoms, repeating

[41] *Ibid.,* I, 604, 633–34.   [42] *Ibid.,* I, 635.   [43] See pp. 156–64, *infra.*

itself in the 1760's. In Adams' words, "There seems to be a direct and formal design on foot to enslave all America. . . . The first step that is intended seems to be an entire subversion of the whole system of our fathers, by the introduction of the canon and feudal law into America." Adams attacked in particular the Stamp Act as contrary to Magna Carta and averred that the supporters of Crown policy were in effect "representing every member of parliament as renouncing the transactions at Runing Mede (the meadow, near Windsor, where Magna Charta was signed) . . . ." [44]

In Virginia, the most important publication to come out of the Stamp Act crisis was Richard Bland's *Inquiry into the Rights of the British Colonies*. Bland was an adherent of the Whig view of history, admiring the Saxon Constitution as having been "founded upon Principles of the most perfect Liberty." Bland urged the right of the colonists to the same privileges and liberties they would enjoy in England, including the right to be subject only to such laws as were made with their consent. His argument was an eclectic one; in arguing that Virginians had the exclusive right to enact their own internal laws, Bland looked to the colonial charters, to the British Constitution, and to natural rights.[45]

Similar calls were heard from the pulpit. One call came from Jonathan Mayhew, of Boston's West Church, a notable figure among the politically minded clerics of his time. Mayhew was well read in the legal rights of Englishmen and carried on a considerable correspondence with Thomas Hollis of Lincoln's Inn, who sent many books to Mayhew. In 1766 Mayhew preached a sermon, *The Snare Broken,* in which he told his listeners that the colonists were Englishmen and, as such, were entitled to fundamental constitutional privileges given them by Magna Carta and confirmed to them by the colonial charters. The Stamp Act, he asserted, violated their rights and offended Magna Carta, the British Constitution, and the charters of the colonies.[46]

---

[44] *The Selected Writings of John and John Quincy Adams,* ed. Adrienne Koch and William Peden (New York, 1946), 23, 20.
[45] Colbourn, *Lamp of Experience,* pp. 145–47.   [46] *Ibid.,* pp. 64–65.

Essays like those of Adams, Otis, and Dulany, like most of the formal resolutions of the various colonial assemblies and those of the Stamp Act Congress, were conceived by their drafters to be nonrevolutionary, in that they were meant to be restatements of a constitutional position. Other public statements were not so restrained. The Sons of Liberty, representing a more unruly element, were passing resolutions with a rather more revolutionary note. The Sons of Liberty in Wallingford, Connecticut, for example, vowed in January 1766 to oppose the Stamp Act "to the last extremity, even to take the field." And the Sons of Liberty of New London, Connecticut, sounded more of Locke and natural rights than of Magna Carta and constitutional rights when they invoked the right of a people, when government exceeded its lawful authority, "to reassume the exercise of that Authority which by Nature they had, before they delegated it to Individuals." [47]

The English defense of the Stamp Act was hardly comforting to Americans already fearful for their rights. An Englishman writing under the nom de plume of "William Pym" in the *London General Evening Post,* lectured the colonists: "[L]et me inform my fellow subjects of America, that a resolution of the British parliament can at any time set aside all the charters that have been granted by our monarchs; and that consequently nothing can be more idle than this pompous exclamation about their charter exemptions. . . ." [48] Pym was talking about colonial charters, but the logic applied to Magna Carta and other royal charters as well. But, even confined to colonial charters, this choice sentiment must have sent chills up the spines (or more likely, made the adrenalin flow in the breasts) of the Americans who read it reprinted in such colonial papers as the *Boston Evening Post* and the *Newport Mercury.*

In August 1765 the Grenville ministry had fallen, and finally in 1766 the Stamp Act was repealed, effective May 1, 1766. The preamble to the repealing statute noted, in what must be one of history's greatest understatements, that repeal was predicated on the finding that the continuance of the Stamp Act "would be attended with many inconveniences." [49]

[47] Morgan, *Prologue to Revolution,* p. 114.　　[48] *Ibid.,* pp. 97–98.
[49] 6 Geo. III, c. 11, *Statutes at Large,* X (London, 1771), 152.

Chapter VIII

Revolutionary Leadership:

Two Adamses

*The "Reluctant Revolution" and
the Role of Leadership*

T HE American Revolution could well be called a "reluctant revolution." In a letter written in 1770, George Mason expressed a widely-held view:

The Americans have the warmest affection for the present royal family, the strongest attachment to the British government and constitution; they have experienced its blessings and prefer it to any that does or ever did exist; while they are protected in the enjoyment of its advantages they can never wish to change. . . . So long as Great Britain can preserve the vigor and spirit of her own free and happy constitution, so long may she, by a mild and equal government, preserve her sovereignty over these colonies.[1]

There were solid reasons for an amiable, even cordial, attitude toward Great Britain. The Americans, after all, were of English descent; their language, laws, and customs bore the stamp of England. Moreover, no colonial people in the world enjoyed greater freedom than did the American colonists. They held land free of feudal tenures. Their charters guaranteed them all the rights they would have enjoyed in England—a parity with the homeland peculiar to the English colonies. They even en-

---

[1] Kate Mason Rowland, *Life of George Mason, 1725–1792* (New York, 1892), I, 150.

joyed, often by virtue of their charters, many rights not yet established in England. And, until the end of the Seven Years' War, they enjoyed a surprising freedom from interference in their government and local affairs.

Great Britain, then, had built up a reservoir of good will which was slow to dissipate. Any sign of British appreciation of colonial grievances typically was met with enthusiasm; many were the toasts drunk to George III on the repeal of the Stamp Act. Hence, for there to be a military revolution there had to be, in the words of John Adams, a revolution in the "minds and hearts of the people." The people had to shake off their accustomed admiration for England as their mother country; it took years of witless and impolitic acts on the part of the British Government before the colonists would see England, not as a "kind and tender parent," but as a "cruel beldam, willing like Lady Macbeth, to 'dash their brains out'. . . ." [2]

The catalyst in what Adams called "the real Revolution"—the changes in the people's attitudes—was the intellectual leadership of the colonies. It may have been a talented Frenchman, the Marquis de Chastellux, who first pointed this out. The Marquis was a man of many parts. At the age of twenty-one he was the first Frenchman to volunteer to submit to inoculation, an act recorded in Diderot's *Encyclopédie*. A welcome guest in Paris *salon* society, he published a two-volume work in philosophy praised fulsomely by Voltaire. In 1780, having served in the Seven Years' War, he was promoted to the rank of *maréchal de camp* and designated as one of the major generals to serve in America under General Rochambeau; in that role he took an active part in the Allied campaign that culminated victoriously at Yorktown.

During his years in America (1780–82), the Marquis de Chastellux kept a journal of his travels, in which he remarked on the task which the leadership, at least in Virginia, had:

It was doubtless no easy matter to persuade this people [Virginians] to take up arms, simply because the town of Boston, three hundred leagues away, did not choose to pay a duty

[2] Letter from John Adams to Hezekiah Niles (Feb. 13, 1818), in *Works of John Adams*, X, 282–83.

upon tea, and was in open rupture with England. . . . People had to be awakened to that idea, which makes every man educated in the principles of the English constitution shudder—the idea of submitting to a tax to which he has not consented. Matters had not reached this stage and only the best informed foresaw that a resort to arms was the aim and the inevitable consequence of the first measures. But how were the people to be convinced of this? By what other motive could they be brought to a decision, if not by the confidence they placed in their leaders? [3]

The Marquis found evidence of this confidence. In his journal, he related a conversation he had with Governor Benjamin Harrison (the father of the future President, William Henry Harrison) in 1782 in Richmond. Harrison recalled that, when he, Thomas Jefferson, and Richard Henry Lee were setting off to attend the First Continental Congress at Philadelphia,

a number of respectable but uninformed inhabitants waited upon them and said: "You assert that there is a fixed intention to invade our rights and privileges; we own that we do not see this clearly, but since you assure us that it is so, we believe it. We are about to take a very dangerous step, but we have confidence in you and will do anything you think proper." [4]

David Ramsay, a historian of the American Revolution, concurred in the judgment that it was the intellectual leadership of the colonies that made the difference. Ramsay noted that before the time of the Stamp Act few native Americans had distinguished themselves as speakers or writers; opposition to British policies soon gave them the practice they needed. Such writings, especially John Dickinson's *Letters from a Pennsylvania Farmer,* were crucial; being widely read, they widely enlightened the colonists on what was at stake. It was these writings, in Ramsay's view, which made success possible:

In establishing American independence, the pen and the press had merit equal to that of the sword. As the war was the people's war, and was carried on without funds, the exertions of the army would have been insufficient to effect the revolution, unless the great body of the people had been prepared for it,

[3] *Travels in North America in the Years 1780, 1781 and 1782,* ed. Howard C. Rice, Jr. (Chapel Hill, N.C., 1963) , II, 429.
[4] *Ibid.*

and also kept in a constant disposition to oppose Great Britain. To rouse and unite the inhabitants, and to persuade them to patience for several years, under present sufferings, with the hope of obtaining remote advantages for their posterity, was a work of difficulty. This was effected in a great measure by the tongues and pens of the well informed citizens, and on it depended the success of military operations.[5]

Given the crucial role played by those who put into words the colonial position between the Stamp Act and the outbreak of fighting, it becomes more important to appreciate the formative influences which operated on the intellectual leadership— Whig history, the constitutional tradition of Magna Carta, the common law of England, and others—and to savor the shape which their arguments took, whether in pamphlets, or speeches, or resolutions of colonial bodies.[6]

The efforts to persuade the people were not, of course, in one direction only. There was, to begin with, pamphleteering by the supporters of British policy, especially in England itself. Moreover, Crown officials in the colonies, notably the judges, did what they could to sway local opinion. In Massachusetts, the justices of the Superior Court of Judicature rode circuit and held sessions in every county in the province at least once a year. Frequently these judges were the only personification of royal authority many communities ever saw, and it was common for the judges to use charges to grand juries to deliver moral or political lectures to develop support for the provincial government and to defend the status quo.[7]

Often the grand jury charges were eulogies of Magna Carta and the British Constitution. In a charge delivered in 1770 to the grand jury at Barnstable, the court told the jury that trial by jury was "part of y[e] English Constitution which may be Justly Reconed one of y[e] best That perhaps any nation in y[e] world Enjoy" and traced the great pains which had been taken to hand that right down to posterity "in y[e] Great Charter Called

---

[5] David Ramsay, *History of the American Revolution* (Philadelphia, 1789), II, 319–20.

[6] See Colbourn, *Lamp of Experience,* p. vii.

[7] See John D. Cushing, "The Judiciary and Public Opinion in Revolutionary Massachusetts," in George Athan Billias, ed., *Law and Authority in Colonial Massachusetts* (Barre, Mass., 1965), p. 168.

Magna Charta." Magna Carta, according to Coke, had been confirmed over thirty times by the Kings of England, and in the reign of Edward I "y⁰ Great Charter was Ordained to be taken as part of the Common Law of England, and all Stat. made against it Declared null & void." Obviously the judge was seeking to suggest the role played by Parliament in defending the liberties assured by Magna Carta, and he closed with an appeal for the colonists' support for the mother country:

And here I cannot but Just hint at y⁰ Gen¹ uneasines which has been & Still Subsists Between America & y⁰ mother Countrey to the Great Disadvantage of both. But I hope those Difficulties will soon be removed as Petitions have been Sent to his maj⁰ from the most Considerable Governments—If not all upon the Continent. I am Satisfied no person of Prudence & Discretion will in y⁰ least Countenance any unjustifiable measures for Redress of their Grievances. The People in General & I believe all in America are well attach't to King George y⁰ 3ᵈ & the Present Royal Family and I hope will always remain so and yʳ this uneasiness will soon subside, Especially as we hear Great preparations are now making in France & Spain & war seems to be Expected.[8]

It is interesting that the practice of using grand jury charges as an occasion for "educating" public opinion continued in Massachusetts after the Revolution. The judges were at the constitutional convention which drafted the Constitution of 1780, and, riding circuit, they were in touch with what the public were thinking. John Cushing has suggested that "all evidence indicates that the judiciary was in a more advantageous position than any other branch of government to bring influence directly to bear upon an appreciable number of people." [9] Thus a charge, apparently made in 1780 when the new state constitution was being drafted, included a few remarks on the merits of the British Constitution, observed that though that constitution was not perfect it had served them well in the past and ought not to be abandoned hastily, and said that the forthcoming Massachusetts Constitution would be an improvement on the past but not a radical departure from it.[10]

[8] Ms. in Massachusetts Historical Society.
[9] Cushing, *op. cit. supra* note 7, p. 181.
[10] Ms. in Massachusetts Historical Society.

John Adams

To some contemporary observers, the youthful John Adams might not have seemed destined for greatness. He did not have a commanding figure—as Vice President he was called "His Rotundity"—and he lacked the personality and charisma which marked his fiery cousin, Samuel. In 1782 Sir John Temple said of Adams, "He is the most ungracious man I ever saw." [11] But, without reference to his career in public office after Independence, Adams' role solely in the years between the Stamp Act and the Declaration of Independence would have earned him a secure niche in the hall of great Americans.

After his graduation from Harvard College in 1755, Adams took up a teaching job in Worcester, where he reflected on the law as a career. At first he suffered real doubts. In April 1756 he wrote his college classmate Charles Cushing:

> Let us look upon a Lawyer. In the beginning of Life we see him, fumbling and raking amidst the rubbish of Writs, indightments, Pleas, ejectments, enfiefed, illatebration and a 1000 other lignum Vitae words that have neither harmony nor meaning. When he gets into Business he often forments more quarrells than he composes, and inriches himself at the expense of impovershing others more honest and deserving than himself. Besides the noise and bustle of Courts and the labour of inquiring into and pleading dry and difficult Cases, have very few Charms in my Eye. [12]

Notwithstanding these dreary forebodings, and despite the fact that he had originally been set by his family on a course aiming for the ministry, Adams in August 1756 contracted with James Putnam, a Worcester lawyer, to study law. Adams was later to describe the study of law in the 1750's as a "dreary Ramble," but he had persevered. He had found his chief handicap a "Want of Books" and had determined to furnish himself, "at any Sacrifice, with a proper Library." He did just that, at

[11] Stephen Hess, *America's Political Dynasties from Adams to Kennedy* (Garden City, N.Y., 1966) , p. 11.
[12] *Adams Legal Papers*, I, lii.

least to his satisfaction, for he declared that by degrees he had built up "the best Library of Law in the State." [13]

The shaping of Adams' thinking on the law had begun long before he undertook formal legal studies. Much of what Adams felt about the constitutional rights of Englishmen, which he was to expound in his own writings and courtroom arguments, he had absorbed as a boy at the knee of his great-uncle Peter, who had been a grown man at the time of the Glorious Revolution in England and who had reminisced to young John of such things as the tyrannies of the Stuarts and the Bloody Assizes.[14]

Even in church Adams had learned of Magna Carta and the rights of Englishmen. The Reverend John Hancock, Adams' Congregationalist minister and the father of the patriot of the same name, pointed to the Massachusetts Charter securing to the people of that colony the liberties of Englishmen. Hancock's successor, the Reverend Lemuel Briant, still in his twenties and fresh out of Harvard, was as apt to sermonize on the things of this earth—on the ways of tyrants and the liberties of the subject—as he was to dwell on celestial glories. Briant wove a tapestry in which God's will and the British Constitution were intertwining threads—a mixture which was to characterize colonial thought through the years leading up to the War of Independence. "Of Magna Carta he spoke often with a stubborn, joyful pride as though he himself had signed it. In reality, young Briant knew very little of what Magna Carta had actually meant to the barons of the thirteenth century. But to him and his Braintree parishioners, Magna Carta was a seal, a symbol of British freedom." [15]

Throughout his legal career, Adams was to be steeped in the traditions of Magna Carta. Coke and his learned commentaries on Magna Carta were well represented in Adams' library.[16] And soon after his admission to the Boston bar, Adams was to hear James Otis, already a distinguished figure in Massachusetts, invoke Coke and Magna Carta in arguing the celebrated case

---

[13] *Adams Diary and Autobiography,* III, 273–74.
[14] Catherine Drinker Bowen, *John Adams and the American Revolution* (Boston, 1950), pp. 30–31.
[15] *Ibid.,* pp. 31–32.   [16] See p. 124, *supra.*

against the writs of assistance. Adams sat in the expectant courtroom and took notes as Otis denounced the writs of assistance as offending the "great Charter" of England. Otis lost and the writs issued, but Adams was to remember what he had heard in that courtroom.[17]

Adams' own practice grew swiftly. Eventually he was to be the busiest lawyer in the province, appearing, for example, in 202 Superior Court cases in all counties in 1772 alone.[18] Before that time, he was to take the plunge into public life. In 1765, with the passage of the Stamp Act, Adams began to put to use the ideas which, through his own reading and the issues of the times, had been forming in his mind. In the last half of 1765 alone, Adams wrote his essay on the canon and feudal law, appearing in four installments in the *Boston Gazette;* he composed the famous Instructions of the Town of Braintree to its representatives in the General Court, attacking the Stamp Act; and he was appointed counsel for Boston to plead its case that the local courts, which had been closed by the British Government, be reopened.

In his diary, Adams gave some suggestion of the form his thoughts were taking. In an entry on Christmas Day, 1765, he reflected on the virtues of the British Constitution:

> At Home. Thinking, reading, searching, concerning Taxation without Consent, concerning the great Pause and Rest in Business. By the Laws of England Justice flows, with an uninterrupted Stream: In that Musick, the Law knows of neither Rests nor Pauses. Nothing but Violence, Invasion or Rebellion can obstruct the River or untune the Instrument.[19]

Turning his thoughts to Magna Carta, Adams set out in his diary the words of the Charter's fortieth chapter: *Nulli vendemus, nulli negabimus, aut deferemus Iustitiam,* adding "Every Writ supposes the King present in all his Courts of Justice." And Adams entered a paraphrase of Coke's account, from Coke's commentaries on Magna Carta, of an Act of Parliament which, because it allowed proceedings upon information rather

---

[17] For Otis' arguments in the writs of assistance case, see pp. 133–38, *supra.*
[18] *Adams Legal Papers,* I, lix.　　[19] *Adams Diary and Autobiography,* I, 273.

than upon presentment by a grand jury, offended "this ancient and fundamental Law." [20]

Adams' *Dissertation on the Canon and Feudal Law* likened the attack on colonists' liberties to the Norman subjugation of the Saxons and the tyranny of the Stuarts. Magna Carta, which had been the rallying cry against oppression in the thirteenth and seventeenth centuries, Adams invoked against the Stamp Act.[21] About the same time that his essay on the canon and feudal law was being serialized in the *Boston Gazette,* Adams became a member of a committee of the Town of Braintree, appointed to draft the town's instructions to its representatives in the General Court of Massachusetts on the question of the Stamp Act.

The Instructions of the Town of Braintree, written by Adams, attacked the Stamp Act on two grounds, taxation without consent, and want of trial by jury. In both respects, Adams wrote, the act violated the British Constitution. The vesting of jurisdiction in the admiralty courts to try offenses under the act Adams labeled "the most grievous innovation of all." Of admiralty courts Adams declared, "In these courts, one judge presides alone! No juries have any concern there!" Law and fact were to be decided by a judge whose commission was at the pleasure of the Crown. This part of the act, because it dispensed with juries, "is directly repugnant to the Great Charter itself. . . ." And in support of this argument Adams quoted Magna Carta, chapter 20, allowing amercements to be imposed only "by the oath of honest and lawful men of the vicinage," and chapter 39's guarantee that no freeman should be condemned "but by lawful judgment of his peers, or by the law of the land." [22]

The Stamp Act had required the payment of a tax on any parchment or paper upon which was written any petition, bill, answer, demurrer, or other pleading in the colonial courts. When the taxes were not paid, the courts were closed. In December 1765 Adams was appointed, together with James Otis

---

[20] *Ibid.,* I, 273–74.   [21] See pp. 148–49, *supra.*
[22] *Works of John Adams,* III, 465–67. For the full text of the Instructions, see Appendix E, *infra.*

and Jeremiah Gridley, to represent Boston in appearing before the Governor to ask that the courts be reopened. Magna Carta, Adams submitted, forbade the closing of the courts. "The Law, the King's writs, cannot be withheld from his subjects. Magna Carta says, *We deny no man justice, we delay no man justice.* Is not the closing of the courts, both denial and delay?" Adams' argument was persuasive, but the Governor's answer was that he had no authority to reopen the courts without using the King's stamps.[23]

In the same month, December 1765, Adams began to make notes for a series of public letters he proposed to write in answer to the English apologist for the Stamp Act, "William Pym," whose writings had appeared in the *London Evening Post* and had been reprinted in the *Boston Evening Post* in November. Pym had dismissed colonial arguments against the Stamp Act with the simple assertion that Parliament could at any time set aside royally granted charters and that it was "idle" for the colonists to speak of charter rights. In his journal, Adams set down his faith in the British Constitution:

And here lies the Difference between the british Constitution and other Constitutions of Government, vizt. that Liberty is its End—the preservation of Liberty is its End, its Use, its Designation, its Drift and scope, as much as Life and Health are the Ends of the Constitution of the human Body, as much as the Mensuration of Time is the End of the Constitution of a Watch, as much as Grinding Corn is the End of a Grist Mill, or the Transportation of Burdens the End of a Ship.[24]

Adams countered Pym's dismissal of the colonists' charter rights by evoking the image of Coke and Magna Carta:

Recollect the old Sage Coke, and recollect Magna Charta which your Tribe used to think more sacred than scripture. Consider once more this hideous Taxation. . . . You tell us that a Resolution of the B[ritish] Parliament can at any Time anull all the Charters of all our Monarcks. But would such an Act of Parliament do no wrong? Would it be obeyed? Would one Member of Parliament who voted for it, return to his Country alive? No You would have been the first Man in the

---

[23] See Bowen, *John Adams and the American Revolution,* p. 289.
[24] *Adams Diary and Autobiography,* I, 298.

Kingdom, when you was in the flesh, to have taken Arms against such a law.[25]

In another diary entry, Adams constructed the same argument against the closing of the courts that he had made before the Governor. The colonists were, Adams wrote, as much deprived of the King's protection of their persons and properties as if there had been an invasion or rebellion. "We are therefore in Effect deprived of the Benefit of Magna Charta." [26] In January 1766 these fragments became the basis for three letters published by Adams in the *Boston Gazette* under the name "Clarendon." [27]

In 1768 John Adams' legal abilities were put at the disposal of the wealthiest merchant in New England, John Hancock, in a case which politically was to be Adams' most significant case until his defense of the British soldiers charged with the Boston Massacre. Active in the importing trade, Hancock had been a leading opponent to British revenue measures and had used his influence with British merchants to press for repeal of the Stamp Act. He took an active part in the mounting colonial resistance to British commercial policy; to show his contempt for the Customs Commissioners who enforced revenue measures in Boston, Hancock (to cite only one incident) refused to have the Cadet Company, of which he was captain, appear at a public dinner if the Commissioners were to be present.

The legal proceedings against Hancock arose out of the seizure of one of his ships, the sloop *Liberty,* by customs officials. On behalf of the Collector of the Port of Boston, Joseph Harrison, a libel was filed against the ship and quantities of oil and tar found aboard her. The grounds for the libel were probably that the ship had unloaded pipes of Madeira wine without having gone through customs formalities and that the oil and tar had been loaded without bond or permit. The ship was declared forfeit, and the next step was an action against Hancock himself. The King's Advocate General, Jonathan Sewall, filed an information against Hancock and five others charging

[25] *Ibid.,* I, 274–75.   [26] *Ibid.,* I, 292.
[27] For the text of the "Clarendon" letters, see *Works of John Adams,* III, 469–83.

them with having assisted in the landing of the Madeira, knowing that the duties had not been paid. The penalty sought was £9,000—treble the value of the wine.

Adams served as Hancock's counsel. The trial proved a long and tiring one, with numbers of witnesses called and examined. Having begun in November 1768, the trial continued, with interruptions, until March 1769, when Sewall moved that the information be withdrawn. Thus judgment was never rendered against Hancock. But the importance of the trial lay not in its outcome, but in the publicity which attended it. From the outset of the trial, the proceedings were reported periodically in newspapers throughout the colonies. The Customs Commissioners were brought into bad repute, while Hancock, his reputation enhanced, went on to become President of the Second Continental Congress and the first signer of the Declaration of Independence.[28]

The case has special significance because of its having been brought, not in the ordinary common law courts, but in the admiralty court, as permitted by the revenue acts. Being heard in a court of admiralty, the case was tried without a jury. In his draft of the argument he would make to the court on Hancock's behalf, Adams urged this fact as the statute's greatest evil. He pointed to the anomaly that in England proceedings under the statute were to be brought in court where juries sat, whereas in America jury trial was denied: "What shall we say to this Distinction? Is there not in this Clause, a Brand of Infamy, of Degredation, and Disgrace, fixed upon every American? Is he not degraded below the rank of an Englishman? Is it not directly, a Repeal of Magna Charta, as far as America is concerned." [29]

To be denied the rights of Englishmen as secured by Magna Carta: this was what made the act "the most rigid and severe" of any law of the Empire. Quoting from Magna Carta's thirty-ninth chapter and from Coke's commentaries, Adams recalled that this chapter of the Charter had "for many Centuries been

---

[28] For accounts of the events leading up to the trial and of the trial itself, see Oliver M. Dickerson, *The Navigation Acts and the American Revolution* (Philadelphia, 1951) , pp. 231–46; *Adams Legal Papers,* II, 173–93.
[29] *Adams Legal Papers,* II, 200.

esteemed by Englishmen, as one of the noblest Monuments, one of the firmest Bulwarks of their Liberties. . . ." Adams could find no kind words for a statute which distinguished "my Clyent from the rest of Englishmen." [30]

Adams may have intended his draft argument to serve wider purposes than its use at trial; perhaps it was meant to be the basis for a pamphlet. Certainly his reliance on Magna Carta, seemingly a constitutional attack on the British revenue laws, recalls the position he had taken in the "Clarendon" letters in 1766. And he relied heavily upon the jury trial arguments in his 1768 trial notes in drafting the Instructions to the Boston Representatives in May 1769. Through the publicity which was given the Hancock trial, the principle of trial by jury and its association with Magna Carta became even more deeply embedded in the American consciousness. Adams' arguments, drafted for the courtroom, were all the more effective outside it because of their constitutional flavor: an appeal to English constitutional principles on behalf of an American subject of the English Crown.

John Adams approached advocacy of American independence more cautiously than did his cousin Samuel. John was always more concerned with constitutional principles, Samuel more attuned to results. In 1770, when Boston was aflame with passion over the so-called Boston Massacre, the contrast between the two men was marked. Sam and his associates put moral and physical pressure on the court to get on with the trial of Captain Preston and his soldiers, even though a fair trial was unlikely until tempers cooled. John, on the other hand, agreed, at obvious cost to his own popularity in Boston, to undertake Preston's defense. We have no reason to doubt Adams' explanation, set down in his autobiography, that he took the case simply because "Council ought to be the very last thing that an accused Person should want in a free Country." [31]

After the American Revolution, John Adams retained his

---

[30] *Ibid.*, II, 200–202.

[31] *Adams Diary and Autobiography*, III, 293. Preston was acquitted of the charges against him. In a separate trial, in which Adams was counsel, the soldiers serving under Preston's command were likewise acquitted of murder charges, although two of the soldiers were found guilty of manslaughter. For an account of the trials, and related source materials, see *Adams Legal Papers*, III.

admiration for the British Constitution. In 1787, while he was serving as the first American minister to the Court of St. James, Adams published *A Defence of the Constitutions of Government of the United States.* This work was an answer to the views of Turgot and other Europeans who had criticized the framework of the American state governments. Drawing heavily on history and comparative government, Adams looked for the reemergence of an idealized British Constitution in Great Britain. Like Montesquieu, Adams thought he saw in the British Constitution a balance of powers, a "mixed" form of government, which made that constitution "the most stupendous fabric of human invention." To the Americans, Magna Carta and the British Constitution were a model. "If, in England, there has ever been any such thing as a government of laws, was it not *magna charta?*" Hence the Americans in their state constitutions had translated the best features of the British Constitution to their own needs and had improved on it; in borrowing these features, said Adams, "the Americans ought to be applauded instead of censured, for imitating it as far as they have." [32]

It had been many years since great-uncle Peter had told young John Adams of English liberties and since John had heard the Reverend Mr. Briant eulogize Magna Carta from the pulpit. It had been over twenty years since Adams had first published his own thoughts on the British Constitution. But neither the Stamp Act nor even the Revolution itself had destroyed his belief in the traditional rights of Englishmen as a model for guaranteeing the rights of Americans.

Samuel Adams

I F JOHN ADAMS was moved by a concern for justice even when its pursuit was not expedient—for example, in his defense of the British soldiers in the Boston Massacre trial—his second cousin, Samuel, was a tough-minded politician to whom con-

[32] *A Defence of the Constitutions of Government of the United States of America* (London, 1794) , I, 70, 126.

cern for ends came more naturally than fastidiousness about means. Although they differed widely in temperament and in political methods, John had considerable respect for Samuel, his elder by thirteen years. John once noted in his diary that Samuel "I believe has the most thorough Understanding of Liberty, and her Resources, in the Temper and Character of the People, tho not in the Law and Constitution, as well as the most habitual, radical Love of it, of any of them—as well as the most correct, genteel and artful Pen." John predicted, in fact, that Samuel's writings "would be more admired than any Thing that has been written in America in this Dispute [the American Revolution]." [33]

Like some other figures in public life—Ulysses Grant and Harry Truman, for example—Samuel Adams had a life marked more by reverses than by success before the events of the times found a place for him. Adams failed at several business ventures and was charged with neglect of his duties as a tax collector in Boston. But with the passage by Parliament of the Revenue Act in 1764, Adams began a swift rise to prominence in the affairs of Massachusetts. He became an implacable opponent of British rule. Even at times—for example, after the repeal in 1770 of the Townshend duties—when the colonies were relatively peaceful, Adams was agitating and scheming for a break with Britain. He was an uncommonly adroit leader of the people and did not hesitate to paint the British, their soldiers, and their officials, in the darkest hues.

Samuel Adams may not have cared for the British Government, and it may have been true, as Cousin John said, that Samuel's love of liberty outstripped his knowledge of law and the constitution, but Samuel's writings reflect a ready willingness to use Magna Carta and the British Constitution, well mixed with natural law, as authorities for his arguments, if only because these were part of the common tongue of the times. Soon after his rise to prominence had begun, Adams drafted the resolutions of the Massachusetts House of Representatives against the Stamp Act. Passed on October 29, 1765,

---

[33] *Adams Diary and Autobiography*, I, 271, II, 385.

these resolutions followed the pattern familiar to the resolutions being adopted by the other colonies. They are interesting because, at the outset, they blend a natural rights argument with the authority of the British Constitution, declaring that the "essential rights of the British Constitution" are "founded in the law of God and nature, and are the common rights of mankind." Moreover, to emphasize that the rights claimed have an origin higher than civil society, the resolutions go on to say that the inhabitants of Massachusetts "are unalienably entitled to those essential rights in common with all men: and that no law of society can, consistent with the law of God and nature, divest them of those rights."[34]

Then natural rights are woven into the British Constitution: it is declared that "no man can justly take the property of another without his consent" and that upon this "original principle" the right to be represented in the body which levies taxes, "one of the main pillars of the British Constitution," is founded. Together with "all other essential rights, liberties, privileges, and immunities of the people of Great Britain," this right has been "fully confirmed to them by Magna Charta."[35]

Similarly, the parity of colonial rights with those of freemen in England is rested upon the twin pillars of natural law and the British Constitution: the resolutions declare that not only does the royal charter give the colonists all the rights, liberties, and immunities of Englishmen, but also "reason and common sense" and "common justice" entitle them to the same liberties as enjoyed by Englishmen.[36]

In January 1768 Samuel Adams, by then the clerk of the lower house of the General Court, wrote that house's address to the Earl of Shelburne and its petition to the King. The address reflects the same intermixture of natural rights and constitutional law that characterized the resolutions of 1765. In the address Adams invoked the royal charters' guarantees of the liberties of Englishmen, the right given by the common law that all subjects should enjoy its benefits, and the "spirit of the

[34] *Writings of Samuel Adams,* ed. Harry Alonzo Cushing (New York, 1904–8), I, 23–24.
[35] *Ibid.,* I, 24.   [36] *Ibid.,* I, 24–25.

law of nature and nations" supposing that "all the free subjects of any kingdom, are entitled equally to all the rights of the constitution. . . ." All these sources of rights, thought Adams, formed one common stream: "It is the glory of the British constitution, that it has its foundation in the law of God and nature." [37]

It is probable that natural law thinking, if only because it was more revolutionary and more malleable than legal and constitutional precedents, was more congenial to Samuel Adams. Let John Adams explore the subtleties of the canon and feudal law to lay an intellectual underpinning for an argument from Magna Carta and the other English statutes; Samuel would see that the colonial case was ultimately grounded in the inalienable rights of mankind. Yet, as already noted, Samuel did not despise the inheritance of the British Constitution. For example, in a message of the House of Representatives to the Governor of Massachusetts in June 1769, attributed to Adams, the sentiment was expressed, "No time can better be employed, than in the preservation of the rights derived from the British constitution. . . . No treasure can be better expended, than in securing that true old English liberty, which gives a relish to every other enjoyment." [38]

To Samuel Adams, the colonial charters formed a useful third leg of the colonists' case, along with natural rights and the British Constitution. In a letter written to a friend in 1765, Adams said that the colonial charters were especially sacred because they were compacts between the King and his subjects. If other evidence were wanting, Adams showed himself in this letter to be a disciple of Locke: "Thus we see that Whatever Government in general may be founded in, Ours was manifestly founded in *Compact*." The charters therefore were as fundamental as Magna Carta. By the charters the colonists and their posterity were declared to be entitled to all the liberties and immunities of free and natural subjects of Great Britain; therefore the charters are to be looked upon by them "to be as sacred to them as Magna Charta is to the People of Britain; as

[37] *Ibid.*, I, 153–56.   [38] *Ibid.*, I, 348.

it contains a Declaration of all their Rights founded in natural Justice." [39] Yet in Adams' later tract, *The Rights of the Colonists* (1772), he treated the colonial charters as dispensable, arguing that "by the laws of God and nature, and by the Common law of England, *exclusive of all charters from the Crown,*" the colonists were entitled to all the essential and inherent rights and liberties of subjects in Great Britain.[40]

In Samuel Adams' writings of 1772—the same year he was responsible for the founding of the Committee of Correspondence in Boston—Adams put Magna Carta and the natural law together at the center of his scheme. In "Candidus," Adams drew heavily on the writings of Coke in maintaining that Magna Carta voided inconsistent statutes of Parliament:

Chromus [the writer of another letter in the *Gazette*] talks of *Magna Charta* as though it were of no greater consequence than an act of parliament for the establishment of a corporation of button-makers. Whatever low ideas he may entertain of the *Great Charter* . . . it is affirm'd by Lord Coke, to be declaratory of the principal grounds of the fundamental laws and liberties of England "It is called *Charta Libertatum Regni, the Charter of the Liberties of the kingdom,* upon great reason . . . because *liberos facit, it makes and preserves the people free."* . . . But if it be declaratory of the principal grounds of the fundamental laws and liberties of England, it cannot be altered in any of its essential parts, without altering the constitution. . . . Vatel tells us plainly and without hesitation that "the supreme legislative cannot change the constitution." . . . If then according to Lord Coke, *Magna Charta* is declaratory of the principal grounds of the *fundamental* laws and liberties of the people, and Vatel is right in his opinion, that the supreme legislative cannot change the constitution, I think it follows, whether Lord Coke has expressly asserted it or not, that an act of parliament made against Magna Charta in violation of its essential parts, is void.[41]

Here is one of a number of links in the chain which leads from Coke's arguments that laws inconsistent with Magna Carta are void to the ultimate enshrinement of this doctrine in American constitutional law, with the Supreme Court having the power to review and strike down acts, whether of the fed-

[39] *Ibid.*, I, 27–28.   [40] *Ibid.*, II, 350, 356.   [41] *Ibid.*, II, 324–26.

eral or state legislatures, incompatible with the fundamental law.

No matter what use he might make of Magna Carta, or the common law, or the colonial charters, Samuel Adams invariably returned to the law of nature as the starting point. "Magna Charta itself," he declared, "is in substance but a constrained Declaration, or proclamation, and promulgation in the name of King, Lord, and Commons of the sense the latter had of their original, inherent, indefeazible natural Rights. . . ." [42]

In an earlier chapter of this book, it was observed how even in the early years in New England there was an interplay between the laws of God and the laws of England, how from the start Americans were becoming accustomed to debating public questions both in terms of natural law and in terms of constitutional documents. In Massachusetts in the 1640's those who called for the rights of Magna Carta were clashing with those who would rule according to the laws of God. It is interesting that in the Massachusetts of one hundred and thirty years later the two traditions of natural law and constitutional law should be invoked on the same side. And it is symbolic that the two traditions can be personified in John Adams and Samuel Adams, for the arguments put by these two men demonstrate how, while the two traditions have often flowed side by side in American history, yet they are never wholly the same.

[42] *The Rights of the Colonists, ibid.,* II, 355.

Chapter IX

From English Rights Restated

to Independence Declared

Prosperity in the American colonies in the early 1770's nearly buried once and for all the efforts of Sam Adams and other colonial agitators to sustain resentment against British colonial policy. Repeal of the Stamp Act brought a wave of jubilation to the colonies and an outpouring of loyal sentiment for George III and for the "Great Commoner," William Pitt, who had moved repeal. In March 1770 Parliament repealed the Townshend Acts, save for a duty on tea, and in colony after colony the nonimportation agreements dissolved. Trade increased by bounds, and money flowed into the coffers of colonial merchants and shopkeepers. From time to time issues arose to stir colonial resentments—for example, the "Boston Massacre" and the *Gaspee* affair (in which some Rhode Islanders boarded and scuttled a British revenue cutter)—but most people were enjoying prosperity too much to make trouble.

Then came the Boston Tea Party. In 1773 Parliament made new arrangements with the East India Company for the importation of tea into the colonies. The Townshend duty of 3*d.* per pound of tea was still in effect, and when the Company's tea ships began arriving in colonial ports the Sons of Liberty went into action. At two ports, Philadelphia and New York, the ships were turned back; at Boston, a mob disguised as Indians and Negroes scurried aboard the ships and dumped quantities of tea into the harbor. A showdown was at hand. Massachusetts had misbehaved, and now it was to be punished.

The punishment took the form of Acts of Parliament. In Britain the statutes had titles which were innocuous enough—the Boston Port Act, the Massachusetts Government and Administration of Justice Acts, the Quartering Act. But to the American colonists they were the "Coercive" or "Intolerable" Acts.

The legislation went before the House of Commons beginning in March 1774, accompanied by a message from George III in which the King, referring to the "violent and outrageous proceedings" in Boston, urged action to put a stop to the disorders, to see to the better execution of the laws, and to secure the "just dependance of the colonies upon the crown and parliament of Great Britain." As the House took up the Boston Port Bill, Lord North named Boston as the ringleader in the disturbances and urged that it be "the principal object of our attention for punishment." Another member, Mr. Van, in committee took an even more vindictive stand. The town of Boston, he said, "ought to be knocked about their ears, and destroyed. *Delenda est Carthago:* said he, I am of opinion you will never meet with that proper obedience to the laws of this country, until you have destroyed that nest of locusts." [1]

Some members defended the American point of view. Colonel Barré, in answer to Van, cautioned the House: "The Bill before you is the first vengeful step that you have taken. We ought to go coolly to this business. . . . [A]s long as I sit here among you I will oppose the taxing of America. . . . Keep your hands out of the pockets of the Americans, and they will be obedient subjects." Mr. Sawbridge denied the right of the British Government to tax America; had they a right to take "a single shilling" out of an American's pocket, they had a right to

---

[1] *Parliamentary History* (London, 1813), XVII, 1159, 1165, 1178. Van was echoing the famous phrase of Marcus Porcius Cato, who, alarmed at the wealth of Carthage, concluded all his speeches in the Roman Senate with the words, "Carthage must be destroyed."

172 The Road from Runnymede

take the whole. On the floor of the House, Edmund Burke looked to the British Constitution as being against the bill. Anticipating pillory for opposing the bill, Burke felt compelled to protest its injustice and hoped some day to see America governed by a plan "not founded upon your laws and statutes here, but grounded upon the vital principles of English liberty." [2]

Several Americans living in London petitioned Parliament not to pass the Boston Port Bill. The petitioners conceived themselves and their fellow subjects in America "intitled to the rights of natural justice, and to the common law of England, as their unalienable birthright. . . ." They complained especially that Boston was about to be punished without being heard in its own defense. This, they submitted, violated the principle of the British Constitution that "no man shall be condemned unheard" (a principle which American courts after the Revolution were to find to be one of the chief American inheritances from Magna Carta). To do what the bill before Parliament proposed would mean that "no man, or body of men, in America, could enjoy a moment's security. . . ." American law, after all, gave a redress for grievances; as as example, the petitioners cited the acquittal of Captain Preston and his soldiers. In sum, the petition warned that the bill would alienate the affections of Americans for the mother country.[3]

Such warnings were in vain. The Boston Port Bill became law, placing Boston under a kind of blockade until it would pay reparations for the jettisoned tea. Ships of the Royal Navy and a garrison of redcoats formed a tangible British presence in Boston to enforce the bill. The other "Intolerable" Acts provided for the commandeering of private houses to quarter British troops and for the appointment by the Governor of the Council, which theretofore had been elected by the whole Assembly and had supported the popular cause.[4]

[2] *Ibid.*, XVII, 1178–79, 1167–68, 1185.   [3] *Ibid.*, XVII, 1189–91.
[4] See Harry A. Cushing, "History of the Transition from Provincial to Commonwealth Government in Massachusetts," in Columbia University, *Studies in History, Economics and Public Law,* VII, 1 (1896). For a brilliant study of the House of Commons at the time of the "Intolerable" Acts, see Sir Lewis Namier and John Brooke, *The House of Commons, 1754–1790* (3 vols.; Oxford, 1964).

Colonial Resolutions

T HE American colonies were quick to rally to the support of Massachusetts. Within weeks of the news of the oppressive British legislation, meetings were being called in colonies up and down the coast to give voice to colonial sentiments and to issue calls for action. On May 24, 1774, a few days before the British statutes punishing Boston were to take effect, the House of Burgesses of Virginia declared its apprehension of the "hostile invasion" of Boston and set aside the first of June, the day the statutes went into effect, as a day of fasting, humiliation, and prayer to implore the Deity to give the colonists "one heart and one mind" to oppose the British policies and to pray that King and Parliament might be dissuaded from a course "pregnant with their ruin." Two days later Governor Dunmore dissolved the Assembly.[5]

Before they left Williamsburg, the Burgesses met in the Apollo Room of the Raleigh Tavern, formed themselves into a committee, and agreed upon a resolution for united action by the colonies. An attack on any of the colonies, the Virginians declared, "is an attack made on all *British America,* and threatens ruin to the rights of all, unless the united wisdom of the whole be applied." Therefore the members recommended that each colony appoint delegates to meet in a general congress to deliberate on such action as the common interests of the colonies might require. Eighty-nine members of the dissolved House of Burgesses affixed their signatures.[6]

The other colonies followed suit. From May through August, 1774, resolutions were passed by conventions in the several colonies, as well as by scores of counties, town, and other localities. Through the medium of the well-organized Committees of Correspondence, the ideas put forth in the resolutions showed a striking likeness, from Georgia in the South to New England in the North. Resolutions passed in different colonies

[5] *American Archives,* 4th ser., ed., Peter Force, I (Washington, D.C. 1837), 350.
[6] *Ibid.,* I, 350–51.

within days of each other reflect the close consultation which took place among all the colonies. Like grievances are aired, like solutions are proposed. Yet when one reads the texts of the various resolutions, one finds that rarely is the wording identical from one to the next. Obviously the resolutions were gone over with great care and were fashioned to put the colonial case in the way that a particular body thought most persuasive.

The resolutions passed in 1774 are typically brief, and what they have in common is easy to identify. For one thing, they reveal that in 1774 the case against the policies and acts of the British Government was still a constitutional one. Occasionally a resolution, especially those of conventions in New England, stressed natural rights rather than the guarantees of the British Constitution. For example, the resolution passed at a town meeting in Providence, Rhode Island, several times invoked the colonists' "natural rights and privileges" but never once mentioned the British Constitution.[7] But is was rare for a resolution not to make the argument a constitutional one. Resolutions of the southern and middle colonies were especially apt to do this; the claim was, as the Georgia resolutions put it, that his Majesty's subjects in America were entitled to "the same rights, privileges, and immunities with their fellow-subjects in *Great Britain.*"[8]

Charter rights were invoked. Middlesex County, Massachusetts, resolved that "when our ancestors emigrated from *Great Britain* Charters and solemn stipulations expressed the conditions; and what particular rights they yielded; what each party had to do and perform; and which each of the contracting parties were equally bound by." The resolution went on to say that the colonists had done nothing to forfeit their charter rights and that therefore the various Acts of Parliament objected to must be considered unconstitutional.[9]

The British Constitution itself was drawn upon, indeed, praised in sometimes fulsome language. The people of Cumberland County, Massachusetts, thought it the duty of every subject to preserve the Constitution inviolate, "for we regard it not

[7] *Ibid.,* I, 333–34.   [8] *Ibid.,* I, 700.   [9] *Ibid.,* I, 750–51.

13. John Adams, after John Singleton Copley. (Courtesy, Museum of Fine Arts, Boston. F. W. Bayley–Seth Kettell Sweetser Residuary Fund.)

14. Samuel Adams, by John Singleton Copley. (Courtesy, Museum of Fine Arts, Boston. City of Boston.)

15. Seal of Massachusetts, 1775–1780. An "English American" holding Magna Carta and a sword. (Courtesy, Secretary of the Commonwealth of Massachusetts.)

16. Provision of the Council of Massachusetts in 1775 for the colony's seal: "Instead of an Indian holding a Tomahawk . . . There be an English American holding a Sword in the right hand and Magna Charta in the Left hand with the Words Magna Charta imprinted on it." (Courtesy, Secretary of the Commonwealth of Massachusetts.)

only as the foundation of all our civil rights and liberties, but as a system of Government the best calculated to promote the people's peace and happiness." [10]

Probably the most explicit discussion of the colonial theory of their constitutional rights was that set out in the resolution of the freeholders and inhabitants of Fairfax County, Virginia. At a meeting chaired by George Washington, the people of Fairfax began their resolutions with the following constitutional doctrine:

Resolved, That this Colony and Dominion of *Virginia* cannot be considered as a conquered country, and, if it was, that the present inhabitants are the descendants, not of the conquered, but of the conquerors. That the same was not settled at the national expense of *England,* but at the private expense of the adventurers, our ancestors, by solemn compact with, and under the auspices and protection of, the *British* Crown, upon which we are, in every respect, as dependent as the people of *Great Britain,* and in the same manner subject to all his Majesty's just, legal, and constitutional prerogatives; that our ancestors, when they left their native land, and settled in *America,* brought with them, even if the same had not been confirmed by Charters, the civil Constitution and form of Government of the country they came from, and were by the laws of nature and Nations entitled to all its privileges, immunities, and advantages, which have descended to us, their posterity, and ought of right to be as fully enjoyed as if we had still continued within the Realm of *England.*[11]

With the resolutions of 1774, American history was repeating itself. Nine years earlier, when resolutions had been passed both by the individual colonies and by a body speaking for all the colonies, the Stamp Act Congress, Americans had declared themselves heirs to their ancestors' right to the liberties, franchises, and immunities of Englishmen. In 1765 two rights had been expressly held to be among those rights of Englishmen: the right to be taxed only upon consent given and the right to trial by jury. In 1774 these same rights were enumerated. And

[10] *Ibid.,* I, 799.
[11] *Ibid.,* I, 597. For the text of the Fairfax County resolutions, see Appendix G, *infra.*

in 1774, as in 1765, the influence of Magna Carta was unmistakable.

North Carolina, for example, declared that it was "of the very essence of the *British* Constitution, that no subject should be taxed, but by his own consent, freely given by himself in person, or by his legal Representatives, and that any other than such a taxation is highly derogatory to the rights of a subject, and a gross violation of the Grand Charter of our liberties." [12] As for the right to trial by jury, her sister colony of South Carolina drew directly on the language of chapter 39 of Magna Carta to hold it "a fundamental right which his Majesty's liege subjects are entitled to, that no man should suffer in his person or property without a fair trial, and judgment given by his peers, or by the laws of the land." [13]

The Continental Congress

THE resolutions were by no means confined to statements of constitutional doctrine. In all cases the resolutions proposed action of some kind, the better to secure redress of the colonists' grievances. The colonies were in agreement with the proposal of the Virginia Burgesses that, as the Pennsylvania convention put it, a "Congress of Deputies" from the several colonies should assemble "to consult together, and form a general plan of conduct to be observed by all the Colonies. . . ." [14] The resolutions, whether of a colony's convention or of a local meeting, commonly called upon the congress, when convened, to consider an agreement not to import from or export to Great Britain until a change in British policies was forthcoming.[15]

Though concerted action was called for, the resolutions remained within the scope of what their proponents conceived to

---

[12] *American Archives*, I, 734.   [13] *Ibid.*, I, 525.   [14] *Ibid.*, I, 556.

[15] See, e.g., among resolutions of colony conventions, those of Maryland and New Jersey, and among local resolutions, those of Albemarle County, Va., and Queen Anne County, Md. *Ibid.*, I, 439–40, 624–25, 637–38, 366. It is interesting that the resolutions passed in New York City, a port city, called for a halt to all trade with Great Britain, while the resolutions passed in Philadelphia were silent on the nonimportation proposals. See *ibid.*, I, 312–13, 426–27.

be a constitutional position. It was common for a resolution to include a profession of loyalty to the Crown. New Jersey, for example, declared that the people of that province were "firm and unshaken in their loyalty to his Majesty King *George* the Third . . . to whom under his royal protection in our fundamental rights and privileges, we owe, and will render all due faith and allegiance." [16] And the resolutions showed a real hope that persuasion might prevail. The colonists knew that they had a number of able advocates among public figures in England, such as William Pitt and Edmund Burke, and Delaware spoke the sentiments of many Americans when its convention resolved its thanks to "those truly noble, honourable, and patriotick advocates in *Great Britain,* who have so generously and powerfully, though unsuccessfully, espoused and defended the cause of *America,* both in and out of Parliament. . . ." [17]

The hope remaining in 1774 that, as Delaware put it, the people of Great Britain and America should remain "one people," [18] was one of the reasons why the resolutions of that year were for the most part couched in constitutional language. There was in the resolutions, as in pamphlets and other colonial arguments of the time, an unquestioned eclecticism—a tendency to draw on charter rights, the British Constitution, and natural rights as several arrows in a sling. Suffolk County, Massachusetts, for example, explicitly stated colonial rights to have been derived from "nature, the Constitution of *Britain,* and the privileges warranted to us in the Charter of the Province." [19] These were by no means looked upon by the colonists as unrelated, since the British Constitution was, as the Georgia resolutions expressed it, simply a statement in positive law of "reason and justice, and the indelible rights of mankind." [20]

That the arguments were essentially constitutional has a corollary of special interest in light of the later development of the American courts' doctrine of judicial review of legislation. The existence of constitutional rights carried with it the corollary of the right, even the duty, to make judgments that a legislative act which passed the bounds of the constitutional

[16] *Ibid.,* I, 624.   [17] *Ibid.,* I, 668.   [18] *Ibid.,* I, 667.
[19] *Ibid.,* I, 776.   [20] *Ibid.,* I, 701.

should be opposed as unconstitutional. The resolutions of 1774 exercised precisely that judgment. The resolutions used various language to characterize the objectionable Acts of Parliament, but it is interesting how often the objections were summed up in the evaluation that the acts were simply "unconstitutional." The Pennsylvania resolutions were characteristic; they set out, in separate numbered paragraphs, each of the British statutes and labeled each of them "unconstitutional." [21] So natural did the colonists find this usage that it is a measure of the extent to which the habit of looking to fundamental law as the measure of the legitimacy of legislative acts had become a well-developed concept and, though not exercised in these 1774 documents by any judicial body, helped pave the way for the assumption by American courts of the power to pass on the constitutionality of statutes.

When the Continental Congress met in September 1774, much of the debate centered on the manner in which the rights of the colonies ought to be expressed. Richard Henry Lee of Virginia argued that the colonists' rights rested on four grounds: natural law, the British Constitution, colonial charters, and immemorial usage. But other delegates, including John Rutledge of South Carolina and James Duane of New York, submitted that the constitutional arguments were to be preferred to those based on the law of nature. John Adams noted in his diary that Duane was "for grounding our Rights on the Laws and Constitution of the Country from whence We sprung," that is, on the rights of Englishmen, "their Birthright and Inheritance." [22]

Duane developed his views in a statement to the committee appointed to draft a statement of the rights of the colonies. Tracing events in the colonies from the Stamp Act to 1774, Duane urged the committee to articulate a constitutional principle. "It is now, sir, essential to place our Rights on a broader and firmer Basis, to advance and adhere to some solid and Constitutional Principle which will preserve us from future Violations—a principle clear and explicit and which is above the Reach of Cunning and the arts of oppression." For Duane

[21] *Ibid.*, I, 556.   [22] *Adams Diary and Autobiography*, II, 128–29.

this principle was the rights of Englishmen, secured to the colonists both by the common and statute law of England and by their own charters. These rights were inherent and the colonists' birthright, "of which they could only be deprived by their free Consent. Every Institution, legislative and Judical, essential to the Exercise and Enjoyment of these Rights and priviledges in constitutional security were equally their Birth right and inalienable Inheritance. They could not be withheld but by lawless oppression. . . ."[23]

John Rutledge proposed to the committee a resolution which would rest colonial rights on the same two bases suggested by Duane: the English common and statute law and the colonial charters. Rutledge's resolution held the colonists entitled not only to such parts of the English laws as existed at the time of the emigration to America and were applicable to conditions there, but also to such statutes enacted after the settlement of America which had as their purpose the securing of the "rights and Liberties of the Subject." Such English law, the colonial charters, and the acts of colonial assemblies—these and these only constituted "the Law of the Land and the Rights and priviledges of the people in the Colonies."[24]

The Congress of 1774 produced a number of documents— resolutions of nonimportation and nonexportation, an address to the people of Great Britain, an address to the inhabitants of Quebec, a petition to the King, and others. Of special significance was the Congress' statement of the rights of the colonies which it held to have been violated by the British Government, a document often referred to as the Declaration and Resolves of the First Continental Congress.[25] These resolutions began by adverting to the claims of Parliament to the right to legislate for the colonies and Parliament's enactment of "impolitic, unjust, and cruel, as well as unconstitutional" statutes. Then the Congress set out the actual resolutions, chief among which was the declaration that their ancestors upon emigrating to Amer-

[23] *Letters of Members of the Continental Congress,* ed. Edmund C. Burnett (Washington, D.C., 1921–36), I, 23, 24, 25.
[24] *Ibid.,* I, 44.
[25] The full text of these resolutions appears in Appendix H, *infra.*

ica carried with them "all the rights, liberties, and immunities of free and natural-born subjects, within the realm of England." [26]

The Congress spelled out what rights they thought these were. First was the right to "a free and exclusive power of legislation in their several provincial legislatures" in all cases of taxation and internal polity, though the Congress "cheerfully" consented to the right of the British Parliament to regulate external commerce. Secondly, the colonists claimed the common law of England, in particular (here paraphrasing Magna Carta), "the great and inestimable privilege of being tried by their peers of the vicinage, according to the course of that law." Thirdly, Americans claimed the benefit of such English statutes as existed at the time of the American colonization and as had been found suited to local circumstances. Fourthly, they would have all privileges granted by the colonial charters. Finally, in a number of separate headings, the Congress resolved that the colonists had a right peaceably to assemble and to petition for redress of grievances, that the colonies should consent to the presence of standing armies in time of peace, and that the principle of the independence of the constituent branches of government (which we would call the separation of powers) required that councils appointed by the Crown not have legislative powers. The Congress supplemented these statements of principle with a list of the specific Acts of Parliament which were thought to infringe the stated colonial rights.[27]

The Debate in the Countryside

THE events which brought the First Continental Congress to Philadelphia occasioned considerable writing and commentary in the country at large. The stream of pamphlets, newspaper articles, and other writings which had begun in earnest about

---

[26] *Journals of the Continental Congress, 1774–1789*, ed. Worthington Chauncey Ford (Washington, D.C., 1904–6), I, 63–68 [hereinafter *Journals of the Continental Congress*].

[27] *Ibid.*, I, 68–73.

the time of the Stamp Act reached its prerevolutionary culmination in 1774. In August 1774 William Henry Drayton of South Carolina wrote a letter signed "Freeman" and addressed to the Continental Congress, which was about to convene. Born in South Carolina, Drayton had been educated in England (Westminster School; Balliol, Oxford; and the Inns of Court). At the time of his 1774 letter, he was serving as one of the King's judges in South Carolina and as a member of the colony's Privy Council. Yet he took up his pen to defend American rights, and his "Freeman" letter is notable as a carefully reasoned legal and constitutional statement of the American case as it had been honed by a decade and more of reflection and argumentation.

The question, as Drayton saw it, was not simply one of taxation, rather it was whether Great Britain had a constitutional right to exercise despotic power over America. Drayton cited the recent Acts of Parliament interfering with American rights of representative government, acts which in effect left it "in the power of the Crown, whether or not, or in what degree, such subjects shall enjoy the benefit of Magna Charta and the Common Law, under a Crown, which is itself limited and controled by Magna Charta and the Common Law!" [28]

Step by step, Drayton analyzed the constitutional bases of American rights, beginning with the claim that "Americans being descended from the same ancestors with the people of England, and owing fealty to the same Crown, are therefore equally with them, entitled to the common law of England formed by their common ancestors. . . ." Accordingly Americans were entitled to all the benefits and rights specified in Magna Carta, the Petition of Right, the Bill of Rights, and the Act of Settlement, all of which, Drayton reasoned, were no more than declaratory of the fundamental laws of England. Indeed, so basic to Drayton's argument were the "ancient and unalienable rights and liberties" of Magna Carta, recognized

[28] "A Letter from 'Freeman' of South Carolina to the Deputies of North America, Assembled in the High Court of Congress at Philadelphia," in R. W. Gibbes, ed., *Documentary History of the American Revolution* (New York, 1855), II, 11, at pp. 14–16.

anew by the seventeenth-century documents, that he thought this source of American freedoms "infinitely more important" than the colonial charters from the Crown.[29]

To recognize the rights of an Englishman was to reject absolutism, either in Britain or America. In Britain, Drayton argued, Parliament could not "annihilate or constitute a sovereign to Magna Charta. The great Coke has said, 'Magna Charta is such a fellow that he will have no sovereign.'" If Parliament could not make the Crown absolute in England, it could not do so in America. Drayton challenged Blackstone's theory that America was a conquered country and the view that therefore the King could make such laws there as he pleased. Drayton could not believe that the Crown could "legally acquire a power over subjects of English blood, destructive of those rights which are peculiar to the blood—rights evidenced by Magna Charta, and defended by the fundamental laws of England."[30]

In the course of his "Letter," Drayton listed those rights which he conceived to be among those specific immunities comprised among the "liberties of Englishmen." This list is significant because it reflects the way in which American notions of what rights should be taken to be fundamental had expanded by the time of the Revolution. It is, indeed, one of the characterstics of Anglo-American constitutionalism that each generation restates for itself the basic tenets of its fundamental law. Just as Magna Carta had grown and developed between 1215 and the Glorious Revolution, so American views of the "rights of Englishmen" had become more comprehensive by 1774. This is so partly because Americans typically claimed the benefit, not only of preemigration statutes like Magna Carta, but also of later enactments such as the Bill of Rights and the Act of Settlement.

Thus Drayton's list of rights included, along with the more ancient claims traced to Magna Carta such as Americans' right to trial by jury and right to tax themselves, newer claims such as the right to an independent judiciary and the illegality of general search warrants or writs of assistance.[31] Since the Ameri-

[29] *Ibid.*, pp. 16–27.   [30] *Ibid.*, pp. 23–24.   [31] *Ibid.*, p. 17.

can state and federal constitutions drafted after the Revolution included both the rights claimed from Magna Carta and the rights conceived in later centuries, Drayton's letter may be viewed as one of the bridges between colonial statements of the "rights of Englishmen" and the eventual statement, in American constitutions, of the rights of Americans.

Drayton's fellow judges felt themselves to have been vilified by the "Letter," which they said must have been written by Drayton, and the Chief Justice and another Justice of the South Carolina Court of Common Pleas laid before the Lieutenant Governor and Council a remonstrance in which they questioned Drayton's fitness to remain on the bench. In his defense, Drayton prepared a carefully documented memorandum of law in which he conceived that, before the question of his removal from office could be reached, there must first be considered two questions, whether the "Letter" was a libel and whether he was the author. Drayton took the position that the Lieutenant Governor could not lawfully be the judge of these two questions, a proposition which Drayton supported "from the authority of the 29th Chapter of Magna Charta." Drayton quoted that chapter, and Coke's commentaries on it, and concluded that the facts in question should be found by a jury according to the "law of the land." And he appealed to the Lieutenant Governor's respect for the laws of England: "I trust your Honor has too much learning, too much virtue, too great veneration for the sovereign laws of your country, to be induced to violate *the great charter of our liberties.*" [32]

Drayton's learning could not prevent action being taken against him, and he was removed both from the bench and from the Council. In the ensuing months he emerged as one of the leaders of the Revolution in South Carolina.[33] He carried the colonists' story even to the Cherokee Indians, whose headmen and warriors he addressed in 1775. The purpose of his talk, he told the tribesmen, was to explain "the causes of the

---

[32] *Ibid.*, pp. 39–40, 69–70.

[33] Drayton's sacrifice of position for his beliefs has an interesting family sequel in the fact that Percival Drayton and Thomas Fenwick Drayton, sons of a cousin of William Henry Drayton, served on opposite sides in the War between the States.

unhappy quarrel between a part of the people in Great Britain, and your brothers the white people living in America," as well as to tell them "why our people have put on their Shot pouches, and hold their Rifles in their hands." [34]

"Before our forefathers left England," Drayton told the Cherokees, "they made an agreement with the Great King; that when they came to America, they and their children after them, should then continue to have and enjoy the same rights and privileges, that the people of England, who you know were their own brothers, did actually enjoy." Because of this agreement the white people in America believed that "the money they have in their pockets is their own." Yet notwithstanding the King's promise, the English were making laws for America and taking the American colonists' money without their consent. Drayton told the Indians of the tax on tea and of other English laws and asked, "Friends and Brother Warriors, —is it not now as plain as the sight at the end of your rifles, that these laws and proceedings are like so many hatchets, chopping our agreement to pieces?" If the English would use their own flesh and blood this way, what treatment, Drayton asked, might the red man expect? [35]

What the Cherokees heard from William Henry Drayton, and what the Continental Congress was debating in 1774, was to be heard even from American pulpits. William Gordon, the pastor of the Third Church in Roxbury, Massachusetts, delivered a sermon in 1774 in which he admitted that a sermon was normally the place to speak of "sin and Satan" but that (like many a modern preacher) he believed that there were occasions when a sermon "may treat of politics." Accordingly, he attacked the British Parliament for taking a position which, unless resisted, would reduce the colonists to a state of slavery. "If the British Legislature is the constitution, or superior to the constitution, Magna Charta, the Bill of Rights, and the Protes-

[34] John Drayton, *Memoirs of the American Revolution . . . as Relating to the State of South Carolina* (Charleston, 1821) , I, 419.
[35] *Ibid.*, I, 420–22. Fuller extracts from Drayton's talk are reprinted as Appendix I, *infra*.

tant Succession, these boasts of Britons are toys to please the vulgar, and not solid securities." [36]

One of the "King's friends" denounced Gordon's sermon as "daring and treasonable . . . audacious and wicked" and concluded, "I must heartily wish, for the peace of America, that he and many others of his profession would confine themselves to gospel truths." [37] But colonial men of the cloth would not keep quiet, no more than would their fellow Americans. Samuel Langdon, president of Harvard College, preached a sermon in 1775 in which he lamented the decline of the British Constitution: "We have lived to see the time when British liberty is just ready to expire, —when that constitution of government which has so long been the glory and strength of the English nation is deeply undermined and ready to tumble into ruins. . . ." And Langdon raised the question of what should be done if the existing government was dissolved. By the law of nature any body of people lacking government could form a civil society. Magna Carta pointed the way: "Thanks be to God that he has given us, as men, natural rights, independent on all human laws whatever, and that these rights are recognized by the grand charter of British liberties." [38]

To Independence

As the authority of the British Government and its officials in the colonies withered in 1775 and 1776, Langdon's advice proved prophetic. The rising spirit of resistance was reflected in an address delivered by James Wilson to a Pennsylvania convention assembled in Philadelphia in January 1775. Resistance, he said, was inspired by Magna Carta. Wilson could not conceal his "emotions of pleasure" when he observed that the objections urged against the colonists' actions would also have

[36] "A Discourse Preached December 15th, 1774," in John Wingate Thornton, *The Pulpit of the American Revolution* (Boston, 1860) , p. 187, at pp, 197, 201.
[37] *Ibid.*, p. 196.
[38] "A Sermon Preached before the Honorable Congress of the Colony of the Massachusetts-Bay in New-England," in *ibid.*, p. 227, at pp. 233–34, 250.

to be raised against "the convention of the barons at Running Meade, where the tyranny of John was checked, and magna charta was signed. . . ." Wilson submitted a resolution declaring that the Acts of Parliament altering the Charter of Massachusetts Bay, closing its port, and quartering soldiers on the populace were "unconstitutional and void" and "that all force employed to carry such unjust and illegal attempts into execution is force without authority: that it is the right of British subjects to resist such force: that this right is founded both upon the letter and the spirit of the British constitution." [39]

As the breach widened, Thomas Paine, in his essay *Common Sense* published in January 1776, voiced his doubts about the "so much boasted constitution of England." It was, he said, a noble advance in the "dark and slavish times" when it had its origin, but Paine thought it now to be "imperfect, subject to convulsions, and incapable of producing what it seems to promise." Therefore Paine thought it time to call a "Continental Conference" for the framing of a "Continental Charter, or Charter of the United Colonies (answering to what is called the Magna Charta of England)." It is interesting that one so critical of the British Constitution should nevertheless, in seeking a metaphor, suggest that an American constitution should take the form of a "Magna Charta." [40]

Americans were indeed moving closer to providing their own governments. In May 1776 the Continental Congress resolved that it be recommended to the respective assemblies and conventions of the several colonies that, where adequate governments were lacking, they create such governments as, in their opinions, should "best conduce to the happiness and safety of their constituents in particular, and America in general." [41] It was also proposed that the Congress adopt a resolution calling for the total suppression of "every kind of authority" under the British Crown. John Adams recorded James Wilson as observing that "in Magna Charta, there is a Clause, which authorises

[39] *Selected Political Essays of James Wilson,* ed. Randolph G. Adams (New York, 1930), pp. 91, 93.

[40] *Writings of Thomas Paine,* ed. Moncure Daniel Conway (New York, 1894–96), I, 72, 98.

[41] *Journals of the Continental Congress,* IV, 342.

the People to seize the K[ing]'s Castles, and opposes his Arms when he exceeds his duty." Wilson predicted that if the resolution passed, "there will be an immediate Dissolution of every Kind of Authority" [42]—an accurate prediction, for one result of the measures of the Congress was the destruction of the proprietary government in Pennsylvania and the formation of a new government there.

The preamble to the Congress' resolution, agreed to on May 15, 1776, in calling for the suppression of British authority in America, gave as its reasons the Crown's having, through the recent Acts of Parliament, "excluded the inhabitants of these United Colonies from the protection of his crown" and having given no answer to the colonies' petitions for the redress of grievances.[43] The way was laid for the declaration, on July 4, 1776, of a bill of particulars against George III: interference with legislatures and the administration of justice in the colonies, taxation without consent, denial of the right to trial by jury, abolition of charters, suppression of "the free system of English laws," and other counts.

After years of colonial petitions and resolutions to King and Parliament, of thorough airing of colonial grievances, the Declaration of Independence could with considerable justice say that the colonies had not "been wanting in attentions to our British brethren. We have warned them, from time to time, of attempts by their legislature to extend an unwarrantable jurisdiction over us. We have reminded them of the circumstances of our emigration and settlement here. We have appealed to their native justice and magnanimity, and we have conjured them by the ties of our common kindred to disavow these usurpations. . . ." [44] But a deaf ear had been turned. Constitutional argument having run its course, the decision was now given into the hands of the gods of war.

[42] *Adams Diary and Autobiography,* II, 240.
[43] *Journals of the Continental Congress,* IV, 357–58.
[44] For the text of the Declaration of Independence, see Richard L. Perry, ed., *Sources of Our Liberties* (Chicago, 1959) , pp. 319–22.

Chapter X

The Colonists' Case

The Rights of Englishmen

or the Rights of Man?

I N 1789 David Ramsay published in Philadelphia his *History of the American Revolution*. Though there have been interpretations of the Revolution by later historians with access to more documents and resources, Ramsay's *History* has stood the test of time rather well. In fact, Page Smith has said of Ramsay, "The generosity of mind and spirit which mark his pages, his critical sense, his balanced judgment and compassion" are such as to entitle Ramsay to a place in the "front rank of American historians." Of Ramsay's work, Smith adds, his "history is a remarkable achievement. In his analysis and interpretation of the events culminating in the Revolution he showed unusual insight and a keen sense of proportion." [1]

Of the crisis between the American colonies and the mother country, especially the phase around 1774, Ramsay pointed to the constitutional debate as "the very hinge of the controversy. The absolute unlimited supremacy of the British parliament, both in legislation and taxation, was contended for on one side; while on the other, no farther authority was conceded than

---

[1] Page Smith, "David Ramsay and the Causes of the American Revolution," 17 *Wm. & Mary Qtly.* (3d ser.) 51, 77, 52 (1960). Richard B. Morris similarly makes a favorable judgment of Ramsay's history. *The American Revolution Reconsidered* (New York, 1967), p. 23.

such a limited legislation, with regard to external commerce, as would combine the interest of the whole empire." [2]

Ramsay states the problem simply and well. The British Government, on the one side, and the colonial spokesmen, on the other, had taken up positions which, once aired and hardened, proved irreconcilable. They had in fact laid bare a conceptual problem of the boundary between the supremacy of Parliament and the independence of the colonies, a border which was best left a mystery and which, once explored, could lead only to a clash.

What was the plane of argument? In an earlier age, it might have been theological, with appeals to the doctrines of St. Thomas Aquinas or the Church Fathers. In a later age, it might have an appeal to class and economic instincts, invoking Marx and Engels, or to racial pride, as in some of the new nations of Africa. The debate of the 1760's and 1770's, of course, took shapes congenial to the thinking of that age. [3]

If one followed Locke, he might tend to use the language of natural rights. If Coke, the language of the law. Either level of discourse would have been familiar to Englishmen and colonists alike at that time. Which did the colonists use? Ramsay, in his *History,* observed that the colonists, from their first settlement in America, were "devoted to liberty, on English ideas, and English principles." But Ramsay seemed to think that the colonists' arguments were essentially based on natural law and natural rights rather than on the British Constitution. By his view, the colonists looked, not to Magna Carta, but to God:

Many of them had never heard of Magna Charta, and those who knew the circumstances of the remarkable period of English history when that was obtained, did not rest their claims to liberty and property on the transactions of that important day. They looked up to Heaven as the source of their rights, and claimed, not from the promises of Kings but, from the parent of the universe. [4]

[2] David Ramsay, *History of the American Revolution* (Philadelphia, 1789), I, 136.

[3] For a brilliant exposition of the character of colonial arguments before the Revolution, see Bernard Bailyn, *The Ideological Origins of the American Revolution* (Cambridge, Mass., 1967).

[4] Ramsay, *History of the American Revolution,* I, 31.

If Ramsay is right, then Magna Carta would seem to play a secondary part in the arguments which preceded the Revolution, at least a less important role than many would have thought.

There is unquestionably ample material which one could draw on to support a thesis that the colonists really looked to Providence, not to the British Constitution, as the origin of their rights, and that the nub of the argument, therefore, was natural rights, not the rights of Englishmen. For example, John Dickinson, in his *Address to the Committee of Correspondence in Barbados* (1766), said that the Americans claimed their rights

from a higher source—from the King of kings, and Lord of all the earth. They are not annexed to us by parchments and seals. They are created in us by the decrees of Providence, which establish the laws of our nature. They are born with us; exist with us; and cannot be taken from us by any human power, without taking our lives. In short, they are founded on the immutable maxims of reason and justice.[5]

Similarly, the idea of natural rights was the principal basis of Dickinson's arguments in his best-known work, *Letters from a Pennsylvania Farmer,* and in his later *Essay on the Constitutional Power of Great Britain,* in which Dickinson tended to argue from the general principles of government, rather than from specific legal or constitutional precedents.[6]

Some, like Tom Paine, were openly critical of the British Constitution. Paine, in *Common Sense* (1776), mounted a slashing attack on the "so much boasted constitution of England." Said Paine: "That it was noble for the dark and slavish times in which it was erected, is granted. When the world was overrun with tyranny the least remove therefrom was a glorious rescue. But that it is imperfect, subject to convulsions, and incapable of producing what it seems to promise, is easily

---

[5] *Writings of John Dickinson,* ed. Paul L. Ford (Philadelphia, 1895), I, 262.
[6] David L. Jacobson, *John Dickinson and the Revolution in Pennsylvania: 1764-1776* (Berkeley, Calif., 1965), pp. 55, 76.

demonstrated." [7] Paine published these words just a few months before the open break with Great Britain, at a time when Americans were far less apt to be admitting to admiration of things British, but he reflects an attitude held by at least some of the colonists that it was better to have Heaven on their side than to have the British Constitution.

Yet enough has been said about Americans' reliance, from the earliest settlements down through the decade between the Stamp Act and the Revolution, on Magna Carta and the "rights of Englishmen" to make the reader pause before accepting the notion that it was, after all, natural rights, and not constitutional rights, which were at stake.

In fact, the gulf is not so great as it might seem. It is true that the leading colonial figures—in congresses and assemblies, in pamphlets and essays—were often of opposing views on the question of whether the colonists ought to argue from natural rights or from the rights of Magna Carta and the colonial charters. But ultimately, eclecticism prevailed, and the various divergent paths tended to merge.

The debates in the Continental Congress in 1774 over how the colonial case against British policy should be stated offer an example. Richard Henry Lee of Virginia submitted that colonial rights in fact rested on *four* foundations—"on Nature, on the british Constitution, on Charters, and on immemorial Usage." John Jay, delegate from New York, agreed that resort should be had to the law of nature and to the British Constitution to ascertain colonial rights, but James Duane of New York thought the constitutional argument sufficient; he was for "grounding our Rights on the Laws and Constitution of the Country from whence We sprung, and Charters, without recurring to the Law of Nature—because this will be a feeble Support. Charters are Compacts between the Crown and the People and I think on this foundation the Charter Governments stand firm." Joseph Galloway of Pennsylvania agreed: "I have looked for our Rights in the Laws of Nature—but could not

[7] *Writings of Thomas Paine,* ed. Moncure Daniel Conway (New York, 1894), I, 72.

find them in a State of Nature, but always in a State of political Society. I have looked for them in the Constitution of the English Government, and there found them. We may draw them from this Soursce securely." [8]

The committee appointed by the Congress to work out a statement of the colonists' rights took the eclectic course. Samuel Ward noted in his diary that, on October 9, he met with the committee and that they "agreed to found our rights upon the laws of Nature, the principles of the English Constitution, and charters and compacts. . . ." [9]

The debate between those who looked to the laws of nature and those who looked to the laws of England, and the dissent of some Americans from the proposition that it was Magna Carta and the British Constitution which formed the basis of their liberties, had a counterpart in some of the English tracts of the time. John Cartwright, an Englishman, wrote *American Independence, the Interest and Glory of Great Britain,* first published in 1774, noting in his preface that even if he derived no other satisfaction from writing his essay it would be enough were his American kindred to say, "There was one Englishman an advocate for our cause." Cartwright referred to a tract entitled *A Letter from a Merchant in London to his Nephew in America,* which said, "Magna Charta is the great foundation of English liberties, and the basis of the English constitution." This, said Cartwright,

I must positively deny. It is indeed a glorious member of the superstructure, but of itself would never have existed, had not the constitution already had a basis, and a firm one too. . . . I have elsewhere observed, that the original and only real foundations of liberty were, by the Almighty architect, laid together with the foundations of the world, when this right was ingrafted into the nature of man at his creation; and therefore it cannot be held, after the manner of an external property or possession, by charters and titles of human fabrick. [10]

[8] *Adams Diary and Autobiography,* II, 128–30. With the outbreak of war Galloway became a Loyalist and died an exile in England. *DAB.*

[9] *Adams Diary and Autobiography,* II, 131, note.

[10] *American Independence, the Interest and Glory of Great Britain* (Philadelphia, 1776), pp. 76–77.

The civil, like the religious, constitution, submitted Cartwright, is founded on the "word of God." As for Magna Carta —"notoriously known to have been extorted by the sword, and formed and ratified in the heat of a hostile contention"—and other statutes, they were less important than the *spirit* of a constitution, which must be *"internal justice and inherent liberty."* [11]

The divergent colonial approaches to a theoretical basis for their rights reflected in good part the different backgrounds and assumptions of leaders from New England and from the southern colonies. In the southern and middle colonies were to be found lawyers whose legal training, frequently received at the Inns of Court, was far superior to that enjoyed by most New England lawyers. The traditions of the common law and a profound respect for the orderly processes of the British Constitution characterized those bars—for example, in South Carolina, Virginia, and Maryland—which had a significant representation of members of the Inns. Their arguments against the policies and acts of the British Government were likely to take channels in which their understanding of the law could be best used.

The revolutionary leaders of New England tended more to abstractions and theory than to legal precedents. They were better philosophers than they were lawyers. Accordingly, the law they looked to was as likely to be natural law as it was to be the statute or common law of England. This attitude of mind was shared by at least one southerner, Thomas Jefferson, who is remembered, and spoke at the time, more as theorist and philosopher than as lawyer. As Vernon Parrington has observed, Jefferson "wrote more convincingly when defending the principles of Locke than in expounding Coke." [12]

A prime example of Jefferson's preference for natural law over the British Constitution as the basis for the colonists' case is found in the Resolutions of the Freeholders of Albemarle County. These were passed in July 1774, at a time when free-

[11] *Ibid.*, p. 77.
[12] *Main Currents in American Thought* (New York, 1930), I, 222. Parrington says the same thing of John Adams, a view of Adams which I do not share. See pp. 156–64, *supra.*

holders of the various counties of Virginia were electing and instructing delegates to a new Assembly scheduled to meet in August (Governor Dunmore having dissolved the previous Assembly in May). Most of the county resolutions made explicit use of constitutional arguments. The Fairfax County Resolutions (already noted) claimed the rights of Englishmen and sought the restoration of America's "constitutional rights and liberties." [13] York County's Resolutions carefully blended the "first principles of the *British* Constitution" with the "eternal and immutable laws of Nature's God." [14] But Jefferson's resolutions for the freeholders of Albemarle dispensed with the British Constitution altogether and instead relied on a kind of social contract theory. Whereas the Fairfax Resolutions had assumed a constitutional connection with the mother country and claimed, as part of that relation, the rights of Englishmen, the Albemarle Resolutions allowed of no dependence on Great Britain or its Constitution:

Resolved, that the inhabitants of the several states of British America are subject to the laws which they adopted at their first settlement, and to such others as have been since made by their respective legislatures, duly constituted and appointed with their own consent; that no other legislature whatever may rightfully exercise authority over them, and that these privileges they hold as the common rights of mankind, confirmed by the political constitutions they have respectively assumed, and also by several charters of compact from the crown.[15]

A more thoroughly Lockean statement could hardly be imagined.

Jefferson's Albemarle Resolutions were, however, atypical. Elsewhere in resolutions and other statements of colonial views,

---

[13] *American Archives* (4th ser.) , I, 597–602.   [14] *Ibid.,* I, 595–97.

[15] *Papers of Thomas Jefferson*, ed. Julian P. Boyd (Princeton, N.J., 1950——) , I, 117. In 1776 the Albemarle County Instructions concerning the Virginia Constitution called the Virginia General Assembly's attention to "all the remains of despotism and barbarism, still existing in the English Constitution (piercing thorns, from which hope to be soon delivered!) "—the thorns including entails, prerogatives, and the established Church. *Ibid.,* VI, 288.

On Jefferson's ideas of natural rights, see Caleb Perry Patterson, *The Constitutional Principles of Thomas Jefferson* (Austin, Texas, 1953) , pp. 45–54. Patterson would resolve the respective claims of natural law and the British Constitutional tradition as shaping forces in American constitutionalism in favor of the preeminence of natural law. *Ibid.,* p. 49.

constitutional and natural law arguments appear together. Usually the reader finds that the two main streams of argument merge. Sometimes the merger is obscure. For example, Christopher Gadsden, one of the representatives of South Carolina at the Stamp Act Congress, wrote Charles Garth, the colony's agent in London, that he had "ever been of opinion, that we should all endeavor to stand upon the broad and common ground of those natural and inherent rights that we all feel and know, as men and as descendants of Englishmen . . . ." Here there is a subtle identification of natural rights, natural because men are men, and rights which spring from English blood. That Gadsden is linking the two sources of rights, natural law and the British Constitution, is evident from his further remark that the colonies should "have a constant eye upon the attacks that may be made upon the essential part of the British Constitution" and to take alarm at an invasion of constitutional rights in any colony, lest presently it be made a precedent for the rest.[16]

Other times the merger of natural rights and constitutional arguments is more explicit. A good example is Alexander Hamilton's first attempt at pamphleteering, *A Full Vindication of the Measures of the Congress,* written in 1774 when Hamilton was not yet twenty and published as an answer to Samuel Seabury's *Free Thoughts.* Hamilton begins with a position drawn from natural law:

That Americans are intitled to freedom, is incontestible upon every rational principle. All men have one common original: they participate in one common nature, and consequently have one common right. No reason can be assigned why one man should exercise any power, or pre eminence over his fellow creatures more than another; unless they have voluntarily vested him with it. Since then, Americans have not by an act of their's impowered the British Parliament to make laws for them, it follows they can have no just authority to do it.[17]

To this, Hamilton added the authority of the British Constitution:

[16] R. W. Gibbes, *Documentary History of the American Revolution* (New York, 1855), II, 8–9.

[17] *A Full Vindication of the Measures of the Congress* (New York, 1774), p. 5.

Besides the clear voice of natural justice in this respect, the fundamental principles of the English constitution are in our favour. It has been repeatedly demonstrated, that the idea of legislation, or taxation, when the subject is not represented, is inconsistent with *that*.[18]

And as a third, and separate, ground of colonial rights Hamilton looked to the colonies' own charters:

Nor is this all, our charters, the express conditions on which our progenitors relinquished their native countries, and came to settle in this, preclude every claim of ruling and taxing us without our assent.[19]

By way of emphasis, Hamilton recapitulated the three elements, urging that "the pretensions of Parliament are contradictory to the law of nature, subversive of the British constitution, and destructive of the faith of the most solemn compacts." [20]

There were good reasons why constitutional argument and philosophical speculation tended to merge. The Englishman who, like Coke, was reflecting on the dimensions of Magna Carta and the common law, and the Englishman who, like Locke, was writing a philosophy of government, were concerned with the same problem: how arbitrary power might be limited so that individual rights might be secured. The tendency of power to expand, and the consequent need to defend liberty, would have been considered by the Englishmen of the time as one of the leitmotivs of English history. Whether they spoke the language of the lawyer, then, or that of the philosopher, they had the same end in view.

The American colonist, conditioned as he was to the Englishman's way of looking at law and society, was, if anything, even more concerned with the uses and abuses of power. Natural rights were to the colonist a restraint on power. The British Constitution was a restraint. John Adams called that constitution "the most stupendous fabric of human invention"; [21] like many American colonists, he took that view because he looked

---

[18] *Ibid.*   [19] *Ibid.*   [20] *Ibid.*
[21] *A Defence of the Constitutions of Government of the United States* (London, 1794), I, 70.

upon the British Government as a "mixed" government. By that theory, government by King, Lords, and Commons represented a blending of the three classical forms of government—monarchy, aristocracy, and democracy. It was to this tripartite mixture that Americans like Adams and theorists like Montesquieu attributed the peculiar virtues of the English system.[22]

If a corollary of natural rights thinking was that there were limits to government and to the arbitrary exercise of power by those who governed, then a constitution which checked and limited power was a natural vehicle for the expression of such natural rights. Thus the American colonists, like many Englishmen, came frequently to identify natural rights and the rights of Englishmen. Charters and the common law came to be viewed as a distillation of inherent rights, concrete statements in legal form of rights which were ordained by God's law or which sprang from the nature of man. By this view, Magna Carta itself was "in substance but a constrained Declaration, or proclamation and promulgation in the name of King, Lords, and Commons of the sense the latter had of their original, inherent, indefeazible, natural Rights. . . ."[23]

Clinton Rossiter has noted the "indiscriminate appeal" by the colonists to every kind of higher law: Magna Carta, colonial charters, common law, the law of God and Nature. And he wonders whether it would have aided the colonial cause to have selected the defense on which they proposed to rest their chief reliance. Implying that it would not have been to their advantage to make such a choice, Rossiter suggests that "at least some of the confusion in colonial arguments must have been calculated to confuse."[24]

Rossiter's point has value, but it requires qualification. Occasionality can have its uses, as any lawyer knows who has in the

[22] See R. W. K. Hinton, "English Constitutional Theories from Sir John Fortescue to Sir John Eliot," and Corinne Comstock Weston, "The Theory of Mixed Monarchy Under Charles I and After," 75 *English Historical Review* 410, 426 (1960).

[23] Samuel Adams, *The Rights of the Colonists*, in *Writings of Samuel Adams*, ed. H. A. Cushing (New York, 1904), II, 355.

[24] Clinton Rossiter, *The Political Thought of the American Revolution* (New York, 1963), pp. 35–36.

same brief offered a court a number of alternative ways—a constitutional claim, a point of statutory construction, an equitable argument—to decide a case his way. And no doubt the colonists wanted to pull all the stops, the better to enjoy the moral advantage which might come from any one of the possible grounds of argument available to them. But whatever they thought of natural law, when it came time for the colonists to "brief" their own case, in the form of memorials and resolutions, their ultimate reliance, certainly down through 1774, was on the ancient rights of Englishmen in the constitutional sense, rather than on the rights of man as given by God or found in nature. Some judges may care everything for abstract notions of justice and nothing for constitutions and statutes, but most will want to be pointed to the language of positive legal instruments (even if typically they will want to be assured by counsel that if they decide his way on the law justice will in fact be done). Similarly, it would be surprising if the American colonists, in selling their case to the King or to Parliament, had preferred the language of natural rights to that of the traditional guarantees of the British Constitution. And in general they did not.

There are some resolutions of colonial assemblies in which appeals to natural law seem to be even more basic to the pattern of the argument than do appeals to constitutional rights. Perhaps the best illustration is the set of resolutions against the Stamp Act passed by the Massachusetts House of Representatives in October 1765. They were written by Samuel Adams and, reflecting that leader's personality, depart somewhat from the pattern of other resolutions against the Stamp Act.

From beginning to end, the Massachusetts resolutions make natural law the substructure and the British Constitution the superstructure (rather like economics and law in Marx). The first resolution proclaims that there are "certain essential rights of the British Constitution of government, which are founded in the law of God and nature, and are the common rights of mankind." The ensuing resolutions follow a similar pattern. The colonists enjoy "essential rights in common with all men"; "no law of society can, consistent with the law of God and nature, divest them of those rights"; the right, protected by the British Constitution, to be represented in the body which levies taxes is founded on the "original principle" that "no man can justly take the property of another without his consent"; "reason and common sense" and "common justice," as much as the colonial charters, entitle the colonists to the liberties enjoyed by Englishmen in England.[25]

But the Massachusetts resolutions are not, in their emphasis on natural rights as the origin of constitutional rights, typical of the colonial resolutions passed in 1765. The Virginia resolutions, which were the forerunner of the other colonies' resolves, were a straightforward constitutional argument: that the first settlers brought with them and transmitted to their posterity all the liberties of Englishmen, that by two royal charters the colonists were entitled to "all Liberties, Privileges, and Immunities" they would have enjoyed in England, that the right of self-taxation was an essential feature of the "ancient Constitution," and that these rights have been "constantly recognized by the Kings and People of *Great Britain.*"[26]

Although the resolutions of the other colonies were somewhat longer than those of Virginia, the Virginia pattern, with variations in language, prevailed. Occasionally a resolution made explicit reference to natural law—e.g., Pennsylvania's evocation of the "natural Rights of Mankind"—but the body of the argument was that of nailing colonial rights to the kinds of authorities that would be most telling to an English reader: Magna Carta, the British Constitution, royal charters to the colonies, customs of the realm.[27]

The Declaration and Resolves of the Continental Congress in 1774 are another case in point. Occasionally the language hints—but no more than hints—at natural rights. The first resolution, for example, speaks of the colonists' right to "life, liberty, & property," and says that they have "never ceded to any sovereign power whatever, a right to dispose of either

[25] *Writings of Samuel Adams*, I, 23–25.

[26] *Journal of the Burgesses*, p. 360. The full text of the Virginia resolutions is set out in Appendix F, *infra*.

[27] For the texts of the various colonies' resolutions, see Morgan, *Prologue to Revolution*, pp. 50–62.

without their consent." Here is implied a Lockean contract theory, a right to decide at the outset whether or not to cede given powers to a sovereign, but it is certainly inexplicit. Similarly, in resolution 4, natural rights are implied when the right to be represented in the legislative councils is said to be, not only a right of Englishmen, but also a right "of all free government." [28]

If natural rights are only hinted at, the argument from charters, the British Constitution, and the rights of Englishmen is explicitly and fully spelled out. The second resolution declares that the original emigrants to the colonies were entitled to "all the rights, liberties, and immunities of free and natural-born subjects, within the realm of England"—virtually word for word the language of the original colonial charters. In resolution 5, the colonists claimed the benefits of "the common law of England, and more especially the great and inestimable privilege of being tried by their peers of the vicinage, according to the course of that law"—an obvious paraphrase of the language of Magna Carta. In the next resolution the Congress claimed the benefit of "such of the English statutes as existed at the time of their colonization" and which were applicable to colonial conditions. In resolution 7, the colonies held themselves to be entitled to "all the immunities and privileges granted & confirmed to them by royal charters." The essentially legal character of the Declaration and Resolves was further underscored by the inclusion, as a kind of bill of particulars, of a list of Acts of Parliament held to violate the rights of the colonists.[29]

This is a legal document, not a philosophical tract. The arguments are constitutional, the very language drawn, virtually verbatim, from constitutional documents—Magna Carta, other English statutes, the colonial charters. Right down to the summer of 1776, the colonists were insisting that their resistance was a constitutional right. They often drew a distinction (one that, unfortunately for the colonial position, had vanished with the Glorious Revolution) between the King and Parliament. When the Continental Congress drafted its petition to the King in October 1774, they implored the King's protection

[28] *Journals of the Continental Congress,* I, 67, 68.　　[29] *Ibid.,* I, 68–73.

against unconstitutional acts by Parliament but were careful to assure the monarch that they did not seek any "diminution of the prerogative" of the Crown. "Your royal authority over us," they continued, "and our connexion with Great-Britain, we shall always carefully and zealously endeavour to support and maintain." [30]

Edmund Burke appreciated the nature of the colonial case. In his "Speech on Conciliation with America" in 1775, he traced the colonists' love of liberty to the fact that they were descendants of Englishmen. "They are therefore not only devoted to liberty, but to liberty according to English ideas, and on English principles. Abstract liberty, like other mere abstractions, is not to be found. Liberty inheres in some sensible object. . . ." [31]

Burke was speaking for that habit, which we often associate with the seventeenth- and eighteenth-century Englishman, of looking for the concrete, rather than the abstract. To see liberty in the form of the British Constitution, rather than in some unfamiliar form, would have been natural to the times. It was natural, too, that, whatever might be their thoughts about natural rights, the colonists should in their formal documents state their case in the specifics of the British Constitution— above all, in Magna Carta and their own charters.

An appeal to charter rights, a cry that an ancient and fundamental law had been violated—these were things which an Englishman could understand. Englishmen, after all, had seen the repeated confirmation of their fundamental law—Magna Carta was confirmed by Parliament over forty times—and recalled all too well the struggles against the Stuart kings for the rights of Englishmen. English cities, like American colonies, had charters, which more than once had themselves been threatened (London temporarily lost its charter for its support of Simon de Montfort). Basing the colonial case squarely on the British Constitution, especially on the Great Charter, carried an historical association and force which appeals to ab-

[30] *Ibid.*, I, 119. See C. H. McIlwain, *The American Revolution: A Constitutional Interpretation* (New York, 1923), pp. 1–5.

[31] *Speech on Conciliation with America*, ed. Charles R. Morris (New York, 1945), pp. 25–26.

stractions would not. It gave the colonists the opportunity to suggest, as did Arthur Lee, a Virginian serving as a colonial agent in London, that what happened to the liberties of Americans could be repeated in England: "May the liberties of Englishmen be immortal—but may Englishmen ever remember, that the same arbitrary spirit which prompts an invasion of the constitution in America, will not long leave that of England unattacked. . . ." [32]

It is fair to say that by the time of the American Revolution the language and values of the law were no longer simply the heritage of lawyers. Debate over British policies and colonial responses could be framed in legal terms, not simply because many colonial leaders were lawyers, but more fundamentally because the best principles of English constitutionalism, as adapted to the colonies, were now part of the structure of American society. As a historian of the bar has commented, from the time of the Revolution on, "all the major issues of American political life would be cast in legal language and, accordingly, would receive their final shape from lawyers rather than from philosophers or political scientists." [33]

[32] *An Appeal to the Justice and Interests of the People of Great Britain* (London, 1774), pp. 62–63.
[33] Chroust, *Legal Profession*, I, 54.

Chapter XI

The State Constitutions

Old Wine in New Bottles

THERE have been many revolutions, and many constitutions, in the history of the modern world. If one takes the French or Russian Revolution as a prototype, a revolution aims at overthrowing an old way of doing things and replacing it with something new. The new constitution is expected to mirror the expectations of the revolution and make the new order a lasting one, safe from counterrevolution, or foreign intervention, or whatever threat the makers of the revolution may foresee. But the American Revolution is a kind of oddity among revolutions. It was fought to preserve old values—indeed, to preserve values which had sprung from the very country rebelled against, but which that country had somehow forgotten.

To make the War for Independence a victory for liberty—that was the task of the constitution-makers. Law and order there must be; a frame of government there must be. But a bill of rights: that came first. Law and order the Americans could have in abundance from the British Government—rather too much law and order for the Sons of Liberty. It was the "rights of Englishmen" for which the Americans had taken up arms, and now the first problem was to set those rights into the mortar of the new American state governments.

Jefferson saw the dimensions of the problem. On May 15, 1776, the Virginia Convention adopted a resolution calling for independence and appointed a committee to draft a plan of government. Writing to Thomas Nelson the same month, Jefferson said that the making of a new state constitution "is the whole object of the present controversy; for should a bad government be instituted for us in future it had been as well to have accepted at first the bad one offered to us from beyond the water without the risk and expence of contest." [1] Jefferson also saw the most likely solution. As he put it in a letter written some years later, "we have employed some of the best materials of the British constitution in the construction of our own government. . . ." [2] Jefferson was correct. While the American political genius was to make enormous original contributions to the new state and federal constitutions written from 1776 onward, the drafters began nevertheless with what they had known and treasured from the British Constitution.

It was natural that the newly independent American states should have written constitutions. Though Great Britain did not then have, and does not today have, a written constitution in the usual sense, it is not paradoxical that the Americans, even while looking to the British Constitution for much of their inspiration, sought to rest their new governments on written documents within the four corners of which all the basic provisions were set out. In reducing the basis of government to a written instrument, the Americans were simply following in this case a different British example: that of the colonial charters, to which as colonists the Americans had so often (for example, in 1765 and 1774) pointed as security for their rights and under which they had lived for six generations.

[1] *Papers of Thomas Jefferson*, ed. Julian P. Boyd (Princeton, N.J., 1950——), I, 292.
[2] Letter to John Norvell, June 14, 1807, in *Writings of Thomas Jefferson*, ed. Paul Leicester Ford (New York, 1892–99), IX, 72. Jefferson, who was not at the convention which drafted Virginia's 1776 constitution, later complained that the constitution was only an ordinance, lacking the assured status of fundamental law. "Notes on the State of Virginia" (1785), in *ibid.*, III, 225–29. In practice the 1776 constitution was treated as fundamental law. *Papers of Thomas Jefferson*, ed. Boyd, VI, 279.

The Contribution of George Mason

Tʜᴇ trail was blazed by the Constitution of Virginia of 1776. Its Declaration of Rights, drafted by George Mason, was adopted by the Virginia Convention in June 1776. In the person of Mason we find one of the links between the struggle of Americans as colonists for the "rights of Englishmen" and their incorporation as an independent people of those same rights into their new constitutions. In 1766 Mason had written a letter to the "Committee of Merchants in London," in which he said that the colonists claimed "nothing but the liberties and privileges of Englishmen, in the same degree, as if we had still continued among our brethren in Great Britain; these rights have not been forfeited by any act of ours; we cannot be deprived of them, without our consent, but by violence and injustice; we have received them from our ancestors, and, with God's leave, we will transmit them, unimpaired, to our posterity." [3]

Mason enjoyed considerable opportunity to be schooled in the precedents and traditions of the British Constitution. On the death of his father when Mason was ten years old, Mason was educated by his uncle, John Mercer of Marlborough, who had a large library of over five hundred volumes dealing with law and history. In 1773 Mason was gathering evidence to fortify his claims to lands in Fincastle County, Virginia, and had occasion to study and make extracts from the several Virginia charters. His notes, which still exist, include extracts, along with Mason's remarks, from the charter provisions guaranteeing the settlers the "Liberties, Franchises and Immunities" of Englishmen.[4] Armed with this knowledge of the early charters, Mason the next year wrote the Fairfax County Resolves, which took note of the destruction of "our ancient laws and liberties, and the loss of all that is dear to British subjects

---

[3] Letter of June 6, 1766, in Kate Mason Rowland, *Life of George Mason* (New York, 1892), I, 387.
[4] *Ibid.*, I, 393–414.

and freemen" and resolved to form a militia for Fairfax County ready to defend "the just rights and privileges of our fellow-subjects, our posterity, and ourselves, upon the principles of the English Constitution." [5]

Little did Mason think, when he wrote his letter to London in 1766 and said that the Americans would transmit the liberties of Englishmen "unimpaired, to our posterity," that ten years later, pen in hand, he would do just that. Significantly, the Declaration of Rights in the Virginia Constitution of 1776 preceded the actual constitution or "form of government." The "form of government"—whether that of Virginia or that of the United States—was to be the characteristically American contribution to the art of government. But the bills of rights, starting with Mason's in 1776, were the repository of English values. There were, of course, in such bills of rights values and guarantees which no Englishman of the time could have pointed to in *his* basic law—for example, the statement that government derives from the people and not the rulers and the guarantee of freedom of conscience and religion. But Allan Nevins is close to the mark in saying that the Virginia Declaration of Rights and the other bills of rights which followed it were in good part "restatement[s] of English principles—the principles of Magna Charta, the Petition of Rights, the Commonwealth Parliament, and the Revolution of 1688." [6]

Mason's Declaration of Rights began with a good, healthy dose of natural rights: that all men are by nature created free and independent; that they enjoy certain inherent rights of which, even in a state of society, they cannot divest their posterity, namely, life, liberty, property, and the pursuit of happiness; that all power derives from the people; that when government

[5] *Ibid.,* I, 427–30. George Washington was closely associated with the Fairfax Resolves. Mason carried the resolutions to Mount Vernon the evening before the meeting at which they were adopted and at which Washington presided. Douglas Southall Freeman, *George Washington* (New York, 1948–57), III, 362. It is interesting that Washington, like so many other leaders, resisted British policies on the grounds of both natural rights and the British Constitution. Those policies, he said, were "not only repugnant to natural right, but subversive of the law and constitution of Great Britain itself. . . ." *Ibid.,* III, 371.

[6] *The American States during and after the American Revolution, 1775–1789* (New York, 1924), p. 146.

fails in its purposes a majority of the people have the inalienable right to alter or abolish it.[7] Then came provisions which must have come easily to the pen of Mason, so recently a defender of the rights of Englishmen. From the principle which Englishmen had built from Magna Carta through the Petition of Right and the Bill of Rights came the provision of the Declaration of Rights that the people cannot be taxed without their consent or that of their representatives. The first section of the English Bill of Rights appeared in the declaration that the laws shall not be suspended without the consent of the people's representatives. Standing armies, thought to be a danger to liberty, were warned against in the 1776 document, recalling the prohibition of the 1689 bill against standing armies in peacetime without consent of Parliament.

Procedural rights (always so near to the core of Anglo-American jurisprudence) were guaranteed. Trial by jury, which Coke and Blackstone had traced to Magna Carta, was assured, and the Great Charter's chapter 39 appeared in the requirement that "no man be deprived of his liberty, except by the law of the land, or the judgment of his peers." The tenth section of the English Bill of Rights became, word for word, the ninth section of Mason's Declaration: "That excessive bail ought not to be required, nor excessive fines imposed, nor cruel and unusual punishments inflicted."

John Adams Writes a Constitution

THE story of the adoption by Massachusetts of its first constitution is an equally interesting one.[8] It begins with a resolution of the Continental Congress passed in June 1775, when there was a kind of hiatus in the government of Massachusetts. The Congress, refusing to acknowledge the legality of Parliament's

[7] Thorpe, VII, 3812–14.
[8] For a full account, with documents, see Robert J. Taylor, ed., *Massachusetts, Colony to Commonwealth: Documents on the Formation of Its Constitution, 1775–1780* (Chapel Hill, N.C., 1961). See also Samuel Eliot Morison, "The Struggle over the Adoption of the Constitution of Massachusetts, 1780," in Massachusetts Historical Society, *Proceedings* (3d ser.) 50 (1916–17), 353.

alteration of the Massachusetts Charter, recommended that the people of that colony hold elections to choose a House of Representatives, that the House in turn choose a Council, and that these two bodies should exercise the powers of government until—since in 1775 there was still hope of a reconciliation with Great Britain—"a Governor, of his Majesty's appointment, will consent to govern the colony according to its charter." [9]

This suggestion was well received by moderate leaders in Massachusetts, but a vocal minority in the western part of the State, called the "Constitutionalists," objected that there was no legitimate basis for the government of Massachusetts since the people had not had any say about the kind of government there should be. A General Court was elected in 1775, as suggested by the Continental Congress, and it in turn elected a Council. After independence had been declared, a constitution for Massachusetts was drafted and submitted to the towns in 1778 but met defeat. The Constitutionalists continued to insist that no government could exist without direct action of the people, and to enforce this claim Berkshire County kept its courts closed.

Faced with this discontent, the General Court sent out an investigating committee to hear representatives of the Berkshire towns state their grievances. Pittsfield, in an address to the committee, insisted on the need for a fundamental constitution tracing that principle to its "imperfect" beginnings in Magna Carta:

In all free Governments duly organized there is an essential Distinction to be observed between the fundamental Constitution, & Legislation. The fundamental Constitution is the Basis & ground work of Legislation, & ascertains the Rights, Franchises, Immunities & Liberties of the people; However & how often officers Civil and military shall be elected by the people, & circumscribing and defining the powers of the Rulers, & so affoarding a sacred Barrier against Tyranny & Despotism. This in antient & corrupt Kingdoms when they have woke out of Slavery to some happy dawnings of Liberty, has been called a Bill of

---

[9] *Journals of the Continental Congress*, II, 83–84.

Rights, Magna Charta etc. which must be considered as imperfect Emblems of the Securities of the present grand period.[10]

Arguments like those of Pittsfield apparently had their effect, for in 1779 the General Court issued the call for the election of a state constitutional convention. The convention, meeting in Cambridge in September, put the task in the hands of a three-man committee, James Bowdoin, Samuel Adams, and John Adams, which in turn left the work largely to John Adams. The result was the Massachusetts Constitution of 1780, a document of which Andrew C. McLaughlin said in his inaugural address as president of the American Historical Society in 1914:

If I were called upon to select a single fact or enterprise which more nearly than any other single thing embraced the significance of the American Revolution, I should select—not Saratoga or the French Alliance or even the Declaration of Independence—I should choose the formation of the Massachusetts constitution of 1780, and I should do so because that constitution rested upon the fully developed convention, the greatest institution of government which America has produced, the institution which answered, in itself, the problem of how men could make governments of their own free will. . . .[11]

The Constitution of 1780 drew heavily on English sources.[12] Magna Carta's principle of "law of the land" was connoted by the provision (Article X) that each individual was entitled to be protected in the enjoyment of his "life, liberty, and property, according to standing laws," a phrase rather like the requirement of the Body of Liberties of 1641 that life, liberty, or property should not be proceeded against save by virtue of "some expresse law of the Country."[13] In fact, "law of the land," was twice guaranteed, in the article already quoted and again in Article XII, which was virtually a verbatim restate-

[10] Taylor, ed., *Massachusetts, Colony to Commonwealth: Documents on the Formation of Its Constitution, 1775–1780,* pp. 98–99.

[11] "American History and American Democracy," 20 *Am. Hist. Rev.* 255, 264–65 (1915). Samuel Eliot Morison has expressed his admiration for the "high degree of political wisdom possessed by the average citizen of Massachusetts in 1780." *Op. cit. supra* note 8, p. 354.

[12] For the Declaration of Rights of the Constitution of 1780, see Appendix K, *infra.*

[13] See p. 37, *supra.*

ment of Magna Carta, chapter 39. The King's promise, in chapter 40 of the Great Charter, "To no one will We sell, to none will We deny or delay, right or justice," appeared in fuller form in the Massachusetts declaration:

Every subject of the Commonwealth ought to find a certain remedy, by having recourse to the laws, for all injuries or wrongs which he may receive in his person, property, or character. He ought to obtain right and justice freely, and without being obliged to purchase it; compleatly, and without any denial; promptly, and without delay; conformably to the laws.

Just compensation for the taking of private property for public use, found in chapter 28 of Magna Carta, was provided for in Article X of the 1780 declaration.

The English Bill of Rights, too, was mined for its constitutional ore. The right to petition for redress of grievances, the provision that only the legislature might suspend the laws, legislators' freedom of speech and debate, frequent legislative sessions, no taxation without the consent of the people or their representatives, no excessive bail or fines, and no cruel and unusual punishments—all had been established in the Bill of Rights of 1689, and all were inserted into the Massachusetts Constitution of 1780.

The English Act of Settlement of 1701—which the British Crown had not wanted to apply to the American colonies—had, among other things, provided for an independent judiciary. One of the charges against George III in the Declaration of Independence was that he had made judges in the colonies "dependent on his will alone, for the tenure of their offices, and the amount and payment of their salaries." Accordingly the Massachusetts Declaration of Rights provided that the judges of the Supreme Judicial Court "should hold their offices as long as they behave themselves well; and that they should have honorable salaries ascertained and established by standing laws."

The language of the 1780 constitution is enough, by itself, to demonstrate quite plainly the origin of those provisions which were drawn from the fundamental British documents. But it is interesting to note a further point—the grouping of these provisions. The articles which Adams took from Magna Carta are all found near the front of the Declaration of Rights—in three consecutive articles, X, XI, and XII. There Adams put the principles drawn from Magna Carta, chapters 28, 39, and 40. The articles which he based on the Bill of Rights of 1689 are similarly grouped—Articles XIX, XX, XXI, XXII, XXIII, XXVI. Finally, just before the end, are a single provision (Article XXVII) drawn from the Petition of Right of 1628 (the ban on quartering troops on the populace in time of peace) and a single article (XXIX) based on the Act of Settlement of 1701 (providing for an independent judiciary).

The scene is easy to reconstruct. There sits John Adams, pen and paper in hand, surrounded by an untidy assortment of books—Magna Carta, the Bill of Rights, Locke's *Second Treatise,* the constitutions of sister States, other sources. A veteran of all those years of a war of words for the rights of Englishmen, Adams knows his way around the English documents as if he had written them. Settling down to his work, he turns first to one, then to another familiar source as he selects what he wants to put in his draft. The results: the distillation of two decades of legal learning since Adams sat in the courtroom in Boston and heard James Otis denounce the writs of assistance and a succinct statement—perhaps as neat a list as exists in any American document—of what rights the American colonist had in mind in the 1760's and 1770's when he claimed the "liberties of Englishmen."

The Principles of Magna Carta

WHAT Virginia and Massachusetts did in their declarations of rights—the products, respectively, of two of the most noted constitutional thinkers of the time—is illustrative of the provisions which one will find in the constitutions drawn up by the other American States. Of the principles which derive from Magna Carta, the most popular among the drafters of the original state constitutions was the guarantee of proceedings according to the "law of the land" or "due process of law." At first the universal usage was "law of the land," either in an article (for example, that of the Maryland Declaration of Rights of 1776) [14] precisely like that of Magna Carta, chapter 39 or in an article (such as that of the Virginia Declaration of Rights of 1776) [15] in which there was also the guarantee of other procedural rights in criminal cases—notice of the nature of the accusation, confrontation of accusers and witnesses, opportunity to present evidence, etc.

Gradually, usages other than "law of the land" were introduced into state constitutions. The precedent for a variation in language had been set in the Fifth Amendment to the Federal Constitution, which, instead of "law of the land," had used "due process of law," the two phrases having the same meaning. New York, in its Constitution of 1821, was the first State to adopt the usage "due process of law," [16] although Mississippi had used the language "due course of law" in its Constitution of 1817. [17] Later, after the War between the States, when state constitutions were revised or newly adopted, the guarantee of "due process of law" was typically stated so as not to be limited (unlike chapter 39 of Magna Carta or the provisions of the early state constitutions) to criminal proceedings. The Fourteenth Amendment simply states that no State shall "deprive any person of life, liberty, or property, without due process of law . . . ," a form which West Virginia, in 1872, was the first State to follow. [18] To take the concept of due process of law out of its criminal context was an open invitation, which the state and federal courts accepted, to create a body of "substantive" due process of law as a limit on the powers of legislatures, for example, in the regulation of property rights. [19] Today, the constitution of every State save one—New Jersey—has, in one form or another, the guarantee of due process of law [20]—a

---

[14] Thorpe, III, 1688.   [15] *Ibid.*, VII, 3813.   [16] *Ibid.*, V, 2648.
[17] *Ibid.*, IV, 2033.
[18] *Ibid.*, VII, 4036. The West Virginia Constitution, unlike the Fourteenth Amendment, goes on to provide for "judgment of his peers."
[19] See pp. 363–67, *infra.*
[20] See Appendix N, *infra*, for table of present state constitutional guarantees of "law of the land" or "due process of law."

thundering tribute to the vitality of an ideal whose formal statement reaches back at least seven hundred and fifty years, to Magna Carta. [1]

Other principles drawn from the Great Charter have had a conspicuous place in the constitutions of the American States. The guarantee of chapter 40 that justice is not to be sold, denied, or delayed has been nearly as popular a provision as due process of law. Massachusetts in 1780 adopted the language already quoted above; most States chose a simpler statement (rather closer to chapter 40), such as Connecticut's assurance in its Constitution of 1818 of "right and justice administered without sale, denial, or delay." [22]

Compensation for property taken for public use, born of Magna Carta's chapter 28, is commonly provided.[23] Equally popular has been the principle of humane punishment in criminal cases. Sometimes this takes the form of the English Bill of Rights' ban on cruel and unusual punishment, for example, in the North Carolina Declaration of Rights of 1776.[24] Less commonly it has been put in language more like that of chapter 20 of Magna Carta, for example, in the provision—inserted to the end that the law be "less sanguinary"—in the South Carolina Constitution of 1778 that punishments should be "in general more proportionate to the crime." [25]

Other principles reminiscent of Magna Carta have taken their place in the state constitutions. Chapter 18 of Magna Carta requires that certain land disputes be tried in their own counties. There are examples—the Georgia Constitution of 1777 is one [26]—of state constitutions requiring cases involving real property to be tried in the county where the property lies. More common is the salutary provision that the trial of criminal cases be had in the locality. This is the case, for example, in the provision of the New Hampshire Constitution of 1784 that

[21] For an exhaustive study of "due process of law," see Rodney L. Mott, *Due Process of Law* (Indianapolis, 1926) .

[22] Thorpe, I, 538. See Appendix O, *infra*, for table of present state constitutional provisions banning the sale, denial, or delay of justice.

[23] See, e.g., Thorpe, I, 569 (Delaware, 1792) .   [24] *Ibid.*, V, 2788.

[25] *Ibid.*, VI, 3257.   [26] *Ibid.*, II, 783.

"the trial of facts in the vicinity where they happen" is essential in criminal cases.[27]

The list would not be complete without mention of the uncommon, but interesting, provision naming free migration to be one of man's inherent rights. Magna Carta, in chapter 42, had guaranteed to the people of England freedom to "leave and return to Our kingdom safely and securely." This states the principle of freedom of movement, rather than migration, but it has something of a counterpart in the later natural right doctrine of free emigration. Pennsylvania, for one, stated this as man's "natural inherent right to emigrate from one state to another" in its Constitution of 1776.[28]

Magna Carta was not, of course, the only English source for principles stated in the American state constitutions. As with the provisions already mentioned in the original declarations of rights of Virginia and Maryland, the constitutions of this country have drawn heavily on the English Bill of Rights, the Petition of Rights, the Habeas Corpus Act, the Act of Settlement, and other documents. Some States, at the early stage when they were faced with the problem of what would be the content of the law which would form the basis of judicial decisions, even declared in their constitutions that the common and statute law of England, or certain parts of it, were to continue as the law of the State. This was true, for example, of the New York Constitution of 1777, which decreed that such parts of the common and statute law of England which formed part of the law of New York on April 19, 1775, should continue in force in New York.[29]

The manner of drafting of the several state constitutions has at least a dual significance. Obviously it was important to the States involved, and to the people who lived in them, that the drafters of the state constitutions looked to English precedents such as Magna Carta in putting together frames of government for the States. But one should not overlook the further significance of the patterns which were being established and the expec-

[27] *Ibid.*, IV, 2455. Of course, there are instances when the defendant's interests are better served by a trial outside the area, as when there has been excessive prejudicial publicity in the locality.
[28] *Ibid.*, V, 3084.   [29] *Ibid.*, V, 2635.

tations which were being aroused as to what kind of basic document should govern the States in their confederated or united condition. When events unfolded leading to the Constitutional Convention at Philadelphia in 1787, the delegates were by no means drawing up the continent's first written constitution. Even if we take no account of colonial charters and other prerevolutionary precedents, the delegates' thinking could not help but be influenced by what they knew of the recently adopted state constitutions. Moreover, when the Federal Constitution would go to the several States for ratification, the peoples of those States might well judge the new instrument by whether it measured up to what they knew of their own state constitutions. That the state constitutions incorporated so many of the "rights of Englishmen" is not without significance when we consider below the heated and close fight over ratification of the Federal Constitution.

Chapter XII

The Federal Constitution

Conserving and Creating

IN 1774 William Hooper, a North Carolina lawyer who had read law in the office of James Otis in Massachusetts after his graduation from Harvard, wrote a prophetic letter to James Iredell, the distinguished Carolinian who later served as Associate Justice of the United States Supreme Court. Hooper believed that the American colonies were "striding fast to independence" and, having cut free of Great Britain, would adopt the British Constitution "purged of its impurities." [1] In a few years, the first part of Hooper's prediction had come true; independence was a fact. It took some years more to test the second proposition: that Americans would take the British Constitution, purge its "impurities," and adopt it as their own. The test came with the call, born of difficulties with the Articles of Confederation, issued by Congress to the States in 1787 to send delegates to a convention to consider revising the Articles.

In May 1787 a remarkable group of men assembled in Philadelphia in answer to Congress' call. It was a young assemblage; five of the fifty-five delegates were under thirty years of age. Many of the most vocal members of the convention were in their early or mid-thirties: Alexander Hamilton, James Madi-

The Philadelphia Convention

[1] J. S. Jones, *A Defence of the Revolutionary History of the State of North Carolina* (Boston, 1834), p. 314.

son, Edmund Randolph, Gouverneur Morris. Yet young though they were, the fifty-five included among them virtually every public figure in America who had any real contribution to make to the art of creating a government. Among the few notable absences were Thomas Jefferson, John Adams, and John Jay, all occupied with the young country's foreign affairs.

The story of the convention is a well-known one and will not be retold here. A spirit of compromise prevailed over issues which, in the hands of lesser men, would have proved impasses. In the four months that they sat, the delegates resolved the interests of large State and small, of men of property and those without, of nationalists who wanted a strong central government and libertarians who feared national authority. The result was truly a "mixed" government of the kind so in favor with theorists of the eighteenth century, a government in which executive, legislature, and judiciary were conceived to have their respective spheres, the better to protect the people's liberties.

Luther Martin, a voluble spokesman at the convention for the interests of the small States,[2] later reported the events at Philadelphia to the Maryland legislature. He remarked that, in debating many of the questions before the convention, "we were eternally troubled with arguments and precedents from the British government. . . ." From this, one would judge that Martin thought analogies to the British Constitution a nuisance and little more. Yet Pierce Butler, one of South Carolina's delegates, wrote a few days after the convention adjourned that the members "in many instances took the Constitution of Britain, when in its purity, for a model, and surely We cou'd not have a better." [3]

There is no doubt, from the notes of James Madison and others remaining to us from the convention of 1787, that to whatever extent the delegates felt they were charting a path unknown to the British Constitution, nevertheless their

---

[2] William Pierce, one of the delegates to the convention, said that Martin was "so extremely prolix, that he never speaks without tiring the patience of all who hear him." *Records of the Federal Convention of 1787*, ed. Max Farrand (New Haven, 1911), III, 93.

[3] *Ibid.*, III, 203, 102.

expressions of esteem for that system, especially among more conservative delegates, were frequent. Charles Pinckney of South Carolina, for example, called the British Constitution "the best constitution in existence." Alexander Hamilton declared that he shared the "opinions of so many of the wise & good, that the British Govt. was the best in the world. . . ." And Madison noted John Dickinson's "warm eulogiums on the British Constitution." [4]

"Warm eulogiums" or not, it takes little sophistication to mark the extent to which the American Constitution departs in so many ways from the British Constitution either of 1787 or of the modern day. Having declared his high regard for that constitution, in the language already quoted, Pinckney went on in the next breath to express his confidence that "it is one that will not or can not be introduced into this Country. . . ." That is, while Pinckney admired what he conceived to be the balance among Crown, Lords, and Commons, it was obvious that the same balance could not be had in a country in which there was neither Crown nor Lords. [5]

Thus, while expressions of esteem and respect for the British Constitution were frequent in the debates, the distinctions drawn between British circumstances and those in America outweighed the similarities adduced. If different conditions, then a different mechanism, whatever the delegates' admiration for the British model. Thus it is common to find in the Philadelphia debates such passages as those in which Elbridge Gerry of Massachusetts warned his fellow delegates that "maxims taken from the British constitution were often fallacious when applied to our situation which was extremely different." In this vein we find James Wilson, the Pennsylvanian who later sat on the United States Supreme Court, refusing to consider the prerogatives of the British monarch as a guide in defining what ought to be the powers of the American executive, and, at another point in the debates, pointing to the "poison" of the inequality of representation in the British Parliament. [6]

In essence, what the delegates thought they were drawing

[4] *Ibid.*, I, 398, 288, 136.   [5] *Ibid.*, I, 398–99.   [6] *Ibid.*, I, 50, 65, 253–54.

from the British Constitution was the theory of a "mixed" government in which the various branches operated as checks on one another. In this understanding of the British system the colonists drew heavily upon Montesquieu, whose *Spirit of the Laws* was widely read in the colonies. When Madison, in the *Federalist* papers, wrote of the question of the separation of powers, he turned to Montesquieu—"the oracle who is always consulted and cited on this subject." For Montesquieu, said Madison, the British Constitution was the "mirror of political liberty"; its secret lay in the fact that the legislative and executive powers were not united in the same hands.[7]

As many observers have pointed out, Montesquieu's description hardly matched what was actually taking place in the development of English government. In the mid-nineteenth century Walter Bagehot wrote, "The efficient secret of the English Constitution may be described as the close union, the nearly complete fusion, of the executive and legislative powers." And at another point he added, "The Americans of 1787 thought they were copying the English Constitution, but they were contriving a contrast to it."[8]

However, that the British Constitution may not, in 1787, have corresponded to this model did not prevent the Philadelphia delegates from thinking that it did and that this was its greatest virtue. If the separation of powers was, as applied to Great Britain, a myth, it was hardy enough to become a reality in the newly drafted American Constitution. Certainly the specifics of the British system, as the Americans of 1787 understood it to operate, were often rejected in favor of some innovation thought more appropriate to a republican system and to a government of limited and delegated powers. Appeals to British experience were as much to avoid British mistakes as to copy British virtues.

Especially noteworthy, in the context of the present study, is the fact that Magna Carta was hardly relevant to the issues

---

[7] *Federalist* No. 47. For a documentation of the influence of Montesquieu at the time of the Revolution, see Paul Merrill Spurlin, *Montesquieu in America: 1760–1801* (University, La., 1940).

[8] *The English Constitution* (London, 1928), pp. 9, 201.

under consideration at the Philadelphia convention. So far as the notes of the debates reveal, Magna Carta may never have been mentioned at all during the debates. This may seem surprising when one recalls the extent to which Americans up to the time of the Revolution relied on the Great Charter in developing their constitutional case against British colonial policy. But the surprise may abate somewhat if one observes that the focus of discussion at Philadelphia was the establishment of the machinery of government, with emphasis on allocation of powers among the executive, legislative, and judicial branches of government, on such restraints on state powers as would ensure a viable Union, on elections and representation in the two houses of Congress, and other such questions.

The delegates at Philadelphia were, in short, creating an entire government. For such a project Magna Carta furnished little guidance. Those who forced that charter on King John were not seeking to alter the shape of the regime or to substitute one government for another. Rather, they were demanding a specific list of safeguards against the caprice of the Crown. Those safeguards granted, the Crown remained the Crown. Hence the document which embodied the settlement of Runnymede could not be a blueprint for the delegates of 1787. At least, it could not be a blueprint for a frame of government. It could, however, furnish guidance in limiting that government, once established.

Herein lay Magna Carta's relevance to the American experience. While the Charter was not in the main concerned with the distribution of governmental powers or with the shape of governmental machinery, it was very much concerned with individual rights and liberties against the state. And it was the failure of the Convention to focus on these very problems of the individual and the state—at least, its failure to provide for the individual's liberties in a bill of rights—which made the ensuing ratification contest the close thing that it was. And it was, as we shall see, in the course of these debates over the rights of Americans that Magna Carta was once again brought into the dialogue.

The Country Debates the New Constitution

Wren the newly drafted Constitution of the United States went to the country for approval or rejection, shades of the British Constitution, like Banquo's ghost, went with it. John Jay, in the *Federalist* papers, sounded the note which the framers of the new Constitution wanted the people to feel characterized their approach to constitution-making: "The history of Great Britain is the one with which we are in general the best acquainted, and it gives us many useful lessons. We may profit by their experience without paying the price which it cost them." [9]

It is schoolboy's lore that the lack of a bill of rights provoked the real fight over ratification. William Pierce, a Georgia member of the Constitutional Convention, wrote to St. George Tucker in September 1787 to relate his view that, since by the constitutional system being erected power was restrained, there was no need of a bill of rights. Defined and limited powers ought to prevent invasion of the people's rights. The guarantee of American liberties, thought Pierce, was the fact that Americans had inherited the English love of liberty:

I set this down as a truth founded in nature, that a nation habituated to freedom will never remain quiet under an invasion of its liberties. The English history presents us with a proof of this. At the Conquest that nation lost their freedom, but they never were easy or quiet until the true balance between liberty and prerogative was established in the reign of Charles the second. The absolute rights of Englishmen are founded in nature and reason, and are coeval with the English Constitution itself. They were always understood and insisted on by them as well without as with a Bill of Rights. This same spirit was breathed into the Americans, and they still retain it, nor will they, I flatter myself, ever resign it to any power, however plausible it may seem.[10]

On the other hand, Pierce thought there were good reasons why some of the "rights of Englishmen" were omitted from the

[9] *Federalist* No. 5.   [10] 3 *Am. Hist. Rev.* 313, 315 (1898).

new Constitution. He noted that some critics of the instrument had complained that it did not provide for trial by jury in civil cases. Pierce admitted that "an Englishman to be sure will talk of it [jury trial] in rapture; it is a virtue in him to do so, because it is insisted on in Magna Charta (that favorite instrument of English liberty) as the great bulwark of the nation's happiness." But Pierce believed that the evils which made jury trial in civil cases valuable in England (as lords' power over tenants) did not obtain in America. "In my idea," Pierce concluded, "the opinion of its [jury trial's] utility is founded more in prejudice than in reason. I cannot but think that an able Judge is better qualified to decide between man and man than any twelve men possibly can be." [11] Pierce was stating a view of "judge-made law" shared by such later figures as Judge Jerome Frank in a running battle over the value of juries in civil cases which continues, if anything with more passion, to this day. [12]

The want of any provision for trial by jury in the Federal Constitution was but one of many objections the Antifederalists had against the document. Only thirty-nine of the fifty-five delegates at the Philadelphia convention signed the Constitution, and most of those who had opposed the Constitution at Philadelphia worked against its ratification. The proponents of the Constitution enjoyed the prestige of such national heroes as George Washington and Benjamin Franklin and the intellect of such luminaries as James Madison and Alexander Hamilton. But the Anti's probably reflected the majority sentiment in the country, had a popular referendum been taken, and they did not lack for talented spokesmen—Patrick Henry, Richard Henry Lee, Luther Martin, and others.

Before the state ratifying conventions met, the country was treated to a torrent of rhetoric in pamphlets, in speeches, in the newspapers. George Mason, the libertarian whose Virginia Bill of Rights had been the model for other States, led the attack on the Constitution, drawing on the historical example of the

[11] *Ibid.*, p. 316. Today most civil cases in England are tried without a jury.
[12] For example, compare the views of Jerome Frank, *Courts on Trial* (Princeton, N.J., 1949), pp. 108–45, with those of Mr. Justice Hugo Black as described in Leon Green, "Jury Trial and Mr. Justice Black," 65 *Yale L.J.* 482 (1956) and as expounded in Black opinions there cited.

English documents, such as Magna Carta and the Bill of Rights, which served to secure the liberties of Englishmen.

The proponents of the Constitution waged an effective paper war of rebuttal. Roger Sherman, in his letters signed "A Countryman," recalled that Magna Carta was but a statute, which each Parliament had the right to repeal, and that the only real security for individual rights was, not a bill of rights, but that the government is as interested in preserving individual rights as are the governed.[13]

The chief argument against the necessity for a bill of rights rested on a contrast between the origin and nature of the proposed Federal Government and that of Great Britain. Robert Yates of New York, writing under the name "Sydney," pointed out that in countries with an implied constitution, such as Great Britain, a declaration of rights might be necessary "to prevent the usurpation of ambitious men," but the Americans, having thrown off British authority, were starting, in effect, in a state of nature, so that the Constitution would operate as a bill of rights.[14]

In the same vein, several writers argued that magna cartas and bills of rights were a function of disputes between kings and subjects over power and liberties and hence irrelevant to a system where government originated with the people. Oliver Ellsworth, later to be Chief Justice of the United States, said that in England such documents were considered as grants from the King; they were unimportant in America, where "all the power government now has is a grant from the people."[15] John Jay took the same line, saying that when monarchs and subjects disputed about prerogatives and privileges, the subjects had to "oblige the former to admit, by solemn acts, called bills of rights, that certain enumerated rights belonged to the people.

---

[13] "Letters of 'A Countryman,'" in Paul Leicester Ford, ed., *Essays on the Constitution of the United States* (Brooklyn, N.Y., 1892), pp. 215–28 [hereinafter Ford, *Essays*]. Sherman's "Letters" were published in the *New-Haven Gazette* in Nov. and Dec., 1787.

[14] *Ibid.*, p. 299. Yates' letters appeared in the *New York Journal* in June 1788. For a similar argument by Hamilton, see *Federalist* No. 84.

[15] "Letters of 'A Landholder,'" in Ford, *Essays*, p. 163. Ellsworth's letters were printed in the *Connecticut Courant* and the *American Mercury* between Nov. 1787 and March 1788.

. . . But thank God, we have no such disputes; we have no monarchs to contend with, or demand admissions from."[16]

But the Antifederalists were not to be put off so easily. Their reading of history, and their philosophy of government, did not suggest to them that tyranny's only garb is the royal purple of monarchy. There was as yet no Lord Acton to coin the famous phrase about the tendency of power to corrupt, but the Antifederalists embraced that attitude wholeheartedly and looked with foreboding on any concentration of power, even if it was in popular hands, and above all looked with misgivings on any neglect to enumerate specifically the rights of individuals. Richard Henry Lee expressed such fears in a letter to Edmund Randolph in October 1787, in which Lee complained of the lack of a bill of rights to secure "that residuum of human rights which is not intended to be given up to society. . . . The rights of conscience, the freedom of the press, and the trial by jury, are at mercy."[17]

The Ratifying Conventions

THE dimensions of the contest marked out by the battle of words in newspapers and pamphlets, the arena now shifted to the ratifying conventions. As one would expect, speakers in these conventions often looked to English history and to the British Constitution to support respectively arguments for and against the proposed American Constitution. It is interesting to note in these debates how Magna Carta was invoked, first on one side to show why no bill of rights was needed in the American Constitution, then on the other to show why one was needed.

Delaware was first off the mark to ratify, in December 1787. Pennsylvania was next, after a convention in which James

---

[16] "Address to the People of the State of New York on the Subject of the Proposed Federal Constitution," in Jonathan Elliot, ed., *Debates in the Several State Conventions on the Adoption of the Federal Constitution* (2d ed.; Washington, D.C., 1836), I, 498 [hereinafter *Elliot's Debates*].

[17] *Ibid.*, I, 503.

Wilson had drawn a rather clear contrast between what he understood to be the way in which Magna Carta and the English Bill of Rights had come into being and the shape which the proposed Federal Government would take:

I confess I feel a kind of pride in considering the striking difference between the foundation on which the liberties of this country are declared to stand in this Constitution, and the footing on which the liberties of England are said to be placed. The Magna Charta of England is an instrument of high value to the people of that country. But . . . from what source does that instrument derive the liberties of the inhabitants of that kingdom? Let it speak for itself. The king says, *"We* have *given* and *granted* . . . these liberties following, to be kept in our kingdom of England forever." When this was assumed as the leading principle of that government, it was no wonder that the people were anxious to obtain bills of rights, and to take every opportunity of enlarging and securing their liberties. But here, sir, the fee-simple remains in the people at large, and by this Constitution they do not part with it.[18]

In Wilson's view, a bill of rights in the American Constitution would not only be unnecessary, it would be imprudent, for to attempt an enumeration would be to imply that everything which was not enumerated was within the power of the Federal Government. Drawing again on the language of Magna Carta, the Petition of Rights, and the Bill of Rights of England, Wilson observed that in both of the latter documents the people's claims are rested upon the foundation of an original "contract" between the King and the people, that is, on Magna Carta. No such compact need be invoked as the basis for the rights of the American people; they may say, to every suggestion concerning a bill of rights, "WE reserve the right to do what we please."[19]

Massachusetts presented an especially critical test for the new Constitution. A straw vote taken shortly after that State's ratifying convention met in January 1788 showed 192 members against the Constitution, 144 for it. The prestigious John Hancock was against, as, for a while, was Samuel Adams. To secure Massachusetts' favorable action, the Federalists agreed to a

[18] *Ibid.*, II, 435.   [19] *Ibid.*, II, 437.

proposal for a bill of rights, and Massachusetts ratified by the not especially comfortable margin of 187 to 168. Maryland ratified in April, also proposing a bill of rights. Among Maryland's proposals was one that the militia not be subject to martial law except in time of war, invasion, or rebellion, an explanatory comment noting that in England it was "contrary to Magna Charta to punish a freeman by martial law, in time of peace, and murder to execute him." [20]

When South Carolina's convention met, the lack of a bill of rights was fully aired. Patrick Dollard, speaking for the people of Prince Frederick's Parish, said that his constituents were to a man opposed to the new Constitution because there was no bill of rights to secure their liberties. His people would have the rights of Englishmen. "They say, that they are by no means against vesting congress with ample and sufficient powers; but to make over to them, or any set of men, their birthright, comprised in Magna Charta, which this new constitution absolutely does, they can never agree to." [21] South Carolina ratified, attaching a list of proposed amendments to the Constitution.

New Hampshire followed, to make the ninth State. By the terms of the Constitution's submission to the States, the instrument was to become effective upon the ratification of nine States. But the battle was not over; four States, among them wealthy and populous Virginia, had not acted. Virginia's convention brought together a roster of the great and to-be-great names of the time—Patrick Henry, James Madison, George Wythe, Benjamin Harrison, John Tyler, Edmund Pendleton, James Monroe, George Mason, John Marshall, Colonel Henry ("Light Horse Harry") Lee, and Edmund Randolph. There was no want of leadership for either the Federalist or Antifederalist sides: Madison, Marshall, and Randolph spoke for the Constitution, Mason and Henry, against it. If class interest played a part in opposition to the Constitution in some state conventions, men like Henry, the coiner of libertarian phrases during the Revolution, and Mason, the architect of the Virginia Bill of Rights, spoke from conviction. As a result, nowhere did the issues surrounding the new Constitution get a fuller airing than in Virginia.

[20] *Ibid.,* II, 552.   [21] *Ibid.,* IV, 321.

Magna Carta figured in the discussion of whether or not the Constitution should have a bill of rights and, to an even greater degree, in the controversy over the question of guaranteeing the right to trial by jury. Patrick Henry, never at a loss for words (his remarks occupy about one-fourth of the printed record of the Virginia debates), led the attack, with special emphasis on the want of a bill of rights. George Nicholas answered by contrasting the underlying assumptions of the English and American constitutions. In America, it was a principle universally agreed upon that all powers not given were retained. In England, however, in disputes between the King and the people, recurrence would be had to the enumerated rights of the people—in Magna Carta, the Bill of Rights, and other statements of rights. If the rights were not found there, then generally speaking they were thought to be within the King's prerogatives. Who, then, was more secure, the people of England or the people of America? The Englishman had Magna Carta and his Bill of Rights, but the American had something better: the knowledge that he had relinquished certain powers for certain purposes and had retained everything else, and the right to resume what he had given, if it were perverted from its intended object.[22]

The debates on the Federal Constitution's provisions respecting federal courts and trial by jury brought considerable analysis, by speakers on both sides, of what security for jury trial was given by Magna Carta and in which country, England or America, trial by jury was more secure. John Marshall, then thirty-two years old, spoke to objections raised by George Mason to the lack of a constitutional guarantee of jury trial. The future Chief Justice argued that, if jury trial was secured to the English by their constitution, yet there was no part of that constitution which Parliament could not change. Nevertheless, jury trial had always been held sacred in England. There was no reason to think the American government would, even without a constitutional mandate, be less sensitive to this right. To Mason's objection that the right to challenge jurors had not been provided for, Marshall pointed out that Magna Carta contained no such provision; in England this privilege

[22] *Ibid.*, III, 246.

was found in ordinary laws. Surely, thought Marshall, this would be sufficient in America.[23]

William Grayson, answering Marshall, disagreed with him that Parliament could in fact—whatever its theoretical powers—tamper with Magna Carta or the right to a jury trial. To the argument that trial by jury could be destroyed by Act of Parliament, Grayson submitted:

I believe the gentleman is mistaken. I believe it is secured by Magna Charta and the bill of rights. I believe no act of Parliament can affect it, if this principle be true,—that a law is not paramount to the constitution. I believe, whatever may be said of the mutability of the laws, and the defect of a written, fixed constitution, that it is generally thought, by Englishmen, that it is so sacred that no act of Parliament can affect it.[24]

With Marshall taking the tack that Magna Carta was a slender reed because it could be repealed by Parliament, Edmund Randolph believed the Antifederalists' reliance on Magna Carta was misplaced for another reason: that Magna Carta's guarantee of trial by jury of peers related only to criminal trials, not civil cases:

I beg those gentlemen who deny this doctrine to inform me what part of the bill of English rights, or Great Charter, provides this right. The Great Charter only provides that "no man shall be deprived of the free enjoyment of his life, liberty, or property, unless declared to be forfeited by the judgment of his peers, or the law of the land." The bill of rights gives no additional security on the subject of trial by jury. Where is the provision made, in England, that a jury shall be had in civil cases? This is secured by no constitutional provision. It is left to the temper and genius of the people to preserve and protect it.[25]

Patrick Henry shifted the attack to another feature of the Constitution: the provision (Article III, section 2) that the trial of criminal cases should be held in the State where the crime was committed. This, thought Henry, was not a trial in the vicinage. In England a subject "has a right to trial by his peers. What is meant by his peers? Those who reside near him,

[23] *Ibid.*, III, 558–59.   [24] *Ibid.*, III, 569.
[25] *Ibid.*, III, 573. In England, at the present day, juries are not generally used in civil cases.

his neighbors, and who are well acquainted with his character and situation in life. Is this secured in the proposed plan before you? No, sir." [26]

William Grayson rejoined the debate, again invoking **Magna Carta**. "As to the trial by jury being safer here than in **England**, that I deny. Jury trials are secured there, sir, by **Magna Charta**, in a clear and decided manner; and that here it is not in express and positive terms, is admitted by most gentlemen who now hear me." Grayson concluded with saying that he doubted that there existed "a social compact upon the face of the earth so vague and so indefinite as the one now on the table." [27]

The Federalists prevailed, and Virginia ratified, by a vote of 89 to 79. A switch of six votes would have blocked Virginia's ratification. The opponents of the Constitution, holding to the end their view that a bill of rights was essential to the cause of liberty, acquiesced in the result with grace. None had fought harder than Patrick Henry, but just before the final vote was taken he told the company: "I will be a peaceable citizen. My head, my hand, and my heart, shall be at liberty to retrieve the loss of liberty, and remove the defects of that system in a constitutional way"—that is, by constitutional amendment.[28]

Three States had not yet acted. The Constitution squeaked through in the New York convention by a margin of three votes. North Carolina and Rhode Island remained, for the time being, hold-outs. The debates in North Carolina turned the delegates' attention to the usual dispute over the necessity for a bill of rights and, consequently, to comparisons between the British and American Constitutions, between Parliament and Congress. The convention debated the point whether Congress, having (by virtue of Article I, section 4) the power to fix the times, places, and manner of elections, might not extend their own term of office, as the British Parliament did in extending their term from three to seven years. Archibald Maclaine contrasted Parliament's power to alter the British Constitution with the limits placed on Congress by the American Constitution. Though the English talked as loudly of constitutional rights as did the Americans, in fact in England they had no

[26] *Ibid.*, III, 579.   [27] *Ibid.*, III, 583.   [28] *Ibid.*, III, 652.

written constitution—only Magna Carta and the Bill of Rights. "These they look upon as their constitution. Yet this is such a constitution as it is universally considered parliament can change." On the contrary, under the American system Congress would be bound by the Constitution and could not pass an act extending their term of office.[29]

Governor Samuel Johnston took the same view. Even Magna Carta could be repealed by Parliament:

> They have no written constitution in Britain. They have certain fundamental principles and legislative acts, securing the liberty of the people. But these may be altered by their representatives, without violating their constitution, in such manner as they think proper. Their legislature existed long before the science of government was well understood. From very early periods you find their parliament in full force. What is their Magna Charta? It is only an act of parliament. Their parliament can at any time, alter the whole, or any part of it. In short, it is no more binding on the people than any other act which has passed. . . .

What Magna Carta lacked, said Johnston, the American Constitution supplied. "The powers of congress are all circumscribed, defined, and clearly laid down. So far they may go, but no farther." [30]

Samuel Spencer called for a bill of rights on the English model. "In Great Britain, when the king attempts to usurp the rights of the people, the declaration and bill of rights are a guard against him. A bill of rights would be necessary here to guard against our rulers." [31] James Iredell, the future Associate Justice of the United States Supreme Court (1790–99), disputed that Magna Carta or the English Bill of Rights was apposite for imitation in a country of which, unlike England, the basic constitution clearly spelled out the limits of governmental power:

> With regard to a bill of rights, this is a notion originating in England, where no written constitution is to be found, and the authority of their government is derived from the most remote antiquity. Magna Charta itself is no constitution, but a solemn instrument ascertaining certain rights of individuals, by the

[29] *Ibid.*, IV, 86–87.   [30] *Ibid.*, IV, 87.   [31] *Ibid.*, IV, 149.

legislature for the time being; and every article of which the legislature may at any time alter. This, and a bill of rights also, the invention of later times, were occasioned by great usurpations of the crown, contrary, as was conceived, to the principles of their government, about which there was a variety of opinions. But neither that instrument or any other instrument ever attempted to abridge the authority of parliament, which is supposed to be without any limitation whatever. Had their constitution been fixed and certain, a bill of rights would have been useless, for the constitution would have shown plainly the extent of that authority which they were disputing about. Of what use therefore can a bill of rights be in this constitution, where the people expressly declare how much power they do give, and consequently retain all they do not?

Iredell concluded that a bill of rights "would not only be incongruous, but dangerous. No man, let his ingenuity be what it will, could enumerate all the individual rights, not relinquished by this constitution." [32]

Iredell was in the minority and was bound to admit, at the convention's close, the uselessness of contending any longer "against a majority that is irresistible." [33] The convention adjourned without taking action on the proposed Constitution, but it met again in November 1789 and decided to join the States that had already ratified. Rhode Island did not call a convention until 1790, at which time it too joined the Union.

Though the Federalists had carried the ratification struggles, the mood of the country in favor of adding a bill of rights to the Constitution was unmistakable. Indeed it is doubtful that some of the more reluctant States, such as Virginia and New York, would have ratified had there not been at least a tacit understanding that amendments would be proposed when the first Congress met under the new government. Most of the ratifying States, following the example of Massachusetts, had drawn up lists of proposed amendments. The lists varied widely in their specifics, but they all carried the hallmarks of the philosophy of John Locke and the constitutional tradition of Magna Carta.

The Virginia ratifying convention appointed a committee of unusual distinction to draft its proposals for amendments to the

[32] *Ibid.,* IV, 158–59.   [33] *Ibid.,* IV, 237.

Federal Constitution. Chaired by the learned George Wythe, America's first professor of law and teacher of Thomas Jefferson and John Marshall, the committee included Benjamin Harrison, Patrick Henry, Governor Edmund Randolph, George Mason, William Grayson, James Madison, John Tyler, John Marshall, James Monroe, and others. The committee reported a declaration of rights and a list of constitutional amendments. The declaration of rights is notable for its eclecticism, for the manner, characteristic of American pamphlets and arguments before the Revolution, of blending philosophical ideals, especially those of a natural law origin, with the traditional precepts of Magna Carta and the British Constitution.[34]

The Virginia proposal for a declaration of rights began with the enumeration, straight from John Locke, of a compact theory of government and of the existence, under that compact, of certain "natural rights"—life, liberty, and property.[35] Power was held to derive from the people, and government was declared to be a trust. Government was proclaimed to be for the common benefit of the people, and the doctrine of nonresistance to arbitrary power was scorned as absurd and destructive of men's happiness.

On this foundation of natural rights the declaration added several provisions drawn directly from Magna Carta, either the original document or the glosses which centuries of constitutional usages had placed on it. As generations of American colonists had invoked Magna Carta against taxation without representation, so the proposed declaration provided that "no aid, charge, tax, or fee, can be set, rated, or levied, upon the people without their own consent, or that of their representatives. . . ."

The procedural guarantees of Magna Carta were carefully included. A criminal defendant was to be assured of "a fair and speedy trial by an impartial jury of his vicinage." Magna Carta's chapter 39 was restated almost verbatim: "That no freeman ought to be taken, imprisoned, or disseized of his freehold,

---

[34] The proposals are to be found in *ibid.*, III, 657–61. For the full text of the proposed declaration of rights, see Appendix L, *infra*.

[35] See John Locke, *Second Treatise of Government* § 135: the law of nature gives no man "Arbitrary Power over the Life, Liberty, or Possession of another."

liberties, privileges, or franchises, or outlawed, or exiled, or in any manner destroyed, or deprived of his life, liberty, or property, but by the law of the land." Chapter 40 of Magna Carta appeared in the guarantee "that every freeman restrained of his liberty is entitled to a remedy, to inquire into the lawfulness thereof, and to remove the same, if unlawful, and that such remedy ought not to be denied or delayed," the injunction against denial or delay of justice being the contribution of chapter 40, the principle of a remedy for unlawful restraint being drawn from the Habeas Corpus Act of 1679.[36]

English liberties as set out in the Bill of Rights of 1689 were also well represented in the Virginia proposals. The Glorious Revolution echoed in such provisions as those which forbade suspension of the laws without the consent of the people's representatives; decreed that excessive bail ought not to be required, nor excessive fines imposed, nor cruel and unusual punishment inflicted; declared the right peaceably to petition for redress of grievances; and warned against the danger of standing armies.[37] A prohibition against the quartering of soldiers on the populace in time of peace recalled not only such practices in the colonial days, but also the comparable provision of the Petition of Right of 1628.[38]

George Washington's journey from Mount Vernon to New York for his inauguration as the first President of the United States was like the triumph of a returning Roman emperor. Allowing for the more limited communications of the time, especially the absence of the all-seeing eye of television, probably no President in history has been the object of greater public interest in his every move. The administration, being without precedents, was making its own, from the great affairs of state to the niceties of protocol. Some Antifederalists, still disgruntled over the failure of their opposition to the Constitution's ratification, were quick to seize upon anything that looked like monarchist instincts on the part of the new President.

[36] For a history of habeas corpus, see Daniel John Meador, *Habeas Corpus and Magna Carta* (Charlottesville, Va., 1966).
[37] For the text of the Bill of Rights of 1689, see Richard L. Perry, ed., *Sources of Our Liberties* (Chicago, 1959), p. 245.
[38] For the Petition of Right, see *ibid.*, p. 73.

No doubt conscious that these suspicions were still alive, Washington intimated in his inaugural address that Congress should, as one of its first orders of business, see to the submission to the States of a bill of rights to the Constitution. Congress picked up the cue, and when it met in its first session, in 1789, James Madison rose on the floor of the House of Representatives to explain the proposed amendments. He admitted that he had never considered a bill of rights so essential as to make it a prerequisite to ratification of the Constitution (there had been, of course, many Antifederalists who had taken this position), but at the same time neither had he considered such amendments, properly thought out, either useless or dangerous.

Some people, Madison noted, had cited the British experience as evidence that the enumeration of rights was hazardous business, but Madison felt the comparison inapposite, chiefly because documents like Magna Carta were only a barrier against the Crown and no deterrent to the legislative branch; nor did it made provision for those rights—such as freedom of the press or of conscience—about which the American people were most concerned:

> In the declaration of rights which that country [Britain] has established, the truth is, they have gone no farther than to raise a barrier against the power of the Crown; the power of the Legislature is left altogether indefinite. Although I know whenever the great rights, the trial by jury, freedom of the press, or liberty of conscience, come in question in that body, the invasion of them is resisted by able advocates, yet their Magna Charta does not contain any one provision for the security of those rights, respecting which the people of America are most alarmed. The freedom of the press and rights of conscience, those choicest privileges of the people, are unguarded in the British Constitution.[39]

Representative James Jackson, of Georgia, characterized by Madison as "unfriendly" to the proposed amendments, objected to the House's going into a committee of the whole, as moved by Madison, to consider the amendments. He felt the House "ought not to be in a hurry with respect to altering the Constitution. . . . What experience have we had of the good or

[39] 1 *Annals of Congress* 436 (Washington, D.C., 1834).

bad qualities of this Constitution?" Jackson objected, too, to the form of the amendments. The original Constitution ought to remain inviolate and "not be patched up, from time to time, with various stuffs resembling Joseph's coat of many colors." It was argued, he continued, that the amendments should be incorporated into the Constitution itself, so that the people might have the whole before them in one view. Jackson cited the experience of England; they had not found it necessary, he argued, to incorporate into Magna Carta successive enactments providing for the liberty of the subject:

> Look at the Constitution of Great Britain; is that all contained in one instrument? It is well known that *magna charta* was extorted by the barons from King John some centuries ago. Has that been altered since by the incorporation of amendments? Or does it speak the same language now, as it did at the time it was obtained? Sir, it is not altered a tittle from its original form. Yet there have been many amendments and improvements in the Constitution of Great Britain since that period. In the subsequent reign of his son, the great charters were confirmed with some supplemental acts. Is the *habeas corpus* act, or the statute *De Tallagio non concedendo* incorporated in *magna charta*? And yet there is not an Englishman but would spill the last drop of his blood in their defence; it is these, with some other acts of Parliament and *magna charta,* that form the basis of English liberty. . . . [The British] Constitution is composed of many distinct acts; but an Englishman would be ashamed to own that, on this account, he could not ascertain his own privileges or the authority of the Government.[40]

William Smith, of South Carolina, answered Jackson's argument by reminding the House that even Magna Carta was subject to repeal by Parliament. The British Constitution, Smith said, "is neither the *magna charta* of John, nor the *habeas corpus* act, nor all the charters put together; it is what the Parliament wills." Smith conceded that in Great Britain there were "rights granted to the subject that cannot be resumed," but the Constitution, or form of government, he con-

[40] *Ibid.,* pp. 425–26, 714.

tended, "may be altered by the authority of Parliament, whose power is absolute without control." [41]

The proposed amendments were submitted to the States. With their ratification by Virginia, the eleventh State to approve them, the Bill of Rights came into being as Amendments I through X to the Constitution. The decade of domestic politics which followed was to produce one more interesting statement by Madison on the extent to which the Federal Constitution, as amended, had gone beyond its distant ancestor, Magna Carta. Increasing American difficulties with France, including a naval war with that country, had their reflection in Federalist fears of intrigue and sedition within the Republic's gates. Federalist anxiety over homegrown and imported Jacobinism—by 1798 there were twenty-five thousand French refugees in the United States, many of them radicals—called forth the Alien and Sedition Acts of 1798.

The Federalists were not especially concerned about discriminating between conspiring Frenchmen and the government's Republican opposition. Several editors and even a member of Congress were silenced by use of the Sedition Act, and men like Thomas Jefferson and James Madison were quick to protest. These two drafted resolutions—Madison the Virginia Resolves, and Jefferson the Kentucky Resolves—which were passed by the legislatures of Virginia and Kentucky condemning the Alien and Sedition Acts as unconstitutional. Madison, in the course of his Report on the Virginia resolutions (made to the Virginia House of Delegates), had occasion to point out, as he had done in the House of Representatives in 1789, that Magna Carta was, in his view, a check on the Crown only, not on Parliament. In Great Britain, he said, Parliament is considered omnipotent. Hence "all the ramparts for protecting the rights of the people, such as their Magna Charta, their Bill of Rights, &c. are not reared against the parliament, but against the royal prerogative. They are merely legislative precaution, against executive usurpation." [42] Madison's point, in the context of the protests against the Sedition Act, was that because the American Constitution was a bulwark against both executive and

[41] *Ibid.*, pp. 715–16.   [42] *Elliot's Debates*, IV, 596.

legislative acts, something which Magna Carta and the British Constitution, in his view, were not, the Sedition Act could not be vindicated by looking at the meaning of "freedom of the press" at common law.

The opinions expressed by American public figures in the period which extended from the drafting of the Federal Constitution through the Virginia and Kentucky Resolutions form an interesting watershed in the American odyssey of Magna Carta. From the first settlements in the early seventeenth century through the opposition to British colonial policies in the 1760's and 1770's, whenever an American was heard to speak of the Great Charter, it was to eulogize it. The colonial American understood his charters to give him the privileges of Magna Carta, his colonial assemblies enacted it into the colonial laws, he fought theocrats and Crown alike to have its benefits, he pleaded it against indictments, to the end of the colonial connection it was the text for his arguments against the overreaching of the mother country. But Independence lent a new perspective. Magna Carta had indeed served as inspiration, and to a great extent it was to serve as model. But now it was not a form of sacrilege to say that Magna Carta was not, after all, the alpha and omega. Americans could learn from Britain, the Constitution could draw on the Great Charter, but they could do even better.

To begin with, Magna Carta suffered from the fact that, in form, it was a grant from the King, not a document created by the people. This is why Oliver Ellsworth was inclined to think the English documents of liberty not all that important to an American because in America any power in the hands of government "is a grant from the people." This was the view expressed by James Wilson in the Pennsylvania ratifying convention. Secondly, it was argued by some that Magna Carta was only one more statute of the realm and that, as Governor Johnston put it in the North Carolina convention, Parliament "can at any time, alter the whole, or any part of it." Thirdly, a related argument, Madison and others considered the Great Charter to be a barrier against the executive only, and no defense against legislative invasion of individual liberties.

These notions about Magna Carta require some qualification. It is, for example, not altogether safe to accept the Blackstonian picture of the omnipotent Parliament, which, if it chooses, can wipe Magna Carta or the Bill of Rights off the books. This is a picture which the modern American looking at Great Britain is quite apt to have.[43] But from the theory of an omnipotent Parliament it does not follow that Parliament can in fact do what it will—for example, disregard any or all of the liberties of Englishmen. The workings of a constitutional system which, though without a written constitution as such, has constitutional conventions which "broaden down from precedent to precedent" is not without its own ways of protecting individual freedoms.[44]

But it is not necessary to resolve the problem of whether the principles of Magna Carta are, despite Blackstone and the rest, somehow sacrosanct so that theoretical omnipotence fades in the face of such virtue. For it is easy to see what James Madison and the others were getting at. If indeed Magna Carta and the other sources of English liberties were not secure from attack (*arguendo*, if you like), this certainly did not have to be the case with the American Constitution. If Americans wanted more, they could have it. And they did. The objections already noted as having been lodged against Magna Carta—that it was a grant from the King, that it could be repealed, that it bound only the executive—are, of course, not tenable against the Constitution of the United States. There is a document which unmistakably emanates from the people—it even begins with the phrase "We the People." It is beyond congressional repeal (even amendment is not easy; the graveyard of would-be amendments is a good-sized one). And it binds all branches of government, federal and state, as John Marshall demonstrated to the discomfort of Thomas Jefferson in *Marbury v.*

[43] Justice Hugo Black, for example, in an essay on the American Bill of Rights, quoted the Leveller John Lilburne ("Free-born John"), who said that the basic defect of Magna Carta was that "that which is done by one Parliament, as a Parliament, may be undone by the next Parliament. . . ." Justice Black also quoted Madison's 1789 statement in the first Congress. "The Bill of Rights and the Federal Government," in Edmond Cahn, ed., *The Great Rights* (New York, 1963), p. 41, at pp. 47, 56.

[44] See pp. 379–80, *infra*.

Madison [45] and Spencer Roane in *Martin v. Hunter's Lessee*.[46]

While the Americans did indeed go beyond anything which Magna Carta, whether in its original dimensions or as shaped by such later figures as Coke, had done or which was thought possible of it, the American debt to Magna Carta in the creation of their own constitutions remains considerable. In 1807 Thomas Jefferson wrote that the Americans had "employed some of the best materials of the British constitution in the construction of our own government. . . ." [47] Nearly a century later one of the great British commentators on American government, Lord Bryce, drew a like conclusion in *The American Commonwealth*. Lord Bryce lavished considerable praise upon the Federal Constitution and the genius of its drafters but added:

The American Constitution is no exception to the rule that everything which has power to win the obedience and respect of men must have its roots deep in the past, and that the more slowly every institution has grown, so much the more enduring is it likely to prove. There is little in this Constitution that is absolutely new. There is much that is as old as Magna Charta.[48]

Innovation and tradition: both played their part in the shaping of the American Constitution. The habit of eclecticism, developed in the prerevolutionary years of argumentation over the Navigation Acts and other British policies, persisted when the framers of the Constitution sat down to their work in Philadelphia. Well read in the history and law of Great Britain, these American statesmen understood the values and limits of the older country's system. If innovation and tradition both had their place, innovation had perhaps the upper hand in the body of the Constitution, where the chief concern was with the creation of a frame of government, and tradition in the Bill of Rights, where government was being limited to ensure the liberties of the individual.

It is in the Bill of Rights, rather than in the body of the Constitution itself, that we find the bridge between Magna

[45] 1 Cranch (5 U.S.) 137 (1803).   [46] 1 Wheat. (14 U.S.) 304 (1816).

[47] Letter to John Norvell (June 14, 1807), in *Writings of Thomas Jefferson*, ed. Paul Leicester Ford (New York, 1892–99), IX, 72.

[48] (3d ed.; New York, 1896), I, 29.

Carta in England and the Charter's legacy in America. As the Supreme Court said over a hundred years after the Bill of Rights went into effect, "The law is perfectly well settled that the first ten amendments to the Constitution, commonly known as the Bill of Rights, were not intended to lay down any novel principles of government, but simply to embody certain guaranties and immunities which we had inherited from our English ancestors. . . ." [49]

Nearly two centuries of jurisprudence have added considerable breadth to the meaning and uses of the provisions of the Bill of Rights. The ever-dynamic patterns of American constitutional law have evolved dimensions for one or another of the first eight amendments which simply did not exist in the English law. But the origin in, and debt to, Magna Carta remains.

[49] Robertson v. Baldwin, 165 U.S. 275, 281 (1897).

Chapter XIII

The Adoption of British Statutes

after the Revolution

The Initial Expedients

Wɪᴛʜ the birth of the American Republic there began a debate over the shape which American law was to take. Americans debated an evolutionary common law versus codification, the English legal inheritance versus a native American jurisprudence, the traditional rights of Englishmen as restated in American terms versus the law of nature. This debate lasted for decades.[1] The assumptions of the two (or more) sides to the debate left traces discernible to this day, for example, in the ever-recurring discussions of "judge-made law." But lawyers and laymen after the Revolution could not wait for the arguments for and against the English legal tradition to run their course. Let scholars dispute the fine points; the plainer people (and the scholars, too) were, after the Revolution as before it, makers of contracts, and drawers of wills, and plaintiffs and defendants in cases civil and criminal. They needed a legal system.

The first reaction of some of the newly independent States was—especially in light of the fact that they were fighting a war for their survival—one both simple and obvious. These States simply declared that all laws theretofore in force should remain in force until altered or repealed. South Carolina, for example,

[1] See Chapter X, *supra.*

made such provision in its Constitution of 1778.[2] A more common reaction was to take a step equally simple and, given the lack of considerable time and resources to pursue alternatives, virtually as obvious: the adoption or retention of British law, common and statute.[3]

While the lawmakers or constitution-drafters in most states agreed on the continuation of the laws they had known—and, in a real sense, gone to war about—as the best solution to the problem of devising a workable legal order for their States, the formulae they adopted differed somewhat from one State to another. New Jersey, for example, provided in its Constitution of 1776 that the common law of England, as well as so much of its statute law as had theretofore been practiced in New Jersey, should remain in force until altered by the legislature, save such features of the English law as might be repugnant to the state constitution itself.[4]

Other States were a bit more specific, saying that English common or statute law in force as of a given date was to remain the law of the State. Maryland, in its Constitution of 1776, limited its adoption of English statutes to those which existed at the time of the first emigration to Maryland which by experience had been found suited to local circumstances; Maryland also adopted such later English statutes as had been "introduced, used and practised" in Maryland courts.[5] New York, in its Constitution of 1777, gave force to such parts of the English common and statute law, as well as colonial laws, as had formed the colony's laws on April 19, 1775.[6] Vermont, by statute in 1782, fixed the date as October 1, 1760—a date chosen apparently out of distaste for George III, as that monarch had succeeded to the throne in October 1760.[7]

To adopt the British law, at least such parts which had been found adapted to American conditions, was, of course, born in good part of the need to do something quick and expedient. The Vermont statute above, for example, cited, as the occasion for its passage, the combined circumstances of the impossibility of legislating immediately all the statute law that might be

[2] Thorpe, VI, 3255.   [3] See Brown, *British Statutes*, pp. 24–26.
[4] Thorpe, V, 2598.   [5] *Ibid.*, III, 1686–87.   [6] *Ibid.*, V, 2635.
[7] See Brown, *British Statutes*, pp. 63–64.

needed in Vermont and the fact that the inhabitants of the State were accustomed to living under the English laws. But there was more than expediency involved. It is significant that the drafters of the Maryland Constitution of 1776 put the adoption of the English common and statute law, not into the body of the constitution entitled "Form of Government," but rather into the Declaration of Rights, along with the enumeration of the individual liberties of the people. Moreover, the Declaration of Rights holds Marylanders to be "entitled" to the common law (as well, in the same clause, as to trial by jury) and to the "benefit" of the English statutes.[8] This is not the language one uses to describe a system adopted solely for convenience; at its adoption, it was simply the historic echo of a long and recent dialogue (in which Marylanders like the Dulanys, father and son, took such a prominent part) over the "rights of Englishmen" and a just-begun war against a British Government which had denied those rights.

By such constitutional or statutory provisions as those cited above, the various American States took the first necessary step: the statement, in general terms, of the source to which their people were to look for guidance in legal matters. But many questions remained to be answered. How, for instance, was one to decide whether a specific British statute was or was not in force in a colony as of a given date? What data had to be adduced, say in court, to show that colonial courts—for which there were virtually no surviving reported decisions—had accepted and acted on such a statute? And so on. Movements got under way, sooner in some States, later in others, either to set about revising the State's laws and stating them in some detail or, alternatively, to undertake to supplement the general adoption of British statutes with an actual list of the particular British statutes to be treated as of force in that jurisdiction.

Virginia, at the urging of Thomas Jefferson, chose revision of the laws. In May 1776 Virginia had by statute declared that the common law of England and all English statutes of a general nature made "in aid of the common law" prior to the fourth year of James I, as well as colonial acts, should be in force in

8 Thorpe, III, 1686–87.

the Commonwealth. In October of the same year the Assembly, at the motion of Jefferson, created a committee to revise the laws of Virginia and by resolution in November appointed Jefferson, Edmund Pendleton, George Wythe, George Mason, and Thomas Ludwell Lee as its members. When the committee reported in June 1779, it indicated that its work had been done by three of its members (Jefferson, Pendleton, and Wythe), one of the original members having died and another having resigned. The three had divided the work among them, Jefferson having the job of deciding what parts of the English common law and statutory law before 1607 should be the basis of Virginia statutes, and the committee in 1779 reported 126 bills.[9] It was some years before the Assembly took final action; at length, in 1792, it passed an "Act Providing for the Republication of the Laws of this Commonwealth" and repealed so much of the act of May 1776 as related to English statutes.[10]

Statements of Statutes in Force

IN most States, at least in the first decades of their existence, the task of revising the laws in their entirety was thought to be too major a project. The more common approach to the problem of a definitive statement of what laws were in force in a given State was, at least insofar as the British statutes were concerned, to draw up a list of those statutes thought to have effect in that State. In Pennsylvania the legislature, by a statute passed in 1807, directed the judges of the state supreme court to report to the legislature which of the British statutes were of force in Pennsylvania. The judges did so, in a report which is appended to a volume of Binney's *Pennsylvania Reports*. The judges observed in their report that the terms of the legislature's reference of the question to the court entailed two inquir-

[9] 9 *Hening* 127, 175 and note. For Jefferson's description of the committee's work, see *Writings of Thomas Jefferson,* ed. Paul Leicester Ford (New York, 1892–99), I, 48–63.

[10] *A Collection of All Such Acts of the General Assembly of Virginia, of a Public and Permanent Nature, as Are Now in Force* (Richmond, 1794), pp. 302–3.

ies: first, to ascertain which English statutes were in force in Pennsylvania, and, second, to give the judges' opinion as to which of the statutes found to be force ought to be incorporated into the State's laws.[11]

The judges began by recalling that, although the charter granted to William Penn had provided that various English laws should be in force in Pennsylvania, nevertheless many of the laws of England would have been inappropriate for an infant colony. "It is the true principle of colonization, that the emigrants from the mother country carry with them such laws as are useful in their new situation, and none other." Thus the judges were of opinion that many of the laws of England, including many relating to property, felonies, the King's prerogative, rights and privileges of nobility and clergy, local commerce and revenue, and other subjects, were never in fact extended to Pennsylvania. Therefore the judges had to examine, not only the English statute books, but also Pennsylvania statutes and cases in order to decide which English statutes were unsuited to local conditions. In particular, the judges made the assumption that English statutes passed since Pennsylvania's settlement had not been extended to the colony unless they had been recognized by acts of assembly or by accepted practice in the courts.[12]

Passing to the second part of their task, the judges trod warily. The task of deciding which of the statutes found to be in force *ought* to be incorporated into Pennsylvania's laws "though very honourable, was very arduous, and in executing it, they have thought themselves bound to proceed with great caution. In works which consist in the alteration of long established usages, it it safer to do too little than too much." Therefore the judges were recommending the repeal of some English statutes, but doubtful cases they left for the lessons of further experience.[13]

A number of states followed a course like that of Pennsylva-

[11] Report of the Judges of the Supreme Court of the Commonwealth of Pennsylvania . . . to the Senate and House of Representatives, 3 Binney 593, 595 (Pa. 1808).
[12] 3 Binney, at 596–97.   [13] 3 Binney, at 597–98.

nia and provided for the listing of those British statutes thought to be in force in those jurisdictions. Sometimes the job was given over to one or more commissioners. North Carolina, for example, by act of assembly of 1817, appointed commissioners to enumerate the British statutes, both pre- and postsettlement, which had been found suitable to conditions in Carolina and had been adopted in the colony.[14]

Listing the English statutes thought appropriate to a given State's legal structure was helpful, but its value was limited if the actual texts of the statutes were not available. In Georgia the legislature in 1784 had adopted the English common law and such statutes as were usually of force in Georgia, but in 1823 the Assembly's Joint Committee on the Judiciary noted that, though fifty years had passed, knowledge of the English statutes was scanty and few copies of them existed in Georgia. The committee believed it "not only compatible with, but indispensably necessary to the liberty and interest of a free people, that the laws by which they are governed should be promulgated and known. . . ." Therefore the committee resolved to have a "fit and proper person" to digest and arrange the English statutes.[15]

The "fit and proper person" they selected was William Schley, who in the preface to his compilation of the British statutes remarked that it was "a matter of some astonishment that the statutes now presented to the public, should have been the law of the land from the time that general Oglethorpe first set his feet upon the soil of Georgia . . . and that they should not have been published and given to the people anterior to this period." The colonists, after all, had claimed the common law of England as their birthright. And in his dedication to the Governor, Schley added, "The magistrates of the country will no longer manifest surprise at the mention of an English statute which they never saw, and to which they had no means of access. These statutes will now become as familiar as our own,

[14] See *Laws of the State of North-Carolina*, ed. Henry Potter, J. L. Taylor, and Bart. Yancey (Raleigh, N.C., 1821), pp. iii–v.

[15] See William Schley, ed., *A Digest of the English Statutes of Force in the State of Georgia* (Philadelphia, 1826), pp. ix–x [hereinafter *Schley's Digest*].

and will, I hope, in part be the means of promoting a spirit of inquiry into the principles and foundations of our excellent system of laws. . . ."[16]

Magna Carta

Magna Carta played a varying role in the various American states' restatements of those British statutes which were thought to form part of the laws of those States. Sometimes the Great Charter contributed one or two lesser provisions; other times it was made a central feature of the digest. It might be noted that the selection of chapters from Magna Carta did not involve the somewhat more complicated problem surrounding British statutes postdating the settlement of a particular American colony. There might be disagreement on the status of British statutes between the emigration and the Revolution, but there was less argument over the premise that when the first emigrants left England they carried with them the existing laws of England, at least insofar as they were applicable to American conditions. Few Americans doubted that, if the settlers brought any English law, they brought Magna Carta. The only remaining question actually was, which of the chapters of Magna Carta (much of which dealt with purely feudal problems) had relevance in the American States.

South Carolina's enumeration of 1837 included five chapters from Magna Carta (chapter numbers are those of the charter of 1225, 9 Henry III) : chapters 8 (how sureties are to be charged to the King), 18 (the King's debtor dying, the King shall be paid first), 28 (no wager of law without a witness), 29 (guarantee of proceedings according to the law of the land and assurance of no sale or denial of justice), and 34 (in what case only a woman shall have an appeal of death).[17] The judges' report in Pennsylvania, by contrast, recommended that chapter 34 be among those provisions which, if thought to be in force in

[16] *Ibid.,* pp. xvii–xx, iii.
[17] *Statutes at Large of South Carolina,* ed. Thomas Cooper (Columbia, S.C., 1837), II, 417. For a discussion of the meaning of the chapters in question, see McKechnie, *Magna Carta,* and Swindler, *Magna Carta.*

Pennsylvania, ought not to be incorporated into the laws of the Commonwealth.[18] A chapter fairly commonly held to be in force was that which guaranteed certain rights to widows.[19]

Some of the compilers and digesters took the occasion for rather full commentaries on the place which Magna Carta occupied in the constitutional and legal inheritance of the American people, especially its relation to individual liberties. Samuel Roberts, in his *Digest of Select British Statutes* (1817), three hundred copies of which were subscribed for by the Pennsylvania legislature, began with Magna Carta, which, with the Charter of the Forest, Roberts held to be "almost universally considered as the bulwark of English liberties; as the pole star to guide the legislature; and in fact, as forming the constitution of the country." Roberts then traced the history of the Great Charter; it is interesting that he did not hold to the view, voiced by so many American colonists before the Revolution, that Magna Carta was meant to revive the ancient Saxon laws.[20]

Like many modern commentators on Magna Carta, Roberts was aware of the great diversity in the nature of the Charter's provisions and the consequent difficulty one has in reducing observations on the Charter to some semblance of regularity. Moreover, Roberts was aware that the majority of Magna Carta's provisions would be of no interest to his readers; indeed many of the chapters would be unintelligible.[21] Nevertheless Roberts was quick to assure his readers that some of the chapters of Magna Carta were "well deserving of notice" in that they lay at the basis of the constitution and laws of America. For one, Roberts traced the ban, found in federal and state

[18] 3 Binney, at 599.

[19] See, e.g., Julian J. Alexander, ed., *A Collection of the British Statutes in Force in Maryland* (Baltimore, 1870), p. 1; 3 Binney, at 599 (Pennsylvania).

[20] *Digest of Select English Statutes* (Philadelphia, 1817), p. 1 [hereinafter *Roberts' Digest*]. The Charter of the Forest came into being in 1217, when the forest clauses originally contained in Magna Carta were split off into a separate charter. The extensive royal forests were a special concern at the time because in those areas a forest law, harsher in many respects than the common law, governed. See Austin Lane Poole, *From Domesday Book to Magna Carta: 1087–1216* (2d ed.; Oxford, 1955), pp. 29–35; Doris M. Stenton, *English Society in the Early Middle Ages* (3d ed.; London, 1962), pp. 97–119.

[21] See A. E. Dick Howard, *Magna Carta: Text and Commentary* (Charlottesville, Va., 1964), pp. 8–9.

constitutions alike, on cruel and unusual punishment not only to the English Bill of Rights but back to its ultimate origin in Magna Carta's requirement that amercements should be proportioned to the offense, a small punishment for a minor default, a greater amercement for a more serious offense.[22]

Roberts paid special tribute to Magna Carta's chapter 29 (chapters 39 and 40 of the charter of 1215), the guarantee that no freeman should be proceeded against save by judgment of his peers or the law of the land and the proscription against the sale, denial, or delay of justice. Said Roberts, "No provisions of the great charter have been viewed by posterity with greater reverence than those contained in this chapter; which explicitly declares the protection which every man might expect from the laws of his country." Roberts took issue with the popular notion, supported by Blackstone among others, that "judgment of peers" meant trial by jury. Whatever may have been the technical meaning of the various parts of chapter 29 through the centuries after Runnymede, Roberts was sure of the chapter's importance to constitutional developments in Pennsylvania: "The framers of the constitution of Pennsylvania doubtless had in view this chapter of Magna Charta, when they provided that right and justice should be administered, without sale, denial, or delay. And that no one should be deprived of his life, liberty, or property, unless by the judgment of his *peers* [evidently intending the *trial by jury*] or the law of the land." [23]

William Schley, in the *Digest of the English Statutes* which he did at the commission of the Georgia legislature in 1826, laid similar stress on Magna Carta as being not just one of a number of British statutes laying down rules of private law but, more importantly, one of the jurisprudential cornerstones of American constitutional law. Schley was fully aware that the purpose of his compilation, under the legislature's mandate, was to state what statutes and what provisions were of force in Georgia and that, by this measure, very few of the substantive provisions of Magna Carta would be included. Nevertheless, he believed that the Great Charter, being the foundation of Eng-

---

[22] *Roberts' Digest*, pp. 3-5.   [23] *Ibid.*, pp. 5-8 (brackets in original).

lish liberty, ought to appear in his digest in its entirety, a course he accordingly adopted "that this great statute might appear entire, and without mutilation." [24]

Having set out the text of Magna Carta, Schley noted that only seven of its chapters were applicable in Georgia: the provisions dealing with waste by guardians, the duty of guardians to maintain an inheritance, widows' rights, amercements, the liberties of freemen and the ban on the sale or denial of justice, treatment to be accorded foreigners, and the ban on giving land to a religious house to be held of that house.[25] But, as he had already indicated, the real significance of Magna Carta to his readers did not lie in these several provisions of substantive law; it lay in the story of developing English liberties of which the Charter was such an intrinsic part. It was, he said, "undoubtedly the foundation, and great corner stone of that system of civil and political liberty, which the English people enjoy in a greater degree, than any other nation, except the citizens of the United States." Indeed Schley thought that two chapters by themselves—the chapter requiring that amercements be proportioned to the default and the chapter guaranteeing the law of the land and justice without sale or denial—"independently of many other valuable provisions in this statute, constitute a firm basis of freedom, and contain almost all the vital principles of liberty." [26]

Schley saw one significant limitation on Magna Carta, a limitation which, as we have noted above, was remarked on by some of the speakers at the conventions called to ratify the Federal Constitution. That was the fact that the Charter was not a declaration of the rights of the people by the people themselves; it was, in Schley's view, "a grant of privileges and immunities, proceeding from the sovereign, as matter of mere grace and favor. . . ." It was the seventeenth century which

---

[24] *Schley's Digest,* p. xxviii.

[25] *Ibid.,* p. 33 note. Schley lists chapters 4, 5, 7, 14, 29, 30, and 36 of the 1225 charter, which correspond to 4, 5, 7, and 8, 20–22, 39 and 40, and 41 of the charter of 1215 (chapter 36 was added in 1217). For a discussion of the meaning of these chapters, see McKechnie, *Magna Carta,* and Swindler, *Magna Carta.*

[26] *Schley's Digest,* p. 52.

Schley thought crucial, for it was then that "Magna Charta was made the foundation of this petition [the Petition of Right of 1628]" after centuries during which the principles of the Great Charter had been often disregarded. Schley sketched these developments the better to show how, "at this fortunate period, the first principles of our own free institutions were conveyed to this western hemisphere." [27]

Magna Carta, in Schley's view, was the American colonists' chief inheritance: "The colonies might with great propriety, be called *'a land of liberty,'*—having at their first emigration brought with them the principles of freedom as contained in the great charter, and successively improved in their political condition, in proportion as the principles of liberty were better understood and enforced in the mother country." Believing as they did in their rights as British subjects, the colonists were content to live under the British Constitution. The colonists therefore were slow to adopt the cause of Independence, and it took nothing less, Schley believed, than the British Government's oppression of the American people, in violation of the laws of England and the charter rights of the colonists, to bring about the Americans' change of attitude toward the mother country.[28]

Having thus shown the manner in which the colonists brought Magna Carta with them and later fought a war of Independence to secure the rights of Englishmen, Schley concluded by commenting on the debt which American constitutionalism owed to the British Constitution, by which Schley specifically had in mind Magna Carta, the Habeas Corpus Act, and the Bill of Rights. A comparison of these documents with American constitutions would reveal that many of the provisions of those constitutions were drawn directly from the British sources. But Schley was careful to repeat one marked difference which he saw between the two systems: "the one is the act of the sovereign conferring privileges on his subjects, and unwillingly consenting to an abridgment of his ancient prerogatives; whilst the other is the act of the people, forming a govern-

[27] *Ibid.,* pp. 53–56.   [28] *Ibid.,* pp. 56–57.

ment of their own choice, and limiting the power of their rulers. . . ." [29]

Influence of the Compilations

THE compilations and digests of the early nineteenth century played a useful part in making it more clear what parts of the statute law of Britain were to be treated as in force in the American States. They had a practical function for the practicing lawyer or the judge; even though frequently the lists were not themselves adopted in statute form they typically had official sanction. They had an educational role as well, especially in the commentaries, like that of Schley, which developed such themes as the place which Magna Carta and the other landmarks of Anglo-American constitutional history played in the development of individual liberties in America. Schley was able, in a short space, to impart to his reader a rather vivid picture of Magna Carta's meaning to an American. One can only speculate on the number of Georgia lawyers who, perhaps consulting Schley's *Digest* for some workaday purpose, stopped to reflect on the history set down in Schley's commentary and thereby to absorb something of his own heritage as lawyer and as citizen.

The importance of the early lists of British statutes was not limited to the few years following their publication. They usually acquired considerable prestige, and from time to time they have been cited in legal decisions down to our own day. For example, the Supreme Court of Pennsylvania in 1897 rejected a party's attempt to rest his case on a statute of James I on the ground that the statute in question was not among those listed in the 1808 report of the Pennsylvania judges. The court conceded that the omission of a statute from that list was not conclusive, but it raised a presumption of very great weight. The court quoted the preface to Binney's *Reports,* in which the judges' report appeared, as having said that, because of the research and deliberation that the judges put into their report,

---

[29] *Ibid.,* p. 59. For the full text of Schley's commentary on Magna Carta, see Appendix M, *infra.*

"a safer guide in practice, or a more respectable, not to say decisive, authority in argument, cannot be wanted by the profession." This, thought the court, remained true; it was "the view which has always been taken by this court, and in citing any of the British statutes as ground of judgment it has been considered sufficient to refer to that report as authority for their continuance as part of the law of the state." [30] Like examples can be cited from recent Pennsylvania reports of the courts of that Commonwealth referring to the judges' report of 1808 to determine if a particular English statute was received into the laws of Pennsylvania.[31] Citation can be made to cases of other States, such as recent Maryland decisions looking to Chancellor William Kilty's report of 1810 or to Julian Alexander's *British Statutes* (1870), based on Kilty.[32]

Over the years, especially in the nineteenth century, but occasionally down to the present time, the courts have had to work out rules of thumb in cases in which a party pleads a British statute. Such tests have had to be evolved judicially whether or not a given State has or had a compilation like the Pennsylvania judges' report of 1808 or a digest like Roberts' or Schley's. The Massachusetts cases are reasonably illustrative. In agreement with cases and commentators generally, the Massachusetts courts early made a distinction between British statutes enacted before the emigration to Massachusetts and those enacted afterward. For example, in an 1804 decision the Supreme Court of Massachusetts rejected a defendant's argument that a Massachusetts justice of the peace, a creature of statute, had no jurisdiction over a common law offense (poisoning cattle) since no Massachusetts statute gave him that jurisdiction. It was enough, said the court, that jurisdiction could be rested on an English statute passed previous to the emigration to Massachusetts. Judge Sedgwick observed, "It appears to me, generally

[30] Gardner v. Kiehl, 182 Pa. 194, 199, 200, 37 Atl. 829, 830 (1897).
[31] See, *e.g.*, Commonwealth v. O'Brien, 181 Pa. Super. 382, 124 A.2d 666 (1956), *appeal dismissed*, 389 Pa. 109, 132 A.2d 265 (1957); Tollinger Estate, 349 Pa. 393, 37 A.2d 500 (1944).
[32] Hitchcock v. State, 213 Md. 273, 131, A.2 714 (1957) (English Natural Healers Act of 1542 listed by Kilty as never having been in force in Maryland); Kelly v. Scott, 215 Md. 530, 137 A.2d 704 (1958) (statute of *De Praerogativa Regis* adopted in Maryland, according to Alexander).

speaking, that the *English statutes* which were in force at the time of the emigration of our ancestors from that country are common law here." [33]

Probably the most oft-quoted judicial statement both of the claim of the colonists to the common law of England and of the different view taken of statutes enacted before the emigration and those enacted afterward is the language of Chief Justice Parsons in *Commonwealth v. Knowlton* (1807):

Our ancestors, when they came into this new world, claimed the common law as their birth right, and brought it with them, except such parts as were judged inapplicable to their new state and condition. The common law, thus claimed, was the common law of their native country, as it was amended or altered by *English* statutes in force at the time of their emigration. Those statutes were never reenacted in this country, but were considered as incorporated into the common law. Some few other *English* statutes, passed since the emigration, were adopted by our courts, and now have the authority of law derived from long practice.[34]

Ultimately, when a party pleads a British statute in a jurisdiction in which British statutes have in some way been made a part of the laws of that jurisdiction, the court has had to decide the question—suggested by the very wording of the constitutional and statutory provisions in which States made British statutes, or some of them, in force—whether the statute is "adapted to the circumstances of the country" or has been "practiced by the courts" of that jurisdiction. For example, courts of the District of Columbia have had to interpret the effect of the provision of the D.C. Code of 1901 making the English common and statute law in force in Maryland on February 27, 1801, effective in the District "so far as it had not become obsolete or unsuited to our conditions." [35] The U.S. Court of Appeals for the District of Columbia has said that British statutes predating the Revolution are to be treated as judicial precedent, not as legislation, but that British statutes

---

[33] Commonwealth v. Leach, 1 Mass. 59, 60 (1804).

[34] 2 Mass. 530, 534 (1807). See also Sackett v. Sackett, 8 Pick. (25 Mass.) 309, 316–17 (1829); Going v. Emery, 16 Pick. (33 Mass.) 107, 115 (1834).

[35] See Burdick v. Burdick, 33 F. Supp. 921, 925 (D. D.C. 1940).

received in the District "must be considered well established rules of law, not to be varied without good reason. Nor do we lightly undertake the task of excepting a particular case from the general rule of a statute—old or new." But the court saw its chief office as reaching a result grounded in "reason and justice" and so, in the case at bar, made an exception to the rule laid down by the statute (which barred a legacy to a person who, having witnessed a will, testified to establish the will) .[36]

Rarely does today's lawyer have occasion to consult a compilation of those British statutes adopted in his jurisdiction. Few are the modern cases, compared to decisions of the nineteenth century, in which British statutes are cited and discussed. Unlike our ancestors in the years after the American Revolution, we have in every state more than enough laws passed by our own legislatures. The need which they felt to borrow from British laws is not felt by us. Increasingly we are reforming the laws we have or passing new laws to deal with problems unknown to people on either side of the Atlantic in the eighteenth century. But as the specific British statutes and laws once in force (and some still remain in force) become more remote, there should be no doubt of the role they played in helping to provide a system of laws while Americans learned the arts of self-government and legislation. Nor should there be doubt of the significance which the use of British statutes in a variety of private law contexts in the nineteenth century had in strengthening the sense of heritage of public law concepts such as those drawn from Magna Carta.

[36] Manoukian v. Tomasian, 237 F.2d 211, 216 (D.C. Cir. 1956) .

Chapter XIV

The Shape of American Law

after the Revolution

J *The Debate over the Common Law* [1]

AMES KENT, better known to posterity as Chancellor Kent, received a letter in 1828 from a lawyer in Nashville, Tennessee, asking the secret of Kent's success. In a long reply, the Chancellor reflected on the time when he had first been appointed to the bench. In February 1798 Kent had accepted Governor Jay's offer of a place on the Supreme Court of New York. Kent recalled that when he came to the bench, "there were no reports or State precedents. The opinions from the Bench were delivered *ore tenus*. We had no law of our own, and nobody knew what it was. I first introduced a thorough examination of cases and written opinions." [2]

Twenty years did not change things very much. In 1814 Kent was appointed as Chancellor of New York. He found that in that post he could chart pretty much the course he pleased. On the uses of precedent, Kent commented in his 1828 letter that "it is a curious fact that for the nine years I was in that office

[1] The several pages which follow draw in part from some of the writings which form the basis of Perry Miller's *The Legal Mind in America* (Garden City, N.Y., 1962) [hereinafter cited as Miller, *Legal Mind*]. The purpose is to suggest to the reader the usefulness of considering Magna Carta's place in nineteenth-century American legal thought against the larger backdrop of the main intellectual debates which occupied lawyers of that day.

[2] William Kent, *Memoirs and Letters of James Kent* (Boston, 1898), p. 117.

there was not a single decision, opinion, or dictum of either of my two predecessors (Ch. Livingston and Ch. Lansing), from 1777 to 1814, cited to me or even suggested. I took the court as if it had been a new institution, and never before known in the United States. I had nothing to guide me, and was left at liberty to assume all such English Chancery powers and jurisdiction as I thought applicable under our Constitution."[3]

The notable lack of published opinions, at least in the form of regular law reports, was anything but unique to New York. Lawyers arguing cases, and judges deciding them, in the early years of the Republic found themselves in the same situation. It was not enough that English cases could be found in regular reports. These could not be a substitute for American law reports for at least two reasons: the extent to which the English common law, though adopted in an American State, had been altered and adapted to meet American needs, and actual hostility, sometimes virulent, to English law in the newly independent American Republic.

Ephraim Kirby, compiler of the first volume of law reports in Connecticut (1789), commented on the first problem. Noting the "uncertainty and contradiction attending the judicial decisions in this state," Kirby recalled that the settlers in America had brought with them the jurisprudence of their mother country but that the contrast between the wealth and extensive commerce of England and the simplicity of manners and unsophisticated economy of America made deviations from the English laws frequently a matter of necessity. Yet no provision was made for reports of the cases, leading to the confusion which Kirby hoped to set right in his reports.[4]

Kirby's contribution to American law was a mixed blessing. The advent of printed reports did indeed make possible a continuity in the rationale and results of judicial decisions. Lawyers could cite or distinguish earlier cases; judges could rely on them or lay them aside. But whichever they did the law gained at least some dimension of predictability and coherence. On the other hand, it is difficult for the modern lawyer, faced with the diluvian outpourings of reported cases which fill the

[3] *Ibid.*, pp. 157–58.   [4] Kirby's Reports iii–iv (Conn. 1789).

shelves of today's law libraries, to think upon Ephraim Kirby and other pioneers of the printed American law report without at least a touch of malice.

The coming of the printed reporter in America sharpened the controversy, whose birthdate surely ought to be marked as no later than Independence itself, over the place and value of English law in American jurisprudence. Chancellor Kent took note of this dispute. When he took his seat on the Supreme Court of New York, "we had but few American precedents. Our judges were democratic. . . . English authority did not stand very high in those early feverish times, and this led me a hundred times to attempt to bear down opposition, or shame it by exhaustive research and overwhelming authority." [5]

Prejudice against the English law did indeed run high after the Revolution, at least in some quarters. Antifederalists in particular thought ill of the influence of English law, a view they developed in opposition to the efforts of some Federalists to implant the notion that there was a federal common law, apart from the common law of the several States. A legal *cause célèbre*, the case of *Livingston v. Jefferson* (1811), illustrates the contending points of view. Edward Livingston had appropriated the "batture" of the Mississippi River adjacent to New Orleans. The "batture" was an alluvial deposit along the river's bank and, until Livingston came on the scene, had been used by the local people as a sort of common wharf. Livingston's acts aroused local resentment, and the matter came to the attention of President Jefferson, who ordered Livingston removed from the property. Livingston brought suit for damages against Jefferson in the Federal District Court for Virginia.

Sitting in the case were John Marshall and John Tyler, the latter the father of the future President. Both rendered opinions. Tyler had always stood for the doctrine that the Revolution had reduced Americans to a "state of nature" and that no English common law applied in America save what was expressly adopted; this view he took in *Livingston v. Jefferson*. Marshall disagreed. He maintained that the common law ex-

[5] Kent, *Memoirs and Letters of James Kent*, p. 118.

isted in Virginia independently of any adoption by convention or the legislature.[6]

Tyler later wrote Jefferson, asking his views on the existence of the English common law in America.[7] Jefferson replied in a vein characteristic of a man who put natural law ahead of English law: "I deride with you the ordinary doctrine, that we brought with us from England the *common law rights.* This narrow notion was a favorite in the first moment of rallying to our rights against Great Britain. . . . The truth is, that we brought with us the *rights of men.* . . ."[8]

What Jefferson chiefly objected to was the use by American lawyers and judges of English authorities dating after the emigration to America and, even more so, after the American Revolution. Feelings on this subject ran so high that attacks on the use of English precedents, at least those of more recent vintage, resulted in statutes passed (though later repealed) in several States forbidding the citation in local courts of British cases decided since the American Revolution.

Passions ran especially high in Pennsylvania. In February 1803 a petition was presented to the state House of Representatives by Thomas Passmore, complaining that he had been arbitrarily fined and imprisoned for a constructive contempt of court in violation of the Pennsylvania Bill of Rights and praying for impeachment of the judges of the state supreme court. The House voted to impeach, and in 1805 the Senate tried the case. The proceedings, in which Caesar Rodney was retained for the prosecution and Jared Ingersoll and Alexander Dallas were defense counsel, turned into a contest over the use of English precedents, since these had figured in the contempt citation. The summing up of Boileau, one of the managers for the House, was an especially violent attack on English precedents and the legal profession. A majority of the Senate voted

---

[6] Livingston v. Jefferson, Case No. 8,411, 15 Fed. Cas. 660 (1811). For an account of the "batture" controversy, not very favorable to Jefferson, see Albert J. Beveridge, *Life of John Marshall* (Boston, 1919), IV, 100–116.

[7] Tyler to Jefferson (May 17, 1812) in Lyon G. Tyler, *Letters and Times of the Tylers* (Richmond, 1884), I, 263–64.

[8] Jefferson to Tyler (June 17, 1812), *ibid.,* I, 265.

to convict, but for want of a two-thirds vote the judges were acquitted.

Soon thereafter, in 1810, Pennsylvania by statute made it unlawful to quote in a Pennsylvania court any British case decided since July 4, 1776. Judge Henry Hugh Brackenridge, a member of the state supreme court, pointed out the obvious absurdity of hearing what an English court had to say years or even centuries before the Revolution but not hearing what had been said more recently by way of explanation or contradiction. But for his unwillingness to enter into a contest with the legislature, the judge would have been disposed to question the constitutionality of an act abridging the right of the judiciary to hear all reason on a question before it. "What is't to us," Brackenridge commented on the legislature's attitude, "though it were said by Trismegistus?" And he defended the English law, saying that "the stream of law in that country, now runs more clear in particular cases than centuries ago. . . ." Ultimately Judge Brackenridge's common sense prevailed, and the act of 1810 was repealed in 1836.[9]

Opposition to the English common law sprang from a number of sources: the recent memory of a war to be free of British rule, awareness of America's own peculiar social and legal needs, a kind of nationalistic pride in a homegrown jurisprudence, a rationalistic belief in the possibilities of common sense, domestic quarrels between Republicans and Federalists, and others. The flavor of these varying reasons is suggested by a toast given at a Fourth of July celebration in Cambridge, Massachusetts, in 1801, "The Common Law of England: may wholesome statutes soon root out this engine of oppression from America," and the refusal of the judges of New Hampshire around 1800 to listen to citations from "musty, old worm-eaten books" on the ground that "not Common Law—not the quirks of Coke and Blackstone but common sense" should govern their decisions.[10]

---

[9] See William H. Loyd, Jr., "The Courts from the Revolution to the Revision of the Civil Code," 56 *U. Pa. L. Rev.* 88 (1908). Hermes Trismegistus, the "thrice great Hermes" of Milton's "Il Penseroso," was the author of mystical doctrines.

[10] Quoted in Warren, *American Bar*, p. 227. The bar itself was the subject of

In the early years of the nineteenth century, a number of calls were issued by various American lawyers and writers for the rejection of the English common law as being unsuited to the kind of society being built in the United States. Jesse Root, an influential lawyer and politician in Connecticut, brought out a volume of Connecticut reports just before the turn of the nineteenth century and used the preface to that volume as an occasion to argue that the law of nature, not the English common law, was the "common law" of Connecticut.[11] He rejected the idea that the original emigrants to America had any obligation to submit to the laws of England, laws which, according to Root, were tainted by the vices of feudalism. With reference to such English documents as Magna Carta, Root echoed the line of argument which had been urged by such people as James Wilson and Oliver Ellsworth in the state conventions called to ratify the Federal Constitution,[12] namely, that in England the privileges of the people were a grant from the Crown, while in America, government springs from the people themselves. Even Magna Carta suffered this defect, for, said Root, it represented privileges "extorted from the kings by the barons" and "confirmed by the great charter of liberties as of his gift and grant."[13]

The principles of English law Root thought ill-suited to a young country where government was in the people, where the public good was the object of government, where land tenure was free, trade small, and crimes rare. Root would have Connecticut ruled by the law of nature—"those rules and maxims of immutable truth and justice, which arise from the eternal fitness of things"—and would hold that positive laws in conflict with the law of nature would be void.[14]

Root was not troubled by the thought that there might be fewer written sources in which to find the law of nature than to find the laws of England; nature's law, he said, "is near us, it is within us, written upon the table of our hearts, in lively and

no small amount of hostility in the early days of the Republic. Many lawyers at the time of the Revolution had been Tories; the exodus of loyalists amounted to perhaps one-fourth of the colonial bar. See Chroust, *Legal Profession*, II, 5–30.

[11] 1 Root's Reports i *et seq.* (Conn. 1898).

[12] See pp. 224–31, *supra.*   [13] 1 Root's Reports iii.

[14] *Ibid.*, pp. iii–iv, ix.

indelible characters. . . ." Nor did he doubt that it would be comprehensive enough to form the basis for a full-blown system of laws. Natural law, he maintained, would serve to "explain the laws, construe contracts and agreements, to distinguish injuries, to determine their degree and the reparation in damages which justice requires." More importantly, it would define the rights and duties of rulers and people. Root concluded that the law of nature would be "the Magna Charta of all our natural and religious rights and liberties." [15] That one arguing for the ousting of the English law should choose Magna Carta as his metaphor is not without interest as a measure of the pervasive influence of the very system which Root was rejecting.

Root's argument, like others of his time, was born in good part of national pride in the young American nation. Root acknowledged that a "great part" of American legal ideas were originally derived from the laws of England, as adapted to American circumstances. And he was willing to study and learn from the history, constitutions, laws, and practices of foreign countries, but he wanted Americans to erect an American system of jurisprudence, to "be what we profess, an independent nation; and not plume ourselves upon being humble imitators of foreigners, at home and in our own country." [16]

Root was not alone in attacking the English legal inheritance. Some attacks came from Republicans, who, like Root, exalted the American genius for law. For example, Charles Jared Ingersoll, son of Jared Ingersoll and a fervent supporter of the American cause in the War of 1812, delivered an address before the American Philosophical Society in 1823 in which he dwelled on the improvements which Americans had wrought in the English common law: such things as the simplification of pleading, amelioration of harsh criminal penalties, and the abandonment of archaic principles of land tenure. [17] Perhaps the bitterest indictment of the common law came from the lips of an Irishman, William Sampson, who had been expelled from Ireland by the British Government and had emigrated to

---

[15] *Ibid.,* p. x.   [16] *Ibid.,* pp. xiii–xiv.
[17] *A Discourse Concerning the Influence of America on the Mind,* in Miller, *Legal Mind,* p. 76.

America. In a speech to the New York Historical Society in 1823 he proposed codification of the laws and heaped scorn on the English common law:

They called it by the mystical and cabalistic name of Common Law. A mysterious essence. Like the Dalai Lama, not to be seen or visited in open day; of most indefinite antiquity; sometimes in the decrepitude of age, and sometimes in the bloom of infancy, yet the same that was, and was to be, and evermore to sit cross-legged and motionless upon its antique altar, for no use or purpose, but to be praised and worshipped by ignorant and superstitious votaries.[18]

A Bostonian, Robert Rantoul, Jr., painted an equally dark picture of the common law. In a Fourth of July oration in 1836, he argued for codification and condemned the common law as "sprung from the dark ages." It was, he said, "judge-made law," and therefore ex post facto law or a species of special legislation. "No one knows what the law is *before* he [the judge] lays it down; for it does not exist even in the breast of the judge. . . . No man knows what the law is *after* the judge has decided it." [19]

Other observers took a more moderate view. If Sampson was blinded by his Irish hatred of all things English, balance was provided by a Frenchman, Peter du Ponceau. Born in France, Du Ponceau came to America during the American Revolution as secretary to Baron Steuben. Du Ponceau settled in Philadelphia, where he studied law, was admitted to the bar, and taught at the Law Academy. In 1824 he wrote a dissertation in which he examined the question of whether the federal courts have an inherent common law jurisdiction. To Du Ponceau the idolatry with which the American colonists had viewed the English common law was clear:

The grievances which induced them to separate from the mother country were considered as violations of the *common law*, and at the very moment when independence was declared, the *common law* was claimed by a unanimous voice as the *birth right* of American citizens; for it was then considered as synony-

[18] *An Anniversary Discourse . . . Showing the Origin, Progress, Antiquities, Curiosities, and the Nature of the Common Law,* in Miller, *Legal Mind,* p. 123.
[19] *Oration at Scituate,* in Miller, *Legal Mind,* pp. 222–24.

mous to the British Constitution, with which their political rights and civil liberties were considered to be identified.[20]

But Du Ponceau observed that Independence brought a changed attitude toward the common law which we have already noted in American attitudes toward Magna Carta before and after the Revolution. Now it was to a written constitution, not to the common law, that Americans looked for the source of the delegated powers of constituted authorities. In the United States the common law became simply a "system of jurisprudence," not the *source* of power or jurisdiction. But if Magna Carta and the other parts of the English common law system were no longer to be looked to as the source of legal rights, they nevertheless remained, in Du Ponceau's opinion, indispensable. He could say "without the fear of contradiction, that it is impossible to abolish the common law." Attempt to do so, and we should "still recur to it for principles and illustrations, and it would rise triumphant above its own ruins, deriding and defying its impotent enemies."[21]

There were others to defend the value of the common law. Henry Dwight Sedgwick, writing in the *North American Review,* gave direct answer to Sampson. Sedgwick admitted that English law was artificial and technical beyond the needs of America but was unwilling to attack the common law. "If we were compelled to make a selection among all existing, or known systems of jurisprudence, we should certainly decide in favor of the common law. Our chief reason for this preference would be, that it is the law of freedom." Nevertheless, Sedgwick acknowledged the seriousness of the question whether the character of the American states had not become so different from conditions in England that Americans, while paying respect to the English contribution, should "declare a final separation, not a nonintercourse, but an independence in jurisprudence. . . ." Sedgwick's answer was, in short, to improve on the English laws, to make the law simple, homoge-

[20] *A Dissertation on the Nature and Extent of the Jurisdiction of the Courts of the United States* (Philadelphia, 1824) , p. ix.
[21] *Ibid.,* pp. x–xi, 105–6.

neous, intelligible, just, and economical, and, at least in the larger States, to codify the law.[22]

Insofar as the debate over the common law led to calls for codification of the law, probably the high point of the controversy in the nineteenth century came with the efforts of David Dudley Field in the middle decades of that century to have the State of New York adopt codes for its procedural and substantive law. In a sense, what Jeremy Bentham was to law reform in England, Field was to law reform in the United States. Field was successful in having a procedural code adopted, but efforts to see the substantive law codified ran into the vigorous opposition of, among others, James Coolidge Carter, a disciple of Friedrich Karl von Savigny and his school of historical jurisprudence.[23]

Field's civil code met with defeat in New York, but the codification movement had begun and gradually spread, especially in the western states.[24] Today much of the energy once directed to codification of the substantive law is channeled into producing "restatements" of the law of the kind produced by the American Law Institute.

Postrevolutionary Study of Law

LEGAL education as a part of a college's or university's curriculum in the common law countries can be traced, on the two sides of the Atlantic, to the establishment of the Vinerian Chair at Oxford and the creation of the first law professorship at the College of William and Mary. William Blackstone was the first occupant of the Vinerian chair, which was created in 1758, in which capacity he delivered the series of lectures which formed the basis for his famous *Commentaries*, published between 1765 and 1769. It was shortly thereafter, in 1779, that

---

[22] "The Common Law," 19 *North American Review* 411–39 (1824).

[23] On Savigny, see Julius Stone, *The Province and Function of Law* (Cambridge, Mass., 1961), pp. 421–48.

[24] For essays on the work and influence of Field, see *David Dudley Field: Centenary Essays*, ed. Alison Reppy (New York, 1949).

George Wythe was named professor of law at William and Mary, the first such professorship in America.

Wythe had played no small part in public events of the formative years before and after the Declaration of Independence. At the time of the Stamp Act, as a member of the House of Burgesses he had served on the committee appointed to draft the House's remonstrances against that statute. He had served in the Continental Congress and had signed the Declaration of Independence. In 1776 he had worked with Thomas Jefferson and Edmund Pendleton to revise the laws of Virginia, at the instance of the General Assembly. Few men of his day were better steeped in the traditions of the ancient rights of Englishmen or the developing liberties of Americans. It is not surprising that, of all his public achievements, he is best remembered as a teacher of law when one considers that Jefferson (who as Governor was responsible for Wythe's appointment to the chair of law) had studied law in Wythe's law office, that among Wythe's pupils at William and Mary was the future Chief Justice of the United States, John Marshall, and that later, after Wythe moved to Richmond, he had as a pupil Henry Clay.[25]

Gradually other colleges followed William and Mary's lead. The College of Philadelphia in 1790 appointed James Wilson, Associate Justice of the Supreme Court, as professor of law, an appointment which occasioned a series of lectures which form a notable contribution to American jurisprudence. In 1793 Columbia College created a professorship of law, naming James Kent, the future great Chancellor of New York, to the post. Yale established a chair of law in 1801, although no lectures were given until 1826, and Harvard Law School began its operations in 1817. The same year Dr. Thomas Cooper was elected temporary professor of law in the University of Virginia, succeeded by a permanent appointee, John Taylor Lomax, when Mr. Jefferson's University opened its doors in 1826.[26]

[25] For a sketch of the life of Wythe, see Oscar L. Shewmake, *The Honorable George Wythe* (Williamsburg, Va., 1950).

[26] See Warren, *American Bar*, pp. 343–64; Chroust, *Legal Profession*, II, 176–223. For an especially literate history of the Harvard Law School, see Arthur

Charles Warren has commented that the years after 1780 were marked by a "broadening of the study of the law," which he calls a "striking and remarkable feature in the history of law in this country." [27] It was a period in which the lawyer was expected to approach the law with something of a scientific method of inquiry. It was also a period in which the old standby of the law student, the works of Coke, began to give way to the study of Blackstone's *Commentaries.* Many were the complaints which students of the time voiced about the difficulties of mastering Coke. Daniel Webster recalled that when he had studied law in New Hampshire in 1801 he had read *Coke upon Littleton* through without understanding a quarter of it; "I really often despaired. I thought I never could make myself a lawyer and was almost going back to the business of school teaching." [28] Webster was not alone in his complaints.[29] Perhaps the most poignant record of a struggle with the lore of Coke came from the pen of the great scholar and commentator on the Constitution, Justice Story, who, while concluding that the mastery of Coke had been well worth the effort, confessed that the path to knowledge could hardly have been rockier:

I confess my heart sunk within me. . . . Then the student, after reading that most elegant of all commentaries, Mr. Justice Blackstone's work, was hurried at once into the intricate, crabbed, and obsolete learning of *Coke on Littleton*. . . . You may judge how I was surprised and startled on opening works where nothing was presented but dry and technical principles, the dark and mysterious elements of the feudal system, the subtle refinements and intricacies of the middle ages of the Common Law. . . . Soon after Mr. Sewall's departure to Washington I took it [*Coke*] up, and after trying it day after day with very little success I set myself down and wept bitterly. . . . I went on and on and began at last to see daylight, ay, and to feel that I could comprehend and reason upon the text and the comments. When I had completed the reading of this most

---

E. Sutherland, *The Law at Harvard: A History of Ideas and Men, 1817–1967* (Cambridge, Mass., 1967).

[27] Warren, *American Bar*, p. 180.   [28] Quoted in *ibid.*, pp. 176–77.

[29] John Quincy Adams, in his journal for March 1788, recorded the drudgery of getting through his folio of Coke. *Mass. Hist. Soc. Proceedings* (2d ser.), 16 (1902), 392.

formidable work, I felt that I breathed a purer air and that I had acquired a new power. . . .[30]

Lord Eldon advised a would-be lawyer that the study of Coke was undoubtedly toil and labor but that a mastery of Coke would lay the world of law before the student. Eldon scorned shortcuts, saying, "At present, lawyers are made good, cheap, by learning law from Blackstone and less elegant compilers." [31] Eldon may have been right in believing that Coke was a far more profound and, if pursued, rewarding subject of study than Blackstone. Thomas Jefferson, who as a student had found Coke hard going, nevertheless wanted the first professor of law at the University of Virginia to be well steeped in Coke.[32] But most American students were quite glad to avoid the anguish which Webster and Story described and take the Blackstonian shortcut. Blackstone's *Commentaries* were published in America as early as 1771–72, and at least a thousand copies of the English edition had been imported before that time. And with the advent of law professors and law schools in America, Blackstone proved a ready tool for teaching law.

American Commentaries

O<small>NE</small> of the American law professors to be impressed by the value of the *Commentaries* was St. George Tucker, who wrote the most notable American commentaries on Blackstone and who earned and deserved the name, "the American Blackstone." He founded one of the most remarkable of American legal families; his sons, Henry St. George and Nathaniel Beverley, were professors of law at the University of Virginia and the College of William and Mary, respectively (both using their father's textbook), and his grandson (John Randolph Tucker) and great-grandson (Henry St. George Tucker) were both presidents of the American Bar Association and both authors of

[30] Quoted in Warren, *American Bar*, pp. 175–76.
[31] Henry Flanders, *Lives and Times of the Chief Justices* (Philadelphia, 1858), I, 35.
[32] Caleb Perry Patterson, *The Constitutional Principles of Thomas Jefferson* (Austin, Texas, 1953), p. 5.

treatises on constitutional law. Of the great-grandson's writing, it has been aptly said that "probably never before was a legal scholar able to rely almost exclusively on authorities from his own ancestors—from his great-grandfather's *Tucker on Blackstone* to his father's *Tucker on the Constitution*." [33]

St. George Tucker put a high premium on the value of Blackstone's *Commentaries*. In 1800 Tucker succeeded his mentor, George Wythe, in the chair of law at William and Mary. He found that there was not sufficient time for him to prepare a full set of original lectures; instead he hit upon the idea of adopting Blackstone as a text and adding remarks upon such passages as might require illustration or explanation because of the divergencies of American law from the English law which was the subject of Blackstone's study. But in his preface to the published version of his commentaries on Blackstone, Tucker took care to say that it was not just the exigencies of time which led to his use of Blackstone, it was also his high opinion of the work. "On the appearance of the COMMENTARIES," said Tucker, "the laws of England, from a rude chaos, instantly assumed the semblance of a regular system." Blackstone could now replace Coke's "crude and immethodical labours," and even though Coke might well be considered a "rich mine of learning" the student no longer need expend the great labors required to extract its "precious ore." [34]

One might well suppose that the laying aside of Coke as the standard work for the student might mean the concurrent downgrading of Magna Carta, in light of the fact that Coke was the chief exponent of the Charter in the seventeenth century, when Magna Carta, after a kind of somnolence, came into its own once again with the clashes between the Stuarts and Parliament. Had that happened, then a generation of American lawyers, and their legal posterity, would have come to the bar unaware of the tradition of Magna Carta which had played such a conspicuous and central role in the colonists' struggles against British policy leading up to the Revolution and in the

[33] Stephen Hess, *America's Political Dynasties: From Adams to Kennedy* (Garden City, N.Y., 1966), pp. 387–88.
[34] *Tucker's Blackstone*, I, iii–iv.

constitution-making which followed. But that did not happen, for Blackstone carefully spelled out the meaning of Magna Carta to English liberties, and American works like *Tucker's Blackstone* made clear to American readers the place in American constitutionalism of the principles inherited from the Great Charter.

Blackstone enumerated three "absolute rights": the rights to life, liberty, and property. Each of these he associated with Magna Carta. To begin with, Blackstone observed that the British Constitution was "an utter stranger to any arbitrary power of killing or maiming the subject without the express warrant of law," quoting from chapter 29 of Magna Carta (chapters 39 and 40 of the 1215 charter). Tucker, in commenting on this passage in Blackstone, showed how this principle of Magna Carta was carried over into both the Federal Constitution and a Virginia statute which, he said, was "a pretty exact translation of this part of the British *Magna Charta.*" Due process of law Blackstone enumerated as another of the essential cornerstones of English liberties, the parallels of which Tucker pointed out in the due process guarantees of the Federal Constitution, the Virginia Constitution, and the laws of Virginia.[35]

The right of property Blackstone denoted as the "third absolute right." By it he meant "the free use, enjoyment, and disposal of all his acquisitions, without any control or diminution, save only by the laws of the land," and he pointed out that Magna Carta was "extremely watchful in ascertaining and protecting this right. Upon this principle the great charter has declared that no freeman shall be disseised, or divested, of his freehold, or of his liberties, or free customs, but by the judgment of his peers, or by the law of the land." Tucker, citing federal and state constitutions and laws, commented that "the means of acquiring and possessing property" had been recognized in America as one of the inherent rights of man. In both

[35] *Ibid.,* I, 133–34. At another place Tucker quoted the Fifth Amendment to the Federal Constitution and said that it should be considered to be "a liberal exposition, and confirmation of the principles of that important chapter of Magna Charta . . . [quoting chapter 29 of the charter of 1225]." *Ibid.,* I, Appendix, 304–5.

countries, the right of property connoted just compensation for property taken by the state. Blackstone traced this protection to Magna Carta: "And by a variety of ancient statutes it is enacted, that no man's lands or goods shall be seised into the king's hands, against the great charter, and the law of the land. . . ." Tucker by way of comment drew a parallel to the just compensation requirements of the United States Constitution and of the laws of Virginia.[36]

Especially important to the concept of a rule of law has been the availability of redress of injuries in courts of justice. This was a central guarantee of Magna Carta, as Blackstone observed:

Since the law is in England the supreme arbiter of every man's life, liberty, and property, courts of justice must at all times be open to the subject, and the law be duly administered therein. The emphatical words of *magna carta,* spoken in the person of the king, who in judgment of law (says Sir Edward Coke) is ever present and repeating them in all his courts, are these: *nulli vendemus, nulli negabimus, aut differemus rectum vel justitiam. . . .*

This promise of Magna Carta—we will not sell, we will not deny or delay, right or justice—found its exact duplicate in the laws of Virginia, which Tucker quoted as guaranteeing that "justice or right shall not be sold, denied, or deferred to any man." [37]

Tucker also took the occasion of his commentaries on Blackstone to note the introduction into the American colonies of the laws of England and, in particular, the assurances contained in the charters of Virginia and the other colonies that the settlers should enjoy "all the rights and privileges of free natives of England." [38]

What one generation of students learned from St. George Tucker the next learned from his son, Henry St. George. The son served for a while in Congress, as well as in the state legislature, where he introduced a bill for emancipation of the slaves which was defeated by only one vote. Never very enthusiastic about the life of politics, Henry St. George Tucker went

[36] *Ibid.,* I, 138–39.   [37] *Ibid.,* I, 141.   [38] *Ibid.,* I, Appendix, pp. 378 ff.

on the bench, eventually becoming, like his father, the president of the Virginia Supreme Court of Appeals. When he left the bar to become a judge, Tucker undertook to supplement his income by delivering a series of lectures on the laws of Virginia. He soon decided that it was not sufficient to give the lectures orally; they should be reprinted. As his father had done, he adopted the course of using Blackstone as the basis for the lectures, annotating them as necessary. While he left out a good deal of material of no interest to the American student, he reprinted in full, with references to the Federal and Virginia Constitutions, Blackstone's discussion of absolute rights and the manner in which Magna Carta served to protect those rights.[39]

While law students in Virginia were learning of Magna Carta and the inheritances of the English law from the Tuckers, James Kent was developing a similar theme for his students at Columbia College in New York. On his retirement in 1823 from the Chancellorship of New York, Kent resumed the professorship which he had earlier held from 1793 to 1798. Out of his lectures at Columbia grew his immensely influential *Commentaries on American Law,* which ran to six editions under his own editorship. Kent was far more interested in commercial law than had been Blackstone (who had in fact devoted little space to this area of the law) ; moreover Kent was an admirer of the civil law, which he had often relied upon in his opinions on the bench and which he made free use of in his *Commentaries.* Still he thought it important that his lectures develop fully the influences of English constitutional guarantees on American constitutional law. Accordingly he recalled some of the highlights of constitutional development in the colonial period and pointed to some of the specific rights of Englishmen which found their place in American constitutionalism.

Kent cited instances in which the inhabitants of colonial Massachusetts had insisted on the "privileges of English freemen" and had relied in particular on doctrines which they had associated with Magna Carta: the right not to have any tax imposed upon them "without the act and consent of their own

[39] See Henry St. George Tucker, *Commentaries on the Laws of Virginia* (Winchester, Va., 1831) , I, 33–44.

legislature"; the principle that justice "ought to be equally, impartially, freely, and promptly administered"; the right of trial by jury; and the assurance that "no person should suffer without express law, either in life, limb, liberty, good name, or estate; nor without being first brought to answer by due course and process of law." Kent recalled how the Stamp Act had brought forth from the Virginia House of Burgesses and from the Stamp Act Congress the claim to the inherent rights and liberties of freeborn English subjects, and the similar declarations of the Continental Congress in 1774.[40]

What the colonists had claimed as subjects of the British Crown, they sought to make part of the fabric of their new constitutions after Independence. They had ready models, said Kent, in Magna Carta "and its generous provisions for all classes of freemen against the complicated oppressions of the feudal system"; the Petition of Right, asserting ancient liberties, especially those in "the great charter of the liberties of England"; and the Bill of Rights. And they used those models. The American devices for protecting the rights of personal security and liberty, which Kent, like Blackstone, counted among the "absolute rights" of men, were "transcribed into the constitutions in this country from *magna carta,* and other fundamental acts of the English Parliament. . . ." Kent then listed a number of the specific constitutional guarantees which he had in mind.[41]

Of all the inheritances from Magna Carta, Kent thought due process of law as basic as any. "Due process of law" and "by the law of the land" Kent, following Coke, held to be interchangeable, and Kent felt that it was "a self-evident proposition, universally understood and acknowledged throughout this country, that no person can be taken, or imprisoned, or disseised of his freehold, or liberties, or estate, or exiled, or condemned, or deprived of life, liberty, or property, unless by the law of the land, or the judgment of his peers." [42]

Kent's special interest in and, even more, his profound knowledge of the civil or Roman law was unusual in a lawyer of

[40] *Commentaries on American Law* (New York, 1826–30) , II, 1–4.
[41] *Ibid.,* II, 4, 9.   [42] *Ibid.,* II, 10.

his or any other day in America. There were few commentators on or professors of law who would have blended the traditions of the English law with the values of the civil law in the way that Kent did in his *Commentaries*. There was indeed a handful of people who, through the early decades of the republic, sought to make the civil law, if not a substitute for, at least the peer of the common law in this country. Peter Stein has admirably traced the history of the efforts of James Wilson and James Kent and others between the Revolution and the middle of the nineteenth century.[43] But the mainstream of American jurisprudence in the nineteenth century was to be, in a very real sense, Anglo-American. A few philosophically minded members of the bar might look to the civil law, but the practicing lawyer, having mastered the mysteries of the common law as revealed in *Tucker's Blackstone* or as given him from the hands of some other preceptor, was quite content to stick pretty much with the system he had been taught. If change was what he yearned for, he was more apt to seek it in codification rather than in outright abandonment of the English legal heritage. And even codification was, for most States and in most areas of the law, a long way off.

Magna Carta and Natural Law

If the civil law never really took hold (save in States like Louisiana and in a few areas of substantive law), natural law was more readily received. Americans in the years before the Revolution had had no trouble merging the mandates of the law of nature and the principles of the British Constitution, the latter simply being a statement of the former. Magna Carta was not opposed to natural rights; rather both stood together as ground from which to shake a colonial fist at British policies. In like measure, Americans after the Revolution found Magna Carta and natural law ready companions. Thus state courts, in some of the earlier decisions, were willing to look to the "higher

[43] "The Attraction of the Civil Law in Post-Revolutionary America," 52 *Va. L. Rev.* 403 (1966).

law" or to the principles of Magna Carta or to both as being
sufficient, even in the absence of a specific constitutional provision, to serve as the basis for legal decision in cases involving
fundamental rights, such as those of property.

The Supreme Court of Georgia, for example, in 1847 referred
to the requirement of the Fifth Amendment to the Federal
Constitution that there be just compensation for the taking of
property and asked, "Does the amended Constitution do anything more than declare a great common law principle, applicable to all governments, both State and Federal, which has
existed from the time of *Magna Charta,* to the present moment?" The eminent domain clause did not, said the court,
create any new principle but simply recognized the existence of
a great common law principle "founded in natural justice,
especially applicable to all republican governments, and which
derived no additional force . . . from being incorporated into
the Constitution of the United States." [44] Four years later the
same court, in a case invalidating a statute allowing the taking without compensation of wild and unenclosed lands for
new roads, said that the requirement of just compensation
"was the law of the land in England, before *Magna Charta*"
and was ensured by the Charter. Therefore it became the law of
Georgia as part of the common law, and it was not necessary to
rest the case on the Federal Constitution. Not only was it part
of the common law, it was a principle inherent "in every other
free government," a principle "admitted by the ablest writers,
as being founded in natural equity and of universal application." [45]

Most judges might be unwilling, however strong their belief
in natural law, to rest an opinion solely on the dictates of
natural justice. But it was easy enough to do as colonial Americans had so often done and intertwine Magna Carta and the
common law rights with natural right and justice and weave

[44] Young v. McKenzie, 3 Ga. 31, 41–42, 44 (1847).
[45] Parham v. The Justices, 9 Ga. 341, 349–50 (1851). Similarly, see Bradshaw v.
Rodgers, 20 Johns. 103 (N.Y. 1822); Sinnickson v. Johnson, 17 N.J.L. 129 (1839);
Henry v. Dubuque & Pac. RR., 10 Iowa 540 (1860). See generally J. A. C. Grant,
"The 'Higher Law' Background of the Law of Eminent Domain," 6 *Wisc. L. Rev.*
67 (1931).

constitutional precedents, including Magna Carta and other British antecedents, with principles drawn from natural right and justice. Eclecticism was as much a characteristic of nineteenth-century American case law as it had been of eighteenth-century American pamphleteering. American constitutional law for a century and more was to be shaped in this Anglo-American tradition.

Judicial Review

To speak of the "shape" of American law after the Revolution, especially with reference to the influence of Magna Carta, is not complete without an examination of the doctrine of judicial review. It is by this doctrine that American courts wield a power possessed by the courts of few countries in the world: the power to strike down a legislative act found to be in violation of the Constitution. Most countries are accustomed to the idea of legislative (or executive) supremacy. In the United States there is a remarkable degree of popular acquiescence in the notion that the law is indeed what the Supreme Court says it is—even when the Court lays down propositions notably unpalatable in many quarters. The Court says that the races may not be segregated in public schools, that criminal defendants must have a wide range of procedural rights against police who would question them, that States may not prescribe the saying of prayers in public schools. The critics call for the Court's wings to be clipped, but the Court's power of judicial review remains undisturbed.

The Court's power to annul legislation is associated, above all, with Chief Justice John Marshall's landmark decision in *Marbury v. Madison*,[46] handed down in 1803. In that case, so bound up in the partisanship of the time, William Marbury, appointed a justice of the peace for the District of Columbia by outgoing President John Adams, sought to have the Supreme Court order the new Republican administration to deliver his commission of office (which had been undelivered before

[46] 1 Cranch (5 U.S.) 137 (1803).

Adams left office) . In his opinion Marshall interpreted an Act of Congress to authorize the bringing of such suits in the original jurisidiction of the Supreme Court. But Marshall went on to hold that the statute, so construed, conflicted with Article III of the Constitution. Decreeing that "a law repugnant to the constitution is void," Marshall concluded that the Court must disregard the Act of Congress and dismiss the case.[47]

On first glance, the case might seem a victory for the Jeffersonians; the Court's ruling left Marbury still without his commission. But one Federalist justice of the peace more or less was a small matter compared to the larger principle established in the case: the power of the Court to declare an Act of Congress unconstitutional. The decision came at a time when the Jeffersonians, victorious in the elections of 1800, were already indignant at outgoing President Adams' having packed the federal judiciary with Federalist appointees. Their hostility mounting, the Jeffersonian House of Representatives voted to impeach Supreme Court Justice Samuel Chase, noted for his conduct of sedition and treason trials. But when the case was tried in the Senate, there were too few votes for conviction. The Jeffersonians' antipathy to Marshall and the Court continued, but both the Court and the principle of *Marbury v. Madison* survived the crisis.[48]

Whence came the principle of judicial review laid down by Marshall in *Marbury v. Madison?* Marshall's biographer proclaimed, "This principle is wholly and exclusively American. It is America's original contribution to the science of law." [49] With respect, one must answer that this is simply not so. It is true that in no country is judicial review what it is in America. It is true that it is perhaps the most characteristic feature of the American constitutional system. But to say, as the quoted statement does, that its origins are exclusively American, cannot be supported.

The influences which lay behind the idea of judicial review,

[47] 1 Cranch (5 U.S.) , at 180.
[48] See John A. Garraty, "The Case of the Missing Commissions," in Garraty, ed., *Quarrels That Have Shaped the Constitution* (New York, 1964) , p. 1.
[49] Beveridge, *The Life of John Marshall*, III, 142.

as it evolved in *Marbury v. Madison*, were many—more indeed than the text of the opinion would indicate. Marshall, in supporting his conclusions, advanced a number of arguments. Some of them were a priori exercises in political theory, for example, that the theory of any written constitution is that "an act of the legislature, repugnant to the constitution, is void," and that, it being "emphatically" the province of the courts to say what the law is, the courts must decide which to apply when a constitution and a statute conflict.[50] Other arguments he advanced were textual, drawn from the language of the Constitution itself. Strongest of the textual arguments was the language of Article VI that only those laws "made in Pursuance" of the Constitution should be the supreme law of the land.[51]

Marshall's opinion is curiously devoid of citations of authority. It depends on analysis and argument, some of it (like the textual arguments) strong, some of it (like the suggestion that written constitutions inevitably connote judicial review) weak. Confining oneself to the face of the opinion, one might well agree with the statement of Marshall's biographer that judicial review was indeed an "original contribution." But the opinion should be considered in conjunction with the English and American jurisprudence and experience which preceded it.

The debates of the Federal Convention of 1787 are not very helpful; even less are they decisive. A number of statements by various delegates are often taken to show that they took it for granted that courts would exercise the power of judicial review to nullify unconstitutional legislation. Such a statement is that of Madison that "a law violating a constitution established by the people themselves, would be considered by the Judges as null & void." [52] But, as Leonard W. Levy has pointed out, the context of the statement shows that Madison was referring to the likelihood that state judges would strike down state statutes

---

[50] 1 Cranch (5 U.S.) , at 177–78.

[51] Treaties made "under the Authority of the United States" are also declared to be the supreme law of the land.

[52] *Records of the Federal Convention of 1787*, ed. Max Farrand (New Haven, 1911) , II, 93. See also statements by Elbridge Gerry, *ibid.*, I, 97, Rufus King, *ibid.*, I, 109, Luther Martin, *ibid.*, II, 76, George Mason, *ibid.*, II, 78, Gouverneur Morris, *ibid.*, II, 299, James Wilson, *ibid.*, II, 73.

violating the Federal Constitution, not to the prospect that federal courts would exercise such power over Congress.[53] And of course delegates can be cited who expressly rejected the doctrine of judicial review; John Francis Mercer, of Maryland, "disapproved of the Doctrine that the Judges as expositors of the Constitution should have authority to declare a law void."[54] Thus while Max Farrand felt able to say that it was "generally assumed" by the leading men in the convention that the federal judiciary would have the power of judicial review,[55] Levy is closer to the mark when he concludes that "decisive evidence cannot be marshalled to prove what the framers had in mind."[56]

But the discussions of judicial review which did take place at the Philadelphia Convention reflect the place which that idea was already coming to have in American constitutional thought. Colonial and postrevolutionary experience played their part in the forming of the concept. There was, for one thing, the fact that Americans as colonists had become accustomed to living under colonial charters—written instruments whose terms were enforced by various means, among them appeals to the Privy Council in England.[57] James B. Thayer, writing in the late nineteenth century, thought this colonial experience under written charters central to the later adoption of the constitutional doctrine of judicial review.[58]

Along with the colonists' own experience under their char-

[53] Leonard W. Levy, ed., *Judicial Review and the Supreme Court* (New York, 1967) , pp. 4–5.

[54] *Records of the Federal Convention of 1787*, ed. Farrand, II, 298. See John Dickinson's agreement with Mercer, *ibid.*, II, 299.

[55] *The Framing of the Constitution of the Unitel States* (New Haven, 1913) , p. 157. For a like conclusion see Edward S. Corwin, *The Doctrine of Judicial Review* (Princeton, N.J., 1914) , pp. 10–13.

[56] *Judicial Review and the Supreme Court*, p. 2. The most notable statement of the case for judicial review made at the time was put forth, not at the Constitutional Convention itself, but during the ratification debate. This was No. 78 of *The Federalist*, written by Alexander Hamilton.

[57] See pp. 20–21, *supra*.

[58] "The Origin and Scope of the American Doctrine of Constitutional Law," 7 *Harv. L. Rev.* 129, 130–31 (1893) . See also Charles Grove Haines, *The American Doctrine of Judicial Supremacy* (2d ed.; Berkeley, Calif., 1932) , pp. 44–59. For a comprehensive account of appeals to the Privy Council, see J. H. Smith, *Appeals to the Privy Council from the American Plantations* (New York, 1950) .

ters was their awareness of English doctrines and precedents. Through Coke, for example, they knew of the early English statutes which declared that if any statute be made contrary to Magna Carta it should be "holden for none." [59] And they knew, too, of Coke's declaration in *Dr. Bonham's Case* that Acts of Parliament against common right and reason were to be judged void.[60] Indeed Corwin has gone so far as to conclude that "all the law and the doctrine" on the question of judicial review "goes back finally to Coke's famous dictum in *Dr. Bonham's* case. . . ." [61]

Thus Magna Carta as interpreted by Coke becomes one of the fundamental sources of the American concept of judicial review. Given a view of Magna Carta as a basic norm by which the validity of other laws might be measured, therein lay an obvious precedent for viewing an American constitution (state or federal) as a fundamental law controlling legislative acts. Both were written documents, both were born of times of crisis in which men believed tyrannical rulers to be threatening their liberties, both were seen by eighteenth-century Americans as embodying natural rights, beyond the reach of positive laws.

The parallel between an American constitution and Magna Carta was obvious, and in Coke's commentaries and jurisprudence there lay ready precedents for establishing in American courts the doctrine of judicial review of legislation. Well before *Marbury v. Madison* there were instances of state judges announcing the power of courts to annul unconstitutional legislation; in these opinions the precedent of Magna Carta has a prominent place.[62]

[59] See pp. 121–22, *supra.*   [60] See p. 121, *supra.*

[61] "The Establishment of Judicial Review," 9 *Mich. L. Rev.* 102, 104 (1910). On the question, discussed p. 121 n. 26, *supra,* whether Coke was stating a constitutional rule, Corwin believes that "Coke was not asserting simply a rule of statutory construction. . . ." "The 'Higher Law' Background of American Constitutional Law," 42 *Harv. L. Rev.* 149, 365, 372 (1928–29).

[62] One should not overstate the extent to which the doctrine of judicial review had become established in state cases decided before the adoption of the Federal Constitution. Leonard W. Levy, disputing the findings of Charles Grove Haines' *The American Doctrine of Judicial Supremacy* (New York, 1914), says that of the seven precedents listed by Haines for the period 1776–1787 several are "spurious" and only two are "legitimate" precedents. *Judicial Review and the Supreme Court* (New York, 1967), pp. 8–10. While Levy's rebuttal to Haines is

In one of the earliest relevant state cases, *Commonwealth v. Caton,* decided in 1782, the Court of Appeals of Virginia upheld the Treason Law of 1776 against the claim that it was unconstitutional. But in the course of the opinion, George Wythe, Marshall's law teacher, gave his view of the court's power to declare a statute unconstitutional:

Nay more, if the whole legislature, an event to be deprecated, should attempt to overleap the bounds, prescribed to them by the people, I, in administering the public justice of the country, will meet the united powers, at my seat in this tribunal; and, in pointing to the constitution, will say, to them, here is the limit of your authority; and, hither, shall you go, but no further.[63]

The precedent of Magna Carta was relied upon in the Rhode Island case of *Trevett v. Weeden,* decided in 1786, a decision which, though unclear, is one of the most famous of the early state cases associated with the doctrine of judicial review. The case arose out of the unrest over paper money. In making paper money legal tender for debts, the state legislature had provided criminal penalties for refusing to take paper and had enacted that trials of a charge of such refusal would be without a jury. Trevett bought meat from Weeden, who refused Trevett's tender of paper money. A complaint was filed against Weeden.

The argument made by James Mitchell Varnum as counsel for Weeden survives, and it reveals how Varnum drew upon Magna Carta in claiming the unconstitutionality of the act under which his client was being prosecuted. Varnum, relying on Blackstone, traced the right to trial by jury to Magna Carta and recalled how later confirmations of the Charter had laid it down that judgments contrary to the Charter should be void. Trial by jury being embedded in the English Constitution, Varnum said, this "sacred right" was transferred to America by settlers who gloried in the laws of England as the "birthright of all the subjects." The Rhode Island Charter, he added, explicitly guaranteed the "liberties and immunities" of Englishmen—a concession which "was declaratory of, and fully con-

---

effective and persuasive, it should be noted that Levy quotes from Haines' original 1914 study; Haines brought out a revised edition in 1932.

[63] 4 Call (8 Va.) 5, 8 (1782).

firmed to the people the Magna Charta, and other fundamental laws of England." The royal charter had required acts to be agreeable to the laws of England, and Varnum submitted that the Revolution had not changed the proposition that the legislature could not deprive citizens of their fundamental right to trial by jury.[64]

Precisely what the court decided in *Trevett v. Weeden* is not clear, for the judges simply ruled that the information against Weeden "was not cognizable before them." But the state legislature treated the court's decision as having ruled an act of the legislature "unconstitutional" and called the judges to appear and account for their decision. A motion to dismiss the judges from office did not pass, and the case, especially Varnum's arguments, received wide publicity.[65]

Invoked by Varnum in Rhode Island, Magna Carta was relied upon by the Superior Court in South Carolina when in 1792 it decided *Bowman v. Middleton.* That case involved a dispute over title to land. The court held that the plaintiffs in the case could not claim under a South Carolina act of 1712 "as it was against common right, as well as against *magna charta,* to take away the freehold of one man and vest it in another, and that, too, to the prejudice of third persons, without any compensation, or even a trial by the jury of the country, to determine the right in question." Such an act, said the court, was void.[66]

Such cases being decided in state courts laid the way for the statement of Justice Chase in *Calder v. Bull,* in 1798, that there are "acts which the *Federal,* or *State,* Legislature cannot do, *without exceeding their authority."* [67] And they laid the way for the decision of Chief Justice Marshall in *Marbury v. Madison.*

The debate stirred by Marshall's decision continues to our own day. At the height of liberal agitation in the 1930's over the Supreme Court's striking down social and economic reform

---

[64] Peleg W. Chandler, *American Criminal Trials* (Boston, 1844), II, 267, 281–325.

[65] *Ibid.,* II, 325–26. See Haines, *The American Doctrine of Judicial Supremacy,* pp. 105–12.

[66] 1 Bay 252, 254 (1792).   [67] 3 Dall. (3 U.S.) 386, 388 (1798).

legislation, Louis B. Boudin wrote *Government by Judiciary,*[68] the burden of which was to question the extent of the Court's power to review legislation. And more recently Judge Learned Hand argued that judicial review was an interpolation into the Constitution. While he believed it a necessary interpolation, necessary to prevent the failure of the undertaking, he doubted that the framers had meant the federal courts to have this power.[69]

Such attacks have brought forth many defenders of the institution of judicial review. To quote only one, Professor Herbert Wechsler, in answer to Judge Hand, affirmed, "I have not the slightest doubt respecting the legitimacy of judicial review, whether the action called in question in a case which otherwise is proper for adjudication is legislative or executive, federal or state." [70]

Whatever the academicians may conclude, the fact of judicial review is undoubted. That it came to pass in this country is a result of more than one historical factor. But central among those factors was the tradition handed down from Magna Carta through the commentators to the hands of the American colonists who laid the legal foundations for the constitutional ideas of the young Republic.

[68] (New York, 1932).

[69] *The Bill of Rights* (Cambridge, Mass., 1958), pp. 1–30.

[70] "Toward Neutral Principles of Constitutional Law," 73 *Harv. L. Rev.* 1, 2 (1959). It is interesting that liberals, inclined in the 1930's to be suspicious of judicial review, tend in the age of the Warren Court to be the doctrine's defenders, whereas conservatives begin to wonder if judicial review is, after all, such a good thing. Boudin's book, *supra* note 68, is an example of a liberal attack on judicial review in the 1930's; for a sample of current conservative thinking, see *The Warren Revolution* (New Rochelle, N.Y., 1966) by L. Brent Bozell, the guiding hand in Barry Goldwater's *Conscience of a Conservative.*

Chapter XV

Justice Neither Sold, Denied,

nor Delayed

A Legacy of Magna Carta

No CHAPTER of Magna Carta has left a greater mark on American constitutional law than chapter 39, the guarantee of "law of the land" and the ancestor of due process of law as we understand it today. But chapter 39, as a seminal provision, is run a close second by chapter 40, the promise of the King, "To no one will We sell, to none will We deny or delay, right or justice." That this provision has had such influence in American jurisprudence may be easily explained. In the first place, on its face and own merits, the promise not to sell, deny, or delay justice has an obvious and inherent appeal. It is a principle which any enlightened system of justice would include as a basic premise.

Secondly, there are historical reasons for this chapter's later influence. It was merged with chapter 39 into what became chapter 29 in Henry III's reissue of Magna Carta in 1225. The new chapter thus combined judgment by peers (later interpreted to mean trial by jury), law of the land, and the ban on sale or denial of justice, all in a few short lines. Coke, Blackstone, and other commentators made much of chapter 29, and when Americans took Magna Carta to be part of their constitutional inheritance they knew chapter 29 better than any other provision. They saw the proscription on sale, denial, or delay of justice as a worthy companion of due process of law; as a result this guarantee of Magna Carta became a typical clause in the constitutions of the new American States.[1]

The state constitutional provisions based on the Great Charter's injunction against the sale, denial, or delay of justice have tended to take either of two basic forms. One is the rather longer statement preferred by the draftsmen of the Massachusetts Constitution of 1780:

Every subject of the Commonwealth ought to find a certain remedy, by having recourse to the laws, for all injuries or wrongs which he may receive in his person, property, or character. He ought to obtain right and justice freely, and without being obliged to purchase it; completely, and without any denial; promptly, and without delay; conformably to the laws.[2]

Some States have preferred a shorter statement, closer to the original language of Magna Carta, such as the guarantee put by Connecticut into its Constitution in 1818 of "right and justice administered without sale, denial, or delay." [3]

Court Costs and Fees

L ITIGATION over these clauses—and the cases have been many —has centered mainly on a party's claim that it is a sale of justice to require filing fees or a surety for costs, to require the payment of costs as a prerequisite to an appeal, or in some other way to extract payment from a litigant at some point in judicial proceedings. In resolving these claims, the courts have typically begun by having recourse to the historical abuses which led to the insertion of chapter 40 into King John's charter in the first place and generally have concluded by upholding the fees in question.

---

[1] See Appendix O, *infra*. In passing it might be noted that in the case law of some of the New England states, another of Magna Carta's provisions, that requiring the removal of fishweirs (chapter 33), has been drawn on in interpreting the common right of fisheries. See, e.g., Weston v. Sampson, 8 Cush. (62 Mass.) 347 (1851); Payne & Butler v. Providence Gas Co., 31 R.I. 295, 77 Atl. 145 (1910).

[2] Thorpe, III, 1891.   [3] Thorpe, I, 538.

The most-cited case has been a Rhode Island decision, *Perce v. Hallett* (1881). There a Rhode Island statute requiring entry fees and continuance fees for suits at law and in equity was challenged as infringing the provision of the Rhode Island Constitution that every person "ought to obtain right and justice freely and without purchase; completely and without denial; promptly and without delay; conformably to the law."

To require the court fees, it was argued, was in fact a sale of justice. The court admitted that the argument might be convincing if the court were at liberty to consider "simply the language of the provision." But the court thought the provision's history illuminating, for as it appeared in Magna Carta it was intended, not to abolish court fees altogether, but rather to put an end to the unjust practice of fees to buy favor:

The provision has a history which sheds light on its meaning. It was borrowed from Magna Charta, and in England the generality of jurists and legislators have supposed and acted on the supposition that it does not prohibit such fees. Reeves' History of the English Law, Finlason's ed. vol. 1, pp. 284–287, and notes. The better opinion is that it was designed to abolish, not fixed fees, prescribed for the purposes of revenue, but the fines which were anciently paid to expedite or delay law proceedings and procure favor. See Thompson's Essay on Magna Charta, p. 230. The character of those fines is copiously exemplified by Madox in the twelfth chapter of his History of the Exchequer. They appear to have been arbitrary exactions, often outrageously oppressive. Madox concludes his twelfth chapter with the following language: "Some men used to pay fines to have or obtain justice or right; others, to have their right or their proceedings or judgment speeded; others, for stopping or delaying of proceedings at law; and others were obliged to pay great and excessive fines (viz., a fourth part, a third part, or half of the debt sued for) to obtain justice and right, according to their several cases, so that the king seemed to sell justice and right to some and to delay or deny it to others. Against these mischiefs a remedy was provided by a clause in the great charters of liberties, made by King John and King Henry III. That clause in each of those charters runs in the same or consonant words, which are these: *Nulli vendemus, nulli negabimus, aut differemus rectum aut justiciam.*" Mag. Char. Joh. 40; Char. Hen. III. 33.[4]

[4] 13 R.I. 363, 364–65 (1881).

The provision of Magna Carta had been widely copied into the declarations of right in American constitutions, yet nowhere, so far as the court knew, had it been held to prohibit court fees. The fees in question were not only moderate in amount but, the court added in a characteristic Yankee insight, "entirely insufficient to reimburse the State for the cost of the administration of justice." The court's conclusion, therefore, was that the constitutional mandate "was intended to prohibit, not fees, like those prescribed in the fee table, but gratuities, or exactions, given or demanded for the direct purpose of influencing the course of legal proceedings." [5]

The state courts have rejected attacks on other kinds of court fees, with reasoning similar to that in *Perce v. Hallett.* The Wisconsin Supreme Court, for example, upheld a statute which required that, on reversal of a plaintiff's judgment on an appeal by the defendant, the cause should be dismissed unless the plaintiff paid the costs on reversal. This, it was held, did not violate a provision of the Wisconsin Constitution virtually identical to that of Rhode Island. Tracing the provision "back to the days of Magna Carta," the court said that it was designed "to prevent a species of official exactions made as the price of delaying or expediting justice" and bore no relation to a system of court costs bearing equally on all litigants.[6] Similarly, an Indiana court, upholding a statute requiring sheriff's fees to be taxed to litigants, distinguished such costs from "the corrupt and disgraceful practices of a corrupt judiciary in demanding oppressive gratuities for giving or withholding decisions in pending cases." [7] And docket fees for appeals have been commonly upheld against the claim that they are a sale of justice.[8]

The key to these cases has sometimes been the reasonableness of the fees or costs. In a case in which a party objected to the payment of a jury fee as a condition to a trial by jury in a civil action, a Minnesota court characterized the argument as being,

[5] 13 R.I. at 365.
[6] Christianson v. Pioneer Furniture Co., 101 Wis. 343, 347, 77 N.W. 174, 175 (1898).
[7] Henderson v. State, 137 Ind. 552, 563, 36 N.E. 257, 260 (1894).
[8] See, e.g., Littlefield v. Peckham, 1 R.I. 500 (1851); In re Lee, 64 Okla. 310, 168 Pac. 53 (1917), the latter case discussing Magna Carta at some length.

not simply an objection to a reasonable fee, but an objection to any fee at all. The court could see no valid complaint against a reasonable fee. "The constitution does not guarantee to the citizen the right to litigate without expense, but simply protects him from the imposition of such terms as unreasonably and injuriously interfere with his right to a remedy in the law, or impede the due administration of justice." [9] Or, as a West Virginia court, interpreting that State's constitutional guarantee of justice "without sale, denial or delay," said, "Of course, common sense tells us that there is a breaking point beyond which an ostensible fee would be so oppressive as to cease to be in reality a fee and become violative of the spirit of the constitution. . . ." [10]

Occasionally, therefore, one does find cases in which a fee is struck down because found to be unreasonable. Cases of probate fees are the principal illustration. In these cases the courts have looked to the constitutional ban on sale or denial of justice as originating in Magna Carta and have acknowledged that this chapter of the charter has been generally taken not to prohibit the imposition of reasonable fees. Nevertheless, the courts in these cases struck down payments which had to be made as a condition precedent to probate of estates and the amount of which the courts thought arbitrary and not bearing a reasonable relation to the benefit conferred upon the estates themselves.[11]

A problem of special concern has been costs which, though modest and reasonable of themselves, are still beyond the reach of a party too poor to pay any costs at all. Sometimes a court has not let this stand in the way of upholding the costs. For example, the Supreme Court of Oklahoma, having already upheld in an earlier case a statute requiring a deposit of $25 for costs as a prerequisite to an appeal to that court, specifically allowed the statute to be applied to a pauper unable to pay the deposit.[12]

Other courts are less willing to see the ax fall in this fashion.

[9] Adams v. Corriston, 7 Minn. 365, 370 (Gilfillan 1862).

[10] McHenry v. Humes, 112 W. Va. 432, 437, 164 S.E. 501, 504 (1932).

[11] State ex rel. Davidson v. Gorman, 40 Minn. 232, 41 N.W. 948 (1889); Malin v. LaMoure County, 27 N.D. 140, 145 N.W 582 (1914).

[12] Howe v. Federal Surety Co., 161 Okla. 144, 17 P.2d 404 (1932).

The Supreme Court of Kentucky, in a case involving a statute requiring the payment of a $5 fee as prerequisite to filing a civil suit, held that the requirement of such an advance fee did not violate the state constitution's guarantee of "right and justice administered without sale, denial or delay." The court rested its holding on the general agreement of American courts that this protection, drawn from Magna Carta, did not prohibit reasonable fees. But the court was careful to add (though strictly it was not part of the holding in the case) that if a litigant was unable to pay the fee he would not be "deprived of his day in court" since he could, upon a proper showing of poverty, proceed *in forma pauperis.*[13]

A Rhode Island case is a more overt interpretation of that State's constitutional ban on the sale or denial of justice. The Supreme Court of Rhode Island had earlier upheld a statute requiring a resident of the State to give surety for costs in a civil case on the ground that "a person cannot be said to purchase justice when he simply secures his opponent's costs in case he fails in the suit." But the court had left open the question whether, if a man was too poor to find a surety, the court "ought to go so far as to dismiss the suit," a question not before the court since there was no allegation of inability to get a surety.[14] The question there left open was answered in a case in which it was conceded that the plaintiff was in fact too poor to procure a surety. "To dismiss the suit in such a case," said the court, "would practically amount to a denial of justice and would be inconsistent with the Constitution." Therefore the court treated the statute as being discretionary, allowing a court, upon a showing by an indigent person that he had a probable cause of action, to waive the requirement of the fee.[15]

Equal Protection of the Laws

Problems of an indigent party unable to pay court costs or other expenses of litigation are today characteristically ap-

---

[13] Harbison v. George, 228 Ky. 168, 169, 14 S.W.2d 405, 406 (1929).
[14] Conley v. Woonsocket Institution for Savings, 11 R.I. 147, 148 (1875).
[15] Spalding v. Bainbridge, 12 R.I. 244, 245 (1879) (per curiam).

proached from the standpoint of the equal protection clause of the Fourteenth Amendment. This is especially true if the proceeding is a criminal one. A good illustration, perhaps the best, is *Griffin v. Illinois* (1956). Illinois law provided appellate review in criminal cases as a matter of right, but in order to obtain review a defendant had to furnish the appellate court with a bill of exceptions or report of the trial proceedings. The defendants in *Griffin*, who were indigent, sought a free transcript; this was denied on the ground that Illinois provided free transcripts only in death cases. The Supreme Court of the United States reversed the decision, holding that the defendants had been denied due process of law and equal protection of the laws.[16]

Justice Black, writing the majority opinion, conceded that a State was not required by the Federal Constitution to have appellate review at all. But once it did it could not discriminate against some convicted defendants on account of their poverty. The same, said Black, would be true of the initial trial: "Surely no one would contend that either a State or the Federal Government could constitutionally provide that defendants unable to pay court costs in advance should be denied the right to plead not guilty or to defend themselves in court. . . . Plainly the ability to pay costs in advance bears no rational relationship to a defendant's guilt or innocence and could not be used as an excuse to deprive a defendant of a fair trial." [17]

A number of later cases have developed the *Griffin* principle and extended it to the right to counsel as well as to a transcript and, moreover, applied it to collateral proceedings as well as direct appeals.[18] Justice Harlan has objected to this process (he dissented in *Griffin* itself), saying that the States are, of course, prohibited from discriminating between "rich" and "poor" as such, but it is a very different thing when the State simply fails to remove existing economic differences.[19] We have yet to see

[16] 351 U.S. 12 (1956).   [17] 351 U.S. at 17–18.
[18] See, e.g., Douglas v. California, 372 U.S. 353 (1963) (counsel on appeal); Lane v. Brown, 372 U.S. 477 (1963) (transcript in coram nobis proceedings). The Court has also had occasion to wrestle with the probem of effective appellate review of indigents' convictions in federal courts. See Coppedge v. United States, 369 U.S. 438 (1962); Hardy v. United States, 375 U.S. 277 (1964).
[19] See 351 U.S. at 29, 34–36; 372 U.S. at 360, 361–63.

whether the concept of equal protection, already rushing to embrace such diverse subjects as racial discrimination, legislative apportionment, and the poll tax, will come to require that the States make rich and poor equal before the bar of justice in civil cases as they have generally been obliged to do in criminal proceedings. If this happens, then the Federal Constitution's guarantee of equal protection, traced by Mr. Justice Black's opinion in *Griffin* to Magna Carta, will have done what the state constitutional guarantees of open courts and of justice without sale or denial, likewise traced by the courts to the Great Charter, did not do.[20]

The Law's Delay

CHAPTER 40 of the Great Charter of 1215 and its progeny in American state constitutions have three elements: justice is not to be sold, denied, or delayed. Most of the state cases, like those already discussed, deal with an alleged sale of justice. Occasionally there are cases, not involving monetary charges, in which a party argues that justice has been denied or delayed. An Oklahoma court has held that a judge against whom a contempt is committed is not disqualified to try and dispose of the contempt charge. For him to do this was held not to violate the requirement of the Oklahoma Constitution that justice be administered without sale, denial, delay, or prejudice. Indeed the court reasoned that summary action by the judge before whom the contempt was committed is necessary to *prevent* the denial or delay of justice:

Contempt proceedings are expressly designated as summary actions, and wisely so, for Gladstone said: "Justice delayed is justice denied." Should we sit idly by and let the lawful orders and mandates of this court be delayed by contempt by a vacillating attitude, and in the meantime permit a rightful suitor to be delayed in his judgment, would be a denial of justice and

[20] For speculation on the extent to which the reasoning of the right to counsel cases might be extended to require other aids to criminal defendants, see Note, 47 *Minn. L. Rev.* 1054 (1963).

a violation of the provisions of our constitutional enactment above quoted. To permit justice to be denied by a vacillating act of the court is to allow the Constitution, its provisions, and the rights of the people to go down to the same grave with the courts. How are fundamental and constitutional guaranties to be upheld without there be a court with courage to stand as a bulwark for constitutional liberties? [21]

One of the ablest of North Carolina jurists, Justice Sam Ervin of that State's supreme court, later elected to the United States Senate, associated the mandate of Magna Carta with the law's policy against piecemeal appellate review of cases. He wrote the North Carolina court's opinion holding that an appeal from a nonappealable interlocutory order did not deprive the trial court of jurisdiction to proceed with the adjudication of the case on its merits. Said Ervin:

Although the law's delay has been a chronic lament among men for centuries, the law itself does not will that justice should be lame. In truth, its consciousness that justice delayed is justice denied arose before this guaranty of *Magna Carta* was exacted from King John at Runnimede: "To no one will we deny justice, to no one will we delay it." The awareness of the law in this respect finds present-day expression in the declaration of our organic law that right and justice shall be "administered without sale, denial, or delay." N.C. Const. Art. I, Sec. 35.

There is no more effective way to procrastinate the administration of justice than that of bringing cases to an appellate court piecemeal through the medium of successive appeals from intermediate orders. The rules regulating appeals from the Superior Court to the Supreme Court are designed to forestall the useless delay inseparable from unlimited fragmentary appeals, and to enable courts to perform their real function, *i.e.,* to administer "right and justice . . . without sale, denial, or delay." N.C. Const. Art. I, Sec. 35.[22]

This being true, Ervin concluded that a litigant could not deprive the trial court of jurisdiction to proceed with a case by appealing a nonappealable order. A contrary decision would

[21] State ex rel. Att'y Gen. v. Owens, 125 Okla. 66, 75, 256 Pac. 704, 713 (1927). Insofar as the *Owens* case held that contempts were to be defined by reference to the common law, rather than statutes, it was overruled by *Best v. Evans,* 297 P.2d 379 (Okla. 1956).
[22] Veazey v. City of Durham, 231 N.C. 357, 363–64, 57 S.E.2d 377, 382 (1950).

involve the paradox of allowing a party to paralyze the administration of justice simply by doing that which the law does not allow him to do.[23] The principle which Ervin laid down is a fundamental one. It is a recognition that an unsophisticated application of Magna Carta's rule that justice shall not be delayed can in fact delay and thwart justice all the more. Hence the general rule that there must be a final judgment to serve as the basis for an appeal. This rule, in turn, must be applied with some sophistication so that the finality rule will not itself work undue hardships, and statutes, rules of courts, and decisions have worked out instances in which appeals which otherwise might be barred by the finality principle will be allowed.[24]

Open Courts and Certain Remedies

CLOSELY associated with the principle that justice shall not be sold, denied, or delayed is the ideal that for every wrong there shall be a remedy and that there should be free access to the courts of justice. In many state constitutions this right is made a constituent part of the clause forbidding the sale or denial of justice. Missouri's Constitution, for example, says that "courts of justice shall be open to every person, and certain remedy afforded for every injury to person, property or character, and that right and justice shall be administered without sale, denial or delay." [25]

Provisions like this, which in one form or another are common in American state constitutions, have given rise to considerable case law. Often a court will say that the language of "certain remedy" is not self-executing and that the function of adjusting remedies to rights is essentially a legislative rather than a judicial one. This was the position taken, for example, by a Rhode Island court in holding that there was no remedy for an invasion of privacy unless the legislature saw fit to create

[23] 231 N.C. at 364, 57 S.E.2d at 382–83.
[24] See, e.g., 28 U.S.C. § 1292 and F.R.C.P. 54 (b) . See generally Henry M. Hart and Herbert Wechsler, *The Federal Courts and the Federal System* (Brooklyn, N.Y., 1953) , p. 1344.
[25] Mo. Const., Art. I, § 14.

one.[26] Similarly, a Missouri decision holds that the guarantee of certain remedies and open courts refers only to such wrongs as are "recognized by the law of the land" and that it does not violate the Missouri Constitution if the legislature chooses to confine appeals in workmen's compensation cases to questions of law, the appellate court being bound by the findings of fact made at trial.[27]

It takes some adjudication to decide what is meant by the guarantee that "courts of justice shall be open to every person." A person aggrieved by the decision of a church body, for example, is apt to find the civil courts holding they have no jurisdiction to review that decision (unless property interests are involved) and that to refuse to hear such cases is not a violation of the constitutional mandate that the courts be open.[28] And there are decisions holding that "civil death" statutes (which perpetuate the old common law rule that convicts under sentence of life imprisonment are "civilly dead" and thus unable to sue in the courts) are not unconstitutional. The Supreme Court of Alabama, in so holding, traced the requirement of open courts to Magna Carta but noted that "civil death" was the rule until changed by statute in England. The court conceded "civil death" to be a "hard" rule, out of harmony with modern views and generally rejected in American courts, but it ruled it constitutional all the same.[29] (That such a statute should present serious due process and equal protection

[26] Henry v. Cherry & Webb, 30 R.I. 13, 73 Atl. 97 (1909). The plaintiff had sought to have the court recognize a "right of privacy" such as was conceived by Samuel D. Warren and Louis Brandeis in 4 *Harv. L. Rev.* 193 (1890). For the Supreme Court's discovery of a constitutional right to privacy, see Griswold v. Connecticut, 381 U.S. 479 (1965).

[27] De May v. Liberty Foundry Co., 327 Mo. 495, 37 S.W.2d 640 (1931).

[28] See Landis v. Campbell, 79 Mo. 433 (1883). See also Richard W. Dusenberg, "Jurisdiction of Civil Courts over Religious Issues," 20 *Ohio St. L.J.* 508 (1959); Note, 75 *Harv. L. Rev.* 1142 (1962).

[29] Quick v. Western Ry. of Ala., 207 Ala. 376, 92 So. 608 (1922). Alabama repealed its civil death statute in 1965. Alabama Laws, 1st Special Sess. 1965, No. 272. On civil death statutes generally, see Note, "Civil Death Statutes—Medieval Fiction in a Modern World," 50 *Harv. L. Rev.* 968 (1937); Note, "The Legal Status of Convicts during and after Incarceration," 37 *Va. L. Rev.* 105 (1951). A task force of The President's Commission on Law Enforcement and the Administration of Justice has called civil death statutes largely an "archaic holdover from the past" and has proposed a number of reforms in the law in this area. *Task Force Report: Corrections* (Washington, D.C., 1967), pp. 89–92.

problems, at least under the Federal Constitution, is obvious.)

Hard-nosed testators make a good deal of law. There is the kind of testator who puts in his will a condition that effects a forfeiture of a bequest if the beneficiary contests the will. Here the legatee has to choose (if such a clause be valid) between accepting a will even though he may think that the testator was mentally incompetent or that there was overreaching or other such circumstances, or challenging the will only to lose everything if unsuccessful. Therefore legatees faced with this dilemma have sometimes claimed that for a court to enforce such a forfeiture would violate the constitutional requirement that persons should have free recourse to the courts. Courts have split on this theory. A Missouri case, for example, holds that such a clause can be enforced without violating that State's constitution.[30] On the other hand, a Wisconsin decision holds that the mandate of open courts overrides in this instance the testator's provision for forfeiture.[31]

The Wisconsin court described the importance of the constitutional guarantee of open courts, especially in a case in which the legatee was claiming the testator's mental incompetence:

This is a basic and valuable guaranty that the courts of the state should be open to all persons who in good faith and upon probable cause believe they have suffered wrongs. Is it not against public policy to permit one person to deprive another from asserting his rights in court? And especially so before it is ascertained that the prohibition against contest is in fact that of the testator and not that of one exercising undue influence over him, or that he was mentally competent to make it?

This policy, the court added, rests on the twin supports of a concern that justice be done to the individual litigant, who should not be penalized for pursuing a claim supported by probable cause, and the public's interest that the true state of facts be ascertained and that valid claims (including the testator's true intentions) be vindicated.[32]

The Supreme Court of the United States has given recognition to the sound policy that there be free access to the courts.

[30] In re Chambers' Estate, 322 Mo. 1086, 18 S.W.2d 30 (1929).
[31] Will of Keenan, 188 Wis. 163, 205 N.W. 1001 (1925).
[32] 188 Wis. at 176, 205 N.W. at 1006.

Thus a State may not require that a corporation, as a condition of doing business in the State, agree not to remove to the federal courts cases brought against it in the courts of the State.[33] While this remains the rule as to the right to remove to federal courts, the more general policy, laid down in earlier Supreme Court cases, is that a party will not be held to his agreement, made in advance, not to take future claims to court. This rule had been recognized in an 1874 case in which the Court said, "Every citizen is entitled to resort to all the courts of the country, and to invoke the protection which all the laws or all those courts may afford him. A man may not barter away his life or his freedom, or his substantial rights." In a given case a person might decide to submit to arbitration; he might, in each recurring case, decide not to go to court. But he might not "bind himself in advance by an agreement, which may be specifically enforced, thus to forfeit his rights at all times and on all occasions, whenever the case may be presented." [34]

Such a rule is in the spirit of Magna Carta's assurance of justice neither sold nor denied and of the state constitutional guarantees of open courts. But today there are many jurisdictions in which the rule does not obtain. Agreements to arbitrate disputes which have not yet arisen are enforceable in an increasing number of jurisdictions.[35] They are commonplace, practical, and in most cases probably just. Certainly they are a well-accepted part of such areas as labor-management relations. But the old rule that a man cannot in advance waive his right to go into court has been disregarded in much harsher circumstances than the agreement to arbitrate made at arm's length by union and employer.[36]

The modern search for the fulfillment of the promise of Magna Carta's chapter 40 is an unending one. Reverting to the

[33] Terral v. Burke Constr. Co., 257 U.S. 529 (1922).

[34] Insurance Co. v. Morse, 20 Wall. (87 U.S.) 445, 451 (1874).

[35] Martin Domke, *Commercial Arbitration* (Englewood Cliffs, N.J., 1965), p. 18, listed 20 States as of 1965. For the origin and evolution of the common-law rule as to arbitration and its modification by statutes, see Charles O. Gregory and Richard M. Orlikoff, "The Enforcement of Labor Arbitration Agreements," 17 *U. Chi. L. Rev.* 233 (1950).

[36] For an especially egregious case, see National Equip. Rental, Ltd. v. Szukhent, 375 U.S. 311 (1964).

theme of an earlier part of this chapter—the law's delay—we are reminded by a recent Supreme Court decision that the principles laid down in chapter 40 are still unfolding. In that case a college professor in North Carolina had taken part in lunch counter sit-ins and had been indicted by a grand jury on a charge of criminal trespass. The professor claimed that the trespass charge had been abated by the Civil Rights Act of 1964, which among other things covered discrimination by various public accommodations.[37] The State's solicitor moved to take a *nolle prosequi* with leave. The effect of this procedure was to leave the charge in a state of suspended animation; the case could be restored to the trial docket whenever the solicitor chose, yet the defendant could neither get a dismissal nor have the case restored to the calendar for trial. Thus he lived from day to day under a cloud, being, in the eye of the law, neither found innocent nor declared guilty.

The Supreme Court, having the case on appeal from the North Carolina courts, held that the right to a speedy trial assured against the Federal Government by the Sixth Amendment was effective against the States by virtue of the Fourteenth Amendment.[38] The North Carolina procedure in this case, the Court concluded, had denied the professor his right to a speedy trial. In so deciding, the Court recalled that the "first articulation" of this right "appears to have been made in Magna Carta (1215), wherein it was written, 'We will sell to no man, we will not deny or defer to any man either justice or right'. . . ." The Court proceeded to trace the evolution of the right to a speedy trial through the writings of Coke and George Mason's Virginia Declaration of Rights of 1776, which "set forth a principle of Magna Carta, using phraseology similar to that of Coke's explication. . . ."[39] Chapter 40 lives on.

---

[37] Pending state convictions in sit-in cases were held to have been abated by the 1964 act in Hamm v. Rock Hill, 379 U.S. 306 (1964).

[38] Klopfer v. North Carolina, 386 U.S. 213 (1967).   [39] 386 U.S. at 223–25.

Chapter XVI

From "Law of the Land"

to "Due Process of Law"

A Cornerstone of American Constitutional Law

No LANGUAGE of the Great Charter of King John is more famous than the words of chapter 39: "No free man shall be taken, imprisoned, disseised, outlawed, banished, or in any way destroyed, nor will We proceed against or prosecute him, except by the lawful judgment of his peers and by the law of the land." Together with chapter 40—"To no one will We sell, to none will We deny or delay, right or justice"—this provision became chapter 29 of Magna Carta in the form in which it was confirmed by Edward I in 1297, when it was placed on the Statute Books of England.

Down through the ages the great commentators on the English law reserved their supreme accolades for chapter 29. Sir Edward Coke concluded his discussion of that chapter with this benediction: "As the goldfiner will not out of the dust, threds, or shreds of gold, let passe the least crum, in respect of the excellency of the metall: so ought not the learned reader to let passe any syllable of this law, in respect of the excellency of the matter." [1] Blackstone was equally glowing in his tribute to this passage of the Charter: "And, lastly, (which alone would have merited the title that it bears, of the *great* charter) it protected every individual of the nation in the free enjoyment of his life,

[1] *Second Institute*, p. 56.

his liberty, and his property, unless declared to be forfeited by the judgment of his peers or the law of the land." [2]

Posterity has endorsed these judgments. What the Great Charter called "law of the land" we would call "due process of law"—with excellent historical sanction, for Coke points out that as early as a statute of Edward III, "law of the land" and "due process of law" meant the same thing.[3] No concept has been so central to American constitutional law as that of due process of law. This is so both because of the historical associations which due process already carried with it when it was written into the Fifth Amendment of the United States Constitution and the comparable clauses of state constitutions and, even more so, because of the vehicle it provided for constitutional development in the hands of American courts. Just as its parent, Magna Carta, had grown and developed with each constitutional crisis in England, especially in the seventeenth century, so did due process of law prove adaptable, for better and worse, to the tides of constitutional litigation and judicial attitudes in the United States from the early nineteenth century onward.

From the start, the American courts, state and federal, approached due process with the express acknowledgment that it sprang from Magna Carta. The Supreme Court of the United States, in the case of *Murray's Lessee v. Hoboken Land and Improvement Co.,* observed that the words "due process of law" in the Fifth Amendment "were undoubtedly intended to convey the same meaning as the words, 'by the law of the land,' in *Magna Charta.*" The Court cited Coke in support of this statement and added that the constitutions of the several States, adopted before the framing of the Federal Constitution, "following the language of the great charter more closely, generally contained the words, 'but by the judgment of his peers, or the law of the land.'" [4]

In like fashion, state courts have often remarked that the provisions ensuring "law of the land" in the state constitutions are, as the Supreme Court of Maine put it, "substantially the

[2] *Blackstone's Commentaries,* IV, 417.   [3] *Second Institute,* p. 50.
[4] 18 How. (59 U.S.) 272, 276 (1856).

same as those found in chapter 29 of Magna Carta, from which they have been borrowed, and incorporated in the federal constitution, and most of the constitutions of the individual states."[5] And numerous state courts have agreed, usually citing Coke, that "due process of law" and "law of the land" are synonymous, both referring to the guarantee of Magna Carta.[6]

The courts' conscious tracing of "due process of law," or "law of the land," to Magna Carta made it likely that the courts would interpret these constitutional provisions in the light of the English history surrounding the concept of "law of the land." Lemuel Shaw, the great Massachusetts jurist, offered this reminder of the fact that "law of the land" was not an invention of American constitution-makers: "This clause, in its whole structure, is so manifestly conformable to the words of *Magna Charta,* that we are not to consider it as a newly invented phrase, first used by the makers of our constitution; but we are to look at it as the adoption of one of the great securities of private right, handed down to us as among the liberties and privileges which our ancestors enjoyed at the time of their emigration, and claimed to hold and retain as their birthright."[7]

Similarly the Supreme Court of the United States pointed out that the prohibition against taking life, liberty, or property without due process of law "is not new in the constitutional history of the English race. It is not new in the constitutional history of this country. . . ."[8] With the historical context of due process of law thus in view, American courts found it natural to develop a doctrine (which will be examined more fully below) that "in giving effect and application to the phrase 'due process of law,' which is held to be equivalent to the

[5] Saco v. Wentworth, 37 Maine 165, 171 (1853).
[6] See, e.g., State v. Rose, 33 Del. 168, 177, 132 Atl. 864, 868–69 (1926); Rhinehart v. Schuyler, 7 Ill. 473, 519 (1845); McKinster v. Sager, 163 Ind. 671, 677, 72 N.E. 854, 856 (1904); Board of Levee Comm'rs v. Johnson, 178 Ky. 287, 298, 199 S.W. 8, 12 (1917); Parish v. East Coast Cedar Co., 133 N.C. 377, 380, 45 S.E. 768, 770 (1903); State ex rel. Att'y Gen. v. Guilbert, 56 Ohio St. 575, 616, 47 N.E. 551, 556 (1897); Christiansen v. Harris, 109 Utah 1, 6, 163 P.2d 314, 316 (1945).
[7] Jones v. Robbins, 8 Gray (74 Mass.) 329, 342 (1857).
[8] Davidson v. New Orleans, 96 U.S. 97, 101 (1877).

phrase 'the law of the land,' the courts of last resort of this country have looked to the English decisions for enlightenment and understanding." [9]

So basic is the concept of due process of law that judges have sometimes commented that it would apply as a limit on governmental power even had it not been made an express part of the States' constitutions. To adopt or retain the common law, as the States did after the Revolution, was to inherit due process of law. William Wallace Thayer, a onetime Governor of Oregon and Chief Justice of that State's Supreme Court in the late nineteenth century, cautioned the bar not to think of due process as a new principle in the law: "it was a part of ancient English liberties, confirmed by Magna Charta on the nineteenth day of June, 1215, which came to the people of the United States as a part of the common law." Therefore it required no constitutional provision to give the people the protection of due process of law.

This provision has been a fundamental rule in the judicial system of every State in the Union which has adopted the common law; and to deprive a person of his property, except by "due process of law," or "by the law of the land," which means the same thing, would be illegal in the absence of the said fourteenth amendment. The people have never delegated any such authority to either the State or federal government. The amendment, therefore, introduces no new principle into the administration of our municipal affairs. It is but declaratory of a rule which has existed beyond the memory of man, and our judicature was builded upon it. [10]

Judge Thayer did not explain, if due process was secured by the common law, how, in the absence of some constitutional provision, it was beyond the reach of the legislature, which could reach and amend other parts of the common law at will. Perhaps he had in mind something of a "natural rights" idea rather like that expressed by the Ninth Amendment to the Federal Constitution, which, though by terms applicable only to the Federal Government, has in the recent Connecticut

[9] Pryor v. Western Paving Co., 74 Okla. 308, 310, 184 Pac. 88, 90 (1919).
[10] Paulson v. Portland, 16 Ore. 450, 454–55, 19 Pac. 450, 453 (1888), *aff'd*, 149 U.S. 30 (1893).

birth-control case been used against state legislation. Whatever the logic of Thayer's thesis, he was not the only judge to express it,[11] and it highlights the deep respect which has always surrounded the concept of due process of law.

Due process of law has been a coat of many colors. It has, in its time, been a coat to protect the propertied classes from the inclement weather of state social and economic legislation, it has been wrapped about criminals and society's outcasts who felt they did not have their day in court, it has restored ousted officeholders to their offices, it has comforted conservatives and liberals alike (though usually at different times in its history), it has been voice of the past and social conscience of the future. It has, in short, had a pervasiveness in American history that no other constitutional provision has come near doing. Possibly some future historian, reading the segregation cases, the poll tax cases, the reapportionment cases, and other cases of post-World War II vintage, will give a like niche to the equal protection clause, but it will be some time, even at the most headlong judicial pace, before the biography of the equal protection clause (a relative judicial newcomer) will be as fat as that of the due process clause.

Due process, as it was developed judicially in the nineteenth century, came to be identified with certain fundamental propositions or, to put it another way, to be recognized as laying down certain rather well agreed-upon assurances to those who claimed its protection. Among these may be included the following: (1) due process served as a limitation on the power of legislative bodies, (2) it served as a restraint on arbitrary power, (3) it carried with it a connotation of like laws applying in like fashion to people in like situations, i.e., it protected a person from being singled out for invidious treatment, (4) it barred bills of attainder and implemented the separation

---

[11] See, e.g., Young v. McKenzie, 3 Ga. 31, 41–2, 44 (1847), which said of the Fifth Amendment, "Does the amended constitution do anything more than declare a great common law principle, applicable to all governments, both State and Federal, which has existed from the time of *Magna Charta,* to the present moment?" Holding that it did not, the court said that the principle "derived no additional force . . . from being incorporated into the Constitution of the United States."

of powers, (5) it required certain procedural safeguards, above all notice and the opportunity to be heard, (6) it gave particular protection to the rights of property, (7) tradition frequently associated due process and trial by jury. The jurisprudence of the due process clause of the Fifth Amendment and of the comparable clauses of the state constitutions found these principles well established even before the adoption of the Fourteenth Amendment to the Federal Constitution, with its own due process clause applying to the States. After that time (1868) the aspects of the development of due process most worthy of notice are the ideas which unfolded in cases decided under the Fourteenth Amendment. That is a story which will be developed separately after a consideration of the basic propositions which nineteenth-century courts drew from due process clauses.

Due Process as a Limit on Legislative Bodies

THE natural connotation of the words "due process," stripped of the case law which surrounds them, would to many people be something to do with procedure, most likely procedure in a court of law. This inference would be all the more natural if one considered not just the phrase "due process," but also the entire provision in Magna Carta which guaranteed proceedings according to the law of the land. Chapter 39 sounds like a provision for the manner in which criminal proceedings shall be conducted before punishments may be meted out: according to the law of the land. Then if one considers that Magna Carta was a restraint on the power of the King, not of Parliament (which did not exist in 1215), then one might well conclude that, although a guarantee of due process of law in an American constitution laid down rules for courts, it was no bar to what a legislative body might do. By such a view, the "law of the land" would be any statute which the legislature chose to enact.

As it happened, this was not the view which American courts took of due process of law. A very few cases—and they were small in number indeed—held the requirement of "law of the land" not to be a limitation on the legislature.[12] But the overwhelming American view was quickly established to be that not any and every act of a legislative body was necessarily to be deemed the "law of the land." [13] The doctrine of judicial review, which had roots in ideas and events before the Revolution, was not long in taking firm hold as a basic concept in American constitutionalism.[14] Magna Carta played its part in the establishment of the American doctrine of judicial power to strike down a legislative act as being contrary to a constitution, and most American courts agreed that the principle of law of the land, or due process of law, was one of the standards against which legislation could be measured and, if found wanting, declared void.

Daniel Webster, in his argument in the *Dartmouth College* case, explained why it could not be correct to say that a legislature might make anything it liked the "law of the land":

Every thing which may pass under the form of an enactment, is not, therefore, to be considered the law of the land. If this were so, acts of attainders, bills of pains and penalties, acts of confiscation, acts reversing judgments, and acts directly transferring one man's estate to another, legislative judgments, decrees, and forfeitures, in all possible forms, would be the law of the land.

To allow this, Webster added, would be to do what was counter to the most basic assumptions of the Federal Constitution, since it would establish "the union of all powers in the legislature." [15]

The courts agreed with Webster about the meaning of "law of the land." Chief Justice Lemuel Shaw of Massachusetts, in the leading case of *Jones v. Robbins* (1857), said that the words "law of the land" could not be taken "in their most bald and literal sense to mean the law of the land at the time of the trial." Such a construction would make the constitutional guarantee wholly nugatory. "The legislature might simply change

[12] See, e.g., Mayo v. Wilson, 1 N.H. 53, 57 (1817).

[13] See, e.g., Trustees of the University of North Carolina v. Foy, 1 Murphey 58, 87, 89 (N.C. 1805).

[14] See pp. 276–83, *supra*.

[15] Trustees of Dartmouth College v. Woodward, 4 Wheat. (17 U.S.) 518, 581–82 (1819).

the law by statute, and thus remove the landmark and the barrier intended to be set up by this provision in the Bill of Rights. It must therefore have intended the ancient established law and course of legal proceedings, by an adherence to which our ancestors in England, before the settlement of this country, and the emigrants themselves and their descendants, had found safety for their personal rights." [16] Similarly the Supreme Court of Maine said that "law of the land" had long had an interpretation "well understood and practically adhered to. It does not mean an Act of the Legislature; if such was the true construction, this branch of the government could at any time take away life, liberty, property and privilege. . . ." [17]

By such statements, courts typically had in mind procedural requirements that legislatures were obliged to honor (though the state courts early used due process to protect property against taking without compensation). But it was not really a long jump, for a court so inclined, to see due process as imposing substantive, as well as procedural, limits on legislative power. When the courts took that leap, they ushered in the era of "substantive due process," a development that is better told as a part of the story of due process after the enactment of the Fourteenth Amendment.[18]

Due Process as a Restraint on Arbitrary Power

$\mathbf{M}$AGNA CHARTA is such a Fellow, he will have no Sovereign." So said Sir Edward Coke. It took no great briefing of authorities by counsel for American courts of the nineteenth century to appreciate that the symbolism of Magna Carta lay, as much as anything else, in being the antithesis of arbitrary rule. The historical circumstances of its origin—the submission of a monarch to the demands of his subjects (or some of them) —were well known to American judges. In a case arising under the due process clause of the Fourteenth Amendment, Mr. Justice Stephen J. Field recalled that "in England the

---

[16] 8 Gray (74 Mass.) 329, 342–43 (1857).
[17] Saco v. Wentworth, 37 Maine 165, 171 (1853).   [18] See pp. 363–67, *infra.*

requirement of due process of law, in cases where life, liberty and property were affected, was originally designed to secure the subject against the arbitrary action of the Crown, and to place him under the protection of the law." [19] With this history in mind, it was natural for the American judge to treat the Charter, especially its provision for due process of law, as laying down the principle that rulers and ruled alike are beneath the law, not above it. What later times tend to speak of as the "rule of law," nineteenth-century courts typically spoke of as freedom from arbitrary power.

Mr. Justice William Johnson, in an 1819 opinion of the Supreme Court of the United States interpreting the "law of the land" guarantee of the Maryland Constitution, thought restraint on arbitrary power the central theme of due process: "As to the words from Magna Charta, incorporated into the constitution of Maryland, after volumes spoken and written with a view to their exposition, the good sense of mankind has at length settled down to this: that they were intended to secure the individual from the arbitrary exercise of the powers of government, unrestrained by the established principles of private rights and distributive justice." [20]

To lay down the principle in the general language used by Mr. Justice Johnson in 1819 was not, of course, much of a guide to how courts in the years that followed would go about deciding when a legislative body had acted arbitrarily. Would it be a vague admonition, incapable of effective judicial application, and therefore little more than a check on the conscience of the legislature? Or would it become a carte blanche, especially with its application to the States in 1868, for judges to play legislators themselves and to declare "arbitrary" such statutes as did not accord with their own particular social or political philosophy? This was to become the most debated problem surrounding the due process clause in the early decades of the twentieth century.[21]

But whatever the specifics of the application of due process,

---

[19] Missouri Pac. Ry. v. Humes, 115 U.S. 512, 519 (1885).
[20] Bank of Columbia v. Okely, 4 Wheat. (17 U.S.) 235, 244 (1819).
[21] See pp. 363–67, *infra*.

bench and bar of the nineteenth century would have been in general agreement on the Supreme Court's analysis in an 1889 case that "the great purpose of the requirement [of due process] is to exclude everything that is arbitrary and capricious in legislation affecting the rights of the citizen." [22] Indeed this was the view most lawyers would have taken of government generally. In an age which shared with John Locke and John Stuart Mill an individualistic philosophy and which was deeply steeped in the heritage of individual rights from English jurisprudence, most would have subscribed to the sentiments of Mr. Justice Samuel Miller in *Loan Association v. Topeka:*

A government which recognized no such rights, which held the lives, the liberty, and the property of its citizens subject at all times to the absolute despotism and unlimited control of even the most democratic depository of power, is after all but a despotism. It is true it is a despotism of the many, of the majority, if you choose to call it so, but it is none the less a despotism.[23]

Due Process as Connoting
General Application of the Laws

Law, to Blackstone, was general in its operation. If, instead of operating on people generally, it singled out one individual, it was a sentence, not a law. A "law," thought Blackstone, must be "not a transient sudden order from a superior to or concerning a particular person; but something permanent, uniform, and universal." [24] This distaste for particularized acts of legislative bodies quickly became, in American decisions, one of the hallmarks of the concept of "law of the land."

The *Dartmouth College* case is remembered principally as a landmark in the development of the prohibition in the Federal Constitution against impairment of the obligation of contracts. But the argument of Daniel Webster, who was counsel for the college ("It is, Sir, as I have said, a small college. And yet there are those who love it."), placed greater emphasis on conten-

---

[22] Dent v. West Virginia, 129 U.S, 114, 124 (1889).
[23] 20 Wall. (87 U.S.) 655, 662 (1874).   [24] *Blackstone's Commentaries,* I, 44.

tions based on the concept of "law of the land." Dartmouth had been founded in 1769 by a royal charter from George III for the education of the American savages. By the charter the college was to be managed by a board of twelve trustees which would be self-perpetuating. After the Revolution, a dispute between the college's young president (a Republican) and the board of trustees involved the state legislature, also Republican, which sought to introduce some element of democratic control by creating a new corporation, with overseers appointed by the legislature, and transferring all the college's rights and property to it. The Supreme Court of New Hampshire, following an earlier New Hampshire decision that "law of the land" is not a limit on the legislature, ruled against the college,[25] and the case went to the Supreme Court of the United States.

There Webster argued that the act infringed the New Hampshire Constitution because in passing the statute the legislature had assumed a judicial power and, further, because property had been taken other than by the "law of the land." The legislature, he maintained, had declared a forfeiture, without trial or hearing. Webster quoted Blackstone on the meaning of "law of the land" and added, "Lord Coke is equally decisive and emphatic. Citing and commenting on the celebrated 29th chap. of *Magna Charta,* he says, 'no man shall be disseized, &c. unless it be by the lawful judgment, that is, verdict of equals, or by the *law of the land,* that is, (to speak it once for all,) *by the due course and process of law.'* " Webster asked, "Have the plaintiffs lost their franchises by 'due course and process of law?' On the contrary, are not these acts 'particular acts of the legislature, which have no relation to the community in general, and which are rather sentences than laws?' " [26]

Then Webster gave what unquestionably has since become the most celebrated, and oft quoted, definition of "law of the land": "By the law of the land is most clearly intended the general law; a law, which hears before it condemns; which

[25] Trustees of Dartmouth College v. Woodward, 1 N.H. 111 (1817).
[26] Trustees of Dartmouth College v. Woodward, 4 Wheat. (17 U.S.) 518, 581 (1819).

proceeds upon inquiry, and renders judgment only after trial. The meaning is, that every citizen shall hold his life, liberty, property, and immunities, under the protection of the general rules which govern society." [27]

Webster had cited Blackstone and Coke on Magna Carta in support of his proposition that due process requires that laws be general in their operation, not particularized. Although the Supreme Court decided the case on another ground, the impairment of the obligation of contracts, other judicial decisions of the time, notably those of state courts, gave judicial imprimatur to Webster's reasoning. The Supreme Court of Tennessee, a few years after the *Dartmouth College* case, held the phrase "law of the land" to mean "a general and public law, equally binding upon every member of the community." [28] That this should be its meaning the court thought best demonstrated by looking at its history, from its origin in Magna Carta, to its repeated denial being the occasion for the American colonists' ultimate decision to declare independence:

The right to life, liberty and property, of every individual must stand or fall by the same rule or law that governs every other member of the body politic. . . . The idea of a people through their representatives making laws whereby are swept away the life, liberty and property of *one* or a *few* citizens, by which neither the representatives nor their other constituents are willing to be bound, is too odious to be tolerated in any government where freedom has a name. Such abuses resulted in the adoption of Magna Charta in England, securing the subject against odious exceptions, which is, and for centuries, has been, the foundation of English liberty. Its infraction was a leading cause why we separated from that country, and its value as a fundamental rule for the protection of the citizen against legislative usurpation was the reason of its adoption as part of our constitution.[29]

Strict application of this meaning of "law of the land" would make what we call "special legislation" impossible. And this, in the early cases, is precisely what often happened. For example, in 1829 the Tennessee legislature passed an act constituting a

[27] *Ibid.*   [28] Vanzant v. Waddel, 10 Tenn. 259, 270 (1829).
[29] 10 Tenn., at 270–71.

special tribunal for trying suits commenced by the Bank of the State against its officers and their sureties, and from whose decision there was no appeal. The act was attacked in the special tribunal. Each of the three judges sitting delivered a separate opinion and, while they differed on other grounds, agreed that the law was unconstitutional because partial in its operations and therefore not the law of the land. In his opinion, Justice William E. Kennedy cited Magna Carta and Coke's *Institutes* and said, "Does this statute apply to *all* the citizens of the state? Does it apply to *all* the debtor class of society? Or to *all* those who are indebted to the bank? It does not. It is intended to affect only a few of those who are indebted to that institution. It cannot therefore with propriety be called *legem terrae*, the law of the land." [30]

Under this approach it would be difficult for a legislature to pass remedial legislation dealing with a particular situation. For example, the Tennessee legislature passed a statute providing that a suit should be dismissed if it was found to have been brought in trust for another, but the act applied only to suits brought in the name of any Indian reservee to recover lands under the provisions of the treaties of 1817 and 1819 between the United States and the Cherokee Nation. The act was passed to deal with those who, the legislature believed, had speculated upon the ignorance and necessities of the Indian reservees and had fraudulently obtained their claims for trifling considerations and were corruptly obtaining false evidence to support nonexistent claims, to the prejudice of purchasers from the State. The state supreme court, declaring that "law of the land" required that "the rights of every individual must stand or fall by the same rule or *law* that governs every other member of the body politic . . . ," said that this statute did not meet that standard. It could not be the "law of the land" because it was "limited in its operation to a comparatively small section of the state, and to a very few individuals claiming a very small portion of the section of country referred to." [31]

This use of due process is a rarity today. The typical state

[30] Bank of the State v. Cooper, 10 Tenn. 599, 621 (1831).
[31] Wally's Heirs v. Kennedy, 10 Tenn. 554, 555–56 (1831).

constitution deals in great detail with the kinds of "special" legislation which the legislature may not pass. The Virginia Constitution of 1902, for example, enumerates twenty kinds of special laws which the General Assembly "shall not enact." [32] Such specificity is a product in part of the trend, which became pronounced in the latter part of the nineteenth and the early part of the twentieth centuries, toward long, detailed state constitutions approaching the complexity of a code of laws, rather than conforming to the older notion, represented by the original state constitutions, that the fundamental document should simply set out basic propositions in fairly general language. Attacks against special legislation in a state court today will, therefore, nearly always rest more heavily upon some specific prohibition against that kind of statute. Even if the advocate also adds a claim sounding in due process, the court's decision will likely turn on an interpretation of the more specific clause. (Actually, as any student of political science knows, in most States constitutional prohibitions against special legislation are notoriously ineffective against special legislation, for example, that which, by clever drafting, can only apply to one county in the entire State, though that is expressly forbidden by the State's constitution.[33])

In the federal courts, since the addition to the Federal Constitution of the equal protection clause, a party's claim of invidious classification or of particularized legislation nearly always is briefed, argued, and decided as being primarily a problem of equal protection, rather than of due process of law. Here the inquiry becomes one of permissible classification, rather than "special" legislation. It is nonsense to suppose that there can never be classifications; if there could not be, then legislators might as well go home. The Supreme Court acknowledged this long ago: "Indeed, the greater part of all legislation is special, either in the extent to which it operates, or the objects sought to be attained by it." [34]

[32] Section 63.
[33] See J. G. Sutherland, *Statutes and Statutory Construction*, ed. Frank E. Horack, Jr. (3d ed.; Chicago, 1943), II, § 2101; Note, 42 *Va. L. Rev.* 860 (1956).
[34] Home Ins. Co. v. New York, 134 U.S. 594, 606 (1890).

Under the equal protection clause, the central question, then, is the "reasonableness" of the statutory classification, having in mind the purposes for which the statute was passed and the traits of the class of people or activities to which the statute applies.[35] Certain kinds of cases—those involving, for example, racial classifications—test statutes by far more rigid standards than those of "reasonableness." In such cases the Supreme Court will not indulge the usual presumptions in favor of the legislative judgment; in a succession of cases the Court has treated racial classifications as being, at best, constitutionally suspect.[36] And increasingly there are coming to be other areas of the law—including the apportionment of state legislatures and the imposition of the poll tax—in which state statutes are measured against far stricter standards then "reasonableness."[37] But outside such areas as these, the usual test is the reasonableness of the classification, a test not difficult to satisfy, especially in instances of economic regulation, where the Supreme Court only once since the so-called "Constitutional Revolution" of the 1930's has struck down on equal protection grounds a state statute regulating economic activities.[38]

Even though questions of classification, so often handled in nineteenth-century state courts as a due process problem, are more likely today to be thought of as involving the equal protection clause, it should not be thought that due process and equal protection are unrelated. Far from it, as the Supreme Court has observed a number of times. In a 1921 case Chief Justice Taft pointed out that there is an overlap between the two clauses and that a violation of one may at times involve a violation of the other. The spheres of protection which they offer are, of course, not coterminous, and they came into the Federal Constitution by different routes—the due process clause originating in Magna Carta and appearing in the Fifth

[35] See Joseph Tussman and Jacobus tenBroek, "The Equal Protection of the Laws," 37 *Calif. L. Rev.* 341 (1949).

[36] See, e.g., McLaughlin v. Florida, 379 U.S. 184, 192 (1964); Bolling v. Sharpe, 347 U.S. 497, 499 (1954); Korematsu v. United States, 323 U.S. 214, 216 (1944).

[37] See, e.g., Reynolds v. Sims, 377 U.S. 533, 561–68 (1964) (legislative apportionment); Harper v. Virginia Board of Elections, 383 U.S. 663 (1966) (poll tax).

[38] Morey v. Doud, 354 U.S. 457 (1957).

Amendment, the equal protection clause being added only with the Fourteenth and thus not, by terms, being a limitation on the Federal Government. But Taft noted that there is clearly an element of equal protection in due process itself: "It, of course, tends to secure equality of law in the sense that it makes a required minimum of protection for every one's right of life, liberty and property, which the Congress or the legislature may not withhold. Our whole system of law is predicated on the general, fundamental principle of equality of application of the law." [39]

It is interesting that Justices Frankfurter and Black, often thought to epitomize contrasting judicial philosophies, have each made similar associations of due process and equal protection and, moreover, have traced both to Magna Carta. Justice Frankfurter put it this way: "The safeguards of 'due process of law' and 'the equal protection of the laws' summarize the history of freedom of English-speaking peoples running back to Magna Carta and reflected in the constitutional development of our people." [40] Justice Black took the occasion of one of his landmark opinions in criminal law, *Griffin v. Illinois*,[41] to develop the same idea. In *Griffin* the Court held that, where a State has appellate review in criminal cases and requires the defendant filing the appeal to furnish a bill of exceptions or a report of the trial proceedings, it must furnish a transcript or some equivalent to an indigent defendant who otherwise would be unable to appeal. Often thought of as an equal protection decision, *Griffin* in fact rested on both the due process and equal protection clauses of the Fourteenth Amendment.

Justice Black discussed the "age-old problem" of providing equal justice for rich and poor, powerful and weak alike. To this ideal Black ascribed, at least in part, "the royal concessions of Magna Charta" in chapter 39, the guarantee of law of the land, and in chapter 40, the promise not to sell, deny, or delay right or justice. "In this tradition," Black continued, "our own

[39] Truax v. Corrigan, 257 U.S. 312, 332 (1921). For a similar statement in a state court decision, see Camden County v. Pennsauken Sewerage Authority, 15 N.J. 456, 469, 105 A.2d 505, 511 (1954).
[40] Malinski v. New York, 324 U.S. 401, 413–14 (1945) (separate opinion).
[41] 351 U.S. 12 (1956).

constitutional guaranties of due process and equal protection both call for procedures in criminal trials which allow no invidious discriminations between persons and different groups of persons. Both equal protection and due process emphasize the central aim of our entire judicial system—all people charged with crime must, so far as the law is concerned, 'stand on an equality before the bar of justice in every American court.' " [42]

In another context, the Supreme Court has reminded us that, were there no equal protection clause, due process could, if a court chose, serve at least a good part of the same function. On May 17, 1954, in *Brown v. Board of Education,* the Court held that the segregation of the races in a State's public schools violates the equal protection clause of the Fourteenth Amendment.[43] In a companion case to *Brown* the Court had to decide what ruling to make as to segregated schools in the District of Columbia. Chief Justice Warren, the author of the *Brown* opinion, also wrote for the Court in the District of Columbia decision, *Bolling v. Sharpe.* He acknowledged that the case could not be rested on the equal protection clause, for only the Fifth, and not the Fourteenth, Amendment applied to the federal enclave, and there was no equal protection clause in the Fifth Amendment. But the Fifth did have a due process clause. True, Warren conceded, "The 'equal protection of the laws' is a more explicit safeguard of prohibited unfairness than 'due process of law,' and, therefore, we do not imply that the two are always interchangeable phrases. But, as this Court has recognized, discrimination may be so unjustifiable as to be violative of due process." [44]

"Liberty," as protected by the due process clause of the Fifth Amendment, Warren urged, "extends to the full range of conduct which the individual is free to pursue, and it cannot be restricted except for a proper governmental objective." Having

[42] 351 U.S., at 16–17. Black also cited the provision of the Illinois Constitution of 1818, Art. VIII § 12, which, based on chapter 40 of Magna Carta, declared that every person "ought to obtain right and justice freely, and without being obliged to purchase it, completely and without denial, promptly and without delay, conformably to the laws." 351 U.S., at 18. The present Illinois Constitution has essentially the same provision. Art. II § 19.

[43] 347 U.S. 483 (1954).   [44] 347 U.S. 497, 499 (1954).

in mind that racial classifications are "constitutionally suspect," Warren concluded that "segregation in public education is not reasonably related to any proper governmental objective, and thus it imposes on Negro children of the District of Columbia a burden that constitutes an arbitrary deprivation of their liberty in violation of the Due Process Clause." Then the Chief Justice added the rather meaningful observation that, in view of the fact that the Court was that very day holding that the States might not maintain segregated schools, "it would be unthinkable that the same Constitution would impose a lesser duty on the Federal Government." [45]

For seven hundred and fifty years due process and equal protection of the laws, by whatever names and with whatever functions, have never been far apart. In the Great Charter of King John, chapter 39 and chapter 40, side by side, promised the freemen of England due process of law and equal treatment in the courts of justice. Within a few years, by the time the Charter had taken the shape it was to have on the statute books of England, the two chapters had been merged into one: chapter 29. So they continued, down through the centuries, picking up as they went the glosses of Coke and Blackstone and others. Into the American States' constitutions went provisions typically drawing word for word on both of the principal parts of chapter 29. The nineteenth century saw due process being used to require legislatures to pass laws of general and equal application. And in our own century we see due process and equal protection, though each having its own area of jurisprudence, nevertheless touching and intertwining again and again.

---

[45] 347 U.S., at 499–500.

Chapter XVII

Due Process of Law

Attainders and Fair Procedures

*Due Process as Barring Bills of Attainder and
as Implementing the Separation of Powers*

THE requirement of the "law of the land" that laws be general in their nature was, as Blackstone put it, to avoid legislative acts which were in effect judicial sentences, operating on individuals, who thereby would be denied the procedural rights which due process of law guaranteed them in a court of law. A number of the earlier state cases make it quite clear that the courts were viewing due process as a ban upon what we would be more apt to call a bill of attainder, that is, a legislative act inflicting penalties without a judicial trial.[1] Moreover, those state courts were viewing due process, as the present-day Supreme Court has viewed the Federal Constitution's ban on bills of attainder, as implementing the separation of powers among the three branches of government, legislative, executive, and judicial.[2]

A number of these cases were counterparts, in one way or another, of the *Dartmouth College* case, for they involved legislative attempts to transfer privileges and property from one set

---

[1] Technically, a bill of attainder at common law included the death sentence; a parliamentary act decreeing penalties short of death for the named persons was a "bill of pains and penalties." In text the phrase of "bill of attainder" is used to describe all legislative penalties inflicting punishment without a judicial trial.

[2] See United States v. Brown, 381 U.S. 437, 442–44 (1965).

of trustees of an educational or charitable institute to a new group of trustees. The cases differed from the New Hampshire decision in *Dartmouth College* in that they invalidated the legislatures' acts; they differed, too, from the United States Supreme Court's *Dartmouth College* decision in that the latter was based on the impairment of the obligation of contracts and the state cases used due process of law.

One case arose in Maryland, where a legislative act of 1825 professed to abolish the corporation of the Regents of the University of Maryland and to appoint a different board of trustees to whom all the corporation's franchises and property should be transferred. The court held the statute invalid, describing it as a "legislative ouster . . . an exercise of judicial power not warranted by the constitution" and as a taking of property other than by the "law of the land." By the "law of the land" the court meant "by the due course and process of the law," quoting Coke's commentary on Magna Carta. This meant a sentence in a court of law. "An act which only affects and exhausts itself upon a particular person, or his rights and privileges, and has no relation to the community, 'is rather a sentence than a law' " (quoting Blackstone) .[3]

A like result was reached in a contemporary South Carolina case. There the Medical Society of South Carolina had been authorized to license applicants to practice medicine and to organize a medical college. In 1831 the legislature passed an act incorporating the Medical College of South Carolina and transferring to the new college all the rights and powers previously conferred on the Society. This, the court held, was a violation of the "law of the land," by which the court understood "a trial had, and a judgment pronounced, in the court of law of this State." [4]

A Pennsylvania case of a few years later was even more explicit in treating such a divestment of privileges by legislative act as a bill of attainder. In that case the legislature divested the trustees of an orphanage of the privileges and franchises

[3] Regents of the University of Maryland v. Williams, 9 Gill & J. 365, 411–12 (Md. 1838) .
[4] State v. Heyward, 3 Rich. 389, 412 (S.C. 1832) .

and gave to others the power to appoint new trustees. The "law of the land" did not mean "bills of attainder in the shape of an act of Assembly, whereby a man's property is swept away from him without hearing trial or judgment. . . . [It means] the law of the individual case, as established in a fair and open trial, or an opportunity given for one in court, and by due course and process of law." Magna Carta required this. "Sir Edward Coke defines the meaning of the words, *by the law of the land*—for they were used in *Magna Charta,* and have been sprinkled with the tears and blood of many patriots—to be a trial by due course and process of law. I do not, therefore, regard an act of Assembly, by which a citizen of Pennsylvania is deprived of his lawful right, as the law of the land." [5]

The Pennsylvania court also connected the constitutional guarantee of "law of the land" to the separation of powers. The Pennsylvania Constitution, it noted, vests the powers of government in three departments, each of which "are confined within the limits of their respective and appropriate spheres of action." Just as the court's attempt to issue general edicts would be usurpation, and the executive's assumption of the power to decide cases would be beyond its power, so the legislature is bound by the requirement of "law of the land" to stay within its proper sphere. [6]

The bulwark of "law of the land" as a barrier against bills of attainder was put to its severest test in the vindictive days which followed the Civil War. Punitive legislation against ex-Confederates or their sympathizers was adopted by Congress and by state legislatures, notably in Missouri, a State where feelings about the war ran especially high. Missouri in 1865 adopted a new constitution, one section of which provided that any person who had in any one of a number of described ways supported the Confederacy could not hold any public office in the State, could not be an officer of a corporation, and was barred from certain professions, including law, teaching, and

[5] Brown v. Hummel, 6 Pa. State Rep. 86, 91 (1847).

[6] 6 Pa. State Rep., at 90. The Supreme Court of North Carolina used this approach to invalidate a statute providing for the election of new clerks in each county of the State before expiration of the old clerks' terms of office. Hoke v. Henderson, 15 N.C. 1 (1833).

the ministry. Not only did the section include overt acts against the United States, it embraced expressions of "sympathy" with those engaged in rebellion against the United States.

A Roman Catholic priest named Cummings refused to take an oath, prescribed by the state constitution, that he had done none of the proscribed acts, and he was indicted and convicted of carrying on his religious calling without having taken the oath. The case went to the Supreme Court of the United States on writ of error, where David Dudley Field, better known to posterity as the proponent of the Field Code in New York, argued the case for Cummings. Citing Coke on chapter 29 of Magna Carta, Field submitted that the Missouri requirement was in fact a bill of attainder, which Field defined as any "legislative act which inflicts punishment without a judicial trial." The Court agreed and reversed Cumming's conviction.[7]

In a companion case, *Ex Parte Garland,* the Court held that an Act of Congress of 1865 providing that no person should be admitted to practice before any federal court unless he first took an oath that he had never given aid to those engaged in armed hostility to the United States Government and had never held any office under any authority hostile to the United States was a bill of attainder as applied to Garland, who had been a member of the bar of the Supreme Court in 1860 and had, during the War between the States, served in the Confederate Congress.[8]

Memories of the recent war, and bitterness toward the defeated Confederates, were too strong for decisions like those in *Cummings* and *Garland* to put an end to the matter. The next year the Supreme Court of Missouri heard arguments in *Blair v. Ridgley,*[9] a case involving a section of the 1865 constitution which, in sweeping terms, refused the vote to those who had given any kind of support to the Confederate States, including the expression of sympathy for their cause. Francis Preston Blair was strongly pro-Union; he had helped keep Missouri in the Union, had risen to the rank of Major General in the Union Army, and had ruined himself financially by spending

---

[7] Cummings v. Missouri, 4 Wall. (71 U.S.) 277 (1866).
[8] 4 Wall. (71 U.S.) 333 (1866).   [9] 41 Mo. 63 (1867).

much of his private means in support of the Union. But after the war he was deeply opposed to the Radical Republicans and their policies for Reconstruction. As one measure of his opposition, Blair refused to take the oath prescribed by the section as a prerequisite to voting and challenged the section as unconstitutional.

Blair's case was argued by Samuel Taylor Glover, a leading member of the Missouri bar and, although (like Blair) he had been anti-slavery and pro-Union, an uncompromising opponent of the oaths required by the state constitution. The oath, he submitted, was against the requirement of "law of the land," which Glover traced to Magna Carta. He reminded the court that the American people had fought a war to secure such rights:

> It is scarcely necessary to say, may it please the court, it was never intended to abate on the part of the American people any portion of the substantial liberties of Englishmen. The war of 1776 grew out of a claim made by America to these liberties ["law of the land" and related guarantees of Magna Carta], and the battles of the revolution were fought to make good that claim. They made it good; and the people preserved it in constitutional guaranties. . . .

In effect, Glover argued, the Missouri oath requirement worked a disfranchisement without any indictment or trial. Quoting Coke on Magna Carta, Glover maintained that "law of the land" affirmed "the right of trial according to the processes and proceedings of the common law." [10]

Glover sensed that some might think it anomalous that, in arguing a question of American constitutional law, he should rely on Magna Carta:

> It is far from being a pleasant reflection that a citizen of the United States, defending himself against arbitrary power, is at this day driven to the great charter of the liberties of Englishmen, extorted from the King who ruled the mother country in the twelfth century, for a definition of his political and personal rights and an acknowledgment that they are in deed his property. But so it is and there may be something salutary after all in the necessity. Lawyers know how destructive of sound law

[10] 41 Mo., at 82, 83, 85.

is the ignorance which knows nothing of the wisdom of the past, as well as the arrogance which, springing from this ignorance, disdains to profit by the thoughts and experience of those who have passed through trials not wholly unlike our own. If those who are placed in stations of trust and power in this country could be so far instructed as to become sensible of the disadvantage they sustain by their ignorance of the lessons of history, many outrages, many follies of a most costly nature, might be avoided. If, in examining into the tenure and qualities of the liberties of freemen, which we have so long claimed to hold by inheritance, and to have enlarged by our own struggles until there is no other nation the people of which enjoy them in so full a measure, we are led to the discovery that we have narrowed rather than extended that inestimable possession, and are in danger of losing it altogether, we may be quickened and prompted, while it is yet time, to the performance of our duty—the re-assertion of our ancient birthright, and the casting off of a yoke to which our necks are not yet accustomed.[11]

Glover quoted in full the language of chapter 29 of Magna Carta (chapters 39 and 40 of the 1215 charter), which he called "one of the most pregnant passages of the whole of that remarkable instrument." And he proceeded to discuss, in some detail, the implications for the case at hand of this part of the Great Charter.[12]

Opposing counsel, C. D. Drake, saw the case quite differently. To him the only issue was whether the people of Missouri had the right to declare "who shall be voters, and who shall not." He disdained Glover's appeals to history, preferring himself "to walk in the light of this age and this country, not in the twilight of old Greece and Rome, or the darkness of medieval Europe, or the gloom of Westminster Hall in its days of attainders, pains, and penalties. America sheds light enough upon her own institutions; and no other country's history or laws can much increase that light, in the grand realm where her people are working out the sublime problem of self-government, as never it was worked out before."[13]

In place of Glover's Magna Carta, Drake offered the horrors of the recent war. The convention which drafted the constitu-

[11] 41 Mo., at 118–19.   [12] 41 Mo., at 119–20.   [13] 41 Mo., at 133–35.

tion of 1865 was not, he said, vengeful; it aimed only "to protect the loyal people of Missouri against their wily, blood-thirsty, and implacable foes." The test oath was necessary to prevent the ex-Confederates from exercising the franchise which they had "utterly and most justly forfeited." Drake's argument is a remarkable courtroom example of what one expects to find in the text of Reconstruction-era campaign speeches, the waving of the "bloody flag":

> In short, there was hardly any form in which treason to coun-try, treachery to friends, faithless to obligations, and disregard of all laws, divine and human, could be manifested, that was not exhibited daily, for years, in this unhappy State. Could there be written a full account of all the crimes of the rebels of Missouri, and the wrongs and outrages inflicted by them upon her loyal inhabitants, during the four years of the rebellion the world would shrink aghast from a picture which has no parallel in the previous history of any portion of the Anglo-Saxon race. . . . The moral sense of all patriots revolts at the thought of the government of a State being controlled by those who, in a war of unheard-of atrocity, had traitorously sought to destroy the Nation of which that State is a part; had ravaged the State itself; had waged cruel and relentless strife against its citizens, solely because they were loyal and faithful; and imbrued their hands for years in the blood of unoffending patriots; had made the land howl with the wails of widows and orphans of mur-dered loyalists; and yet, after all this, would, with the impu-dence of the arch-fiend himself, demand equal rights at the ballot box with those whose hands were 'guiltless of their coun-try's blood,' and who in every hour of that country's peril were found faithful and true to its cause.[14]

One might suppose that, faced with the Supreme Court of the United States' decision in *Cummings,* the Missouri court would have held for Blair. It was not to be so. In its decision in the *Blair* case, the Missouri court acknowledged that it had been reversed in *Cummings* but observed that the decision had been 5 to 4 and that the dissenting opinion was one "which for ability, logic, and admirable judicial criticism, has rarely been excelled even in that august tribunal"—a somewhat florid way

[14] 41 Mo., at 142–43, 151–52.

of saying that the four Supreme Court dissenters had voted to affirm, rather than reverse, the earlier Missouri decision.[15]

Moreover, the Missouri court in *Blair* thought that there was a significant distinction between the pursuit of a profession, the subject matter of *Cummings,* and the right to vote, which was at issue in *Blair*. And the court set out to show that, if Mr. Glover could cite Magna Carta in his client's behalf, the court could reply in kind, using Magna Carta to bolster its case. The court observed that *Cummings* had involved a "natural and inalienable right," the right to pursue a calling or profession. "When the sturdy barons wrested from a despotic king *magna charta,*" the court said, they inserted the guarantee of "law of the land." This same principle the court traced through Coke's *Institutes* into American constitutional law, in which it might be said that a man has a "special property" in his calling or profession. But the court could not conceive the right to vote to be a "natural, absolute, or vested" right, since (unlike property) it could not exist in a state of nature. Thus, the court concluded, the right to vote "may be enlarged or restricted, granted or withheld, at pleasure, and with or without fault." [16]

Glover failed to persuade the Missouri court in *Blair,* but he was more successful in a contemporary case in which he himself was the litigant. Glover felt that, in good conscience, he could not take the attorney's oath required by the 1865 Missouri Constitution. Seeking to test the constitutionality of the oath, Glover wrote the local prosecuting attorney, advising him that Glover was practicing without having taken the oath, and asked the prosecutor to institute an indictment. Glover offered to make such admissions or proofs as would aid in putting the oath's "constitutionality to the judicial test that I desire." [17]

Glover was indicted, convicted, and fined $500, the sentence to be stayed pending Glover's appeal to the supreme court of the State. There Glover's counsel argued that the oath was in effect a bill of attainder and treated the court to an extensive discussion of the history of bills of attainder. To the proposi-

[15] 41 Mo., at 170–71.   [16] 41 Mo., at 172–74, 178.
[17] Letter of Sept. 11, 1865, quoted in letter from State Historical Society of Missouri to author, May 26, 1966.

tion that the requirement of the oath imposed no "punishment," counsel characterized the State as saying, "We will not punish thee—we are merciful! But go—we proclaim thee an outlaw, disabled from following thy past calling. . . . No punishment? I defy the history of the world to invent a punishment more refined and ingenious than to punish a man through his love of truth, his adherence to his word." And counsel ended with a theatrical touch, rather more to the taste of the nineteenth century than to that of our own time, comparing the State's "benediction" to the "outlawed" attorneys to the Inquisitors' *"requiescat in pace"* to the brother they had just walled up alive in his death-cell.[18]

Counsel's argument probably was less of a factor in the Missouri court's ultimate decision than the court's awareness that the United States Supreme Court's decisions in *Garland* and *Cummings*, taken together, clearly called for reversal of Glover's conviction. The court expressed some misgivings but, acknowledging the force of the Supreme Court cases, rendered judgment in Glover's favor.[19]

If recent cases have been correctly decided, then bills of attainder are not simply historic relics to be associated with sixteenth- and seventeenth-century England or with nineteenth-century America. In the 1950's, with the passage by Congress of a variety of legislative measures aimed at the Communist conspiracy in the United States, challenges to statutes as being bills of attainder have come once again into their own. The landmark case of this post-World War II era is *United States v. Brown*,[20] decided by the Supreme Court in 1965. Decided, like the *Cummings* and *Garland* decisions of almost exactly a century before, by a 5 to 4 vote, *Brown* followed a decade and more of litigants' unsuccessful attempts to use the bill of attainder clause of the Constitution against state or federal measures dealing with Communism and subversion.[21]

---

[18] Murphy and Glover Test Oath Cases, 41 Mo. 339, 360–62 (1867).
[19] 41 Mo., at 362–88.   [20] 381 U.S. 437 (1965).
[21] See, e.g., American Communications Assn. v. Douds, 339 U.S. 382, 413 (1950); Joint Anti-Fascist Refugee Comm. v. McGrath, 341 U.S. 123, 143 (1951); Garner v. Board of Public Works, 341 U.S. 716. 722 (1951); Barsky v. Board of Regents, 347 U.S. 442, 459 (1954); Peters v. Hobby, 349 U.S. 331, 352 (1955);

In *Brown* an Act of Congress making it a crime for a member of the Communist Party to serve as an officer or employee of a labor union was held to be a bill of attainder and therefore unconstitutional.

As already noted, the nineteenth-century cases often viewed due process as both barring bills of attainder and implementing the separation of powers. It is interesting, by way of a jurisprudential continuum, that the Court in *Brown* made a like connection between bills of attainder and separation of powers. Writing for the majority, Chief Justice Warren believed that the drafters of the Constitution meant for the prohibition against bills of attainder to be "an implementation of the separation of powers, a general safeguard against legislative exercise of the judicial function, or more simply—trial by legislature." And the Court quoted James Madison as having said, in the *Federalist* No. 47, that the "accumulation of all powers, legislative, executive, and judiciary, in the same hands, whether of one, a few, or many, and whether hereditary, self-appointed, or elective, may justly be pronounced the very definition of tyranny." [22]

The Court's decision in *Brown* raises some serious analytical problems for the legislative draftsman who would, in good faith, avoid the ban on bills of attainder, as Mr. Justice White's dissenting opinion demonstrates.[23] But, laying this question aside (the reader is invited to study the majority and dissenting opinions himself), *Brown* is of interest to the present discussion because it is a reminder of the way in which different constitutional provisions have one end in view: a restraint on the power of those in power. The constitutional assurance of due process of law, born of Magna Carta's promise of "law of the land"; the ban, evoked by the lessons of English history, on bills of attainder; the safeguard of separation of powers, a contribution of

---

Uphaus v. Wyman, 360 U.S. 72, 108 (1959) ; Barenblatt v. United States, 360 U.S. 109, 160 (1959) ; DeVeau v. Braisted, 363 U.S. 144, 160 (1960) ; Flemming v. Nestor, 363 U.S. 603, 612–21 (1960) ; Communist Party v. Subversive Activities Control Bd., 367 U.S. 1, 82–88 (1961) .

[22] 381 U.S., at 442, 443. In this analysis (even to quoting Madison) , as in many other particulars (both of argument and sources) , the majority opinion in *Brown* owes an obvious debt to the note in 72 *Yale L.J.* 330 (1962) .

[23] See 381 U.S., at 462.

eighteenth-century thought—all form part of the history of devices fashioned to ensure that tyranny and arbitrary government should have no place in England or the United States.

Due Process as Requiring Notice and Hearing

Wｅｂｓｔｅｒ's classic definition of "law of the land" in the *Dartmouth College* case included the requirement of a law "which hears before it condemns; which proceeds upon inquiry, and renders judgment only after trial." No concept is more basic to Anglo-American jurisprudence than the necessity for adequate notice and opportunity to be heard in one's defense before being subjected to some penalty. And none of the various meanings which have attached to due process is more closely identified with its origins in Magna Carta.

The invocation of Magna Carta as assuring the right to notice and opportunity to be heard was common well before the American Revolution. In 1724 John Checkley of Massachusetts put on sale a tract entitled *A Short and Easy Way with the Deists*. Checkley was an Anglican, and his book was offensive to the Puritans. The Council of Massachusetts directed the Attorney General to draw up a presentment against the book as a "scandalous libel." Checkley was convicted and appealed to the Court of Assize, where the conviction was affirmed and Checkley fined.

Checkley's argument before the appellate court is of interest for his use of Magna Carta. During the argument, Checkley began a long discussion of Greek and Roman history and was interrupted by the Chief Justice, who said that "the Court can't spend their time in hearing you talk about the *Greeks* and *Romans*. It is nothing to your Case." Checkley objected to being thus cut off: "No Man ought to be condemned without Answer," urged Checkley, citing Magna Carta and Coke's *Institutes*. "I was not suffered to defend my self in Inferiour Court; I beseech your Honours to let me make my Defence." The Chief Justice said that Checkley might continue. He did—drawing on the histories of Athens, Sparta, Rome, Babylonia, Assyria, and other lands! [24]

The noted Maryland lawyer, Daniel Dulany the Elder, was another who looked to Magna Carta as assuring the right to be heard. The Lord Proprietary of Maryland granted 750 acres to Walter Bayne, the proprietor's surveyor laid off the acreage, and a land grant issued. When Bayne died in 1673, he devised the land to his daughter Eleanor, then six years old. A writ issued out of the Chancery Court alleging that Bayne had fraudulently procured the grant knowing that it was reserved to the proprietor; the writ ordered the sheriff to warn the heirs of Bayne to show cause why the letters patent for the land ought not to be revoked. Bayne's widow, by her son-in-law, appeared and surrendered the grant, which was ordered revoked. Eleanor, however, was not represented, and some years later she and her husband brought suit to recover the land.

Daniel Dulany argued the case for the claimants. His principal argument was that the judgment revoking the grant was void because rendered against a minor who was not called to make a defense, "a right to which every one living is entitled to." In support of his argument Dulany quoted the full text (in Latin) of chapter 29 of the 1225 version of Magna Carta, as found in Coke's *Second Institute*. Moreover Dulany argued that to make the unheard party bring suit to attack such a void judgment would be a sale of justice, contrary to Magna Carta. "It is a fundamental and immutable principle of *Magna Charta* that justice must not be sold. So it is, that no man ought to be condemned unheard." If, argued Dulany, a judgment passed against a person unheard was, until reversed, to have the same force and effect as a judgment rendered after a court had heard both parties' evidence, then "to put a man to the expense and fatigue of a formal proceeding to reverse such a judgment, is surely a selling him justice, or which is the same thing, putting him under the necessity of buying it." The court found

24 Prince Society, *John Checkley* (Boston, 1897), II, 21–22. Checkley also cited Magna Carta's guarantee of the rights of Holy Church as being among the authorities for his argument that the Church of England was established in the colonies. *Ibid.*, II, 34.

that Eleanor had not agreed to the surrender of the grant and gave judgment in her favor.[5] Two years after the judgment in this case Dulany published his influential *The Right of the Inhabitants of Maryland to the Benefit of the English Laws.*[26]

Soon thereafter, a quit-rent act passed in North Carolina in 1738 was assailed as violating Magna Carta's assurance of the right to be heard. The Board of Trade received, from the hands of Henry McCulloch, the agent for North Carolina, a statement on those clauses of the quit-rent act conceived to be inconsistent with the laws of England and the rights of His Majesty's subjects in the colonies. The act provided that all land patents must be registered within eight months of the act's ratification; otherwise they would be void unless the party claiming under them was able to prove to the satisfaction of the Governor and Council that the grant had been complete. McCulloch's message called this "one of the greatest and most violent Breaches, that has been ever attempted since the Restoration, on the Laws & Constitution of this Kingdom." By giving the Governor and Council the power to determine and defeat the title of grantees under the Crown "in a summary way, & without being held to legal proof, or any other proof, than what may be to the satisfaction of the Govr and Council, is against the first principles of Law, destructive of ye undoubted Rights & Libertys of the subject, breaks in on Magna Charta, & all the Laws of Great Britain. . . ." McCulloch submitted that the act was wholly without precedent in any of the plantations. The Lords Justices in Council voided the act, although on grounds other than those urged by McCulloch.[27]

The idea that Magna Carta underwrote the right to be heard became a basic presupposition of the case law which, after the Revolution, interpreted the constitutional right to due process of law. In an 1897 case arising out of a dispute over an award made by the commission which, under the treaty of 1871 with Great Britain, settled the *Alabama* claims, certain persons re-

---

[25] Digges's Lessee v. Beale, 1 H. & McH. 67 (Md. 1726).

[26] See pp. 61–63, *supra.*

[27] *Colonial Records of North Carolina,* ed. William L. Saunders and Walter Clark (Raleigh, N.C., 1886–1914), IV, 425–34.

fused to pay a sum of money into court when ordered to do so. The court, on motion, held them in contempt and ordered their answer in the pending action to be stricken, resulting in a default judgment against them. When the Supreme Court decided the case, it commented that "at common law no man was condemned without being afforded opportunity to be heard." In support of this statement the Court quoted from Coke's commentary on Magna Carta's guarantee of the "law of the land" and from later English cases laying down the rule that "a party has the right to be heard for the purpose of explaining his conduct."[28] Fifth Amendment due process, said the Court (quoting Story), was "but an enlargement of the language of Magna Charta" assuring proceedings according to the "law of the land." The Court concluded, on the facts of the case before it, that it was not proper for a lower court, on the theory that a party has been guilty of a contempt of court, to strike his answer, suppress his testimony, and allow a default judgment to go against him.[29]

Countless state cases have traced procedural due process to the guarantees of Magna Carta, usually quoting from Coke on Magna Carta and pointing out that, even without evidence of the well-known historical origins of due process, a simple comparison of the language of a state constitution's provision for due process or law of the land and that of Magna Carta would make the ancestry obvious. These cases hold that if due process as drawn from the Great Charter means anything, it means notice and an opportunity to be heard. Typical is a Delaware case which noted that "the expression, 'due process of law,' as it appears in the Constitution of the United States, and the expression, 'law of the land,' as used in many of the State Constitutions, have been generally held to mean the same; in fact, both terms have been held to be the equivalent of the expression 'per legem terrae,' as used in Magna Charta." What this requires, the court concluded, is "summons or notice such as is ordinarily given upon the institution of a suit, due appearance

28 Capel v. Child, 2 Cromp. & J. 558, 574 (1832). See also Bonaker v. Evans, 16 Q.B. 162, 171 (1850).
29 Hovey v. Elliott, 167 U.S. 409, 415–17 (1897).

of the parties in interest, pleading of the facts to issue and a determination thereof by a jury." [30]

Even to give a representative sampling of the factual situations in which courts have held procedural due process to have been lacking because sufficient notice or opportunity to be heard was not given would be far beyond the scope of this study. The cases are many in number and in variety of settings. Some idea of the breadth of the concept may be had by mentioning several factual situations taken only from cases in which the court explicitly traced its idea of procedural due process to Magna Carta and found that, on the facts of the case, due process had been violated: a statute failing to give notice or opportunity to be heard on assessments for levee improvements; [31] a system of registration of land titles (a modified Torrens system) which would cut off vested property interests but which did not provide for issuance of judicial process to give notice to all who might make adverse claims; [32] forfeiture and sale of an automobile without notice to the owner, who was in no way connected with the offense (unlawful transportation of liquor) committed by the defendant; [33] and a statute imposing absolute liability without fault upon a railroad for death of livestock upon its right-of-way.[34]

The reader should by no means assume that the specific fact situations chosen for illustration above would necessarily be held by a given court today to involve a violation of due process. For instance, the reasoning of the court in the case (decided in 1889) involving absolute liability without fault (that to prevent a party from averring or proving his lack of negligence denied due process of law) would be shared by few courts today, when legislatures and courts alike are much more receptive to the notion of spreading the burden of industrial risks and accidents without regard to traditional notions of fault.

[30] State v. Rose, 33 Del. 168, 178, 132 Atl. 864, 868–69 (1926).

[31] Board of Levee Comm'rs v. Johnson, 178 Ky. 287, 199 S.W. 8 (1917).

[32] State ex rel. Att'y Gen. v. Guilbert, 56 Ohio St. 575, 47 N.E. 551 (1897).

[33] State v. Rose, 33 Del. 168, 132 Atl. 864 (1926).

[34] Jensen v. Union Pac. Ry., 6 Utah 253, 21 Pac. 994 (1889). Arguably, this could be considered an application of substantive due process. However, the court talked as if the problem were one of procedural due process, the statute being held to deny the railroad its "day in court."

But changing views on some specific factual situations in no way lessens the central importance to Anglo-American jurisprudence of the requirement of notice and hearing as the key to procedural due process. Thus, in reversing a summary contempt conviction in a "one-man grand jury" investigation, the Supreme Court relied (along with the fact that the hearing had been in secret) on their finding that the defendant had not been given a reasonable opportunity to defend himself. Speaking for the majority, Mr. Justice Black said, "A person's right to reasonable notice of a charge against him, and an opportunity to be heard in his defense—a right to his day in court—are basic in our system of jurisprudence." [35] In another case the Court reviewed a conviction for violation of a section of a statute dealing with unlawful assembly. The state supreme court had affirmed the conviction on the ground that the petitioners had violated another section of the statute, relating to the use of force and violence. The United State Supreme Court unanimously reversed, saying, "It is as much a violation of due process to send an accused to prison following conviction of a charge on which he was never tried as it would be to convict him upon a charge that was never made." [36]

So the principle of procedural fairness, above all, of notice and opportunity to be heard in one's defense, born of Magna Carta and nurtured through centuries of English and American cases, remains one of the cherished presuppositions of our system of justice. Few would disagree with the judgment of the Kentucky court which said that the guarantees of due process of law "have come to be regarded as so fundamental a part of every enlightened system of government that no free people would dare to leave them out of their organic law and no court would now be so bold as to attempt to set them aside or deprive them of the meaning they have been universally adjudged to have since their insertion in the constitutions of the state and the nation, and indeed, long before written constitutions were thought of." [37]

[35] In re Oliver, 333 U.S. 257, 273 (1948).
[36] Cole v. Arkansas, 333 U.S. 196, 201 (1948).
[37] Board of Levee Comm'rs v. Johnson, 178 Ky. 287, 298, 199 S.W. 8, 12 (1917).

Chapter XVIII

Due Process of Law

Property and Jury Trial

Due Process as a Protection for Property

I N AN essay written on the occasion of the 750th anniversary of Magna Carta, Gottfried Dietze traced the close connection between the Charter and property. Cataloguing the various provisions of Magna Carta, Dietze suggested that as many as thirty-eight chapters (of a total of sixty-three) were concerned in one way or another with property. Dietze's thesis is that there is a close relationship between property rights and other rights of the individual, so that "by commemorating Magna Carta as a document of free government, we commemorate it as a charter of property." The corollary, in Dietze's view, is that a decline in the protection accorded property rights may herald a like weakening of other individual rights.[1]

The two relationships thus suggested—the connection between Magna Carta and property, and the relation of property rights to individual liberties in general—are a marked feature of the history of due process in America. The veneration of the American colonists for Magna Carta may not have been matched, in each individual colonist's case, by a belief in the sanctity of property; after all, every man could claim the bene-

[1] *Magna Carta and Property* (Charlottesville, Va., 1965), pp. 37, 7, 83. Dietze's views on property are more fully developed in his *In Defense of Property* (Chicago, 1963).

fits of Magna Carta, but not every colonist counted himself among the propertied classes. But by and large, the opinion that counted in pre- and postrevolutionary America, at least the opinion on the part of those that drafted constitutions, sat on courts, and ran the business of government generally, was very much in favor of property.

This was only natural. It was a case of economic interest, philosophical bent, and legal tradition pointing in the same direction. It certainly was not economics alone. Enough doubt has been cast on Charles A. Beard's economic interpretation of the Constitution to suggest that.[2] Economics and class interest aside, the American was steeped in the Lockean idea that the chief end of government was the preservation of men's property (by which Locke meant life and liberty, as well as estate). If he had read Blackstone, the American knew that Blackstone included property (in the usual sense) along with life and liberty among the "absolute rights" of men. He knew, again from the pages of Blackstone, if not otherwise, that property was protected by Magna Carta and the common law of England. American leaders were convinced that rights of property were as indispensable as any other rights of the individual and formed a root of the Tree of Liberty without which that tree would languish. So they carefully wrote protections for property into their federal and state constitutions, in the form of the due process clause.

In the early years of the Republic, Alexander Hamilton had occasion to draw upon Magna Carta as a protection for property rights. The Jay Treaty, agreed to in 1794 by the United States and Great Britain, provided, among other things, that debts or moneys owing to individuals in either nation should not be confiscated in event of differences arising between the two countries. The treaty aroused a storm of protest among the Republicans, the party in opposition, and in 1795 Hamilton wrote a series of essays signed "Camillus" in defense of the treaty. Referring to the virulence with which the article in question had been attacked, Hamilton declared, "No powers of

[2] See p. 3, *supra*.

language at my command can express the abhorrence I feel at the idea of violating the property of individuals. . . ." Hamilton feared that the confiscation of debts owed the enemy might be the first step in a general "war upon credit, eventually upon property. . . . From one violation of justice to another, the passage is easy."

In this respect Hamilton thought Magna Carta had done something in 1215 which the Federal Constitution of 1787 ought to have emulated but had not. He cited that "liberal and excellent provision" in Magna Carta which declared that in the event of a war foreign merchants and their goods in England should not be harmed so long as English merchants in the enemy country were safe. Observing that Montesquieu had said, "It is noble that the English nation have made this one of the articles of its liberty," Hamilton lamented, "How much it is to be regretted, that our magna charta is not unequivocally decorated with a like feature; and that, in this instance, we, who have given so many splendid examples to mankind, are excelled in constitutional precautions for the maintenance of justice." [3]

American courts after the Revolution were quick to find their role as champions of property rights. In this role, from the earliest cases, the courts looked to Magna Carta and due process to supply the standard of decision. One of the earliest cases is among the most interesting. *Lindsay v. Commissioners,* a South Carolina case of 1796, involved a motion for a prohibition to restrain commissioners appointed by the City Council of Charleston from opening a new street. The applicants for the writ objected to the enabling act, which authorized the commissioners to take freehold for public use without compensation, arguing that the act violated that section of the South Carolina Constitution which provided that no freeman should be disseized of his freehold or in any manner deprived of his property save by the "law of the land." [4]

---

[3] *Works of Alexander Hamilton,* ed. H. C. Lodge (New York, 1904), V, 405–8. For Hamilton's constitutional principles, see Clinton Rossiter, *Alexander Hamilton and the Constitution* (New York, 1964).

[4] 2 Bay 38, 40 (S.C. 1796).

Arguing for the city, the City Recorder distinguished the case in which the legislature might attempt to take A's property and give it to B. To do that would be "against both *magna charta* and our own constitution." But the power of the state to lay off roads and highways for the public use and convenience was a different matter; that power, the recorder submitted, "was the law of the land long before *magna charta* was ever thought of, or our constitution promulgated. . . . In fact, it is a part of the ancient law of the land, recognized by *magna charta* and confirmed to the state by our own constitution." [5]

The panel of four judges divided evenly. Two judges admitted the power of eminent domain, but only upon payment of fair compensation, and therefore were for granting the motion. The other two judges held that the power of laying off roads "was neither against *magna charta,* nor the state constitution, but part of the *lex terrae,* which both meant to defend and protect. The so much celebrated *magna charta* of *Great Britain,* was not a concession of rights and privileges, which had no previous existence; *but a restoration and confirmation* of those, which had been usurped, or had fallen into disuse. It was therefore only declaratory of the well-known and established laws of the kingdom." And one of these, they believed, was the state's right to lay off highways. The judges being equally divided, the prohibition did not issue. [6]

In *Lindsay* Magna Carta was invoked to uphold the particular taking of property challenged. As more cases of taking found their way into American courts, Magna Carta, or its derivative, due process, continued to be the standard, but the typical case was to be that in which Magna Carta or due process was held to forbid the taking, unless there was compensation. A notable early case (1805) from North Carolina will serve to illustrate what virtually from the start was the characteristic nineteenth-century judicial attitude to property. *Trustees of the University of North Carolina v. Foy* [7] involved two North Carolina statutes: one of 1789, which granted to the trustees of the university all property which might escheat to

---

[5] 2 Bay, at 42.   [6] 2 Bay, at 56–58, 62.   [7] 1 Murphey 58 (N.C. 1805).

the State, and a second, of 1800, by which all escheated property which had passed to the trustees but had not been sold by them was to revert to the State.

The case was argued by a lawyer named Haywood, probably John Haywood, a distinguished member of the North Carolina bar, whom John Marshall considered one of the ablest lawyers of his day.[8] Haywood maintained that once the property was vested in the trustees the legislature could not take it away without the trustees' consent. His argument was a panegyric of property. Citizens are industrious, he said, because of their expectations that what that industry provides will be peculiarly their own. Just compensation is the duty of the sovereign that would take private property. Individuals must be assured of the sanctity of property, which should be the "most sacred" maxim of free governments. "North-Carolina will find by fatal experience, the oftener her Legislature breaks in upon this great principle, the nearer will she approach to this representation of despotism." [9]

Haywood traced the history of the provision in the North Carolina Constitution for proceedings according to the "law of the land," citing its origin in Magna Carta and Sir Edward Coke's commentary on it. "Law of the land," Haywood reasoned, could not mean simply an act of the legislature, else the constitutional clause would be of no effect at all. "Thank God, no man in North-Carolina can be deprived of his life or property but by the regular judgment of a lawful court. . . . As to private property, therefore, I may venture to affirm it is beyond the reach of the Assembly, and cannot be taken from the owner by any act they can pass for the purpose." Haywood carried the day. The court agreed with him that "law of the land" places limits on the legislature, and it held the trustees entitled to the property.[10]

Chancellor Kent of New York showed a similar sensitivity for the rights of property. His *Commentaries on American Law* were frequently cited by American courts and contained, for

---

[8] See Samuel A. Ashe, *Biographical History of North Carolina* (Greensboro, N.C., 1905–17), VI, 274.
[9] 1 Murphey, at 63.   [10] 1 Murphey, at 73–76, 87–89.

example, this passage cited in the early twentieth century by the Supreme Court of Indiana:

The natural and active sense of property pervades the foundation of social improvement. It leads to the cultivation of the earth, the institution of government, the establishment of justice, the acquisition of the comforts of life, the growth of the useful arts, the spirit of commerce, the productions of taste, the erections of charity, and the display of the benevolent affections.[11]

Kent, both in his *Commentaries* and in his judicial opinions, used Magna Carta to support property against taking without compensation. In 1816, when he was Chancellor of New York, he decided a case involving a statute which allowed a village to enter upon land to provide a water supply for the village. The act provided for compensation for the owners of land entered upon and for owners of land where the source of the water was situated, but no compensation for owners of land through which the stream flowed for the injury they would suffer from the diversion of their water supply. On the complaint of a landowner thus uncompensated for his injury, the Chancellor held that he must be compensated.

A right to a stream of water is as sacred as a right to the soil over which it flows. It is a part of the freehold, of which no man can be disseised "but by lawful judgment of his peers, or by due process of law." This is an ancient and fundamental maxim of common right to be found in *Magna Charta,* and which the Legislature has incorporated into an act declaratory of the rights of the citizens of this state.

If Magna Carta were not enough, Kent also cited Grotius, Pufendorf, Bynkershoek, Blackstone, several state constitutions, European constitutions, and the United States Constitution, all to support Kent's conclusion that the requirement of just compensation "is adopted by all temperate and civilized governments, from a deep and universal sense of its justice." [12]

What state courts were saying about property was being echoed by the highest court in the land. In an 1829 case the

[11] McKinster v. Sager, 163 Ind. 671, 679, 72 N.E. 854, 857 (1904).
[12] Gardner v. Village of Newburgh, 2 Johns. Ch. 162, 165–67 (N.Y. 1816).

Supreme Court said that "government can scarcely be deemed to be free, where the rights of property are left solely dependent upon the will of a legislative body, without any restraint. The fundamental maxims of a free government seem to require, that the rights of personal liberty and private property should be held sacred." Magna Carta guaranteed as much. "In a government professing to regard the great rights of personal liberty and of property . . . it would not lightly be presumed that the great principles of Magna Charta were to be disregarded, or that the estates of its subjects were liable to be taken away without trial, without notice, and without offence." [13]

The support given private property was not confined to judicial decisions. One of the great jurists of the century, Joseph Story, had this to say about property in an address delivered on the occasion of his inauguration as Dane Professor of Law in Harvard University:

The sacred rights of property are to be guarded at every point. I call them sacred, because, if they are unprotected, all other rights become worthless or visionary. What is personal liberty, if it does not draw after it the right to enjoy the fruits of our own industry? . . . What is the privilege of a vote, if the majority of the hour may sweep away the earnings of our whole lives, to ratify the rapacity of the indolent, the cunning, or the profligate, who are borne into power upon the tide of a temporary popularity? [14]

Probably no judge or commentator of the period had more influence in molding legal thinking about the protection which due process should accord to property than Thomas McIntyre Cooley. One of the first law professors at the University of Michigan, Cooley served on the Michigan Supreme Court and was the first chairman of the Interstate Commerce Commission. But he is best known for his prolific and influential writings, the most noted of which was his treatise on *Constitutional Limitations*. One writer has said that this book, which ran to six editions in Cooley's lifetime, "was by far the most important treatise in the entire development of the American idea of due

[13] Wilkinson v. Leland, 2 Pet. (27 U.S.) 627, 657 (1829).
[14] Quoted in Miller, *Legal Mind*, p. 180.

process of law. In many respects he did for constitutional thought in the United States what Coke had done in England two centuries before." [15] One of the things that Cooley did was to emphasize the use of due process to guard property rights, as he foresaw the rising tide of attacks on, and litigation concerning, property. His ideas were congenial to the legal profession, generally of a conservative bent, and no work of the time was more frequently cited in American courts, as any lawyer who has had occasion to look at nineteenth-century reports will agree. Indeed it is common to see Cooley's *Constitutional Limitations* cited in twentieth-century cases decided long after his death.

Bench and bar today have become accustomed, since 1961, to the near-rush of cases "incorporating" or applying to the States, through the due process clause of the Fourteenth Amendment, various specific commands of the Bill of Rights previously applicable as such only to the Federal Government. This has happened, for example, with the Sixth Amendment's requirement of the right to counsel,[16] the privilege against self-incrimination of the Fifth Amendment,[17] the search and seizure standards of the Fourth Amendment,[18] and the Eighth Amendment's ban on cruel and unusual punishment.[19] Cases like these are a sure sign of the concern of modern times with criminal justice and the rights of defendants.

In contrast, it is interesting to recall, by way of catching the special values of the nineteenth century, that the first real "incorporation" case, that is, the first case to apply to the States via Fourteenth Amendment due process some command of the Bill of Rights (though the case was not written in the language of incorporation) was *Chicago, B. & Q. R.R. v. Chicago,*[20] which held that the appropriation of private property for public use without just compensation was a taking of property without due process of law, in violation of the Fourteenth Amendment. The Fifth Amendment in express terms forbade

[15] Rodney L. Mott, *Due Process of Law* (Indianapolis, 1926), p. 184.
[16] Gideon v. Wainwright, 372 U.S. 335 (1963).
[17] Malloy v. Hogan, 378 U.S. 1 (1964).
[18] Mapp v. Ohio, 367 U.S. 643 (1961).
[19] Robinson v. California, 370 U.S. 660 (1962).   [20] 166 U.S. 226 (1897).

the Federal Government to do that, but the Fifth Amendment did not apply to the States. Nevertheless the Court, in an opinion by the first Mr. Justice Harlan (quoting Story), believed the requirement of just compensation to be but "an affirmance of a great doctrine established by the common law for the protection of private property. It is founded in natural equity, and is laid down as a principle of universal law. Indeed, in a free government almost all other rights would become worthless if the government possessed an uncontrollable power over the private fortune of every citizen." [21]

Until late in the nineteenth century, concern for property rights had been centered on actual takings, usually under the power of eminent domain. But with the rise of state and federal regulatory agencies (the prototypes being the state railroad commissions and the Interstate Commerce Commission) and the swelling demands for social, labor, and welfare legislation, attention turned to due process as a barrier for property against regulation. The forty years which followed *Chicago, B. & Q. R.R.* were the high-watermark of judicial protection of property against regulatory statutes, until changing times and changing Supreme Court personalities altered the jurisprudence of due process.[22]

Due Process and Trial by Jury

WHEN King John put the Great Seal to Magna Carta in 1215, trial by jury as we know it today had not yet taken shape, although its roots can be found in the inquisition, an administrative device whereby the Crown obtained information on local affairs from the sworn testimony of local men. But if "judgment of his peers" in Magna Carta did not refer to trial by jury, it is not surprising, in light of the language of chapter 39, that once the jury system had developed Englishmen should have interpreted the language of "judgment of his peers" to mean trial by jury. Blackstone, for example, said that trial by

---

[21] 166 U.S., at 236.   [22] See pp. 363–67, *infra.*

jury is a "trial by the peers of every Englishman, which, as the great bulwark of his liberties, is secured to him by the great charter. . . ." [23]

Americans before and after the Revolution connected trial by jury and Magna Carta. We have already seen how the resolutions passed by colonial bodies against such British measures as the Stamp Act asserted that to restrict the right to jury trial was, to quote the resolution of Pennsylvania, "contrary to *Magna Charta,* the great Charter and Fountain of *English* Liberty, and destructive of one of their most darling and acknowledged Rights, that of Trials by Juries." [24] The declarations of the Stamp Act Congress maintained that trial by jury was "confirmed by the Great CHARTER of *English* Liberty." [25] Similar claims were made in courts of law. In a Maryland case of 1774, an appeal from a conviction in county court of throwing ballast into the Potomac River, the Attorney General said, "By *Magna Charta* a man is not to be condemned but by the judgment of his peers. . . ." [26]

A noted case heard in Pennsylvania on the eve of the adoption of the Federal Constitution is of special interest. A newspaper publisher, Eleazer Oswald, inserted into his newspaper several anonymous pieces calling into question the character of Andrew Browne, the master of a female academy in Philadelphia. Browne brought a libel action. While the case was pending, Oswald published an address to the public, in which he said that freedom of the press was at stake and questioned the impartiality of the court. Oswald was charged with contempt of court, and there followed an argument on whether an attachment should issue against him.

Oswald's counsel contended that the Bill of Rights of the Pennsylvania Constitution entitled Oswald to a jury trial on the question, citing the constitutional mandate of a trial by an impartial jury of the country and the ban against any man's

---

[23] *Blackstone's Commentaries,* IV, 342–43. For a history of the jury, see Theodore F. T. Plucknett, *A Concise History of the Common Law* (5th ed.; Boston, 1956), pp. 106–38. For a study of judgment by peers as a feudal institution, see Barnaby C. Keeney, *Judgment by Peers* (Cambridge, Mass., 1949).

[24] Morgan, *Prologue to Revolution,* p. 52.   [25] *Ibid.,* p. 65.

[26] Miller v. Lord Proprietary, 1 H. & McH. 543, 548 (Md. 1774).

being deprived of his liberty "except by the laws of the land, or the judgment of his peers." If the attachment issued, it was argued, Oswald would not receive a jury trial. Opposing counsel replied that Oswald's argument "went so far as to assert, that there could be no such offence as a contempt even in *England*, since the very words inserted in the constitution of *Pennsylvania*, were used in the *Magna Charta* of that kingdom. . . ." [27]

The court decided that attachment was proper, but Oswald refused to answer interrogatories put to him and for this refusal was fined £10 and sentenced to a month's imprisonment. Oswald then took his case to the General Assembly of Pennsylvania, asking the legislature to determine whether the court had infringed his constitutional rights. The Assembly resolved itself into a committee of the whole house to hear evidence. One member of the house defended the court by arguing that the use of attachment was "as ancient as the laws themselves, and that it was confirmed by *Magna Charta*. . . ." He also made the interesting argument (anticipating one of the fine points disputed by modern Magna Carta scholars) that the Pennsylvania Constitution made "laws of the land" and "judgment of his peers" *alternatives* by using the word "or" between them. [28] "This very sentiment, expressed in the same words, appears in the *Magna Charta* of *England;* and yet *Blackstone* unequivocally informs us, that the process of *attachment* was *confirmed* by that celebrated instrument." Another member thought it unnecessary "to explore the dark and distant periods of juridical history" and argued that the attachment of Oswald had violated the state constitution. The house, however, finally resolved that there was "no just cause" for impeaching the justices. [29]

Joseph Story, in his *Commentaries on the Constitution of the*

[27] Respublica v. Oswald, 1 Dall. (1 U.S.) 319, 322–23 (Pa. 1788).

[28] For discussions of the proper rendering of "vel" in Magna Carta, see Arthur L. Goodhart, *"Law of the Land"* (Charlottesville, Va., 1965), p. 29; J. C. Holt, *Magna Carta* (Cambridge, 1965), p. 227 n. 9; McKechnie, *Magna Carta*, pp. 381–82; Walter Ullmann, *Principles of Government and Politics in the Middle Ages* (London, 1961), pp. 165–66.

[29] The debate in the Pennsylvania legislature appears in Respublica v. Oswald, 1 Dall. (1 U.S.) 319, 329 note.

United States, traced trial by jury to Magna Carta and said that
it was brought to America as one of the rights of Englishmen
claimed by the colonists:

The right constitutes the fundamental articles of Magna
Charta, in which it is declared, . . . no man shall be arrested, nor
imprisoned, nor banished, nor deprived of life, &c. but by the
judgment of his peers, or by the law of the land. The judgment
of his peers here alluded to, and commonly called in the quaint
language of former times a trial *per pais,* or trial by the country,
is the trial by a jury, who are called the peers of the party accused,
being of the like condition and equality in the state. When our
more immediate ancestors removed to America, they brought
this great privilege with them, as their birth-right and inheritance, as a part of that admirable common law, which had
fenced round, and interposed barriers on every side against the
approaches of arbitrary power.[30]

Nineteenth-century American cases often agreed with Story;
an 1880 Supreme Court case, for example, quoted Blackstone
on the origin of trial by jury in the Great Charter.[31] But courts
began to have doubts. A New York court in 1899, in upholding
a statute providing for a special jury in criminal cases, observed
that Magna Carta had been "generally credited with establishing, or defining, the right of trial by jury." But the court went
on to say that "the correctness of this belief is somewhat open to
doubt; inasmuch as the provision more probably referred to the
existing custom of a trial by peers." [32]

Before the nineteenth century was out, the Supreme Court of
the United States had in effect severed the historic tie between
due process of law and trial by jury. The Seventh Amendment
to the Federal Constitution requires jury trial in certain civil
cases, but the Court in 1875 held that a jury trial in civil cases
in state courts is not essential to due process of law:

A State cannot deprive a person of his property without due
process of law; but this does not necessarily imply that all trials
in the State courts affecting the property of persons must be by
jury. This requirement of the Constitution is met if the trial is

[30] (Boston, 1833) , III, 652–53.
[31] Strauder v. West Virginia, 100 U.S. 303, 308 (1880) .
[32] People v. Dunn, 157 N.Y. 528, 533, 52 N.E. 572, 573 (1899) . See Keeney,
Judgment by Peers, pp. 49–68.

had according to the settled course of judicial proceedings. *Murray's Lessee v. Hoboken L. & I. Co.,* 18 How. 280. Due process of law is process due according to the law of the land. This process in the States is regulated by the law of the State. Our power over that law is only to determine whether it is in conflict with the supreme law of the land. . . .[33]

The Court found no conflict.

In criminal cases the right to trial by jury is assured by Article III, Section 2, and the Sixth Amendment of the Constitution. It has been held that this right is to a trial by jury as understood at common law and includes all the essential elements of jury trial as they were recognized in England and America when the Constitution was adopted, including twelve men "neither more nor less," the assistance of a judge, and a unanimous verdict.[34] Yet Fourteenth Amendment due process has been held not to require that state juries have the traditional characteristics.[35] All state constitutions in fact provide for jury trial in criminal cases,[36] but this does not mean— especially with so many guarantees of the Bill of Rights being applied to the States via the Fourteenth Amendment—that the Supreme Court may not be called upon to decide anew whether due process does, after all, require trial by jury in state courts in those cases in which it would be constitutionally mandated in federal cases. If the Court ever does so hold, then it will have brought together once again two concepts, trial by jury and due process of law, which a mixture of history and popular tradition have associated with the phrases "judgment of his peers" and "law of the land" found side by side in chapter 39 of Magna Carta.[37]

[33] Walker v. Sauvinet, 92 U.S. 90, 92–93 (1875).

[34] Patton v. United States, 281 U.S. 276 (1930).

[35] See Maxwell v. Dow, 176 U.S. 581 (1900), upholding a Utah conviction by a jury of eight.

[36] See Turner v. Louisiana, 379 U.S. 466, 471 (1965).

[37] After this book was in page proofs, the Supreme Court did indeed bring jury trial in state criminal cases into Fourteenth Amendment due process. The Court held that due process guarantees the right of jury trial in all criminal cases which—were they tried in a federal court—would come within the jury trial guarantee of the Sixth Amendment. Duncan v. Louisiana, 36 U.S.L. Week (Sup. Ct.) 4414 (May 20, 1968). In its opinion the Court noted that historically jury trial had carried "impressive credentials" traced by many to Magna Carta but that historians "no longer accept this pedigree." *Ibid.,* p. 4416 and note.

Chapter XIX

Due Process of Law

The Coat of Many Colors

A Dynamic Concept

THROUGHOUT its history from its statement in Magna Carta's "law of the land" to the time it entered the stream of American constitutionalism, due process as a part of English law was a dynamic concept. The very words "due process" invite a judge to evaluate a process according to standards of history or natural justice or reasonableness or the sense of the community or whatever other measure might be a suitable means by which to discover that which is "due." In any event "due process" carries with it no qualities of exactness of definition. While the phrase came into American constitutions with centuries of historical associations, there was never any serious danger that due process would, in the hands of American jurists, be an altogether static concept.

Though it has never been static, due process has, even to the present day, carried with it some connotations of tradition or history, in the sense that people have come to expect certain things of a system of justice and, whatever else the concept may include, due process at least seeks to satisfy those minimal expectations. It may do, and in recent years has done, a great deal more. But it has never done less. That is why, for example, the view that due process requires notice and an opportunity to be heard has throughout the history of due process in this country been such a consistent thread in the cases; it is such a fundamental expectation that no court has ever paused to wonder seriously whether, as a general principle, it is a good idea or not.

As American courts began to develop a jurisprudence of due process, implementing the guarantees of federal and state constitutions, it was natural that, given the inclination of American judges to respect the English law and given the historical "halo effect" surrounding due process as a fundamental guarantee of the English Constitution, the American cases should look to the English common law to decide whether due process had been afforded in a given case. The earlier cases were largely concerned with procedure, the standard for which was the procedure allowed by the English law.

The States Interpret "Due Process of Law"

STATE constitutional mandates of "law of the land" and of due process of law were the subject of judicial decision well before the Supreme Court had occasion to interpret the due process clause of the Fifth Amendment. (Webster's "law of the land" argument in *Dartmouth College,* for example, was not based on the Federal Constitution, nor was it the subject of the Court's ultimate decision.) State courts early marked the path which the Federal Supreme Court was to follow. In an Alabama case of 1838, for example, an attorney named Dorsey challenged an Alabama statute which required each attorney-at-law to take an oath that he had never given or accepted a challenge to fight a duel. The report of the case does not record whether Dorsey was given to dueling; at any rate, he moved to dispense with the oath, urging the act's unconstitutionality.[1]

Before the Supreme Court of Alabama, Dorsey said that to interpret "due process of law" the court should look to the English common law because that law was the source of so many safeguards for individual liberties:

[1] In re Dorsey, 7 Port. 293 (Ala. 1838).

[W]e find many of our principles, precedents, definitions, and customs, are drawn from the English system of jurisprudence, which has furnished us sound and rational principles of civil liberty. Under it, our fathers lived and prospered, and from it they imbibed, and I hope I may say transmitted to us, that lively sense of individual rights, which is inculcated by its generous institutions. We must therefore refer to the English common law, to explain the technical language and the sound import of our laws and institutions.

This approach to interpreting American law, Dorsey pointed out, had been adopted by the report of the Virginia legislature in 1799 on the resolutions against the Alien and Sedition Acts, a report which Dorsey termed "one of the most luminous and masterly documents that ever emanated from the pen of an American statesman." [2]

Dorsey's principal submission was that the Alabama act requiring the oath violated that section of the Alabama Declaration of Rights assuring that no man should be deprived of life, liberty, or property "but by due course of law." This clause Dorsey traced to the twenty-ninth chapter of Magna Carta, the origin of which, he said, was "familiar to lawyers and politicians. It was intended to limit the power of the crown, and check encroachments on the liberty of the subject." [3]

Characterizing the attorney's interest in his office as a "vested right," Dorsey denied the power of the legislature to deprive him of it "without due course of law." And what due course of law required was the proper judgment of a court:

The learned Bracton, in his explanations of Magna Charta, defines due course of law, to be a judgment—a verdict of equals. Sullivan expounds the words—a proceeding to judgment in a court of justice—[citing Coke's *Second Institute*]—Due course of law, as that phrase has been understood ever since Magna Charta, means a correct and established course of judicial proceedings. [4]

The three judges delivered separate opinions, one of them discussing Coke's decision in *Dr. Bonham's Case;* all three agreed on the unconstitutionality of the oath.

In the Alabama case the court, by giving judgment for Dor-

[2] 7 Port., at 303–04.   [3] 7 Port., at 328.   [4] 7 Port., at 328–29.

sey, may be taken to have implied its agreement with Dorsey's analysis of due process. Other decisions are more explicit. The Supreme Court of Illinois, confronted with a party's argument that a summary tax sale of his land was against the "law of the land," observed that the clause of the Illinois Constitution requiring proceedings according to the "law of the land" was in the language of the corresponding chapter of Magna Carta. Therefore, "in order to give a proper exposition to these words, it will be necessary to examine, and ascertain when, and under what circumstances magna charta was obtained, and what meaning has been adopted by the judges and ancient law writers in England, from whence it derives its origin." [5]

After examining various commentaries, including those of Coke, the court summed up its understanding of the purposes of Magna Carta:

> The effect of the *magna charta,* which was in the nature of a constitution or bill of rights, was to impose a limitation upon the improper exercise of the king's prerogative; and the objects intended to be secured by this important concession on the part of crown, have been classed under six general heads:
> 1. To secure the personal liberty of the subjects;
> 2. To preserve his landed property from forfeiture;
> 3. To defend him against unjust outlawry;
> 4. To prevent unjust banishment;
> 5. To secure him against all manner of destruction; and
> 6. To restrict and regulate criminal prosecutions at the suit of the king, by securing to the subject a proper administration of justice through the means of courts and juries, conformable to the principles and usages of the common law, independent of the will and caprice of the sovereign power.[6]

The court thought it "evident from the language of Lord Coke . . . that these expressions in magna charta were intended to apply to criminal, and not to civil proceedings." Further, said the court, if they did have application to civil proceedings, it must be limited; the court referred to such proceedings in England as summary distress for rent. This conclusion was

---

[5] Rhinehart v. Schuyler, 7 Ill. 473, 517–18 (1845).   [6] 7 Ill., at 519.

reinforced by looking at the practice of sister States, all but one of whom provided for the sale of land for taxes by summary procedures.[7]

English Usage as the Measure of Due Process

It was in an 1855 case, *Murray's Lessee v. Hoboken Land and Improvement Co.,* involving the constitutionality of summary proceedings under a distress warrant (to levy on the lands of a government debtor) that the Supreme Court of the United States approached the problem of interpreting due process as assured by the Fifth Amendment.[8] Mr. Justice Benjamin R. Curtis, the author of the opinion, was an unusually scholarly lawyer. When he was appointed to the Supreme Court, he brought with him the Whig view of history as an "affirmance of the ancient standing laws of the land, as they had existed among the Saxons" before the "subtlety of Norman lawyers" had aided Norman power in stripping the English nation of "their ancient civil and political institutions." [9] It was natural, then, that in writing the opinion in *Murray's Lessee* he should approach due process from the standpoint of its English development.

Curtis began by equating Fifth Amendment "due process" with Magna Carta's "law of the land," quoting Coke's *Second Institute*. He noted that the constitutions of the several States, drawn up before the drafting of the Federal Constitution, followed the Great Charter more closely, generally using the phrase "law of the land," used also in the Northwest Ordinance of 1787.[10] Curtis explained the Fifth Amendment's departure from this normal usage; trial by jury (which Curtis took to be the meaning of "judgment of his peers") had already been provided for in other sections of the Constitution, and to use

---

[7] 7 Ill., at 520–22.   [8] 18 How. (59 U.S.) 272 (1855).

[9] G. T. Curtis, ed., *Life and Writings of Benjamin Robbins Curtis* (Boston, 1879), II, 43.

[10] See Reed v. Wright, 2 G. Greene 15 (Iowa 1849), interpreting the Northwest Ordinance's guarantee of "law of the land" by reference to Coke and Magna Carta.

"law of the land" without its usual context might have been misleading. Better, then, to use "due process," words which "the great commentator on *Magna Charta* had declared to be the true meaning of the phrase, 'law of the land' . . . ." [11]

Curtis proceeded to explain how a court went about the task of deciding what constituted "due process of law":

That the warrant now in question is legal process, is not denied. It was issued in conformity with an act of Congress. But is it "due process of law?" The constitution contains no description of those processes which it was intended to allow or forbid. It does not even declare what principles are to be applied to ascertain whether it be due process. It is manifest that it was not left to the legislative power to enact any process which might be devised. The article is a restraint on the legislative as well as on the executive and judicial powers of the government, and cannot be so construed as to leave congress free to make any process "due process of law," by its mere will. To what principles, then, are we to resort to ascertain whether this process, enacted by congress, is due process? To this the answer must be twofold. We must examine the constitution itself, to see whether this process be in conflict with any of its provisions. If not found to be so, we must look to those settled usages and modes of proceeding existing in the common and statute law of England, before the emigration of our ancestors, and which are shown not to have been unsuited to their civil and political condition by having been acted on by them after the settlement of this country. [12]

Accordingly, Curtis sketched the history of distress proceedings in England, including the provision of Magna Carta for the procedure by which debts owed the King should be satisfied. Curtis found that there had been no period in England when the law of the land had not allowed a summary method for recovering debts owed the Crown and in fact that the law of the land allowed a kind of execution bearing a close resemblance to that authorized by Congress in the case at bar. Looking also into the practice in American jurisdictions, the Court concluded that "tested by the common and statute law of England prior to the emigration of our ancestors, and by the laws of many of the States at the time of the adoption of this amend-

[11] 18 How. (59 U.S.), at 276.   [12] 18 How. (59 U.S.), at 276–77.

ment [the Fifth], the proceedings authorized by the act of 1820 cannot be denied to be due process of law. . . ." Nor were there any other constitutional provisions standing in the way.[13]

The historical approach of Mr. Justice Curtis, had it been adhered to by the Court in later cases, would have laid fairly obvious limits on the capacity of the due process clause for growth. Strictly applied, it would neither have given scope for new procedures unknown to the English law nor have protected substantive, as opposed to procedural, claims. In fact when the Court began to hear cases arising under the newly adopted due process clause of the Fourteenth Amendment, it looked as if the limited view of due process would persist. *Davidson v. New Orleans*,[14] decided in 1877, if not approaching the Fourteenth Amendment in quite the way that *Murray's Lessee* had treated the Fifth, was not a break with that case.

Mr. Justice Miller, like Mr. Justice Curtis, began *Davidson* with Magna Carta, tracing due process to the Charter's assurance of "law of the land." Like Curtis, Miller saw due process as a limitation on the legislature as well as the executive. To hold that a state legislature could, simply by its act, make anything "due process of law" would be to hold "that the prohibition to the States is of no avail, or has no application where the invasion of private rights is effected under the terms of State legislation." But Miller seemed to leave the door open for a broader approach to due process than that espoused by Curtis. He observed that the meaning of "due process of law" remained without the satisfactory precision which judicial decisions had given to "nearly all the other guarantees of personal rights" in federal and state constitutions.[15]

If there was going to be a move away from English historical practice as a measure, it was not yet clear. For example, in the leading case of *Munn v. Illinois* (1876), the Court, in holding that Illinois constitutionally might fix maximum charges to be made by grain elevators, pointed out that, while due process as a limit upon the power of the States might be relatively new in the Constitution, it was a principle as old as Magna Carta.

[13] 18 How. (59 U.S.), at 280.　　[14] 96 U.S. 97 (1877).
[15] 96 U.S., at 101–2.

Therefore the Court, by Chief Justice Morrison R. Waite, supported its upholding the Illinois regulations by referring to the practice "customary in England from time immemorial, and in this country from its first colonization," to regulate common carriers, innkeepers, ferries, and others, and to fix maximum charges.[16]

Toward a More Flexible Concept of Due Process:
"Fundamental" Rights

CURTIS's test of due process, as formulated in *Murray's Lessee,* had a tendency to formalism, a capacity for shackling courts with procedures devised for the needs of another era. That due process was to be a more flexible concept than this was made clear by the Supreme Court's landmark decision in *Hurtado v. California.*[17] Hurtado was tried and convicted of first degree murder and challenged his conviction on the ground that he had not been indicted by grand jury but had been proceeded against upon an information filed by the district attorney. Due process of law, as derived from Magna Carta and as laid down by usage, included, Hurtado maintained, not only the general principles of public liberty and private right, but also "the very institutions which, venerable by time and custom, have been tried by experience and found fit and necessary for the preservation of those principles. . . ." One of those institutions, he claimed, was indictment by grand jury.[18]

Mr. Justice Stanley Matthews, writing for the majority in *Hurtado,* conceded that there was some respectable authority for Hurtado's position, notably the decision of Chief Justice Lemuel Shaw of Massachusetts in *Jones v. Robbins* holding that Massachusetts' constitutional guarantee of "law of the land" ("a transcript of *Magna Charta* in this respect," commented Matthews) required indictment by grand jury in felony cases. Shaw had relied heavily upon the statement of Coke that "law of the land" intended indictment or presentment of

[16] 94 U.S. 113, 123–25 (1876).   [17] 110 U.S. 516 (1884).
[18] 110 U.S., at 521.

good and lawful men. But Matthews said that this was a misreading of Coke; in fact, the passage in question did not assert indictment to be essential to due process of law but was "only mentioned as an example and illustration of due process of law." In expansion of his point, Matthews then devoted several pages of the Court's opinion to a discussion of Coke and of the English cases.[19]

Hurtado also argued that the Supreme Court's decision in *Murray's Lessee* furnished an "indispensable test" of due process: that any proceeding not sanctioned by usages which had existed in English common and statute law before the emigration to America and had also been found suited to conditions in this country could not be regarded as due process of law. This argument the Court rejected. "The real syllabus of the passage quoted [from *Murray's Lessee*] is, that a process of law, which is not otherwise forbidden, must be taken to be due process of law, if it can show the sanction of settled usage both in England and in this country; but it by no means follows that nothing else can be due process of law." To hold that only traditional procedures can constitute due process of law "would be to deny every quality of the law but its age, and to render it incapable of progress or improvement. It would be to stamp upon our jurisprudence the unchangeableness attributed to the laws of the Medes and Persians."[20]

Magna Carta itself, thought Mr. Justice Matthews, was the best illustration of his point, for "the words of Magna Charta stood for very different things at the time of the separation of the American colonies from what they represented originally." At first, for example, "judgment of peers" had no reference to trial by jury. And as for the grand jury, Matthews traced it to the Assize of Clarendon (1164) and the Assize of Northampton (1176) and observed that accusation by a grand jury (which heard no witnesses but proceeded on its own knowledge) meant the accused had to undergo the ordeal of water (and lose a hand and a foot if he failed the ordeal) and was banished from

[19] 110 U.S., at 521–27. Jones v. Robbins is reported at 8 Gray (74 Mass.) 329 (1857).

[20] 110 U.S., at 528–29.

the country (even if he was acquitted by the ordeal). Matthews concluded dryly that it seemed therefore "better not to go too far back into antiquity for the best securities for our 'ancient liberties.' "[21]

Rather, the best approach was that which, like Magna Carta itself, gave opportunity for growth and improvement in the law:

> This flexibility and capacity for growth and adaptation is the peculiar boast and excellence of the common law. Sir James Mackintosh ascribes this principle of development to Magna Charta itself. To use his own language: "It was a peculiar advantage that the consequences of its principles were, if we may so speak, only discovered slowly and gradually. It gave out on each occasion only so much of the spirit of liberty and reformation as the circumstances of succeeding generations required and as their character would safely bear. For almost five centuries it was appealed to as the decisive authority on behalf of the people, though commonly so far only as the necessities of each case demanded." 1 Hist. of England, 221.
> The Constitution of the United States was ordained, it is true, by descendants of Englishmen, who inherited the traditions of English law and history; but it was made for an undefined and expanding future, and for a people gathered and to be gathered from many nations and of many tongues. And while we take just pride in the principles and institutions of the common law, we are not to forget that in lands where other systems of jurisprudence prevail, the ideas and processes of civil justice are also not unknown. . . . There is nothing in Magna Charta, rightly construed as a broad charter of public right and law, which ought to exclude the best ideas of all systems and of every age; and as it was the characteristic principle of the common law to draw its inspiration from every fountain of justice, we are not to assume that the sources of its supply have been exhausted. On the contrary, we should expect that the new and various experiences of our own situation and system will mould and shape it into new and not less useful forms.[22]

Justice Matthews also repeated what many American lawyers and jurists had observed about Magna Carta from the time the state and federal constitutions were drafted, namely, that American constitutionalism had improved on Magna Carta. Where

---

[21] 110 U.S., at 529–30.   [22] 110 U.S., at 530–31.

in England Magna Carta had been only a limit on the Crown and not on Parliament, in the United States "the provisions of Magna Charta were incorporated into Bills of Rights," which became limits on the powers of all branches of government. Therefore since these maxims of liberty served a different and more comprehensive office in America than in England, "it would be incongruous to measure and restrict them by the ancient customary English law. . . ." They must be held to guarantee, "not particular forms of procedure, but the very substance of individual rights to life, liberty, and property." [23]

The due process clause of the Fourteenth Amendment, Matthews concluded, can be summed up as policing "the limits of those fundamental principles of liberty and justice which lie at the base of all our civil and political institutions. . . . It follows that any legal proceeding enforced by public authority, whether sanctioned by age and custom, or newly devised in the discretion of the legislative power, in furtherance of the general public good, which regards and preserves these principles of liberty and justice, must be held to be due process of law." The conclusion was that indictment by grand jury is not one of the requirements of due process of law, and Hurtado's conviction was affirmed.[24]

Another landmark decision in procedural due process was *Twining v. New Jersey* (1908), in which the Court once again made it clear that it was going to measure due process by a broader standard than simply what had been accepted at English common law. At issue was the question whether the privilege against self-incrimination, secured against the Federal Government by the Fifth Amendment, was protected by the Fourteenth Amendment against abridgment by the States. The Court took the position that some of the rights safeguarded by the Bill of Rights against federal action might also be protected against the States because the rights were so fundamental as to be included in the very conception of due process of law. (The Court had indeed already applied to the States the requirement of just compensation for the taking of private property, in the

[23] 110 U.S., at 531–32.   [24] 110 U.S., at 535, 537.

Chicago, B. & Q. R.R. case.) The Court declined, as it had declined before, to essay a comprehensive definition of due process, preferring gradually to ascertain its meaning "by the process of inclusion and exclusion in the course of the decisions of cases as they arise." [25]

Mr. Justice William H. Moody, writing the majority opinion, did think it useful to approach the case in the light of certain well-settled general principles which "grow out of the proposition universally accepted by American courts on the authority of Coke, that the words 'due process of law' are equivalent in meaning to the words 'law of the land'" found in Magna Carta. Supreme Court cases could be found to have drawn several conclusions about due process of law:

(1) There was the test adopted by Mr. Justice Curtis in *Murray's Lessee:* an examination of "those settled usages and modes of proceedings" in the English law which had not been found unsuited to American conditions. A proceeding sanctioned by usage would be due process of law.

(2) It did not follow, however, that a settled English usage brought to and practiced in America by the colonists was an essential element of due process of law.

(3) Nevertheless, no change in ancient procedure could be made which disregarded those fundamental principles which, as ascertained by the courts, guard the citizen against arbitrary acts of government. [26]

Turning to the case before it, the Court first applied Curtis' test of English usage and found, after a review of English practice since Magna Carta, that the privilege against self-incrimination was "not regarded as a part of the law of the land of Magna Carta" but came into existence simply as a rule of evidence. But the Court, "without repudiating or questioning the test proposed by Mr. Justice Curtis for the court, or rejecting the inference drawn from English law," preferred to rest its decision on broader grounds, that is, on an inquiry whether the privilege against self-incrimination was "a fundamental principle of liberty and justice which inheres in the very idea of free

[25] 211 U.S. 78, 99–100 (1908).   [26] 211 U.S., at 100–101.

government." On this broad ground the Court noted that none of the fundamental English documents—Magna Carta, the Petition of Right, the Bill of Rights—referred to it. Only four of the thirteen States ratifying the Constitution had insisted that the privilege ought to be included in that document. On this and other evidence, the Court concluded that the privilege was not one of those fundamental rights safeguarded against state action by the due process clause of the Fourteenth Amendment.[27]

Mr. Justice Harlan, who had dissented in *Hurtado,* dissented here, too. He took the view that the end of compulsory self-incrimination in England had placed English liberties on a firmer basis and that when the United States came into being "the wise men who laid the foundations of our constitutional government would have stood aghast at the suggestion that immunity from self-incrimination was not among the essential, fundamental principles of English law." Harlan recalled the claims of the colonists, stated, for example, in the resolutions of the Continental Congress of 1774, to the rights of Englishmen and the guarantees against self-incrimination which Virginia put into its Bill of Rights in 1776 and which other States put into theirs. Harlan concluded that compelling a person to incriminate himself "shocks or ought to shock the sense of right and justice of every one who loves liberty" and that surely the privilege against self-incrimination must be counted among the fundamental rights protected by the Fourteenth Amendment.[28]

Twining, with its three-point analysis of how cases involving claims of procedural due process should be handled, simply made explicit a process which was already well under way and was to characterize procedural due process cases for some time to come. It remained common before and after *Twining* for the Court, in sustaining a given state practice against an argument that it offended due process, to show that the practice had been sanctioned by English practice before the American Revolution. In this manner, for example, the Court upheld the collection of taxes by distress proceedings;[29] a statute providing that,

---

[27] 211 U.S., at 102–14.   [28] 211 U.S., at 114–23.
[29] Palmer v. McMahon, 133 U.S. 660 (1890).

when a prosecution had been instituted maliciously and without probable cause, the prosecuting witness should pay costs;[30] the use of quo warranto as a civil proceeding;[31] and the finality, with only limited judicial review, of the amount of damages awarded by commissioners for changes in street grades.[32] Cases like these kept alive the approach used by Mr. Justice Curtis in *Murray's Lessee.*

At the same time, the Court said repeatedly that due process should not be thought to require any particular form of procedure, so long as there is adequate notice and opportunity to be heard.[33] By such cases as these the Court was issuing constant reminders of what it had said in *Hurtado* and in *Twining*, that due process was not limited to what had been accepted at English law and that it was flexible enough to accommodate the innovations of later ages. For example, in what apparently was the Court's first approval of a substantial deviation from common law procedures in criminal cases, the Court approved a New Jersey statute which allowed a "struck jury" in a murder case, a procedure whereby the court selected from the jury list 96 names, the prosecution and the defense each struck 24, and the trial jury was drawn in the usual way from the remainder. Commenting that a State is not bound to common law practices and procedures, the Court thought the New Jersey statute operated to secure an impartial jury, and that was what due process entitled the defendant to have.[34]

State courts followed a path like that of the Federal Supreme Court in *Hurtado* and *Twining*. A number of States held, for instance, that indictment by grand jury is not essential to due process of law. In so doing these courts explicitly rejected arguments which, drawing on Magna Carta and the English law at the time of the adoption of the American States' constitutions, maintained that "due process of law" was to be construed with

[30] Lowe v. Kansas, 163 U.S. 81 (1896).
[31] Standard Oil Co. v. Missouri, 224 U.S. 270 (1912).
[32] Crane v. Hahlo, 258 U.S. 142 (1922).
[33] Eg., Iowa Central Ry. v. Iowa, 160 U.S. 389, 393 (1896); Rogers v. Peck, 199 U.S. 425, 435 (1905); Garland v. Washington, 232 U.S. 642, 645 (1914); Frank v. Mangum, 237 U.S. 309, 326 (1915).
[34] Brown v. New Jersey, 175 U.S. 172 (1899).

reference to the English usages.[35] Instead the courts took the position that due process does not "confine the states to a particular mode of procedure in judicial proceedings. . . ." [36]

While the Supreme Court of the United States was developing the principle that innovation was permissible, the Court continued to adhere to the other dimension of *Hurtado* and *Twining*, that new procedures still must measure up to the requirement that rights fundamental to our system of jurisprudence be safeguarded. For example, in *Powell v. Alabama* (1932), the Court held that at least in some circumstances there was a right to counsel which was essential to due process; in those circumstances, counsel must be appointed if a defendant was too poor to hire his own. The Court came to this holding despite the fact that at the time of the adoption of the American Constitution there did not exist at English law any comparable right. This history was not controlling because the Court viewed a hearing as one of the indispensable elements of due process and believed that the right to be heard would be an empty privilege if it did not comprehend the right to be heard by counsel.[37]

The view of due process as protecting "fundamental" rights received perhaps its most classic modern statement at the hands if Mr. Justice Cardozo in *Palko v. Connecticut* (1937). Palko had been indicted for first degree murder and convicted of murder in the second degree. The prosecution, as it was permitted to do under Connecticut law, appealed, and the state supreme court reversed the judgment. On retrial, Palko was convicted of murder in the first degree, which was affirmed by the State's highest court. Appealing to the Supreme Court of the United States Palko argued that his retrial had placed him twice in jeopardy for the same offense and thus had denied him due process of law. The Court understood Palko's thesis to be that whatever would violate the original Bill of Rights (Amendments 1 through 8) if done by the Federal Government would be a denial of due process if done by a State.

Mr. Justice Cardozo rejected this argument. Pointing to a

[35] See, e.g., State v. Stimpson, 78 Vt. 124, 62 Atl. 14 (1905).
[36] Rowan v. State, 30 Wis. 129, 149 (1872).   [37] 287 U.S. 45 (1932).

number of guarantees of the Bill of Rights—among them, indictment by grand jury, the privilege against self-incrimination, trial by jury in civil and criminal cases—which had already been held not to be binding on the States, Cardozo said that the test was whether an immunity valid against the Federal Government by virtue of the Bill of Rights was "implicit in the concept of ordered liberty" and therefore binding on the States. Such rights as had been "absorbed" by Fourteenth Amendment due process, such as freedom of speech, had been absorbed on the premise that "neither liberty nor justice would exist if they were sacrificed." This could not be said of such things as indictment by grand jury; similarly, the Court concluded, to allow the State to appeal in Palko's case did not violate any fundamental principle of liberty and justice.[38]

The "Incorporation" of the Bill of Rights

A FULL-SCALE judicial debate over the value of the traditional approach to due process erupted with the Supreme Court's decision in *Adamson v. California* (1947). There Adamson, who had been convicted of first degree murder, alleged that he had been denied due process of law by the California rule which allowed the court and counsel to comment on a defendant's failure to take the stand. The Court assumed for the purposes of argument that to allow such comment in federal court would infringe the privilege against self-incrimination guaranteed by the Fifth Amendment. Nevertheless, the Court, by a 5–4 vote, held that it did not seem "unfair" to require a defendant to explain adverse evidence or to suffer comment on his failure to do so.[39]

Mr. Justice Black, dissenting, attacked the majority's treatment of due process, which he traced to *Twining v. New Jersey*, as holding that the Constitution endows the Supreme Court with "boundless power under 'natural law' periodically to expand and contract constitutional standards to conform to the

[38] 302 U.S. 319, 324–28 (1937).   [39] 332 U.S. 46 (1947).

Court's conception of what at a particular time constitutes 'civilized decency' and 'fundamental liberty and justice.' " Attaching an historical appendix to his dissent, Black urged his own view of Fourteenth Amendment due process: that the Amendment was intended, at the time of its passage, to apply to the States in their entirety the guarantees of the Bill of Rights.[40]

Justice Black's *Adamson* dissent made the "incorporation" theory famous. In *Adamson* Black won the concurrence of three other Justices, one short of what was needed to make his view the prevailing one. The Court has in fact never adopted Black's theory in its entirety, but beginning in 1961 a kind of "selective" incorporation process (which Black in *Adamson* had said was a second-best approach) reached full tide. Actually, selective incorporation of sorts had begun in 1897, when the Court in *Chicago, B. & Q. R.R. v. Chicago* had used the Fourteenth Amendment to impose upon the States the obligation of just compensation for the taking of private property which the Fifth Amendment put upon the Federal Government.[41] The Court had also slid obliquely into "incorporation" and application to the States of the rights of the First Amendment.[42] But from 1961 on one provision after another of the Bill of Rights (though by no means all of them) have been applied to the States: the exclusionary standards of the Fourth Amendment's ban on unreasonable searches and seizures;[43] the Eighth Amendment's proscription of cruel and unusual punishment;[44] the Sixth Amendment's assurance of the right to counsel;[45] the privilege against self-incrimination of the Fifth Amendment;[46] the Sixth

[40] 332 U.S., at 68, 69–89. For an article disagreeing with Justice Black's review of the history of the Fourteenth Amendment, see Charles Fairman, "Does the Fourteenth Amendment Incorporate the Bill of Rights? The Original Understanding," 2 *Stan. L. Rev.* 5 (1949).

[41] 166 U.S. 226 (1897).

[42] This process began with Gitlow v. New York, 268 U.S. 652, 666 (1925), where the Court said it could "assume" for purposes of that case that freedom of speech and press were among the "fundamental" rights protected by the Fourteenth Amendment.

[43] Mapp v. Ohio, 367 U.S. 643 (1961).

[44] Robinson v. California, 370 U.S. 660 (1962).

[45] Gideon v. Wainwright, 372 U.S. 335 (1963).

[46] Malloy v. Hogan, 378 U.S. 1 (1964).

Amendment's assurance of the right to confront adverse witnesses;[47] and the Sixth's guarantees of a speedy trial and of an accused's right to have compulsory process for obtaining witnesses in his favor.[48]

Such cases represent a break with the holdings of a number of the earlier landmark decisions. For instance, the 1964 decision that the privilege against self-incrimination applies to the States required the discarding of the holding in *Twining v. New Jersey*. But the language of the new decisions does not represent such a clean break with the earlier cases. Cases such as *Twining* and *Palko* had developed the principle that Fourteenth Amendment due process included only those rights which were "fundamental." The "selective incorporation" cases, while overruling some of the earlier precedents, use similar language. In *Gideon v. Wainwright* (1963), for example, Mr. Justice Black, in holding that the Fourteenth Amendment applied to the States the Sixth Amendment's guarantee of right to counsel, overruled *Betts v. Brady* (1942),[49] which had held counsel not essential to a fair trial save in special circumstances. Black said that the Court accepted the assumption of *Betts* that a provision of the Bill of Rights which is "fundamental and essential to a fair trial" is binding on the States through the Fourteenth Amendment but thought *Betts* wrong in thinking the right to counsel not to be such a fundamental right.[50] Black used similar language two years later in the opinion which referred to *Gideon* and held that "the Sixth Amendment's right of an accused to confront the witnesses against him is likewise a fundamental right and is made obligatory on the States by the Fourteenth Amendment." [51]

It would strain a point to suggest any direct influence of Magna Carta in the debate between Frankfurterians and those of the Black school over "incorporation" of the Bill of Rights into the Fourteenth Amendment. At this point, Magna Carta, which gave formal birth to the principle of "law of the land,"

[47] Pointer v. Texas, 380 U.S. 400 (1965).
[48] Klopfer v. North Carolina, 386 U.S. 213 (1967); Washington v. Texas, 388 U.S. 14 (1967).
[49] 316 U.S. 455 (1942).   [50] 372 U.S. 335, 342 (1963).
[51] Pointer v. Texas, 380 U.S. 400, 403 (1965).

fades into the background. As long as the Supreme Court measured due process by English standards, references to the Great Charter were frequent and indeed of precedential value. When the Court moved to the broader plane of "fundamental" rights and then, though retaining the language of fundamentality, to the process of selective incorporation, Magna Carta became simply a genial godfather watching that same historical process in which Magna Carta itself underwent centuries of growth carry the search for justice even further.[52]

"Substantive" Due Process

AN ACCOUNT of due process of law would not be complete without a word about so-called "substantive" due process (as opposed to due process in its aspect involved with questions of fairness and right in procedure). Substantive due process is a concept which, whether applied to property rights or other things, puts certain matters, so to speak, out of bounds for legislatures. Thus, by the use of substantive due process, a statute can be declared unconstitutional even though the procedures it sets up are altogether scrupulous and fair if, in the judgment of a court, the statute is "arbitrary" or "unreasonable." The genesis of substantive due process in America was a fairly slow one, partly because the words "due process" would seem to imply procedure, not substance, partly because there was not until 1868 a federal due process guarantee against the States, and, perhaps most of all, because state regulation of the use of private property and of economic activities was infrequent before the late nineteenth century.

At first it looked as if Fourteenth Amendment due process would indeed be confined to questions of procedure. In *Davidson v. New Orleans* Mr. Justice Miller tried to put to rest the "strange misconceptions" litigants had about the Fourteenth Amendment. Although Fifth Amendment due process had been

---

[52] The Court, of course, continues to resort to English history in dealing with concepts of English origin, e.g., habeas corpus, see McNally v. Hill, 293 U.S. 131, 136 (1934), and bill of attainder, United States v. Brown, 381 U.S. 437, 441–42, 458 (1965).

little invoked in a century of its existence, Miller observed that only a few years after the Fourteenth Amendment's adoption,

the docket of this court is crowded with cases in which we are asked to hold that State courts and State legislatures have deprived their own citizens of life, liberty, or property without due process of law. There is here abundant evidence that there exists some strange misconception of the scope of this provision as found in the fourteenth amendment. In fact, it would seem . . . that the clause under consideration is looked upon as a means of bringing to the test of the decision of this court the abstract opinions of every unsuccessful litigant in a State court of the justice of the decision against him, and of the merits of the legislation on which such a decision may be founded.

Miller viewed due process as being limited to procedure; if a party had "a fair trial in a court of justice, according to the modes of proceeding applicable to such a case," then it was not possible to say that he had not had due process of law.[53]

The Court several times voiced concern about the "strange misconceptions" of the due process clause, saying, on one occasion, "the hardship, impolicy, or injustice of State laws is not necessarily an objection to their constitutional validity. . . . This court is not a harbor where refuge can be found from every act of ill-advised and oppressive State legislation." [54] Notwithstanding such dicta, the Court did in fact offer just such a refuge. The gate to the sanctuary began to open with cases invalidating state-fixed railroad rates on the ground that they had been set unreasonably low and therefore amounted to a taking of property without due process of law.[55] Then, soon after the turn of the century, the Court made the first application of its substantive due process doctrine to a state statute regulating labor conditions. In *Lochner v. New York* (1905), the Court struck down a New York statute limiting employment in bakeries to ten hours a day on the view that such a statute was an arbitrary interference with freedom to contract. The test of whether a state regulatory statute was compatible

[53] 96 U.S. 97, 104, 105 (1877).
[54] Missouri Pac. Ry. v. Humes, 115 U.S. 512, 520–21 (1885).
[55] Reagan v. Farmers' Loan & Trust Co., 154 U.S. 362 (1894); Smyth v. Ames, 169 U.S. 466, *modified on rehearing,* 171 U.S. 361 (1898).

with due process was stated to be: "Is this a fair, reasonable and appropriate exercise of the police power of the State, or is it an unreasonable, unnecessary and arbitrary interference with the right of the individual to his personal liberty . . . ?" [56]

Mr. Justice Holmes, one of four dissenters, objected to this decision as embodying the particular economic philosophies of the majority. "The Fourteenth Amendment," he objected, "does not enact Mr. Herbert Spencer's Social Statics." [57] For thirty years the Holmesian view was to be in the minority. The Court invalidated, under the due process clause, a variety of state social and economic legislation. Minimum wages for women,[58] the outlawing of "yellow dog" contracts in labor relations,[59] the fixing of the weight of loaves of bread,[60] the requirement of a certificate of convenience and necessity for those in the business of making ice,[61] and the prohibition of the use of shoddy in the manufacture of bedding [62] were among the state statutes which fell before the scythe.

The "Constitutional Revolution" of the 1930's, occasioned in part by the pressing demands for the use of state police power to deal with the crisis of a major depression and by new faces and new attitudes on the Court, changed all this. Many of the old substantive due process cases involving regulation of social and economic conditions have been overruled.[63] And clearly the philosophy of the earlier cases is moribund. The Court now takes the view that, as far as economic questions are concerned, it will "not sit as a super-legislature to weigh the wisdom" of state legislation [64] and that, before the Court will act, the state statute must be shown, not simply to be unreasonable, but to have "no rational relation" to the object the legislature seeks to attain.[65] With this test, it is not surprising that no statute

[56] 198 U.S. 45, 56 (1905) .   [57] 198 U.S., at 75.
[58] Adkins v. Children's Hospital, 261 U.S. 525 (1923) .
[59] Coppage v. Kansas, 236 U.S. 1 (1915) . "Yellow dog" contracts required that employees agree not to join a labor union.
[60] Jay Burns Baking Co. v. Bryan, 264 U.S. 504 (1924) .
[61] New State Ice Co. v. Liebmann, 285 U.S. 262 (1932) .
[62] Weaver v. Palmer Bros. Co., 270 U.S. 402 (1926) .
[63] See, e.g., West Coast Hotel Co. v. Parrish, 300 U.S. 379 (1937) , *overruling* Adkins v. Children's Hospital, 261 U.S. 525 (1923) .
[64] Day-Brite Lighting, Inc. v. Missouri, 342 U.S. 421, 423 (1952) .
[65] Williamson v. Lee Optical Co., 348 U.S. 483, 491 (1955) .

regulating economic affairs has been invalidated on substantive due process grounds since 1937.

But it would be a mistake to suppose that substantive due process is dead. It may have been banished from the arena of economic regulation, but it persists elsewhere. In the 1920's, at the height of the Court's affinity for substantive due process, the doctrine was used in certain noneconomic areas. For example, in *Meyer v. Nebraska* (1923), in which the Court invalidated a state statute prohibiting the teaching in schools of any language but English, Mr. Justice James C. McReynolds wrote that "liberty" as protected by the Fourteenth Amendment includes not only certain economic rights such as the right to contract but also the right "to acquire useful knowledge, to marry, establish a home and bring up children, to worship God according to the dictates of his own conscience, and generally to enjoy those privileges long recognized at common law as essential to the orderly pursuit of happiness by free men." [66]

Meyer was favorably invoked forty years later when in 1965 the Supreme Court in the *Griswold* case decided that Connecticut could not constitutionally prohibit the use of contraceptives. This law, said Mr. Justice Douglas for the majority, invaded the sanctity of the marriage relationship, a relationship lying within the "penumbra" of rights created by several constitutional provisions (the First, Third, Fourth, Fifth, and Ninth Amendments). Douglas' opinion purports to avoid the *Lochner* kind of reasoning, but he says that the Constitution, in noneconomic areas, does protect rights which are not expressly mentioned in the Constitution, including the "right of privacy." [67] Mr. Justice Harlan concurred in the result but would have rested squarely on the due process clause, holding that the State had, in the words of *Palko,* invaded a value "implicit in the concept of ordered liberty." [68] Mr. Justice Goldberg added a discussion of the Ninth Amendment ("The enumeration in the Constitution of certain rights, shall not be construed to deny or disparage others retained by the people"), which, he believed,

[66] 262 U.S. 390, 399 (1923).
[67] Griswold v. Connecticut, 381 U.S. 479, 484–86 (1965).
[68] 381 U.S., at 499–502.

showed that there were certain protected fundamental rights other than those enumerated in the Bill of Rights.[69]

Mr. Justice Black dissented from all this. He observed that he found the Connecticut anti-birth-control law "every bit as offensive" as did his brethren but believed that whether one used due process or the Ninth Amendment the result was the same: the conferring on the Court of the power "to invalidate any legislative act which the judges find irrational, unreasonable or offensive." He specifically equated reliance on such cases as *Meyer* with the "natural law due process philosophy" of *Lochner*.[70]

And so the debate over due process goes on. Procedural due process goes from that which was "law of the land" in England to that which is "fundamental" to that which is taken over from the Bill of Rights. Substantive due process appears on the scene to defend property and liberty of contract from social activists and then, having been read out of the Constitution as an economic philosophy, remains to protect the values which another generation of jurists find to be basic. Coke saw to it that Magna Carta was adapted to the crises of later ages, and American courts have taken the Charter's gift of due process and done with it things which would never have crossed the minds of King John and his barons.

[69] 381 U.S., at 486–99.   [70] 381 U.S., at 507–27.

Epilogue

I N WRITING this book, I have consciously chosen to go from the specific to the general: from the occasions of the use of Magna Carta to the implications and consequences of that use. One could just as readily go from the general to the specific, that is, begin with a discussion of the great themes of American constitutional development and then look for the instances on which Magna Carta has had a role in the unfolding of those themes. I have chosen to proceed as I have in hopes of avoiding preconceptions about the place which ought to be assigned to Magna Carta in the history of American constitutionalism.

Frankly, I began this study with the assumption that I would find that the use of Magna Carta had been largely symbolic. That, after all, is its primary use today, whether in judicial opinions or in Law Day speeches. But I hope the reader, having followed the story through over three and a half centuries of American history, will agree that in formative periods of American constitutional thought the Charter has left a mark deeper than that associated with symbolism.

I have sought, then, to look for the occasions of the uses of Magna Carta and from those occasions to unfold the extent to which significant principles and ideas in American constitutional thought show the imprint of Magna Carta. In the concluding pages which follow, I would like to do at least three things: to comment on the process whereby Magna Carta came to play a part in American constitutional development, to sum up some of the specific constitutional precepts associated with the Charter, and, finally, to speak of the larger constitutional themes to which it has in such significant measure contributed.

Quite apart from the specific ways in which Magna Carta has influenced our constitutions and laws, the process whereby it came to do so is itself of no mean significance for our constitutional system. To begin with, the story of Magna Carta in this country carries throughout the stamp of England. The English settlers began their lives in the New World enjoying a relationship with their mother country not known in the colonies of other lands. Their charters guaranteed them the rights of Englishmen and shaped colonial thinking along English lines, if their race and sentiments did not already suffice. Through the seventeenth and eighteenth centuries, in colony after colony, one traces the colonists' call for the liberties of the Englishman—a call heard alike in the early days of Massachusetts Bay and over a century later in the resolutions of the colonies and of the Continental Congress against British policy. Thus it must appear from what has been written here that, were one's scope to be enlarged beyond Magna Carta (for example, to speak in detail of the Petition of Right, the English Bill of Rights, the Act of Settlement, etc.), an enormous volume—or shelf of volumes—could be written detailing the myriad ways in which a whole catalogue of English rights came to be enjoyed or desired in the American colonies and later to be incorporated into American constitutions.

In the second place, the story of Magna Carta in America brings into focus the enormous influence of individual thinkers and leaders in the spreading of basic ideas. Much mention has been made here, for example, of the writings of Sir Edward Coke. That the Magna Carta of the seventeenth century was not the Magna Carta of the days of King John is owing to Coke, if anyone. What Americans from the first settlements to the eve of Revolution knew of the Great Charter, they knew, with due allowance to Henry Care and others, because of Coke. Had

Coke not brought his antiquarian interests and intellectual powers to bear during the constitutional struggles against the Stuarts, the present book probably would not have been worth writing. The proof of this lies in the pervasive place Coke had in the libraries, arguments, and writings of American lawyers and other leaders at critical junctures in our history.

If Coke helped to preserve and interpret Magna Carta, it was through the intellectual leadership of the American colonies that the Charter's lore came into the mainstream of American thought. Instances come readily to hand: William Penn, his thinking forged in a courtroom in London, leaving his personal stamp on the laws and attitudes of Pennsylvania, James Otis arguing against the writs of assistance, George Mason penning a bill of rights which would be the model for other States, John Adams drafting a state constitution embodying the best of the English inheritance. What Coke did in making Magna Carta a cornerstone of English constitutionalism, these men did in laying a similar foundation in this country.

That Magna Carta has survived the centuries and has had such influence in American constitutional thought, in times and circumstances so vastly different from those of thirteenth-century England, is a clue to the Charter's most notable quality: its adaptability and capacity for growth. When the American colonists, in attacking the Stamp Act, grounded their asserted right to trial by jury and to being taxed only with their consent in Magna Carta, they were not necessarily guilty of bad history. That trial by jury as we understand it now was not guaranteed by the Magna Carta of 1215 does not mean that it was not part of the Charter as interpreted in the eighteenth century. Fundamental ideas evolve, and fundamental documents, unless they are to die, must have the capacity to absorb and give direction to such evolution. That Magna Carta was expected to have this capacity for growth is witnessed, to choose random examples, by William Penn's ability at his trial to ground such a range of procedural rights in the Charter and by William Henry Drayton's recognition in his "Freeman" letter that Magna Carta must be read in the light of seventeenth-century documents reaffirming it. The United States Supreme

Court, in the *Hurtado* case, acknowledged Magna Carta's "capacity for growth," and the whole history of the interpretation of due process of law in the United States is in this tradition.

In becoming a part of the American constitutional tradition, Magna Carta had a double hurdle to jump: not only did it have to prove capable of growth to meet new problems unknown to the thirteenth century, but also it had to prove adaptable to the problems of a new continent. Seldom has the process of assimilation of an ancient document to new times and new places been so deliberate. As with other features of the common law, much of Magna Carta proved unsuited to American needs. That which remains part of our constitutional tradition is, in effect, but a fragment of Magna Carta of 1215, most of whose provisions died with the feudalism which gave rise to them. But that fragment is a significant one, for it embraces such central concepts as due process of law, evenhanded administration of justice, a humane system of punishments, compensation for the taking of private property, and accessible justice.

To survive to modern times, principles derived from the English law had to overcome at least three obstacles. First, there were the provisos in the colonial charters that English laws could be modified as local conditions required; strengthening this exception was the natural tendency of men living in a frontier condition to discard the less suitable laws of an older, more settled country. Second, there was the appeal of the philosophy of natural rights as an independent force in the development of legal and constitutional thought; this philosophy did not lack for able proponents on either side of the Atlantic, notably John Locke and Thomas Jefferson. Third, after the American Revolution, English concepts had to surmount nationalism and anti-English sentiments, as well as the competition of efforts to introduce civil law concepts into America.

The constitutional principles which we derive from Magna Carta had to surmount just such obstacles as these. The time of the adoption of the Federal Constitution marked the most notable watershed in the fortunes of the Charter in America.

The failure of Magna Carta to figure in the debates at the Philadelphia convention is in marked contrast to its ubiquity in colonial arguments before 1776. This underlines the fact that the Charter, by its very history, is more relevant to limits on government than to creating a structure of government. It is the Bill of Rights, not the body of the Federal Constitution, which is the principal repository of English values. Even viewed as a restraint on the power of government, Magna Carta was found by Americans to have what they considered notable limitations: its being a grant from a king, rather than originating in the people; its being subject to repeal; its being a barrier against the executive branch only.

Limitations or no, Magna Carta did survive. And it survived as more than simply a symbol. From the earliest days in colonial America, the demands for the rights of Englishmen tended to be stated in the specific form of demands for Magna Carta or certain of its guarantees. In the colloquy between Robert Child and the governors in Massachusetts in 1646, both sides looked to the Charter to found their case, the government taking pains in its "parallels" to demonstrate that the people of the colony already enjoyed the rights of the Charter. Just as Magna Carta had seen regular use in lawsuits in medieval England, so in colonial America it was pleaded in private actions, in indictments against Crown officials, in complaints against colonial governors.

In the documents of the colonial and republican periods alike one can trace the survival of specific principles originating in Magna Carta. Due process of law, the descendant of chapter 39's guarantee of "law of the land," appears again and again: in the Body of Liberties of 1641, in the successive Pennsylvania Acts of Privileges to a Freeman, in the Virginia Bill of Rights of 1776 and the other state constitutions, in the Fifth Amendment to the Federal Constitution. And so with other derivatives of Magna Carta: the principle that justice should be available without denial or delay (chapter 40), compensation for the taking of private property (chapter 28), and others.

Having in mind the capacity of Magna Carta for growth,

special note should be taken of two principles, that of the people's right not to be taxed without their consent, and that of trial by jury. It took a fair amount of evolution and interpretation for the requirement of chapter 12 that no scutage or aid be imposed save by "common counsel" of the kingdom (a provision omitted in the reissue of the Charter in 1216) to become the right to being taxed only by consent. Similarly it was some time after 1215 before chapter 39's guarantee of judgment by peers became equated with trial by jury. Yet over and over the American colonists rested these rights on Magna Carta, as in the resolutions against the Stamp Act and in their resolutions in 1774.

The specific principles of constitutional law identified with Magna Carta, such as due process of law, are therefore readily identified and traced through some of the principal documents and events of American history. It remains to say something of the larger principles properly associated with the Charter, principles not so much related to any one chapter of the Charter as to the Charter as a whole.

To begin with, Magna Carta retained in America an association which it early acquired in England: that of being a fundamental law by which other laws should be tested. The Charter carried this potential from the start, being a permanent grant enjoined upon all parties with the greatest solemnity. By the time of Coke, that commentator was able to point to the statutes making the Charter the standard for other enactments and judgments. Americans picked up the theme, spelling out more clearly a theory of supreme law. William Penn looked to Magna Carta as unalterable, fundamental law, and by the time of the Revolution Americans, as in the Pennsylvania resolutions of 1774, found it natural to speak of the "unconstitutionality" of a law. The foundation was laid for the American doctrine of judicial review; in the laying of that foundation Magna Carta had an unquestioned part.

Secondly, Magna Carta is part of a tradition which might be called legalism. This is the fondness, by no means confined to this country, of citing the explicit language of charters and legal documents as the foundation for asserted rights. Coke and the parliamentarians in their citations of ancient authority understood the uses of legalism, as indeed had the barons of Runnymede, who in putting forth their program looked back to the Coronation Charter of Henry I. It was in a naturally inherited tradition of legalism that the colonists put so much reliance on and quoted verbatim the guarantee in their charters of the "liberties, franchises, and immunities" of Englishmen.

Allied with legalism is the tradition of constitutionalism. In American history this tradition has become manifest in a number of ways. For one thing, there was the habit, well established by Independence, of looking to written documents as fundamental law. Magna Carta was the archetype. With it, for the colonists, went the colonial charters, so that in the colonists' resolutions of the 1760's and 1770's the Great Charter and their own charters lent complementary support to their case against Britain. When the time came to set up their own governments, Americans had in Magna Carta, the English Bill of Rights, the colonial charters, and other such documents ready precedents for building new polities on written documents. Parchment barriers they might be, but the Americans, because of what they knew of liberty documents, were prepared to put their trust in them.

Another concomitant of the tradition of constitutionalism was the historical attitude. In history as written by Sidney, in law as illumined by Coke, the American colonists saw Magna Carta idealized. In history and tradition Americans were apt to find the weapons with which to fight what they saw as tyranny. Their use of history is a reminder that history is by no means necessarily on the side of reaction and the status quo; it can equally be, and often has been, used as a liberating, creative force. History in the hands of Coke, and history in the hands of eighteenth-century Americans, should suggest as much.

Further, to explore, through Magna Carta, the tradition of constitutionalism in America is at many points to touch another powerful tradition, that of natural law. It has been noted how these traditions are sometimes antagonists, as in the hands of the governing party and their opponents in early Massachusetts. At other times the two traditions are allies, as in the resolutions of 1774. Some Americans, the towering figure being that of Jefferson, have always put natural law first. Others, their lawyers' habits showing, have thought first in constitutional terms. Still others, Sam Adams being a likely instance, put results first, welcoming any argument that might carry the day. Advocacy and eclecticism have played such a strong part in American intellectual history that it may be impossible to sort out the levels of argument and specious to assign priorities among them. But for modern speculation about fundamental law and fundamental rights there remains significance in the fact that, when arbitrary government (homegrown or beyond the seas) has threatened, a constitutional case has seemed a good one.

That significance appears when one attempts to say what it is which is at the heart of Magna Carta and the Constitution alike. There might be many suggestions, but few present as good a case as a concern about arbitrary government, a government of discretion rather than of laws. The provisions of Magna Carta—indeed the very fact of the Charter—reflect this concern. One need only consider, for example, the assurance of judgments according to the "law of the land," the promise not to sell, deny, or delay justice, the pledge to appoint only such men to office as knew the law of the land and would keep it well. The same concern about arbitrary government runs through American history. It motivated those who in more than one theocratically oriented colony called for the rights of Magna Carta. It underlies many of the provisions and features of the Federal Constitution, such as the separation of powers, and it is the essence of the concept of due process as interpreted by American courts.

Its substantive contribution to American law assured, Magna Carta continues to appear in the decisions of the United States Supreme Court. Its use is now in good measure symbolic, evocative of the ancient origins which a judicial opinion-writer would ascribe to some principle or point of law being put forth in that case. Citations to Magna Carta appear in a variety of contexts in modern opinions. For example, in a 1958 opinion, Mr. Justice Douglas traced the right to travel to Magna Carta,[1] and in the same year in another case Chief Justice Warren observed that the constitutional ban on cruel and unusual punishments has its origins ultimately in that document.[2] More recently Mr. Justice Black has urged that the right to have a case tried locally and to be spared the imposition of having to litigate in a distant or burdensome forum is as ancient as chapters 17, 18, and 19 of the Charter.[3] And more recently still, the Court, in holding that the Sixth Amendment's guarantee of the right to a speedy trial applies to the States by virtue of the Fourteenth Amendment, suggested that the "first articulation" of this right was in the King's promise in 1215 not to deny or delay justice to any man.[4]

So pervasive is the influence of Magna Carta among the Justices that it is as readily cited by a Justice who believes in the "fundamental fairness" concept of Fourteenth Amendment due process as by one who holds to the "incorporation" theory. Justice Frankfurter, who spoke for an evolving and flexible approach to due process, observed in a 1945 opinion that the "safeguards of 'due process of law' and 'the equal protection of the laws' summarize the history of freedom of English-speaking peoples running back to Magna Carta and reflected in the constitutional development of our people." [5] On the question of "incorporating" the specific guarantees of the Bill of Rights into the Fourteenth Amendment, Justice Black has always been Justice Frankfurter's arch-opponent. Yet the Frankfurterian school has by no means preempted the use of Magna Carta, for no Justice is more fond of relying on the Charter than Justice

[1] Kent v. Dulles, 357 U.S. 116, 125 (1958).
[2] Trop v. Dulles, 356 U.S. 86, 99–100 (1958).
[3] National Equip. Rental, Ltd. v. Szukhent, 375 U.S. 311, 318, 325 (1964) (dissent).
[4] Klopfer v. North Carolina, 386 U.S. 213, 223 (1967).
[5] Malinski v. New York, 324 U.S. 401, 413–14 (1945) (separate opinion).

Black. Indeed, in a recent concurring opinion in which he attacked the "fundamental fairness" concept of due process of law as giving judges too much power, Justice Black looked to "law of the land" as used in Magna Carta to illumine his understanding of the present-day application of due process of law.[6]

The paradox is not as great as it seems. Magna Carta survived through the centuries in England because it embraced certain basic ideals, notably that of restraints on arbitrary government, which were a continuing force in the development of English constitutional principles. Similarly the Charter became embedded in the thought and jurisprudence of English America and the United States because it evoked such a consensus on fundamental liberties. For all the divisions on the Supreme Court—the 5-to-4 opinions, the heated dissents, the supposed "liberal" and "conservative" camps—there is a consensus there, too. The most active of the "judicial activists" and the most restrained of the Court's "restrainers" are heir to a common constitutional tradition: the ideal of a rule of law. This is a tradition which binds judges as well as kings, and while some Justices may well be more faithful to the tradition than are others they all understand it; none deny that it is essential. Hence all have good cause to call on Magna Carta as they fashion the nation's jurisprudence.

Yet that most men, judges and others, can agree that Magna Carta is among the "good things" in our constitutional heritage does not lay to rest the recurrent issues which have brought people at various points in English and American history to look to the Charter and the ideas associated with it. To take but one example: we have by no means heard the last of the arguments between those who think in natural law terms and those who look to a more legalistic constitutional tradition. That natural law is not a spent force in legal discourse is evident when one sees leaders of the Negro civil rights movement of the 1960's relying on the "higher law" as a justification

[6] In re Gault, 387 U.S. 1, 59, 62 (1967) (concurring opinion). See also Black's use of Magna Carta in Griffin v. Illinois, 351 U.S. 12, 16–17 (1956).

for civil disobedience. In *Letter from Birmingham Jail*, Martin Luther King, Jr., answers his critics by an appeal to the natural law:

> You express a great deal of anxiety over our willingness to break laws. This is certainly a legitimate concern. Since we so diligently urge people to obey the Supreme Court's decision of 1954 outlawing segregation in the public schools, at first glance it may seem rather paradoxical for us consciously to break laws. One may well ask: "How can you advocate breaking some laws and obeying others?" The answer lies in the fact that there are two types of laws: just and unjust. I would be the first to advocate obeying just laws. One has not only a legal but a moral responsibility to obey just laws. Conversely, one has a moral responsibility to disobey unjust laws. I would agree with St. Augustine that "an unjust law is no law at all."

To make it clear that he is appealing beyond positive law to a "higher law," King defines a "just" law as one that "squares with the moral law or the law of God." [7]

Much has been written on the implications, the virtues and vices, of the doctrine of civil disobedience. [8] But one issue which the doctrine poses for the legal order is clear: the place in a constitutional system for appeals to another, and extra-constitutional, fundamental law.

The argument over the legitimacy of natural law concepts in the constitutional framework takes place within the Supreme Court, too. In his long-standing fight for "incorporation" of the Bill of Rights so that those amendments become the measure of Fourteenth Amendment due process, Mr. Justice Black has attacked the "fundamental fairness" approach to due process of law as endowing the Court with a power under "natural law" to gear constitutional interpretation to the Court's current notion of what is reasonable and just. [9] Similarly, when his brethren drew on the Ninth Amendment and the "penumbra" of the

[7] M. L. King, Jr., *Why We Can't Wait* (New York, 1964), p. 82.

[8] Representative of the articles on the subject are Morris Keeton, "The Morality of Civil Disobedience," 43 *Tex. L. Rev.* 507 (1965); Burke Marshall, "The Protest Movement and the Law," 51 *Va. L. Rev.* 785 (1965); Lewis F. Powell, Jr., "A Lawyer Looks at Civil Disobedience," 23 *Wash. & Lee L. Rev.* 205 (1966).

[9] See, e.g., Adamson v. California, 332 U.S. 46, 68 (1947) (dissent); Rochin v. California, 342 U.S. 165, 174 (1952) (concurring opinion).

Bill of Rights[10] to strike down Connecticut's law forbidding the prescribing or use of devices to prevent contraception,[11] Black, dissenting, again objected to the Court's assumption of the power to read its ideas of "natural justice" into the Constitution.[12]

In weighing theories like those of Martin Luther King's and decisions like the Connecticut birth-control case, we are forced once again to decide what place in our system to give respectively to the natural law tradition and that of constitutionalism. Appeals to natural law, as American history demonstrates, have often been used as a liberalizing and creative force. But natural law as a standard has its flaws, simply because it *lacks* standards. This is not to say that natural law is not a legitimate and healthy feature of our legal system; rather, it is to say that in a system predicated on the rule of law natural law requires the disciplining influence of the tradition of constitutionalism. The rule of law can no more survive unfettered discretion on the part of those who live under the laws than it can the complete discretion of those who make the laws. That discretion and arbitrary will must have unmistakable limits is one of the lessons of Magna Carta.

So the issues which gave rise to Magna Carta, and the traditions which it fostered, continue as major themes in America. It remains to be asked, how does the Charter fare in the country which gave it birth? England, as is well known, prides itself on preserving individual liberties without the need of a written constitution. Sir Ivor Jennings has written that in England it is not so much the laws and institutions which protect the liberties of the subject, it is an "attitude of mind."[13] On the 750th anniversary of Magna Carta, Sir Ivor made the same point:

[10] The Ninth Amendment states that the "enumeration in the Constitution, of certain rights, shall not be construed to deny or disparage others retained by the people." The "penumbra" theory was advanced by Justice Douglas, who, writing the opinion for the Court, relied on the "emanations" from the First, Third, Fourth, Fifth, and Ninth Amendments.

[11] Griswold v. Connecticut, 381 U.S. 479 (1965).

[12] 381 U.S. at 507. See A. E. Dick Howard, "Mr. Justice Black: the Negro Protest Movement and the Rule of Law," 53 *Va. L. Rev.* 1030 (1967).

[13] *The British Constitution* (Cambridge, 1941), p. 220.

"The fundamental principles of Magna Carta, as elaborated by legislation and the common law, have become part of the common stock of ideas; they are principles accepted by social convention." [14]

Sometimes doubts are expressed. In a talk on the BBC's Third Programme, a professor of law at Oxford related how the English courts (until reversed by the House of Lords in its capacity as an appellate court) [15] had held that a Chief Constable could be summarily dismissed without any hearing. The professor commented, "Much as we prize our unwritten constitution, there are occasions when we miss the help of a comprehensive Bill of Rights to remind us of our own fundamental laws." [16] He was, of course, relieved and buoyed by the final outcome of the case, which was a vindication for the fundamental principle that no man should be condemned unheard.

The right to be heard before judgment—a right inherent in Magna Carta's guarantee of judgments according to the "law of the land"—was upheld on this occasion. But 1965, the 750th anniversary of the Charter, saw a correlative right called into question—the right not to have a judgment of a court taken away contrary to the guarantees of due process of law. In that year Parliament passed the War Damage Act, a measure which reversed a judicial decision which the Burmah Oil Company had won against the Crown. The company's oil refineries in Burma had been destroyed by the British government in 1942 to deny their use to the advancing Japanese forces. After the war other companies whose property had been destroyed accepted partial compensation from a claims commission established for the purpose. But Burmah Oil, wanting full com-

[14] *Magna Carta and Its Influence in the World Today* (London, 1965), p. 23. In lectures originally delivered at Cornell in 1938–39, Charles Howard McIlwain suggested that the reason why England had never adopted a formal constitution was that "limitations on arbitrary rule have become so firmly fixed in the national tradition that no threats against them have seemed serious enough to warrant the adoption of a formal code." *Constitutionalism: Ancient and Modern* (rev. ed.; Ithaca, N.Y., 1947), p. 15.

[15] Ridge v. Baldwin [1963] 2 All E.R. 66.

[16] H. W. R. Wade, "The Due Process of Law," *The Listener*, Aug. 8, 1963, pp. 195, 196.

pensation, took its case to the British courts (as it was legally entitled to do) and fought the case all the way to the House of Lords, where the company won a judgment against the Crown.[17]

The reaction of the Government was to introduce the War Damage Bill, to take away in Parliament what the company had won in the courts. At stake was the principle that the Crown and its subjects are equal before the law and that, once the issue is joined in court, both are bound by the judge's decision. Since there is in Britain, unlike the United States, no formal separation of powers, the independence of the judiciary depends upon the convention that the Crown will abide by the decisions of its judges whether it likes them or not. Lord Devlin voiced grave concern about the bill:

If this Bill becomes law, it will shatter the simple belief that we in Britain are blessed among nations in that we do not have to rely for our liberties upon the provisions of a written Constitution since they are enshrined for ever in the hearts of the governors as of the governed. If now we want to preserve some of the few restraints we have left on the power of the executive to do exactly as it likes, we should do well, on the 750th anniversary of Magna Carta, to get something in writing.[18]

The bill became law.[19]

The point of retelling the Burmah Oil episode here is neither to elicit sympathy for the company nor to suggest that the liberty of the subject in Great Britain is a fiction. Britain remains one of the freest places on earth; certainly America's record of civil liberties is not so untarnished that it can afford gibes hurled in the direction of its sister nation across the Atlantic. The point quite simply is that in both countries,

[17] Burmah Oil Co. v. Lord Advocate [1964] 2 All E.R. 348. For comments see 1964 *Camb. L. J.* 180; 27 *Mod. L. Rev.* 709 (1964).

[18] "Justice in Danger?" *The Observer* (London), May 16, 1965, p. 11, col. 5. See also Lord Ogmore, "The Law and the Lawmakers: the Burmah Oil Company Affair," *Contemporary Review,* July 1965, p. 30.

[19] 13 & 14 Eliz. 2, c. 18. One need not, of course, be an oil company to rely on Magna Carta. John Price, a British motorist, urged Magna Carta as the basis for refusing to pay a 1s. toll over a narrow waterway. Like Burmah Oil, Price lost. The court said that he must pay the toll because of a precedent even older than Magna Carta—a decree of King Canute in 1023. *New York Times,* April 6, 1968, p. 13, col. 5.

Britain and the United States, even the most basic of constitutional concepts—due process of law, equality before the bar of justice, and others—are never to be taken for granted. Magna Carta had to be renewed again and again so that its principles might survive. Similarly its modern legacy, the traditions of constitutionalism and the rule of law which it engendered, can bring ordered liberty only to those who care to be free.

Appendixes

Table of Cases

Index

Appendix A

Relevant Chapters of Magna Carta

SELECTED chapters of Magna Carta of 1215 are set out below. Chapters of no special relevance to the subject of the present book have been omitted. The provisions set out below are taken from A. E. Dick Howard, *Magna Carta: Text and Commentary* (Charlottesville, Va., 1964), where the full text of the 1215 Charter can be found.

It might be noted that the original Charter was not divided into chapters. The chapter numbers appearing below are those of the 63 chapters into which by tradition the 1215 Charter is divided.

1. *Rights of the Church; grant of liberties to free men of the kingdom.*

We have, in the first place, granted to God, and by this Our present Charter confirmed for Us and Our heirs forever—That the English Church shall be free and enjoy her rights in their integrity and her liberties untouched. And that We will this so to be observed appears from the fact that We of Our own free will, before the outbreak of the dissensions between Us and Our barons, granted, confirmed, and procured to be confirmed by Pope Innocent III the freedom of elections, which is considered most important and necessary to the English Church, which Charter We will both keep Ourself and will it to be kept with good faith by Our heirs forever. We have also granted to all the free men of Our kingdom, for Us and Our heirs forever, all the liberties underwritten, to have and to hold to them and their heirs of Us and Our heirs.

12. *No aids save by common counsel of the kingdom.*

No scutage or aid shall be imposed in Our kingdom unless by common counsel thereof, except to ransom Our person, make Our eldest son a knight, and once to marry Our eldest daughter, and for these only a reasonable aid shall be levied. So shall it be with regard to aids from the City of London.

13. *Liberties of London and other towns.*

The City of London shall have all her ancient liberties and free customs, both by land and water. Moreover, We will and grant that all other cities, boroughs, towns, and ports shall have all their liberties and free customs.

14. *Calling of council to consent to aids.*

For obtaining the common counsel of the kingdom concerning the assessment of aids (other than in the three cases aforesaid) or of scutage, We will cause to be summoned, severally by Our letters, the archbishops, bishops, abbots, earls, and great barons; We will also cause to be summoned, generally, by Our sheriffs and bailiffs, all those who hold lands directly of Us, to meet on a fixed day, but with at least forty days' notice, and at a fixed place. In all letters of such summons We will explain the cause thereof. The summons being thus made, the business shall proceed on the day appointed, according to the advice of those who shall be present, even though not all the persons summoned have come.

17. *Justice to be had at a fixed place.*

Common Pleas shall not follow Our Court, but shall be held in some certain place.

18. *Land disputes to be tried in their counties.*

Recognizances of novel disseisin, mort d'ancestor, and darrein presentment shall be taken only in their proper counties, and in this manner: We or, if We be absent from the realm,

Our Chief Justiciary shall send two justiciaries through each county four times a year, and they, together with four knights elected out of each county by the people thereof, shall hold the said assizes in the county court, on the day and in the place where that court meets.

19. *Conclusion of assizes.*

If the said assizes cannot be held on the day appointed, so many of the knights and freeholders as shall have been present on that day shall remain as will be sufficient for the administration of justice, according as the business to be done be greater or less.

20. *Fines to be measured by the offense.*

A free man shall be amerced for a small fault only according to the measure thereof, and for a great crime according to its magnitude, saving his position; and in like manner a merchant saving his trade, and a villein saving his tillage, if they should fall under Our mercy. None of these amercements shall be imposed except by the oath of honest men of the neighborhood.

21. *Same for barons.*

Earls and barons shall be amerced only by their peers, and only in proportion to the measure of the offense.

22. *Same for clergymen.*

No amercement shall be imposed upon a clerk's lay property, except after the manner of the other persons aforesaid, and without regard to the value of his ecclesiastical benefice.

28. *Compensation for taking of private property.*

No constable or other of Our bailiffs shall take corn or other chattels of any man without immediate payment, unless the seller voluntarily consents to postponement of payment.

30. *No taking of horses without consent.*

No sheriff or other of Our bailiffs, or any other man, shall take the horses or carts of any free man for carriage without the owner's consent.

31. *No taking of wood without consent.*

Neither We nor Our bailiffs will take another man's wood for Our castles or for any other purpose without the owner's consent.

35. *Uniform weights and measures.*

There shall be one measure of wine throughout Our kingdom, and one of ale, and one measure of corn, to wit, the London quarter, and one breadth of dyed cloth, russets, and haberjets, to wit, two ells within the selvages. As with measures so shall it also be with weights.

39. *Guarantee of judgment of peers and proceedings according to the "law of the land."*

No free man shall be taken, imprisoned, disseised, outlawed, banished, or in any way destroyed, nor will We proceed against or prosecute him, except by the lawful judgment of his peers and by the law of the land.

40. *Guarantee of equal justice.*

To no one will We sell, to none will We deny or delay, right or justice.

41. *Free movement for merchants.*

All merchants shall have safe conduct to go and come out of and into England, and to stay in and travel through England by land and water for purposes of buying and selling, free of illegal tolls, in accordance with ancient and just customs, except, in time of war, such merchants as are of a country at war with Us. If any such be found in Our dominion at the outbreak of war, they shall be attached, without injury to their persons or goods, until it be known to Us or Our Chief Justiciary how Our merchants are being treated in the country at war with Us, and if Our merchants be safe there, then theirs shall be safe with Us.

42. *Freedom to leave and reenter the kingdom.*

In the future it shall be lawful (except for a short period in time of war, for the common benefit of the realm) for anyone to leave and return to Our kingdom safely and securely by land and water, saving his fealty to Us. Excepted are those who have been imprisoned or outlawed according to the law of the land, people of the country at war with Us, and merchants, who shall be dealt with as aforesaid.

45. *Appointment only of those who know the law.*

We will appoint as justiciaries, constables, sheriffs, or bailiffs only such men as know the law of the land and will keep it well.

60. *Liberties to be granted to lesser tenants.*

All the customs and liberties aforesaid, which We have granted to be enjoyed, as far as in Us lies, by Our people throughout Our kingdom, let all Our subjects, whether clerks or laymen, observe, as far as in them lies, toward their dependents.

63. *Oath to observe rights of Church and people.*

Wherefore We will, and firmly charge, that the English Church shall be free, and that all men in Our kingdom shall have and hold all the aforesaid liberties, rights, and concessions, well and peaceably, freely, quietly, fully, and wholly, to them and their heirs, of Us and Our heirs, in all things and places forever, as is aforesaid. It is moreover sworn, as well on Our part as on the part of the barons, that all these matters aforesaid shall be kept in good faith and without deceit. Witness the above-named and many others. Given by Our hand in the meadow which is called Runnymede, between Windsor and Staines, on the fifteenth day of June in the seventeenth year of Our reign.

Appendix B

The First Charter of

the Virginia Company (1606)[1]

JAMES, by the grace of God [King of England, Scotland, France, and Ireland, Defender of the Faith], etc. Whereas our loving and weldisposed subjects, Sir Thomas Gates and Sir George Somers, Knightes; Richarde Hackluit, Clarke, Prebendarie of Westminster; and Edwarde Maria Winghfeilde,[2] Thomas Hannam and Raleighe Gilberde, Esquiers; William Parker and George Popham, Gentlemen; and divers others of our loving subjects, have been humble sutors unto us that wee woulde vouchsafe unto them our licence to make habitacion, plantacion and to deduce a colonie of sondrie of our people into that parte of America commonly called Virginia, and other parts and territories in America either appartaining unto us or which are not nowe actuallie possessed by anie Christian prince or people, scituate, lying and being all along the sea coastes between fower and thirtie degrees of northerly latitude from the equinoctiall line and five and fortie degrees of the

[1] *The Three Charters of the Virginia Company of London* (Williamsburg, Va., 1957), pp. 1–12. The text of the Charter may also be found in Francis Newton Thorpe, ed., *Federal and State Constitutions, Colonial Charters, and Other Organic Laws of the States, Territories, and Colonies Now or Heretofore Forming the United States of America* (Washington, D.C., 1909), VII, 3783–89.

[2] Throughout, this and the following two names are spelled as "Wingfield," "Hanham," and "Gilbert" in Stith.

same latitude and in the maine lande between the same fower and thirtie and five and fourtie degrees, and the ilandes thereunto adjacente or within one hundred miles of the coaste thereof;

And to that ende, and for the more speedy accomplishemente of theire saide intended plantacion and habitacion there, are desirous to devide themselves into two severall colonies and companies, the one consisting of certaine Knightes, gentlemen, marchanntes and other adventurers of our cittie of London, and elsewhere, which are and from time to time shalbe joined unto them which doe desire to begin theire plantacions and habitacions in some fitt and conveniente place between fower and thirtie and one and fortie degrees of the said latitude all alongest the coaste of Virginia and coastes of America aforesaide; and the other consisting of sondrie Knightes, gentlemen, merchanntes, and other adventurers of our citties of Bristoll and Exeter, and of our towne of Plymouthe, and of other places which doe joine themselves unto that colonie which doe desire to beginn theire plantacions and habitacions in some fitt and convenient place betweene eighte and thirtie degrees and five and fortie degrees of the saide latitude all alongst the saide coaste of Virginia and America as that coaste lieth;

Wee, greately commending and graciously accepting of theire desires to the furtherance of soe noble a worke which may, by the providence of Almightie God, hereafter tende to the glorie of His Divine Majestie in propagating of Christian religion to suche people as yet live in darkenesse and miserable ignorance of the true knoweledge and worshippe of God and may in tyme bring the infidels and salvages living in those parts to humane civilitie and to a settled and quiet governmente, doe by theise our lettres patents graciously accepte of and agree to theire humble and well intended desires;

And doe, therefore, for us, our heires and successors, grannte and agree that the saide Sir Thomas Gates, Sir George Sumers, Richarde Hackluit and Edwarde Maria Winghfeilde, adventurers of and for our cittie of London, and all suche others as are or shalbe joined unto them of that Colonie, shalbe called the Firste Colonie, and they shall and may beginne their saide firste plantacion and seate of theire firste aboade and habitacion at anie place upon the saide coaste of Virginia or America where they shall thincke fitt and conveniente betweene the saide fower and thirtie and one and fortie degrees of the saide latitude; and that they shall have all the landes, woods, soile, groundes, havens, ports, rivers, mines, mineralls, marshes, waters, fishinges, commodities and hereditamentes whatsoever, from the said first seate of theire plantacion and habitacion by the space of fiftie miles of Englishe statute measure all alongest the saide coaste of Virginia and America towardes the weste and southe weste as the coaste lieth, with all the islandes within one hundred miles directlie over againste the same sea coaste; and alsoe all the landes, soile, groundes, havens, ports, rivers, mines, mineralls, woods, marrishes [marshes], waters, fishinges, commodities and hereditamentes whatsoever, from the saide place of theire firste plantacion and habitacion for the space of fiftie like Englishe miles, all alongest the saide coaste of Virginia and America towardes the easte and northeaste [or toward the north] as the coaste lieth, together with all the islandes within one hundred miles directlie over againste the same sea coaste; and alsoe all the landes, woodes, soile, groundes, havens, portes, rivers, mines, mineralls, marrishes, waters, fishinges, commodities and hereditamentes whatsoever, from the same fiftie miles everie waie on the sea coaste directly into the maine lande by the space of one hundred like Englishe miles; and shall and may inhabit and remaine there; and shall and may alsoe builde and fortifie within anie the same for theire better safegarde and defence, according to their best discrecions and the direction of the Counsell of that Colonie; and that noe other of our subjectes shalbe permitted or suffered to plante or inhabit behinde or on the backside of them towardes the maine lande, without the expresse licence or consente of the Counsell of that Colonie thereunto in writing firste had or obtained.

And wee doe likewise for us, our heires and successors, by theise presentes grannte and agree that the saide Thomas Hannam and Raleighe Gilberde, William Parker and George Popham, and all others of the towne of Plymouthe in the countie of

Devon, or elsewhere, which are or shalbe joined unto them of
that Colonie, shalbe called the Seconde Colonie; and that they
shall and may beginne theire saide firste plantacion and seate
of theire first aboade and habitacion at anie place upon the
saide coaste of Virginia and America, where they shall thincke
fitt and conveniente, betweene eighte and thirtie degrees of the
saide latitude and five and fortie degrees of the same latitude;
and that they shall have all the landes, soile, groundes, havens,
ports, rivers, mines, mineralls, woods, marishes, waters, fishinges, commodities and hereditaments whatsoever, from the
firste seate of theire plantacion and habitacion by the space of
fiftie like Englishe miles, as is aforesaide, all alongeste the said
coaste of Virginia and America towardes the weste and south-
west, or towardes the southe, as the coaste lieth, and all the
islandes within one hundred miles directlie over againste the
saide sea coaste; and alsoe all the landes, soile, groundes, havens, portes, rivers, mines, mineralls, woods, marishes, waters,
fishinges, commodities and hereditamentes whatsoever, from
the saide place of theire firste plantacion and habitacion for the
space of fiftie like miles all alongest the saide coaste of Virginia
and America towardes the easte and northeaste or towardes the
northe, as the coaste liethe, and all the islandes alsoe within one
hundred miles directly over againste the same sea coaste; and
alsoe all the landes, soile, groundes, havens, ports, rivers,
woodes, mines, mineralls, marishes, waters, fishings, commodities and hereditaments whatsoever, from the same fiftie miles
everie waie on the sea coaste, directlie into the maine lande by
the space of one hundred like Englishe miles; and shall and
may inhabit and remaine there; and shall and may alsoe builde
and fortifie within anie the same for theire better saufegarde
according to their beste discrecions and the direction of the
Counsell of that Colonie; and that none of our subjectes shalbe
permitted or suffered to plante or inhabit behinde or on the
backe of them towardes the maine lande without the expresse
licence or consente of the Counsell of that Colonie, in writing
thereunto, firste had and obtained.

Provided alwaies, and our will and pleasure herein is, that
the plantacion and habitacion of suche of the saide Colonies as

shall laste plante themselves, as aforesaid, shall not be made within one hundred like Englishe miles of the other of them that firste beganne to make theire plantacion, as aforesaide.

And wee doe alsoe ordaine, establishe and agree for [us], our heires and successors, that eache of the saide Colonies shall have a Counsell which shall governe and order all matters and causes which shall arise, growe, or happen to or within the same severall Colonies, according to such lawes, ordinannces and instructions as shalbe in that behalfe, given and signed with our hande or signe manuell and passe under the Privie Seale of our realme of Englande; eache of which Counsells shall consist of thirteene parsons [3] and to be ordained, made and removed from time to time according as shalbe directed and comprised in the same instructions; and shall have a severall seale for all matters that shall passe or concerne the same severall Counsells, eache of which seales shall have the Kinges armes engraven on the one side there of and his pourtraiture on the other; and that the seale for the Counsell of the saide Firste Colonie shall have engraven rounde about on the one side theise wordes: Sigillum Regis Magne Britanie, Francie [et] Hibernie; on the other side this inscripture rounde about: Pro Consillio Prime Colonie Virginie. And the seale for the Counsell of the saide Seconde Colonie shall alsoe have engraven rounde about the one side thereof the foresaide wordes: Sigillum Regis Magne Britanie, Francie [et] Hibernie; and on the other side: Pro Consilio Secunde Colonie Virginie.

And that alsoe ther shalbe a Counsell established here in Englande which shall in like manner consist of thirteen parsons to be, for that purpose, appointed by us, our heires and successors, which shalbe called our Counsell of Virginia; and shall from time to time have the superior managing and direction onelie of and for all matters that shall or may concerne the govermente, as well of the said severall Colonies as of and for anie other parte or place within the aforesaide precinctes of fower and thirtie and five and fortie degrees abovementioned; which Counsell shal in like manner have a seale for matters concerning the Counsell [or Colonies] with the like armes and

[3] *I.e.,* "persons."

purtraiture as aforesaide, with this inscription engraven rounde about the one side: Sigillum Regis Magne Britanie, Francie [et] Hibernie; and rounde about the other side: Pro Consilio Suo Virginie.

And more over wee doe grannte and agree for us, our heires and successors, that the saide severall Counsells of and for the saide severall Colonies shall and lawfully may by vertue hereof, from time to time, without interuption of us, our heires or successors, give and take order to digg, mine and searche for all manner of mines of goulde, silver and copper, as well within anie parte of theire saide severall Colonies as of the saide maine landes on the backside of the same Colonies; and to have and enjoy the goulde, silver and copper to be gotten there of to the use and behoofe of the same Colonies and the plantacions thereof; yeilding therefore yerelie to us, our heires and successors, the fifte parte onelie of all the same goulde and silver and the fifteenth parte of all the same copper soe to be gotten or had, as is aforesaid, and without anie other manner of profitt or accompte to be given or yeilded to us, our heires or successors, for or in respecte of the same.

And that they shall or lawfullie may establishe and cawse to be made a coine, to passe currant there betwene the people of those severall Colonies for the more ease of traffique and bargaining betweene and amongest them and the natives there, of such mettall and in such manner and forme as the same severall Counsells there shall limitt and appointe. And wee doe likewise for us, our heires and successors, by theise presents give full power and auctoritie to the said Sir Thomas Gates, Sir George Sumers, Richarde Hackluit, Edwarde Maria Winghfeilde, Thomas Hannam, Raleighe Gilberde, William Parker and George Popham, and to everie of them, and to the saide severall Companies, plantacions and Colonies, that they and everie of them shall and may at all and everie time and times hereafter have, take and leade in the saide voyage, and for and towardes the saide severall plantacions and Colonies, and to travell thitherwarde and to abide and inhabit there in everie of the saide Colonies and plantacions, such and somanie of our subjectes as shall willinglie accompanie them, or anie of them, in the saide voyages and plantacions, with sufficiente shipping and furniture of armour, weapon, ordonnance, powder, victall, and all other thinges necessarie for the saide plantacions and for theire use and defence there: provided alwaies that none of the said parsons be such as hereafter shalbe speciallie restrained by us, our heires or successors.

Moreover, wee doe by theise presents, for us, our heires and successors, give and grannte licence unto the said Sir Thomas Gates, Sir George Sumers, Richarde Hackluite, Edwarde Maria Winghfeilde, Thomas Hannam, Raleighe Gilberde, William Parker and George Popham, and to everie of the said Colinies, that they and everie of them shall and may, from time to time and at all times for ever hereafter, for theire severall defences, incounter or expulse, repell and resist, aswell by sea as by lande, by all waies and meanes whatsoever, all and everie suche parson and parsons as without espiciall licence of the said severall Colonies and plantacions shall attempte to inhabit within the saide several precincts and limitts of the saide severall Colonies and plantacions, or anie of them, or that shall enterprise or attempt at anie time hereafter the hurte, detrimente or annoyance of the saide severall Colonies or plantacions.

Giving and grannting by theise presents unto the saide Sir Thomas Gates, Sir George Somers, Richarde Hackluite, and Edwarde Maria Winghfeilde, and theire associates of the said Firste Colonie, and unto the said Thomas Hannam, Raleighe Gilberde, William Parker and George Popham, and theire associates of the saide Second Colonie, and to everie of them from time to time and at all times for ever hereafter, power and auctoritie to take and surprize by all waies and meanes whatsoever all and everie parson and parsons with theire shipps, vessels, goods and other furniture, which shalbe founde traffiqueing into anie harbor or harbors, creeke, creekes or place within the limitts or precincts of the saide severall Colonies and plantacions, not being of the same Colonie, untill such time as they, being of anie realmes or dominions under our obedience, shall paie or agree to paie to the handes of the Tresorer of the Colonie, within whose limitts and precincts theie shall soe traffique, twoe and a halfe upon anie hundred of anie thing soe by them traffiqued, boughte or soulde; and being stranngers and not subjects under our obeysannce, untill they shall paie five upon everie hundred of suche wares and commoditie as theie shall traffique, buy or sell within the precincts of the saide severall Colonies wherein theie shall soe traffique, buy or sell, as aforesaide; which sommes of money or benefitt, as aforesaide, for and during the space of one and twentie yeres nexte ensuing the date hereof shalbe whollie imploied to the use, benefitt and behoofe of the saide severall plantacions where such trafficque shalbe made; and after the saide one and twentie yeres ended the same shalbe taken to the use of us, our heires and successors by such officer and minister as by us, our heires and successors shalbe thereunto assigned or appointed.

And wee doe further, by theise presentes, for us, our heires and successors, give and grannte unto the saide Sir Thomas Gates, Sir George Sumers, Richarde Hachluit, and Edwarde Maria Winghfeilde, and to theire associates of the saide Firste Colonie and plantacion, and to the saide Thomas Hannam, Raleighe Gilberde, William Parker and George Popham, and theire associates of the saide Seconde Colonie and plantacion, that theie and everie of them by theire deputies, ministers and factors may transport the goods, chattells, armor, munition and furniture, needful to be used by them for theire saide apparrell, defence or otherwise in respecte of the saide plantacions, out of our realmes of Englande and Irelande and all other our dominions from time to time, for and during the time of seaven yeres nexte ensuing the date hereof for the better reliefe of the said severall Colonies and plantacions, without anie custome, subsidie or other dutie unto us, our heires or successors to be yeilded or paide for the same.

Alsoe wee doe, for us, our heires and successors, declare by theise presentes that all and everie the parsons being our subjects which shall dwell and inhabit within everie or anie of the saide severall Colonies and plantacions and everie of theire children which shall happen to be borne within the limitts and precincts of the said severall Colonies and plantacions shall have and enjoy all liberties, franchises and immunites within anie of our other dominions to all intents and purposes as if they had been abiding and borne within this our realme of Englande or anie other of our saide dominions.

Moreover our gracious will and pleasure is, and wee doe by theise presents, for us, our heires and successors, declare and sett forthe, that if anie parson or parsons which shalbe of anie of the said Colonies and plantacions or anie other, which shall trafficque to the saide Colonies and plantacions or anie of them, shall at anie time or times hereafter transporte anie wares, marchandize or commodities out of [any] our dominions with a pretence and purpose to lande, sell or otherwise dispose the same within anie the limitts and precincts of anie of the saide Colonies and plantacions, and yet nevertheles being at the sea or after he hath landed the same within anie of the said Colonies and plantacions, shall carrie the same into any other forraine countrie with a purpose there to sell or dispose of the same without the licence of us, our heires or successors in that behalfe first had or obtained, that then all the goods and chattels of the saide parson or parsons soe offending and transporting, together with the said shippe or vessell wherein suche transportacion was made, shall be forfeited to us, our heires and successors.

Provided alwaies, and our will and pleasure is and wee doe hereby declare to all Christian kinges, princes and estates, that if anie parson or parsons which shall hereafter be of anie of the said severall Colonies and plantacions, or anie other, by his, theire, or anie of theire licence or appointment, shall at anie time or times hereafter robb or spoile by sea or by lande or doe anie acte of unjust and unlawfull hostilitie to anie the subjects of us, our heires or successors, or anie of the subjects of anie king, prince, ruler, governor or state being then in league or amitie with us, our heires or successors, and that upon suche injurie or upon juste complainte of such prince, ruler, governor or state or their subjects, wee, our heires or successors, shall make open proclamation within anie the ports of our realme of Englande, commodious for that purpose, that the saide parson or parsons having committed anie such robberie or spoile shall, within the terme to be limitted by suche proclamations, make full restitucion or satisfaction of all suche injuries done, soe as the saide princes or others soe complained may houlde themselves fully satisfied and contented; and that if the saide parson or parsons having committed such robberie or spoile shall not make or cause to be made satisfaction accordingly with[in] such time soe to be limitted, that then it shalbe lawfull to us, our heires and successors to put the saide parson or parsons having committed such robberie or spoile and theire procurers, abbettors or comfortors out of our allegeannce and protection; and that it shalbe lawefull and free for all princes and others to pursue with hostilitie the saide offenders and everie of them and theire and everie of theire procurors, aiders, abbettors and comforters in that behalfe.

And finallie wee doe, for us, our heires and successors, grannte and agree, to and with the saide Sir Thomas Gates, Sir George Sumers, Richarde Hackluit and Edwarde Maria Winghfeilde, and all other of the saide Firste Colonie, that wee, our heires or successors, upon peticion in that behalfe to be made, shall, by lettres patents under the Greate [Seale] of Englande, give and grannte unto such parsons, theire heires and assignees, as the Counsell of that Colonie or the most part of them shall for that purpose nomminate and assigne, all the landes tenements and hereditaments which shalbe within the precincts limitted for that Colonie, as is aforesaid, to be houlden of us, our heires and successors as of our mannor of Eastgreenwiche in the countie of Kente, in free and common soccage onelie and not in capite.

And doe, in like manner, grannte and agree, for us, our heires and successors, to and with the saide Thomas Hannam, Raleighe Gilberd, William Parker and George Popham, and all others of the saide Seconde Colonie, that wee, our heires [and] successors, upon petition in that behalfe to be made, shall, by lettres patentes under the Great Seale of Englande, give and grannte unto such parsons, theire heires and assignees, as the Counsell of that Colonie or the most parte of them shall for that purpose nomminate and assigne, all the landes, tenementes and hereditaments which shalbe within the precinctes limited for that Colonie as is afore said, to be houlden of us, our heires and successors as of our mannor of Eastgreenwich in the countie of Kente, in free and common soccage onelie and not in capite.

All which landes, tenements and hereditaments soe to be passed by the saide severall lettres patents, shalbe, by sufficient assurances from the same patentees, soe distributed and devided amongest the undertakers for the plantacion of the said severall Colonies, and such as shall make theire plantacion in either of the said severall Colonies, in such manner and forme and for such estates as shall [be] ordered and sett [downe] by the Counsell of the same Colonie, or the most part of them, respectively, within which the same lands, tenements and hereditaments shall ly or be. Althoughe expresse mencion [of the true yearly value or certainty of the premises, or any of them, or of any other gifts or grants, by us or any our progenitors or predecessors, to the aforesaid Sir Thomas Gates, Knt. Sir George Somers, Knt. Richard Hackluit, Edward-Maria Wingfield, Thomas Hanham, Ralegh Gilbert, William Parker, and George Popham, or any of them, heretofore made, in these presents, is not made; or any statute, act, ordnance, or provision, proclamation, or restraint, to the contrary hereof had, made, ordained, or any other thing, cause, or matter whatsoever, in any wise notwithstanding.] In witnesse wherof [we have caused these our letters to be made patents;] witnesse our selfe at Westminister the xth day of Aprill [1606, in the fourth year of our reign of England, France, and Ireland, and of Scotland the nine and thirtieth.]

[Lukin]

Exactum per breve de private sigillo [etc.]

Appendix C

The Massachusetts "Parallels" of 1646[1]

A DECLARATION of the General Court holden at Boston 4
(9) 1646, concerning a Remonstrance and Petition exhibited
at last Session of this Court by Doctor Child, Thomas Fowle,
Samuel Maverick, Thomas Burton, John Smith, David Yale,
and John Dand.

In this Petition and Remonstrance (as they call it) which is the
first of the sorte that we have received, and (as we conceive without president in any plantation or established commonwealth, as
will appear by the smale cause of such remonstrance, and as
little reason for what is petitioned. . . .

For our government itselfe, it is framed according to our
charter, and the fundamental and common lawes of England,
and carried on according to the same (takeing the words of eternal truth and righteousnes along with them, as that rule by which
all kingdomes and jurisdictions must render account of every act
and administration, in the last day) with as bare allowance for
the disproportion between such an ancient, populous, wealthy
kingdome, and so poore an infant thinne colonie, as common
reason can afford. And because this will better appeare by
compareing particulars, we shall drawe them into a parallel. In

[1] Prince Society, *Hutchinson Papers* (Albany, 1865), I, 223–47.

the one columne we will sett downe the fundamental and common lawes and customes of England, beginning with Magna Charta, and so goe on to such others as we had occasion to make use of, or may at present suite with our small beginnings: In the other columne we will sett downe the summe of such lawes and customes as are in force and use in this jurisdiction, shewing withall (where occasion serves) how they are warranted by our charter. As for those positive lawes or statutes of England, which have been from tyme to tyme established upon the basis of the common law, as they have been ordained upon occasions, so they have been alterable still upon like occasion, without hazarding or weakening the foundation, as the experience of many hundred yeares hath given proofe of. Therefore there is no necessity that our owne positive lawes (which are not fundamental) should be framed after the patterne of those of England, for there may be such different respects, as in one place may require alteration, and in the other not.

For ourselves, we must professe our insufficiencie for so greate matters (as the remonstrants also judge of us) and that in the lawes of England we have but the knowledge of novices, which is mixed with ignorance, and therefore such faileings may appeare either in our collection of those lawes, or in conforming our owne to that patterne, are to be imputed to our want of skill. If we had able lawyers amongst us, we might have beene more exact.

Magna Charta.

1. The Church shall enjoy all her liberties.

Fundamentalls of the Massachusetts.

1. All persons orthodoxe in judgment and not scandalous in life, may gather into a church estate according to the rules of the gospell of Jesus Christ. Liberty, 1.

Such may choose and ordaine theire owne officers, and exercise

Magna Charta.	*Fundamentalls of the Massachusetts.*
	all the Ordinances of Christ, without any injunction in doctrine, worship or discipline. Liberty, 2 & 38.
2. No man shall be condemned but by lawfull tryall; Justice shall not be sould, deferred nor denyed to any man. All mens liberties and free customes shall be reserved.	2. No mans life, honor, liberty, wife, children, goods or estate shall be taken away, punished or endamaged, under colour of lawe, or countenance of authoritie, but by an expresse lawe of the generall court, or in defect of such lawe, by the word of God, &c. Liberty, 1.
	Every person within this jurisdiction, &c. shall enjoy the same justice and lawe, &c. without partiality or delay. Liberty, 2.
	All lands and hereditaments shall be free from all fines, forfeitures, &c. Liberty, 10.
	Every man may remove himselfe and his familie, &c. if there be no legal impediment. Liberty, 17.
3. All cities and townes shall have theire liberties and free customes.	3. The freemen of every towne may dispose of theire towne lands, &c. and may make such orders as may be for the well ordering of their townes, &c. and may choose their constables and other officers. (1) mo 1635.
4. There shall be one measure of corne and wine throughout the kingdome.	4. One measure is appointed through the country, according to the Kings standard. (3) 1631 and 1638.
5. Courts of judicature shall be kepte in a place certaine.	5. Courts of judicature shall be kept at Boston for Suffolk, at Cambridge for Middlesex, at Salem and Ipswich for Essex, &c. upon certaine dayes yearly. (1) 1635.
6. Difficult cases shall be deter-	6. Difficult cases are finally de-

Magna Charta.

mined by the justices of the bench, which was then the highest court of judicature.

7. No amerciament shall be, but for reasonable cause, and according to the quantity of the offence; saveing to a freeman his freehould, and to a merchant his merchandize; and no such amerciament to be assessed but by the oaths of good and lawful men of the vicenage.

8. No wager of lawe shall be allowed without witnesses.

9. Merchants shall have safe conducts.

The Common Lawes of England.

1. The supreame authoritie is in the high court of parliament.

2. In the parliament the people are present by theire deputies, the Knights and burgesses of the house of commons, that nothing can passe without theire allowance.

3. These deputies are chosen for all the people, but not by all the people; but only by certaine

Fundamentalls of the Massachusetts.

terminable in the court of assistants, or in the general court by appeale or petition, or by reference from the inferiour court. Liberty, 31 & 36.

7. Upon unjust suites the plaintiff shall be fined proportionable to his offence. Liberty, 37.

No mans goods shall be taken away, but by a due course of justice. Liberty, 1. In criminal causes it shall be at the liberty of the accused partie, to be tryed by the bench or by a jury. Liberty, 23.

We doe not fine or sentence any man, but upon sufficient testimonie upon oath, or confession. Custome.

8. Wager of lawe is not allowed, but according to this lawe, and according to Exod. 22. 8.

9. Letters testimonial are granted to merchants, when there is occasion. Custome.

Fundamentalls of the Massachusetts.

1. The highest authoritie here is in the general court, both by our charter, and by our owne positive lawes. (3) 1634, &c.

2. In our general court the people are present by theire deputies, so as nothing can passe without theire allowance. Charter, and (1) 1635.

3. Our deputies are chosen for all the people, but not by all the people, but only by the com-

The Common Lawes of England.

freehoulders and free burgers, in shires and corporations.

4. Both parts of this court, viz. the aristocraticall and democraticall part make but one court; yet each of them sitt and consult and act apart, and each hath a like negative power.

5. The acts of this court bind all the people, as well forraigne as free borne; as well such as have no libertie in the election of the members of the court as the freehoulders, &c. who choose them.

6. The fundamentall frame of Englands politie in the subordinate exercise thereof, is either in courts of justice or out of court.

7. In courts of judicature, all causes both civill and criminall are determinable either by the judges or jury, or by the judges alone in some cases, as upon demurrer in law, confession, overt act, or not tendring traverse, &c. or in other cases, as appointed by speciall statute.
8. Out of court the standing councell doe order all affairs of state in the vacancie of the parliament.

9. The justices of peace have power out of court to preserve the peace, &c.

10. The ordinary ministeriall

Fundamentalls of the Massachusetts.

panie of freemen according to our charter.

4. The governor and assistants being the aristocraticall, and the deputies the democraticall part, yet make but one court, though they sitt and act apart, and either of them hath a like negative power. Charter, and (1) 1635.
5. The acts of this generall court do bind all within this jurisdiction, as well no-freemen who have no vote in election of the members of the court, as the free men who doe choose them. By the charter.
6. This government in the subordinate exercise thereof is either in court of judicature or out of court. By the charter and many positive lawes.

7. In our court of judicature all causes civill and criminall are determinable, either by the judges and jury, or by the judges alone, &c. as in England. This is both by custome and by divers lawes established according to our charter, as Liberty, 29. &c.

8. In the vacancie of the generall court, the governor and assistants are the standing councell to take order in all such affaires. By the charter and (8) 1644.
9. The governor and assistants have power out of court to preserve the peace &c. By the charter and custome, and divers speciall lawes.

10. Our ministeriall officers are

The Common Lawes
of England.

Fundamentalls
of the Massachusetts.

officers are sheriffs, constables, marshalls, bailieffs, clarkes, &c.

11. The ordinary processe are summons, attachments, distresses, &c.

12. In all criminall cases where no certaine penalty is prescribed by law, the judges have power to impose arbitrary fines or penalties, according to the nature and merit of the offences.

13. Notorious and greate felonies, as treason, murther, witchcraft, sodomie, &c. are punished capitally, but simple theft and some other felonies are not punished with death, if the offender can reade in scripture.

14. Adultery is referred to the canon or spirituall lawe.

15. All publick charges are borne by the publick revenue or treasury.

16. Where the publick treasury will not suffice, all necessary charges are supplied by subsidies, &c. granted by parliament.

17. These subsidies are intended to be equally imposed upon all places and persons, yet in some cases they prove very unequall, yet they are collected, and such as refuse are distreined.

18. The parliament is not bound to give account to any

marshalls, constables, clerks, &c. By the charter.

11. Our ordinary processe are summons, attachments, distresses, &c. By charter.

12. In all criminall offences, where the law hath prescribed no certaine penaltie, the judges have power to inflict penalties, according to the rule of God's word. Liberty 1. and by charter, &c.

13. Treason, murther, witchcraft, Sodomie, and other notorious crimes are punished with death: But theft, &c. is not so punished, because we reade otherwise in the scripture. Capitalls, &c.

14. Adultrey is punished according to the canon of the spirituall law, viz. the scripture. Capitalls, &c.

15. All publicke charges are defrayed out of the publick stocke. Custome, and Liberty, 63.

16. When we have no publick stock, we supply our necessary public charges by assessment raised by the generall court.

17. The generall court intends an equall assessment upon every towne and person, and indeavours it, by the best meanes they can invent (yet in some cases there falls out inequalitie) this is levyed by distresse of such as are able and yet refuse to pay. Custome & order of court.

18. The generall court is not bound to give account of the ex-

The Common Lawes of England.

Fundamentalls of the Massachusetts.

of the improvement of these subsidies.

pence of these assessments; yet they doe sometimes for all mens satisfaction.

19. It is a fundamentall lawe that a man is not to be imprisoned if he tender sufficient bayle, &c. except in some cases capitall, and some other special cases.

19. No mans person shall be restrained or imprisoned, &c. before the lawe hath sentenced him thereto, if he can put in sufficient baile, &c. except in crimes capitall, &c. Liberty, 18.

20. The full age of man or woman for passing lands is twenty one yeares.

20. The full age, for passing lands, giveing votes, &c. is twenty one yeares. Liberty, 53.

21. A marryed woman cannot dispose of any lands or other estate without her husband, nor can sue or be sued without him.

21. Married women cannot dispose of any estate, &c. nor can sue or be sued, without the husband. Custome and Liberty, 14.

22. In civill actions a man may appeare and answer by his attorney.

22. In civill actions a man may appeare and answer by his atturney. Custome.

1. The eldest sonne is preferred before the younger in the ancestors inheritance.

1. The eldest sonne is preferred before the younger in the ancestors inheritance. Liberty, 81.

2. Daughters are coparceners in the inheritance.

2. Daughters shall inherit as coparceners. Liberty, 82.

3. Prescription is not allowed in cases morally and legally civill.

3. No custome or prescription shall ever prevail, &c. to maintaine any thing morally sinnfull. Liberty, 65.

4. Civill authoritie hath power over any officer or member of the church in all cases civill and criminall.

4. Civill authority may deale with any church member or officer, in a way of civill justice. Liberty, 59.

5. No man is to be twice punished for the same offence.

5. No man shall be twice sentenced by civill justice, for the same offence. Liberty, 42.

6. No oath or covenant of a publick nature can be put upon the subject but by act of parliament.

6. No man shall be urged to take any oath, or subscribe any articles, covenant, or remonstrance of a publick and civill nature, but such as the generall court

The Common Lawes *of England.*	*Fundamentalls* *of the Massachusetts.*
	hath considered, allowed and re- quired. Liberty, 3.
7. Publick records are open to every subject.	7. Publick records are open to all inhabitants. Liberty, 48.

By this it may appeare that our politie and fundamentalls are framed according to the lawes of England, and according to the charter; so that the petitioners (if they had not cast off all modesty) must needs be ashamed of this complaint, as also of those which follow, viz. Arbitrarie government, the negative vote, Illimited oaths, Unjust taxes, Illegall committments, &c. For the first we use to say, Rome was not built in a day: Nay, they could write of it many hundred yeares after, *Tantae molis erat*, &c. Let them produce any colonie or commonwealth in the world, where more hath beene done more 16 yeares. Let them shew where hath beene more care and strife to prevent all arbitrarines, and to bring all judgements to a certaine rule, so farre as may be. Let them confesse theire ignorance of the judiciall proceedings in England, or theire malice which setts them on, to take up any thing to throw at us, though it cutt theire owne fingers, as the practise of England (which they would seeme so much to adhere unto) will most certainely doe, if they looke into any of those courts of judicature (except it be the common pleas) but especially the chauncery (which is the highest court of judicature) the court of requests, the chauncery of the exchequer and of the dutchie, in which courts they are not tyed to the common lawes or statutes of England, but doe judge arbitrarily (*secondum aequum et bonum*) according to equitie. If they can give no reasonable answer here (as we are sure they cannot) they must either harden theire hearts or confesse theire guilt, and be as carefull to reforme theire arbitrary obedience, as we are to keepe off arbitrary government. We may say the same for the second, the negative vote. Sure these men would seeme to have misteries of state in theire heads, and they meane to keepe them there. They tell us of a destructive negative vote, but they neither shew where nor what this daunger is, nor what remedie for it. It may be they have found out a way how a mixt government may subsist without a negative vote, which this court (with all the help of all the elders, and other the wisest in the country, after two or three years endeavour) could not attaine; nor would the farre deeper wisdome of the parliament of England ever attempt it (and that these remonstrants are not ignorant of) nor do they affect a democracie. Therefore this must needs be put in only as a fine device (*ad faciendum populum*) to please the people. For the third, viz. Illimited oathes, and covenants not explained by lawe: They should have done well to have tould us what oathes and covenants they meane, for (*dolus versatur in universalibus*) deceit lyes hid in generalls. We know no oathes we impose upon any, other than such as are allowed by our charter, and were in practice by the company in London (as occasion required) before we came into these parts. And for covenants of a civill nature, there hath not beene so much as any mention of any such amongst us these many yeares, save only, the last yeare, a motion was made in court of complying with our native country in the nationall covenant there, which was referred to further consideration. As for our church covenant, that shall be spoken to in its proper place. Besides (to prevent all such burdens) we have established a lawe to that end, as appears here before. 5thly, For unjust taxes, there is none that come amongst us, or heare of our condition and affaires, but will marvaile for what purpose such great summes should be raised upon the country, as should occasion this grievance; seeing we attempt nothing of chardge, but what is necessarie, and what the freemen and members of the court contribute unto, as largely as any other. We spend nothing superfluously in buildings, feastings, pensions, public gratuities, officers fees, or the like; nay we are ashamed sometimes at our penuriousnes, but that we had rather beare shame and blame, than overburden the people. Such as are in cheife office amongst us are content to live beneath the honour of their places that they might ease the common charge. All our publick expences have beene about some small fortifications, makeing lawes, dispenseing justice, some expeditions against the Indians, who by their injuries and insolencies have provoked us thereunto, and some forraigne occasions of late, which accidentally fell upon us. If the remonstrants have knowne of any lavish wasting or mispence of the publick treasure, it had beene fitt they should have mentioned it, otherwise they deale unjustly and injuriously with us, to expect we should provide for theire peace and safety, and yet deny us the meanes whereby we should accomplish it. 6thly, For illegall committments, theire complaint pretends frequencie, otherwise it were not a public grievance, therefore we conceive they might have produced some cleare instances in this kind. But let them bring forth one: Or let them charge any of the courts or magistrates with corruption in theire places, or manifest injustice in their sentences: Or the government with allowance of any thing that is morally evill. If not; they are impudent slanderers and deeply guilty of the breach of the 5th commandment which (without serious repentance) God will require of them. 7thly, These remonstrants would be thought to be a representative part of all the non-freemen in the countrie; but when we have pulled off theire vizards, we find them no other but Robert Child, Thomas Fowle, &c. For first, although their petition was received with all gentlenes, yet we heare of no other partners that have appeared in it, though it be four months since it was presented. Againe we know that divers of the non-freemen have lived some in Virginia and other plantations, where the government hath not been so easy to them as they have found it here. Others have lived in Kent, under the lawes of Gavelkind, more repugnant to the common lawes of England than any of ours. Others have had to doe in maritime affaires; others in causes testamentrie and matrimoniall; others in the chancery, and others in London and other corporations, and so have found by experience that Englishmen may live comfortably and securely under some other lawes besides the common and statute lawes of England; and that all the priviledge of a freeborne English subject is his interest in the lawes, without right of election of publick officers, which they were never acquainted with there, and yet payd their equall proportions to all publick charges, &c. These non-freemen also are well satisfyed (as we conceive) and doe blesse God for the blessings and priviledges they doe enjoy under this government. They think it is well, that justice is equally administred to them with the freemen; that they have equall share with them in all towne lotts, commons, &c. that they have like libertie of accesse to the church assemblies, and like place and respect there, according to theire qualities, as also in all neighbourly meetings for maintenance of love, as also like freedome of trade and commerce. So that we have good cause to be perswaded, that there are not many of these discontented remonstrants within our jurisdiction, nor in New England. . . .

In theire conclusion, these remonstrants prognosticate what peace and felicitie we may certainely expect both in church and common wealth, if theire petition be granted, viz. that every man be left to his owne libertie, and no distinctions or qualifications observed, &c. which they might have illustrated by some examples, which we marvaile they omitted, especially haveing one so neere and fresh; we shall therefore help theire memory. They well know that some eight yeares since, here were a certaine companie (which were petitioners and remonstrants also though in another kind) who out of theire tendernes of libertie of conscience, and civill libertie withall, made greate disturbance both in church and civill state, but not obtaineing theire desire, and fearing such a ruine to come upon us as these remonstrants foresee, they removed to Rhode-Island, where haveing given equall priviledge to all and established this as their basis, &c. that no man should ever be molested for professing his judgment, &c. they thought themselves the onely happy concording people under heaven. But, alas! it was but a dreame; it was not of God and therefore could not stand. For this liberty and equallity so fomented naturall corruption, as they presently fell at variance among themselves, and grew into three or foure opposite parts, which continue to this day; and instead of establishing church and civill state have overthrowne both.

Such peace, unity, prosperity, &c. is that which we may expect, if we will cast off the rules of Gods word, the civill prudence of all nations, and our owne observation of the fruite of other mens follies, and hearken to the counsell of these new statesmen. From which the Lord deliver us, and all the seed of Israell to the comeing of Christ Jesus. AMEN.

By the generall court,

Increase Nowell, Sec.

Appendix D

Excerpts from William Penn's

The Excellent Priviledge

of Liberty & Property Being the Birth-Right of

the Free-Born Subjects of England (1687)[1]

To the Reader

IT may reasonably be supposed that we shall find in this part of the world, many men, both old and young, that are strangers, in a great measure, to the true understanding of that inestimable Inheritance that every *Free-born Subject* of *England* is Heir unto by *Birth-right,* I mean that unparalell'd Priviledge of *Liberty* and *Property,* beyond all the Nations in the world beside; and it is to wisht that all men did rightly understand their own happiness therein; in pursuance of which I do here present thee with that antient Garland, the *Fundamental Laws of England,* bedeckt with many precious Priviledges of *Liberty* and *Property,* by which every man that is a Subject to the Crown of *England,* may understand what is his Right, and how to preserve it from unjust and unreasonable men: whereby appears the eminent Care, Wisdom and Industry of our Progenitors in providing for themselves and Posterity so

---

[1] *The Excellent Priviledge of Liberty and Property Being a Reprint and Facsimile of the First American Edition of Magna Charta* (Philadelphia, 1897). Only the introduction and commentary on Magna Carta are reproduced here. The pamphlet also includes Edward I's confirmation of Magna Carta, the statute *De Tallageo non Concedendo,* an abstract of the King's patent to Penn for Pennsylvania, and Penn's Charter of Liberties for Pennsylvania.

In the portion entitled "To the Reader" emphasis is as in the original. In the portions beginning with "Introduction," emphasis was so frequent in the original that, to make reading easier, emphasis has been omitted.

good a Fortress that is able to repel the *Lust, Pride* and *Power* of the *Noble,* as well as *Ignorance* of the *Ignoble;* it being that excellent and discreet Ballance that gives every man his even proportion, which cannot be taken from him, nor be dispossessed of his *Life, Liberty* or *Estate;* but by the tryal and judgment of *Twelve* of his *Equals,* or *Law of the Land,* upon the penalty of the bitter Curses of the whole People; so great was the zeal of our Predecessors for the preservation of these Fundamental Liberties (contained in these Charters) from encroachment, that they imployed all their Policy and Religious Obligations to secure them intire and inviolable, albeit the contrary hath often been endeavoured, yet providence hitherto hath preserved them as a Blessing to the *English Subjects.*

The chief end of the Publication hereof is for the information and understanding (what is their native Right and Inheritance) of such who may not have leizure from their Plantations to read large Volumns; And beside, I know this Country is not furnished with Law-Books, & this being the Root from whence all our wholesom English Laws spring, and indeed the Line by which they must be squared, I have ventured to make it publick, hoping it may be of use and service to many Free-men, Planters and Inhabitants in this Country, to whom it is sent and recommended, wishing it may raise up Noble Resolutions in all the Freeholders in these new Colonies, not to give away any thing of *Liberty* and *Property* that at present they do, (or of right as Loyal English Subjects, ought to) enjoy, but take up the good Example of our Ancestors, and understand, that it is easie to part with or give away great Priviledges, but hard to be gained, if once lost. And therefore all depends upon our prudent Care and Actings to preserve and lay sure Foundations for our selves and the Posterity of our Loyns.

Philopolites

Introduction

IN France, and other Nations, the meer Will of the Prince is Law, his Word takes off any mans Head, imposeth Taxes, or seizes any mans Estate, when, how and as often as he lists; and if one be accused, or but so much as suspected of any Crime, he may either presently Execute him, or Banish, or Imprison him at pleasure; or if he will be so gracious as to proceed by form of their Laws, if any two Villians will but swear against the poor Party, his Life is gone; nay, if there be no witness, yet he may be put on the Rack, the Tortures whereof make many an innocent Person confess himself guilty, and then with seeming Justice is executed. But,

In England the Law is both the measure and the bound of every Subjects Duty and Allegiance, each man having a fixed Fundamental-Right born with him, as to Freedom of his Person and Property in his Estate, which he cannot be depriv'd of, but either by his Consent, or some Crime, for which the Law has impos'd such a penalty or forfeiture. For all our Kings take a solmn Oath (1.) At their Corenation, To observe & cause the Laws to be kept: (2.) All our Judges take an Oath, wherein among other points they swear, To do equal Law and Right to all the Kings Subjects, Rich and Poor, and not to delay any person of common Right for the Letters of the King, or of any other Person, or for any other cause: Therefore saith Fortescue, (who was first chief Justice, and afterwards L. Chancellor to K. Henry 6.) in his Book de Laudibus Legum Anglia, cap. 9. Non potest Rex Anglia, &c. The King of England cannot alter nor change the Laws of his Realm at his pleasure; For why, he governeth his people by Power not only Royal, but also Politick: If his Power over them were only Regal, then he might change the Laws of his Realm, and charge his Subjects with Tallage and other Burthens, without their consent; but from this much differeth the Power of a King whose Government is Politick; for he can neither change Laws without the consent of his Subjects, nor yet charge them with Impositions against their wills. With which accords Bracton, a learned Judge & Law-Author, in the Reign of K. Henry the 3d, saying, Rex in Regno suo superiores habet Deum & Legem; i.e., The King in his Realm hath two superiors, God and the Law; for he is under the Directive, tho' not Co-ercive Power of the Law.

'Tis true, the Law it self affirms, The King can do no wrong, which proceeds not only from a presumption, that so excellent a Person will do none, but also because he acts nothing but by Ministers, which (from the lowest to the highest) are answerable for their doings; so that if a K. in passion should command A. to kill B. without process of Law, A. may yet be prosecuted by Indictment or upon an Appeal (where no Royal Pardon is allowable) and must for the same be executed, such Command notwithstanding.

This original happy Frame of Government is truly and properly call'd an English mans Liberty, a Priviledge not exempt from the Law, but to be freed in Person & Estate from Arbitrary Violence and Oppression. A greater Inheritance (saith Judg Cook) is deriv'd to every one of us from our Laws than from our Parents; For without the former, what would the latter signifie? And this Birth-right of English-men shines most conspicuously in two things:

1. *PARLIAMENTS.*
2. *JURIES.*

By the First the Subject has a share by his chosen Representatives in the Legislative (or Lawmaking) Power; for no new laws bind the People of England, but such as are by common consent agreed on in that great Council.

By the Second, he has a share in the Executive part of the Law, no Causes being tryed, nor any man adjudged to loose Life, Member or Estate, but upon the Verdict of his Peers or Equals his Neighbours, and of his own Condition: These two grand Pillars of English Liberty, are the Fundamental vital Priviledges, whereby we have been, and are preserv'd more free and happy than any other people in the World, and (we trust) shall ever continue so: For whoever shall dengn to impair, pervert or undermine either of these, do strike at the very Constitution of our Government, and ought to be prosecuted and punished with the utmost Zeal and Rigour. To cut down the Banks let in the Sea, or to poyson all the Springs and Rivers in the Kingdom, could not be a greater Mischief; for this would only affect the present Age, but the other will Ruin and enslave all our Posterity.

But beside these Paramount Priviledges which the English

are estated in by the Original Constitution of their Government, there are others more particularly declared and expressed in divers Acts of Parliament too large to be inserted in this place.

.   .   .   .

The Comment on Magna Charta

THIS excellent Law holds the first place in our Statute Books, for though there were, no doubt, many Acts of Parliament long before this, yet they are not now extant; 'tis called Magna Charta, or the great Charter, not in respect of its bulk, but in regard of the great importance and weight of the matters therein contained; it is also stiled, Charta Libertatum Regni, The Charter of the Liberties of the Kingdom; And upon great Reason (saith Cook in his Proem) is so called, from the effect, quia Liberus facit, because it makes and preserves the People free. Though it run in the stile of the King, as a Charter, yet (as my L. Cook well observes on the 38 chap.) it appears to have passed in Parliament; for there was then a fifteenth granted to the King by the Bishops, Earls, Barrons, free Tenants and People, which could not be, but in parliament, nor was it unusual in those times to have Acts of Parliament in a form of a Charter, as you may read in the Princes Case, Coo. Rep. l. 8.

Likewise, though it be said here, That the King hath given and granted these Liberties, yet they must not be understood as meer Emanations of Royal favour, or new Bounties granted, which the People could not justly challange, or had not a right unto before; for the Lord Cook in divers places asserts, and all Lawyers know, that this Charter is for the most part only Declaratory of the principal ground of the Fundamental Laws and Liberties of England; No new Freedom is hereby granted, but a Restitution of such as lawfully they had before, and to free them of what had been usurped and encroached upon them by any Power whatsoever; and therefore you may see this

Charter often mentions sua jura, their Rights and Liberties, which shews they had them before, and that the same now were confirmed.

As to the occasion of this Charter, it must be noted, that our Ancestors, the Saxons, had with a most equal poize and Temperament, very wisely contrived their Government, and made excellent Provisions for their Liberties, and to preserve the People from Oppression; and when William, the Norman, made himself Master of the Land, though he be commonly called the Conqueror, yet in truth he was not so, and I have known several Judges that would reprehend any Gentleman at the Bar that casually gave him that Title; for though he killed Harrold the Usurper, and routed his Army, yet he pretended a right to the Kingdom, and was admitted by compact, and did take an Oath to observe the Laws and Customs.

But the truth is, he did not perform that Oath so as he ought to have done, & his Successor William Rufus, King Stephen, Henry the 1st, & Richard likewise made frequent encroachments upon the Liberties of their People; but especially King John made use of so many illegal devices to drain them of Money, that wearied with intollerable Oppressions, they resolved to oblige the King to grant them their Liberties, and promise the same should be observed, which King John did in Running-Mead between Saints and Windsor, by two Charters, one called, Charta Libertatum, The Charter of Liberties (the form of which you may read in Matthew Paris, fol. 246. and is in effect the same with this here recited) the other, The Charter of the Forrest, Copies of which he sent into every County, and commandeth the Sheriff, &c. to see them fulfilled.

But by ill Council he quickly after began to violate them as much as ever, whereupon Disturbances and great Miseries arose, both to himself and the Realm. The Son and Successor of this King John, was Henry the third, who in the 19th Year of his Reign, renewed and confirmed the said Charters; but within two Years after cancelled them by the pernicious Advice of his Favourites, peticularly Hubert de Burgh, whom he had made Lord chief Justice; one that in former times had been a great lover of his Country, and a well-deserving Patriat, as well as learned in the Laws, but now to make this a step to his Ambition (which ever Rideth without Reins) perswaded and humoured the King, that he might avoid the Charters of his Father King John, by Duress, and his own Great Charter, and Charta de Foresta also, for that he was within Age, when he granted the same; whereupon the King in the eleventh Year of his Reign, being then of full Age, got one of the Great Charters, and of the Forrest into his Hands, and by the Counsel principally of this Hubert his Chief Justice, at a Council holden at Oxford, unjustly cancelled both the said Charters, (notwithstanding the said Hubert de Burgh was the Primary Witness of all Temporal Lords to both the said Charters) whereupon he became in high favour with the King, insomuch that he was soon after (viz. the 10th of December in the 13th Year of that King) created (to the highest Dignity that in those times a Subject had) to be an Earl, viz. of Kent: But soon after (for Flatterers & Humorists have no sure foundation) he fell into the King's heavy Indignation, and after many fearful and miserable Troubles, he was justly, and according to Law, sentenced by his Peers in an open Parliament, and justly degraded of that Dignity, which he unjustly had obtained by his Counsel, for cancelling of Magna Charta, and Charta de Foresta.

In the 9th Chapter of this Great Charter, all the Ancient Liberties and Customs of London are confirmed and preserved, which is likewise done by divers other Statutes, as 14 Edw. 3. Chap. 2 &c.

The 29th Chapter, NO FREE-MAN SHALL BE TAKEN, &c. Deserves to be written in Letters of Gold; and I have often wondred the Words thereof are not Inscribed in Capitals on all our Courts of Judicature, Town-Halls, and most publick Edifices; they are the Elixer of our English Freedoms, the Store-house of all our Liberties. And because my Lord Cook in the second part of his Institutes, hath many excellent Observations, his very Words I shall here Recite.

This Chapter containeth Nine several Branches.

First. That No man be taken or imprisoned, but per legem terrae; that is, by the Common-Law, Statute-Law, or Custom of England; for these words, per legem terrae, being towards the end of this Chapter, do refer to all the precedent matters in this Chapter; and this hath the first place, because the Liberty of a man's Person is more precious to him, than all the rest that follow, and therefore it is great Reason that he should by Law be relieved therein, if he be wronged, as hereafter shall be shewed.

2dly. No man shall be desseised; that is, put out of Seisin, or dispossessed of his Free-hold, that is, Lands or Livelihood, or of his Liberties, or free Customs, that is, of such Franchises and Freedoms, and free Customs as belong to him, by his free Birth-right, unless it be by the lawful Judgment, that is, Verdict of his Equals (that is, of men of his own Condition) or by the Law of the Land, that is (to speak it once for all) by the due Course and Process of Law.

3dly. No man shall be Out-lawed, made an Ex lex, put out of the Law, that is, deprived of the Benefit of the Law, unless he be Out-lawed according to the Law of the Land.

4thly. No man shall be Exiled or Banished out of his Country, that is, nemo predit patriam, no man shall lose his Country, unless he be Exiled according to the Law of the Land.

5thly. No man shall in any sort be destroyed, (Destruere id est qod prius structum & factum suit penitus Evertere Exdiruere) unless it be by the Verdict of his Equals, or according to the Law of the Land.

6thly. No man shall be condemned at the King's Suite, either before the King in his Bench, where the Pleas are Coram Rege (and so are the Words, nec super eum ibimus, to be understood) nor before any other Commissioner or Judge whatsoever; and so are the words, nec super eum Mitimus, to be understood, but by the Judgment of his Peers, that is, equals, or according to the Law of the Land.

7thly. We shall sell to no man Justice or Right.

8thly. We shall deny to no man Justice or Right.

9thly. We shall defer to no man Justice or Right.

Each of these we shall briefly explain:

1st; No man shall be taken, (that is) restrained of Liberty by Petition, or suggestion to the King or his Council, unless it be by Indictment or Presentment of good and lawful men, where such Deeds be done. This Branch, and divers other parts of this

Act, have been notably Explained and Construed by divers Acts of Parliament.

2dly; No man shall be Disseised, &c. Hereby is intended that Lands, Tenements, Goods and Chattels, shall not be seised into the King's hands contrary to this Great Charter, and the Law of the Land; nor any man shall be disseised of his Lands or Tenements, or dispossessed of his Goods or Chattels, contrary to the Law of the Land.

A Custom was alledged in the Town of C. that if the Tenant cease by two years, that the Lord should enter into the Freehold of the Tenant, and hold the same until he were satisfied of the Arrearages. It was adjudged a Custom against the Law of the Land, to enter into a mans Freehold in that case, without Action or Answer.

King Henry the 6th, granted to the Corporation of Dyers within London, Power to search, &c. And if they found any Cloth dyed with Log-Wood, that the Cloth should be forfeit. And it was adjudged, that this Charter Concerning the Forfeiture, was against the Law of the Land, and this Statute; for no Forfeiture can grow by Letters Pattents.

No man ought to be put from his Livelihood, without Answer.

3dly, [No man Out-lawed] that is, barred to have the benefit of the Law. And note, to this word Out-lawed, these words, unless by the Law of the Land, do refer [of his Liberties:] This word hath three Significations.

1st, As it hath been said, it signifieth the Laws of the Realm, in which respect this Charter is called Charta Libertatum, as afore-said.

2dly, It signifieth The Freedom the Subjects of England have: for example, the company of Merchant-Taylors of England, having power by their Charter to make Ordinances, made an Ordinance, That every Brother of the same Society should put the one half of his Cloaths to be dressed by some Cloath-worker free of the same Company, upon pain to forfeit ten Shillings, &c. And it was adjudged that this Ordinance was against Law, because it was against the Liberty of the Subject, for every Subject hath freedom to put his Cloaths to be dressed by whom he will, &c. sic de similibus. And so it is, if such, or the like Grant had been made by the Letters Pattents.

3dly, Liberties signifie the Franchizes & Priviledges, which the Subjects have of the Gift of the King, as the Goods & Chattels of Fellons, Out-laws, and the like, or which the Subject claims by Prescription, as Wrack, Waif, Stray, and the like.

So likewise, and for the same Reason, if a Grant be made to any man, to have the sole making of Cards, or the sole dealing with any other Trade, that Grant is against the Liberty and Freedom of the Subject, that before did, or lawfully might have used that Trade, and consequently against this Great Charter.

Generally all Monopolies are against this great Charter, because they are against the Liberty and Freedom of the Subject, and against the Law of the Land.

4thly, [No man Exiled] that is, Banisht, or forced to depart, or stay out of England, without his consent, or by the Law of the Land: No man can be exiled, or banished out of his Native Country, but either by Authority of Parliament, or in case of Abjuration for Fellony, by the Common-Law: And so when our Books, or any Records, speak of Exile or Banishment, other than in case of Abjuration, it is to be intended to be done by Authority of Parliament, as Belknap and other Judges, &c. banished into Ireland in the Reign of Richard the second.

This is a beneficial Law, and is construed benignely; And therefore the King cannot send any Subject of England against his Will to serve him out of the Realm, for that should be an Exile; and he should perdere patriam: No, he cannot be sent against his Will into Ireland, to serve the King or his Deputy there, because it is out of the Realm of England; for if the King might send him out of his Realm to any place, then under pretence of Service, as Ambassador, or the like, he might send him into the furthest parts of the World, whom being an Exile, is prohibited by this Act.

5thly, [No man destroyed] that is, Fore-judged of Life or Limbs, or put to torture or death, every Oppression against Law, by colour of any usurped Authority, is a kind of Destruction, and the words aliquo modo, any otherwise, are added to the verb destroyed, and to no other Verb in this Chapter; and therefore all things, by any manner of means, tending to Destruction, are prohibited: As if a man be accused or indicted of Treason or Fellony, his Lands or Goods cannot be granted to any, no, not so much as by promise, nor any of his Lands or Goods seized into the Kings hand, before he is attainted; for when a Subject obtaineth a promise of the forfeiture, many times undue means, and more violent Prosecution is used for private Lucre, tending to destruction, than the quiet and just proceeding of the Law would permit; and the party ought to live of his own until Attainder.

6thly, [By lawful judgment of his Peers] that is, by his equals, men of his own Rank and Condition. The general division of Persons, by the Law of England, is, either one that is Noble, and in respect of his Nobility, of the Lords House of Parliament, or one of the Commons, and in respect thereof, of the House of Commons in Parliament. And as there be divers degrees of Nobility, as Dukes, Marquesses, Earls, Viscounts and Barrons, and yet all of them are comprehended under this word Peers, and are Peers of the Realm; so of the Commons, they be Knights, Esquires, Gentlemen, Citizens and yeomen, and yet all of them of the Commons of the Realm. And as every of the Nobles one is a Peer to another, though he be of a severall degree, so it is of the Commons; and as it hath been said of Men, so doth it hold of Noble Women, either by Birth or Marriage.

And forasmuch as this Judgment by Peers is called lawful, it shews the Antiquity of this manner of Tryal: it was the antient accustomed legal course long before this Charter.

7thly, [Or by the Law of the Land] that is, by due Process of Law, for so the words are expresly expounded by the Statute of 37 Edw. 3. Chap. 8. and these Words are especially to be refered to those fore-going, to whom they relate; As, none shall be Condemned without a lawful Tryal by his Peers, so none shall be Taken, or Imprisoned, or put out of his Freehold, without due Process of the Law; that is, by the Indictment or Presentment of good and lawful men of the place, in due manner, or by Writ original of the Common-Law.

Now, seeing that no man can be Taken, Arrested, Attached,

or Imprisoned, but by due Process of Law, and according to the Law of the Land; these Conclusions hereupon do follow:

1. That the Person or Persons which commit any, must have Lawful Authority.

2. It is necessary that the Warrant or Mittimus be Lawful, and that must be in Writing under his Hand and Seal.

3. The Cause must be contained in the Warrant, as for Treason, Fellony, &c. suspicion of Treason or Fellony, or the like perticular Crime: for if it do not thus specifie the Cause, if the Prisoner bring his Habeas Corpus, he must be discharged, because no Crime appears on the return; nor is it in such case any Offence at all, if the Prisoner make his escape, whereas if the Mittimus contain the Cause; the escape would respectively be Treason or Fellony, though in truth he were not Guilty of the first Offence, and this mentioning the Cause, is agreeable to Scripture, Acts 5.

4. The Warrant or Mittimus, containing a lawful Cause, ought to have a lawful Conclusion, viz. And him safely to keep until he be delivered by Law, &c. and not until the party committing shall further order.

If a man by colour of any Authority, where he hath not any in that perticular case, shall presume to Arrest or Imprison any man, or cause him to be arrested or imprisoned, this is against this Act, and it is most hateful, when it is done by Countenance of Justice. King Edward the sixth did Incorporate the Town of St. Albans, and granted to them to make Ordinance, &c they made a by-Law upon pain of Imprisonment, and it was adjudged to be against this Statute of Magna Charta; so it had been, if such an Ordinance had been contained in the Pattent it self.

[We will sell to no man, deny to no man, &c.] This is spoken in the Person of the King, who in Judgment of Law in all Courts of Justice is present; and therefore every Subject of this Realm, for Injury done to him in Bonis, Terris, vel Persona, in Person, Lands or Goods, by any other Subject, Ecclesiastical or Temporal what-ever he be, without exception, may take his Remedy by the Course of the Law, and have Justice and Right for the Injury done him, freely without Sale, fully without any denyal,

and speedily without delay; for Justice must have three Qualities, it must be Libera, free; for nothing is more odious then
Justice set to sale; plena, full, for Justice ought not to limp, or
be granted piece-meal and Celeris, speedily: quia Dilatio est
quaedam negatio, Delay is a kind of denyal: And when all these
meet, it is both JUSTICE and RIGHT.

[We will not deny or delay any man, &c.] These Words have
been excellently expounded by latter Acts of Parliament, that
by no means Common-Right or Common-Law should be disturbed or delayed; no, though it be commanded under the
Great Seal, or Privy Seal, Order, Writ, Letters, Messuge, or
Commandment whatsoever, either from the King, or any other;
and that the Justices shall proceed, as if no such Writs, Letters,
Order, Message, or other Commandment were come to them;
All our Judges swear to this: for 'tis part of their Oaths, so that
if any shall be found wresting the Law to serve a Courts turn,
they are Perjured, as well as Unjust; the common Laws of the
Realm should by no means be delayed, for the Law is the surest
Sanctuary that a man can take, and the strongest Fortress to
protect the weakest of all; Lex est tutissima Cassis, the Law is a
most safe Head-piece: And sub Clypeo legis nemo decipitur, no
man is deceived whilst the Law is his Buckler; but the King
may stay his own Suit; as a Capias pro fine, for he may respit
his Fine, and the like.

All Protections that are not Legal, which appear not in the
Register, nor warranted by our Books, are expresly against this
Branch, nulli differemus, we will not delay any man, as a protec-
tion under the Great Seal granted to any man directly to the
Sheriff, &c. and commanding them, that they shall not Arrest
him, during a certain time, at any other man's Suit; which hath
Words in it, Perprarogativam nostram quant nolumus esse Ar-
guendam, by our Prerogative, which we will not have disputed;
yet such Protections have been argued by the Judges, according
to their Oath and Duty, and adjudged to be void; as Mich. 11
H.7. Rot. 124. a Protection granted to Holmes a Vintner of
London, his Factors, Servants and Deputies, &c. resolved to be
against Law, Pas. 7 H. 8. Rot. 66. such a Protection disallowed,
and the Sheriff amerced for not Executing the Writ, Mich. 13.

and 14 Eliz. in Hitchcock Case, and many other of latter time: And there is a notable Record of antient time in 22 E. 1. John de Marshalls case; Non pertinet ad vicecomitem de protectione Regis Judicare, imo ad Curiam.

[Justice or right] We shall not sell, deny or delay Justice and Right, neither the end, which is Justice; nor the mean whereby we may attain to the end, and that is the Law: Right is taken here for Law, in the same sence that Justice often is so called, 1. Because it is the right Line, whereby Justice distributive, is guided and directed; and therefore all the Commissioners of Oyer and Terminer, of Goal-delivery, of the Peace, &c. have this clause, Facturi quod Justitiam pertinet, secundum legem & consuetudinem Angliæ, i.e. to do Justice and Right, according to the Rule of the Law & Custom of England; & that which is called common Right in 2 E. 3. is called common Law in 14 E. 3. &c. and in this sense it is taken, where it is said, Ita quod stat Rectus in Curia, id est Legi in Curia.

2. The Law is called Rectum, because it discovereth that which is tort, crooked or wrong; for as Right signifieth Law, so tort, crooked or wrong signifieth Injuries, and Injuria est contra Jus, Injury is against Right. Recta linea est index sui & obliqui, a right line is both declaratory of it self and the oblique. Here by the crooked Cord of that which is called discretion appeareth to be unlawful, unless you take it, as it ought to be, discretio est discernere per Legem, quid sit Justum, discretion is to discern by the Law what is just.

It is called Right, because it is the best Birthright the Subject hath, for thereby his Goods, Lands, Wife & Children, his Body, Life, Honour & Estimation are protected from Injury & wrong. Major Hœreditas venit unicung; nostrum a Jure & Legibus, quam a Parentibus; A greater Inheritance descends to us from the Laws, than from our Progenitors.

Thus far the very words of that Oracle of our Law, the sage and learned Cook; which so fully and excellently explains this incomparable Law, that it will be superfluous to add any thing further thereunto.

Appendix E

Instructions of the Town of Braintree to Their Representative (1765), Drafted by John Adams[1]

To Ebenezer Thayer, Esq.

SIR,—In all the calamities which have ever befallen this country, we have never felt so great a concern, or such alarming apprehensions, as on this occasion. Such is our loyalty to the King, our veneration for both houses of Parliament, and our affection for all our fellow-subjects in Britain, that measures which discover any unkindness in that country towards us are the more sensibly and intimately felt. And we can no longer forbear complaining, that many of the measures of the late ministry, and some of the late acts of Parliament, have a tendency, in our apprehension, to divest us of our most essential rights and liberties. We shall confine ourselves, however, chiefly to the act of Parliament, commonly called the Stamp Act, by which a very burthensome, and, in our opinion, unconstitutional tax, is to be laid upon us all; and we subjected to numerous and enormous penalties, to be prosecuted, sued for, and recovered, at the option of an informer, in a court of admiralty, without a jury.

We have called this a burthensome tax, because the duties are so numerous and so high, and the embarrassments to business in this infant, sparsely-settled country so great, that it

[1] *Works of John Adams*, ed. Charles Francis Adams (Boston, 1865), III, 465–68.

would be totally impossible for the people to subsist under it, if we had no controversy at all about the right and authority of imposing it. Considering the present scarcity of money, we have reason to think, the execution of that act for a short space of time would drain the country of its cash, strip multitudes of all their property, and reduce them to absolute beggary. And what the consequence would be to the peace of the province, from so sudden a shock and such a convulsive change in the whole course of our business and subsistence, we tremble to consider. We further apprehend this tax to be unconstitutional. We have always understood it to be a grand and fundamental principle of the constitution, that no freeman should be subject to any tax to which he has not given his own consent, in person or by proxy. And the maxims of the law, as we have constantly received them, are to the same effect, that no freeman can be separated from his property but by his own act or fault. We take it clearly, therefore, to be inconsistent with the spirit of the common law, and of the essential fundamental principles of the British constitution, that we should be subject to any tax imposed by the British Parliament; because we are not represented in that assembly in any sense, unless it be by a fiction of law, as insensible in theory as it would be injurious in practice, if such a taxation should be grounded on it.

But the most grievous innovation of all, is the alarming extension of the power of courts of admiralty. In these courts, one judge presides alone! No juries have any concern there! The law and the fact are both to be decided by the same single judge, whose commission is only during pleasure, and with whom, as we are told, the most mischievous of all customs has become established, that of taking commissions on all condemnations; so that he is under a pecuniary temptation always against the subject. Now, if the wisdom of the mother country has thought the independency of the judges so essential to an impartial administration of justice, as to render them independent of every power on earth,—independent of the King, the Lords, the Commons, the people, nay, independent in hope and expectation of the heir-apparent, by continuing their commissions after a demise of the crown, what justice and impar-

tiality are we, at three thousand miles distance from the fountain, to expect from such a judge of admiralty? We have all
along thought the acts of trade in this respect a grievance; but
the Stamp Act has opened a vast number of sources of new
crimes, which may be committed by any man, and cannot but
be committed by multitudes, and prodigious penalties are annexed, and all these are to be tried by such a judge of such a
court! What can be wanting, after this, but a weak or wicked
man for a judge, to render us the most sordid and forlorn of
slaves?—we mean the slaves of a slave of the servants of a
minister of state. We cannot help asserting, therefore, that this
part of the act will make an essential change in the constitution
of juries, and it is directly repugnant to the Great Charter
itself; for, by that charter, "no amerciament shall be assessed,
but by the oath of honest and lawful men of the vicinage;" and,
"no freeman shall be taken, or imprisoned, or disseized of his
freehold, or liberties of free customs, nor passed upon, nor
condemned, but by lawful judgment of his peers, or by the law
of the land." So that this act will "make such a distinction, and
create such a difference between" the subjects in Great Britain
and those in America, as we could not have expected from the
guardians of liberty in "both."

As these, sir, are our sentiments of this act, we, the freeholders
and other inhabitants, legally assembled for this purpose, must
enjoin it upon you, to comply with no measures or proposals for
countenancing the same, or assisting in the execution of it, but
by all lawful means, consistent with our allegiance to the
King, and relation to Great Britain, to oppose the execution of
it, till we can hear the success of the cries and petitions of
America for relief.

We further recommend the most clear and explicit assertion
and vindication of our rights and liberties to be entered on the
public records, that the world may know, in the present and all
future generations, that we have a clear knowledge and a just
sense of them, and, with submission to Divine Providence, that
we never can be slaves.

Nor can we think it advisable to agree to any steps for the
protection of stamped papers or stamp-officers. Good and

wholesome laws we have already for the preservation of the peace; and we apprehend there is no further danger of tumult and disorder, to which we have a well-grounded aversion; and that any extraordinary and expensive exertions would tend to exasperate the people and endanger the public tranquillity, rather than the contrary. Indeed, we cannot too often inculcate upon you our desires, that all extraordinary grants and expensive measures may, upon all occasions, as much as possible, be avoided. The public money of this country is the toil and labor of the people, who are under many uncommon difficulties and distresses at this time, so that all reasonable frugality ought to be observed. And we would recommend particularly, the strictest care and the utmost firmness to prevent all unconstitutional draughts upon the public treasury.

Appendix F

Resolutions of the House of Burgesses

of Virginia against the Stamp Act (1765)[1]

*R*esolved, That the first Adventurers and Settlers of this his Majesty's Colony and Dominion of *Virginia* brought with them, and transmitted to their Posterity, and all other his Majesty's Subjects since inhabiting in this his Majesty's said Colony, all the Liberties, Privileges, Franchises, and Immunities, that have at any Time been held, enjoyed, and possessed, by the people of *Great Britain*.

Resolved, That by two royal Charters, granted by King *James* the First, the Colonists aforesaid are declared entitled to all Liberties, Privileges, and Immunities of Denizens and natural Subjects, to all Intents and Purposes, as if they had been abiding and born within the Realm of *England*.

Resolved, That the Taxation of the People by themselves, or by Persons chosen by themselves to represent them, who can only know what Taxes the People are able to bear, or the easiest Method of raising them, and must themselves be affected by every Tax laid on the People, is the only Security against a burthensome Taxation, and the distinguishing Characteristick of *British* Freedom, without which the ancient Constitution cannot exist.

[1] *Journals of the House of Burgesses of Virginia, 1761–1765,* ed. John Pendleton Kennedy (Richmond, 1907) , p. 360.

Resolved, That his Majesty's liege People of this his most ancient and loyal Colony have without Interruption enjoyed the inestimable Right of being governed by such Laws, respecting their internal Polity and Taxation, as are derived from their own Consent, with the Approbation of their Sovereign, or his Substitute; and that the same hath never been forfeited or yielded up, but hath been constantly recognized by the Kings and People of *Great Britain.*

Appendix G

Fairfax County Resolutions (1774)[1]

AT A General Meeting of the Freeholders and other Inhabitants of the County of *Fairfax,* at the Court House in the Town of *Alexandria,* on *Monday,* the 18th day of *July,* 1774:

GEORGE WASHINGTON, Esquire, *Chairman,* and
ROBERT HARRISON, Gentleman, *Clerk.*

Resolved, That this Colony and Dominion of *Virginia* cannot be considered as a conquered country, and, if it was, that the present inhabitants are the descendants, not of the conquered, but of the conquerors. That the same was not settled at the national expense of *England,* but at the private expense of the adventurers, our ancestors, by solemn compact with, and under the auspices and protection of, the *British* Crown, upon which we are, in every respect, as dependent as the people of *Great Britain,* and in the same manner subject to all his Majesty's just, legal, and constitutional prerogatives; that our ancestors, when they left their native land, and settled in *America,* brought with them, even if the same had not been confirmed by Charters, the civil Constitution and form of Government of the country they came from, and were by the laws of nature and

---

1 *American Archives* (4th ser.) , ed. M. St. Clair Clarke and Peter Force (Washington, D.C., 1837) , I, 597–602.

Nations entitled to all its privileges, immunities, and advantages, which have descended to us, their posterity, and ought of right to be as fully enjoyed as if we had still continued within the Realm of *England.*

Resolved, That the most important and valuable part of the *British* Constitution, upon which its every existence depends, is the fundamental principle of the people's being governed by no laws to which they have not given their consent by Representatives freely chosen by themselves, who are affected by the laws they enact equally with their constituents, to whom they are accountable, and whose burthens they share, in which consists the safety and happiness of the community; for if this part of the Constitution was taken away, or materially altered, the Government must degenerate either into an absolute and despotick monarchy, or a tyrannical aristocracy, and the freedom of the people be annihilated.

Resolved, Therefore, as the inhabitants of the *American* Colonies are not, and from their situation, cannot be represented in the *British* Parliament, that the Legislative power here can, of right, be exercised only by our Provincial Assemblies, or Parliaments, subject to the assent or negative of the *British* Crown, to be declared within some proper limited time; but as it was thought just and reasonable that the people of *Great Britain* should reap advantages from the Colonies adequate to the protection they afforded them, the *British* Parliament have claimed and exercised the power of regulating our trade and commerce, so as to restrain our importing from foreign countries such articles as they could furnish us with, of their own growth and manufacture, or exporting to foreign countries such articles and portions of our produce as *Great Britain* stood in need of, for her own consumption or manufacture. Such a power directed with wisdom and moderation, seems necessary for the general good of that great body politick of which we are a part, although in some degree repugant to the principles of the Constitution. Under this idea, our ancestors submitted to it, the experience of more than a century, during the government of his Majesty's royal predecessors, have proved its utility, and the reciprocal benefits flowing from it produced mutual uninterrupted harmony and good will between the inhabitants of *Great Britain* and her Colonies, who during that long period always considered themselves as one and the same people; and though such a power is capable of abuse, and in some instances hath been stretched beyond the original design and instutition, yet to avoid strife and contention with our fellow-subjects, and strongly impressed with the experience of mutual benefits, we always cheerfully acquiesced in it while the entire regulation of our internal policy, and giving and granting our own money, were preserved to our own Provincial Legislatures.

Resolved, That it is the duty of these Colonies, on all emergencies, to contribute in proportion to their abilities, situation, and circumstances, to the necessary charge of supporting and defending the *British* Empire, of which they are a part; that while we are treated upon an equal footing with our fellow-subjects, the motives of self-interest and preservation will be a sufficient obligation, as was evident through the course of the last war; and that no argument can be fairly applied to the *British* Parliament's taxing us, upon a presumption that we should refuse a just and reasonable contribution, but will equally operate in justification of the Executive power taxing the people of *England,* upon a supposition of their Representatives refusing to grant the necessary supplies.

Resolved, That the claim lately assumed and exercised by the *British* Parliament for making all such laws as they think fit to govern the people of these Colonies, and to extort from us our money without our consent, is not only diametrically contrary to the first principles of the Constitution and the original compacts by which we are dependent upon the *British* Crown and Government, but is totally incompatible with the privileges of a free people and the natural rights of mankind, will render our own Legislatures merely nominal and nugatory, and is calculated to reduce us from a state of freedom and happiness to slavery and misery.

Resolved, That taxation and representation are in their nature inseparable; that the right of withholding, or of giving and granting their own money, is the only effectual security to a free people against the encroachments of despotism and tyranny;

and that whenever they yield the one, they must quickly fall a prey to the other.

Resolved, That the powers over the people of *America,* now claimed by the *British* House of Commons, in whose election we have no share; in whose determinations we have no influence; whose information must be always defective, and often false; who in many instances may have a separate, and in some an opposite interest to ours; and who are removed from those impressions of tenderness and compassion, arising from personal intercourse and connection, which soften the rigours of the most despotick Governments, must, if continued, establish the most grievous and intolerable species of tyranny and oppression that ever was inflicted upon mankind.

Resolved, That it is our greatest wish and inclination, as well as interest, to continue our connection with, and dependence upon, the *British* Government; but though we are its subjects, we will use every means which Heaven hath given us to prevent our becoming its slaves.

Resolved, That there is a premeditated design and system formed and pursued by the *British* Ministry to introduce an arbitrary Government into his Majesty's *American* Dominions, to which end they are artfully prejudicing our Sovereign and inflaming the minds of our fellow-subjects in *Great Britain,* by propagating the most malevolent falsehoods, particularly that there is an intention in the *American* Colonies to set up for independent states, endeavouring at the same time, by various acts of violence and oppression, by sudden and repeated dissolutions of our Assemblies, whenever they presume to examine the illegality of Ministerial mandates, or deliberate on the violated rights of their constituents, and by breaking in upon the *American* Charters, to reduce us to a state of desperation, and dissolve the original compact, by which our ancestors bound themselves and their posterity to remain dependent upon the *British* Crown; which measures, unless effectually counteracted, will end in the ruin, both of *Great Britain* and her Colonies.

Resolved, That the several Acts of Parliament for raising a revenue upon the people of *America,* without their consent; the erecting new and dangerous jurisdictions here; the taking away our trials by jury; the ordering persons, upon criminal accusations, to be tried in another country than that in which the fact is charged to have been committed; the Act inflicting Ministerial vengeance upon the town of *Boston;* and the two Bills lately brought into Parliament for abrogating the Charter of the Province of *Massachusetts Bay,* and for the protection and encouragement of murderers in the said Province, are part of the abovementioned iniquitous system; that the inhabitants of the town of *Boston* are now suffering in the common cause of all *British America,* and are justly entitled to its support and assistance; and, therefore, that a subscription ought immediately to be opened, and proper persons appointed, in every county in this Colony, to purchase provisions and consign them to some gentlemen of character in *Boston,* to be distributed among the poorer sort of the people there.

Resolved, That we will cordially join with our friends and brethren of this and the other Colonies, in such measures as shall be judged most effectual, for procuring a redress of our grievances; and that, upon obtaining such redress, if the destruction of the tea at *Boston* be regarded as an invasion of private property, we shall be willing to contribute towards paying the *East India* Company the value; but, as we consider the said Company as the tools and instruments of oppression in the hands of Government, and the cause of the present distress, it is the opinion of this meeting, that the people of these Colonies should forbear all further dealings with them, by refusing to purchase their merchandise, until that peace, safety, and good order, which they have disturbed, be perfectly restored; and that all tea now in this Colony, or which shall be imported into it, shipped before the first day of *September* next, should be deposited in some store-house, to be appointed by the respective Committees of each county, until a sufficient sum of money be raised, by subscription, to reimburse the owners the value, and then to be publickly burnt and destroyed; and if the same is not paid for and destroyed as aforesaid, that it remain in the custody of the said Committees, at the risk of the owners, until the Act of Parliament imposing a duty upon tea for raising a revenue in *America,* be repealed; and immediately afterwards be delivered unto the several proprietors thereof, their agents or attornies.

Resolved, That nothing will so much contribute to defeat the pernicious designs of the common enemies of *Great Britain* and her Colonies, as a firm union of the latter, who ought to regard every act of violence or oppression inflicted upon any one of them, as aimed at all; and to effect this desirable purpose, that a Congress should be appointed, to consist of Deputies from all the Colonies, to concert a general and uniform plan for the defence and preservation of our common rights, and continuing the connection and dependence of the said Colonies upon *Great Britain,* under a just, lenient, permanent, and constitutional form of Government.

Resolved, That our most sincere and cordial thanks be given to the patrons and friends of liberty in *Great Britain,* for their spirited and patriotick conduct in support of our constitutional rights and privileges, and their generous efforts to prevent the present distress and calamity of *America.*

Resolved, That every little jarring interest and dispute which hath ever happened between these Colonies, should be buried in eternal oblivion; that all manner of luxury and extravagance ought immediately to be laid aside, as totally inconsistent with the threatening and gloomy prospect before us; that it is the indispensable duty of all the gentlemen and men of fortunes to set examples of temperance, fortitude, frugality, and industry, and give every encouragement in their power, particularly by subscriptions and premiums, to the improvement of arts and manufactures in *America;* that great care and attention should be had to the cultivation of flax, cotton, and other materials for manufactures; and we recommend it to such of the inhabitants as have large stocks of sheep, to sell to their neighbours at a moderate price, as the most certain means of speedily increasing our breed of sheep and quantity of wool.

Resolved, That until *American* grievances be redressed, by restoration of our just rights and privileges, no goods or merchandise whatsoever ought to be imported into this Colony, which shall be shipped from *Great Britain* or *Ireland,* after the first day of *September* next, except linens not exceeding fifteen pence per yard, coarse woollen cloth, not exceeding two shillings sterling per yard; nails, wire, and wire cards, needles and pins, paper, saltpetre, and medicines, which may be imported until the first day of *September,* 1776; and if any goods or merchandise, other than those hereby excepted, should be shipped from *Great Britain* after the time aforesaid, to this Colony, that the same, immediately upon their arrival, should either be sent back again by the owners, their agents or attornies, or stored and deposited in some warehouse, to be appointed by the Committee for each respective county, and there kept at the risk and charge of the owners, to be delivered to them when a free importation of goods hither shall again take place; and that the merchants and venders of goods and merchandise within this Colony ought not to take advantage of our present distress, but continue to sell the goods and merchandise which they now have, or which may be shipped to them before the first day of *September* next, at the same rates and prices they have been accustomed to do within one year last past; and if any person shall sell such goods on any other terms than above expressed, that no inhabitant of this Colony should, at any time forever thereafter, deal with him, his agent, factor, or storekeeper, for any commodity whatsoever.

Resolved, That it it is the opinion of this meeting, that the merchants and venders of goods and merchandise within this colony should take an oath not to sell or dispose of any goods or merchandise whatsoever which may be shipped from *Great Britain* after the first day of *September* next, as aforesaid, except the articles before excepted; and that they will, upon the receipt of such prohibited goods, either send the same back again by the first opportunity, or deliver them to the Committees of the respective counties, to be deposited in some warehouse, at the risk and charge of the owners, until they, their agents, or factors, shall be permitted to take them away by the said Committees; and that the names of those who refuse to take such oath, be advertised by the respective Committees, in the counties wherein they reside; and to the end that the inhabitants of this colony may know what merchants and venders of goods and merchandise have taken such oath, that the respective Committees should grant a certificate thereof to every such person who shall take the same.

Resolved, That it is the opinion of this meeting, that during our present difficulties and distress, no slaves ought to be imported into any of the *British* Colonies on this Continent; and we take this opportunity of declaring our most earnest wishes to see an entire stop forever put to such a wicked, cruel, and unnatural trade.

Resolved, That no kind of lumber should be exported from this Colony to the *West Indies,* until *America* be restored to her constitutional rights and liberties, if the other Colonies will accede to a like resolution; and that it is recommended to the general Congress to appoint as early a day as possible for stopping such exports.

Resolved, That it is the opinion of this meeting, if *American* grievances be not redressed before the first day of *November,* 1775, that all exports of produce from the several Colonies to *Great Britain,* should cease; and to carry the said resolution more effectually into execution, that we will not plant or cultivate any tobacco after the crop now growing, provided the same measure shall be adopted by the other Colonies on this Continent, as well as those who have heretofore made tobacco, as those who have not. And it is our opinion, also, if the Congress of Deputies from the several Colonies shall adopt the measure of non-exportation to *Great Britain,* as the people will be thereby disabled from paying their debts, that no judgments should be rendered by the Courts in the said Colonies, for any debt, after information of the said measures being determined upon.

Resolved, That it is the opinion of this meeting, that a Solemn Covenant and Association should be entered into by the inhabitants of all the Colonies, upon oath, that they will not, after the time which shall be respectively agreed on at the general Congress, export any manner of lumber to the *West Indies;* nor any of their produce to *Great Britain;* or sell or dispose of the same to any person who shall not have entered into the said Covenant and Association; and also, that they will not import or receive any goods or merchandise which shall be shipped from *Great Britain,* after the first day of *September* next, other than the before enumerated articles; nor buy or purchase any goods, except as before excepted, of any person whatsoever, who shall not have taken the oath herein before recommended to be taken by the merchants and venders of goods; nor buy or purchase any slaves hereafter imported into any part of this Continent, until a free exportation and importation be again resolved on by a majority of the Representatives or Deputies of the Colonies; and that the respective Committees of the counties in each Colony, so soon as the Covenant and Association becomes general, publish by advertisements in their several counties, a list of the names of those, (if any such there be) who will not accede thereto, that such traitors to their country may be publickly known and detested.

Resolved, That it is the opinion of this meeting, that this and the other associating Colonies should break off all trade, intercourse, and dealings, with that Colony, Province, or town, which shall decline or refuse to agree to the plan which shall be adopted by the general Congress.

Resolved, That should the town of *Boston* be forced to submit to the late cruel and oppressive measures of Government, that we shall not hold the same to be binding upon us, but will, notwithstanding, religiously maintain, and inviolably adhere to, such measures as shall be concerted by the general Congress, for the preservation of our lives, liberties, and fortunes.

Resolved, That it be recommended to the Deputies of the general Congress, to draw up and transmit an humble and dutiful Petition and Remonstrance to his Majesty, asserting in decent firmness our just and constitutional rights and privileges, lamenting the fatal necessity of being compelled to enter into measures disgusting to his Majesty and his Parliament, or injurious to our fellow-subjects in *Great Britain;* declaring, in the strongest terms, our duty and affection to his Majesty's person, family, and Government, and our desire forever to continue our dependence upon *Great Britain;* and most humbly conjuring and beseeching his Majesty not to reduce his faithful subjects of *America* to a state of desperation, and to reflect, that from our Sovereign there can be but one appeal. And it is the opinion of this meeting, that after such Petition and Remonstrance shall have been presented to his Majesty, the same shall be printed in the public papers in all the principal towns in *Great Britain*.

Resolved, That *George Washington,* Esquire, and *Charles Broadwater,* Gentleman, lately elected our Representatives to serve in the General Assembly, attend the Convention at *Williamsburg,* on the first day of *August* next, and present these Resolves as the sense of the people of this county upon the measures proper to be taken in the present alarming and dangerous situation of *America*.

Resolved, That *George Washington,* Esquire, *John West, George Mason, William Rumney, William Ramsay, George Gilpton, Robert Hanson Harrison, John Carlyle, Robert Adam, John Dalton, Philip Alexander, James Kirk, William Brown, Charles Broadwater, William Payne, Martin Cockburne, Lee Massey, William Hartshorne, Thomas Triplett, Charles Alexander, Thomas Pollard, Townsend Dade,* Junior, *Edward Payne, Henry Gunnell,* and *Thomas Lewis,* be a Committee for this county; that they, or a majority of them, on any emergency, have power to call a general meeting, and to concert and adopt such measures as may be thought most expedient and necessary.

Resolved, That a copy of these Proceedings be transmitted to the Printer at *Williamsburg,* to be published.

Appendix H

Resolutions of the Continental Congress

$(1774)^1$

WHEREAS, since the close of the last war, the British parliament, claiming a power of right to bind the people of America, by statute in all cases whatsoever, hath in some acts expressly imposed taxes on them, and in others, under various pretences, but in fact for the purpose of raising a revenue, hath imposed rates and duties payable in these colonies, established a board of commissioners, with unconstitutional powers, and extended the jurisdiction of courts of Admiralty, not only for collecting the said duties, but for the trial of causes merely arising within the body of a county.

And whereas, in consequence of other statutes, judges, who before held only estates at will in their offices, have been made dependant on the Crown alone for their salaries, and standing armies kept in times of peace:

And it has lately been resolved in Parliament, that by force of a statute, made in the thirty-fifth year of the reign of king Henry the eighth, colonists may be transported to England, and tried there upon accusations for treasons, and misprisions, or concealments of treasons committed in the colonies; and by a

---

¹ *Journals of the Continental Congress: 1774–1789*, ed. Worthington Chauncey Ford (Washington, D.C., 1904), pp. 63–73.

late statute, such trials have been directed in cases therein mentioned.

And whereas, in the last session of parliament, three statutes were made; one, intituled "An act to discontinue, in such manner and for such time as are therein mentioned, the landing and discharging, lading, or shipping of goods, wares & merchandise, at the town, and within the harbour of Boston, in the province of Massachusetts-bay, in North-America;" another, intituled "An act for the better regulating the government of the province of the Massachusetts-bay in New-England;" and another, intituled "An act for the impartial administration of justice, in the cases of persons questioned for any act done by them in the execution of the law, or for the suppression of riots and tumults, in the province of the Massachusetts-bay, in New-England." And another statute was then made, "for making more effectual provision for the government of the province of Quebec, &c." All which statutes are impolitic, unjust, and cruel, as well as unconstitutional, and most dangerous and destructive of American rights.

And whereas, Assemblies have been frequently dissolved, contrary to the rights of the people, when they attempted to deliberate on grievances; and their dutiful, humble, loyal, & reasonable petitions to the crown for redress, have been repeatedly treated with contempt, by his majesty's ministers of state:

The good people of the several Colonies of New-hampshire, Massachusetts-bay, Rhode-island and Providence plantations, Connecticut, New-York, New-Jersey, Pennsylvania, Newcastle, Kent and Sussex on Delaware, Maryland, Virginia, North Carolina, and South Carolina, justly alarmed at these arbitrary proceedings of parliament and administration, have severally elected, constituted, and appointed deputies to meet and sit in general congress, in the city of Philadelphia, in order to obtain such establishment, as that their religion, laws, and liberties may not be subverted:

Whereupon the deputies so appointed being now assembled, in a full and free representation of these Colonies, taking into their most serious consideration, the best means of attaining the ends aforesaid, do, in the first place, as Englishmen, their ancestors in like cases have usually done, for asserting and vindicating their rights and liberties, declare,

That the inhabitants of the English Colonies in North America, by the immutable laws of nature, the principles of the English constitution, and the several charters or compacts, have the following Rights:

Resolved, N. C. D.[2] 1. That they are entitled to life, liberty, & property, and they have never ceded to any sovereign power whatever, a right to dispose of either without their consent.

Resolved, N. C. D. 2. That our ancestors, who first settled these colonies, were at the time of their emigration from the mother country, entitled to all the rights, liberties, and immunities of free and natural-born subjects, within the realm of England.

Resolved, N. C. D. 3. That by such emigration they by no means forfeited, surrendered, or lost any of those rights, but that they were, and their descendants now are, entitled to the exercise and enjoyment of all such of them, as their local and other circumstances enable them to exercise and enjoy.

Resolved, 4. That the foundation of English liberty, and of all free government, is a right in the people to participate in their legislative council: and as the English colonists are not represented, and from their local and other circumstances, cannot properly be represented in the British parliament, they are entitled to a free and exclusive power of legislation in their several provincial legislatures, where their right of representation can alone be preserved, in all cases of taxation and internal polity, subject only to the negative of their sovereign, in such manner as has been heretofore used and accustomed. But, from the necessity of the case, and a regard to the mutual interest of both countries, we cheerfully consent to the operation of such acts of the British parliament, as are bona fide, restrained to the regulation of our external commerce, for the purpose of securing the commercial advantages of the whole empire to the mother country, and the commercial benefits of

---

[2] *Nemine contradicente,* i.e., unanimously.

its respective members; excluding every idea of taxation, internal or external, for raising a revenue on the subjects in America, without their consent.

Resolved, N. C. D. 5. That the respective colonies are entitled to the common law of England, and more especially to the great and inestimable privilege of being tried by their peers of the vicinage, according to the course of that law.

Resolved, 6. That they are entituled to the benefit of such of the English statutes as existed at the time of their colonization; and which they have, by experience, respectively found to be applicable to their several local and other circumstances.

Resolved, N. C. D. 7. That these, his majesty's colonies, are likewise entitled to all the immunities and privileges granted & confirmed to them by royal charters, or secured by their several codes of provincial laws.

Resolved, N. C. D. 8. That they have a right peaceably to assemble, consider of their grievances, and petition the King; and that all prosecutions, prohibitory proclamations, and commitments for the same, are illegal.

Resolved, N. C. D. 9. That the keeping a Standing army in these colonies, in times of peace, without the consent of the legislature of that colony, in which such army is kept, is against law.

Resolved, N. C. D. 10. It is indispensably necessary to good government, and rendered essential by the English constitution, that the constituent branches of the legislature be independent of each other; that, therefore, the exercise of legislative power in several colonies, by a council appointed, during pleasure, by the crown, is unconstitutional, dangerous, and destructive to the freedom of American legislation.

All and each of which the aforesaid deputies, in behalf of themselves and their constituents, do claim, demand, and insist on, as their indubitable rights and liberties; which cannot be legally taken from them, altered or abridged by any power whatever, without their own consent, by their representatives in their several provincial legislatures.

In the course of our inquiry, we find many infringements and violations of the foregoing rights, which, from an ardent desire, that harmony and mutual intercourse of affection and interest may be restored, we pass over for the present, and proceed to state such acts and measures as have been adopted since the last war, which demonstrate a system formed to enslave America.

Resolved, N. C. D. That the following acts of Parliament are infringements and violations of the rights of the colonists; and that the repeal of them is essentially necessary in order to restore harmony between Great-Britain and the American colonies, viz:

The several acts of 4 Geo. 3. ch. 15, & ch. 34.—5 Geo. 3. ch. 25.—6 Geo. 3. ch. 52.—7 Geo. 3. ch. 41, & ch. 46.—8 Geo. 3. ch. 22, which impose duties for the purpose of raising a revenue in America, extend the powers of the admiralty courts beyond their ancient limits, deprive the American subject of trial by jury, authorize the judges' certificate to indemnify the prosecutor from damages, that he might otherwise be liable to, requiring oppressive security from a claimant of ships and goods seized, before he shall be allowed to defend his property, and are subversive of American rights.

Also the 12 Geo. 3. ch. 24, entituled "An act for the better securing his Majesty's dock-yards, magazines, ships, ammunition, and stores," which declares a new offence in America, and deprives the American subject of a constitutional trial by a jury of the vicinage, by authorizing the trial of any person, charged with the committing any offence described in the said act, out of the realm, to be indicted and tried for the same in any shire or county within the realm.

Also the three acts passed in the last session of parliament, for stopping the port and blocking up the harbour of Boston, for altering the charter & government of the Massachusetts-bay, and that which is entituled "An act for the better administration of Justice," &c.

Also the act passed in the same session for establishing the Roman Catholick Religion in the province of Quebec, abolishing the equitable system of English laws, and erecting a tyranny there, to the great danger, from so total a dissimilarity of Religion, law, and government of the neighbouring British colonies, by the assistance of whose blood and treasure the said country was conquered from France.

Also the act passed in the same session for the better providing suitable quarters for officers and soldiers in his Majesty's service in North-America.

Also, that the keeping a standing army in several of these colonies, in time of peace, without the consent of the legislature of that colony in which such army is kept, is against law.

To these grievous acts and measures, Americans cannot submit, but in hopes that their fellow subjects in Great-Britain will, on a revision of them, restore us to that state in which both countries found happiness and prosperity, we have for the present only resolved to pursue the following peaceable measures:

Resolved, unanimously, That from and after the first day of December next, there be no importation into British America, from Great Britain or Ireland of any goods, wares or merchandize whatsoever, or from any other place of any such goods, wares or merchandize.[3]

1st. To enter into a non-importation, non-consumption, and non-exportation agreement or association.

2. To prepare an address to the people of Great-Britain, and a memorial to the inhabitants of British America, &

3. To prepare a loyal address to his Majesty; agreeable to Resolutions already entered into.

[3] This paragraph was struck out.

Appendix I

Extract from William Henry Drayton's

Explanation of the "Rights of Englishmen"

to the Cherokee Indians (1775)[1]

F RIENDS, and Brother Warriors,—I take you by the hand, in witness, of the peace and friendship which has so long subsisted between your brothers the White People of this country, and you and your people—and, I hold your hand fast, in testimony, that your brothers the white people wish, that our peace and friendship with you and your people may continue.

I sent a talk to you in your nation, to desire that you would come to see me at the Congarees, in order that we might talk together face to face. When I sent to you, I thought to have been here, before you could have arrived; but, some of our people did not understand the things, about which I intend to speak to you; and to explain which to them I came into the country; my stay among those people was therefore longer, than I expected. This being the case, I make no doubt but that you will readily excuse my absence, which I assure you, was as disagreeable to myself, as it could possibly be to you.

I sent to you, to come to me, that I might explain to you, the causes of the unhappy quarrel between a part of the people in Great Britain, and your brothers the white people living in America. Also, that I might tell you, why our people have put

[1] John Drayton, *Memoirs of the American Revolution, From Its Commencement to the Year 1776, Inclusive; As Relating to the State of South-Carolina* (Charleston, S.C., 1821), I, 419–23.

on their Shot pouches, and hold their Rifles in their hands.

The causes of this unhappy quarrel are very plain, as you will see as I go on with my talk; but, in order that you may see them, and understand them, clearly, I must first talk of the time before any of our white people came to this country, and, what was then done.

Before our forefathers left England, they made an agreement with the Great King; that when they came to America, they and their children after them, should then continue to have and enjoy the same rights and privileges, that the people of England, who you know were their own brothers, did actually enjoy. And, to this agreement, the Great King put his hand and seal; and declared, that all the Great Kings after him, should be bound by the agreement he had made.

Now, in consequence of this agreement, your brothers the white people in America say, the money they have in their pockets is their own; and the Great King has no right whatsoever to send or to order any officers to take this money or any part of it out of our pockets, or to make any laws to bind us, but by our own consent, given by our wise men whom we ourselves elect and appoint to make laws for us. And we say so, for this plain and good reason; because, the Great King has no right to send any officers to take any money out of the pockets of our brothers the people of England, or to bind them by any laws, but by their own consent given by their wise men, whom they themselves elect and appoint to make laws for them. For, as this is the right and priviledge of our brothers in England, so, this agreement declares we have the same right and priviledge.

But, notwithstanding these things, the men about the Great King, have persuaded him, that he and the men in England whom we never elected and appointed to make laws for us, have a right to take our money, out of our pockets without our consent, and to make laws to drag us away from our own country, across the Great Water; and all this, without asking us any thing about the matter, and violently against our consent and good liking. And, unjust and wicked as all this is, yet this is not the worst part of their usage to us. They have by other laws broken our agreement in whatever particular part they pleased; and these men about the Great King, have so teazed and persuaded him, that the Great King and the men in England, whom as I told you before, we never appointed to make laws for us, have made one law, which says, the Great King and those men, have a right to bind us by laws of their making, in all cases whatsoever: which is as much as to say, they have a right to treat us and every thing belonging to us, just as they please. And this you know is as much as to say, they have a right to take all our money, all our lands, all our cattle and horses and such things; and not only all such things, but our wives and children, in order to make servants of them; and, beside all these things, to put us in strong-houses, and to put us to death, whenever they please.

Friends and Brother Warriors,—is it not now as plain as the sight at the end of your rifles, that these laws and proceedings are like so many hatchets, chopping our agreement to pieces? Are not these, unjust things? Enough, to make us put on our shot pouches—and especially, when we find, that our brothers over the Great Water, will not only not harken to the many good talks which we have sent them about these matters; but have really sent over people to take the hatchet up against us.

Oh, my *Brother Warriors,* it is a lamentable thing, that our brothers beyond the Great Water, should use us in this cruel manner. If they use us, their own flesh and blood, in this unjust way, what must you expect—you, who are Red People—you, whom they never saw—you, whom they know only, by the hearing of the ear—you, who have fine lands? You see, by their treatment to us, that agreements even under hand and seal go as nothing with them. Think of these things, my friends, and reflect upon them, day and night.

Having told you, that the men about the Great King persuaded him, that he and the men in England have a right to take our money out of our pockets, without our consent; I must now tell you the contrivances they have fallen upon to take this money, whether we will or not. In order to take this money from us, they have ordered that we must pay a duty upon this and that thing, that we are accustomed to purchase; which is as much as to say, that upon those things we purchase, we must pay to the Great King against our consent, a sum of money above the real value of those things. And in particular, they ordered that if we drink tea, we must pay so much money to the Great King. I must tell you, this tea is somewhat like your Black-Drink. But, as we know, that this order is contrary to our agreement; and also, as we know the evil consequences of our paying this money; so, your brothers the white people in America have resolved that they will not pay it. And, therefore, the men about the Great King have persuaded him to send soldiers to Boston, and we are told some are coming here, to force the people here to give their money without their consent; and thereby to give up their rights and privileges, which are mentioned in the agreement.

Some foolish people, say it is better to pay this money for the tea, than to go to war about it. But I tell you, it is not about this money alone that we quarrel; for the money itself, we do not regard as two corn stalks: but, we are afraid bad consequences will follow, if we pay the money; as I will show you directly.

We find that the men in England talk among themselves, that they intend to make us in America pay to them, a great sum of money every year. The way they intend to raise this money, is as I have told you already, by making us pay a duty upon this and that thing, that we are accustomed to purchase. Now, this duty upon tea, brings in but a very small part of that great sum of money they want to make us pay to them; and therefore, we refuse to pay this money for the tea; lest if we paid it, they would be encouraged to go on time after time, to lay duties upon a great many other things, which we are accustomed to purchase; in order, that they may at last get from us, that great sum of money which they want, and which perhaps, is all we have. By which means, as your brothers the white people will be obliged to give more money than usual, for those blankets, strouds, checks, linens, guns, powder, paint, and rum with which you are supplied; so, if money is thus taken out of our pockets without our consent, and against our agreement, it is plain and certain, that you and your people must pay two and three deer skins for those goods, which you used to purchase of the traders for one deerskin. And thus you see, that we do not quarrel only upon our own account; but that we have put on our shot pouches, not only to preserve our money, but also, to preserve your deer skins.

Appendix J

Virginia Declaration of Rights (1776)[1]

A DECLARATION of rights made by the representatives of the good people of Virginia, assembled in full and free convention; which rights do pertain to them and their posterity, as the basis and foundation of government.

SECTION 1. That all men are by nature equally free and independent, and have certain inherent rights, of which, when they enter into a state of society, they cannot, by any compact, deprive or divest their posterity; namely, the enjoyment of life and liberty, with the means of acquiring and possessing property, and pursuing and obtaining happiness and safety.

SEC. 2. That all power is vested in, and consequently derived from, the people; that magistrates are their trustees and servants, and at all times amenable to them.

SEC. 3. That government is, or ought to be, instituted for the common benefit, protection, and security of the people, nation, or community; of all the various modes and forms of government, that is best which is capable of producing the greatest degree of happiness and safety, and is most effectually secured against the danger of maladministration; and that, when any

[1] Francis Newton Thorpe, ed., *Federal and State Constitutions, Colonial Charters, and Other Organic Laws of the States, Territories, and Colonies Now or Heretofore Forming the United States of America* (Washington, D.C., 1909), VII, 3812–14.

government shall be found inadequate or contrary to these purposes, a majority of the community hath an indubitable, inalienable, and indefeasible right to reform, alter, or abolish it, in such manner as shall be judged most conducive to the public weal.

SEC. 4. That no man, or set of men, are entitled to exclusive or separate emoluments or privileges from the community, but in consideration of public services; which, not being descendible, neither ought the offices of magistrate, legislator, or judge to be hereditary.

SEC. 5. That the legislative and executive powers of the State should be separate and distinct from the judiciary; and that the members of the two first may be restrained from oppression, by feeling and participating the burdens of the people, they should, at fixed periods, be reduced to a private station, return into that body from which they were originally taken, and the vacancies be supplied by frequent, certain, and regular elections, in which all, or any part of the former members, to be again eligible, or ineligible, as the laws shall direct.

SEC. 6. That elections of members to serve as representatives of the people, in assembly, ought to be free; and that all men, having sufficient evidence of permanent common interest with, and attachment to, the community, have the right of suffrage, and cannot be taxed or deprived of their property for public uses, without their own consent, or that of their representatives so elected, nor bound by any law to which they have not, in like manner, assembled, for the public good.

SEC. 7. That all power of suspending laws, or the execution of laws, by any authority, without consent of the representatives of the people, is injurious to their rights, and ought not to be exercised.

SEC. 8. That in all capital or criminal prosecutions a man hath a right to demand the cause and nature of his accusation, to be confronted with the accusers and witnesses, to call for evidence in his favor, and to a speedy trial by an impartial jury of twelve men of his vicinage, without whose unanimous consent he cannot be found guilty; nor can he be compelled to give evidence against himself; that no man be deprived of his liberty, except by the law of the land or the judgment of his peers.

SEC. 9. That excessive bail ought not to be required, nor excessive fines imposed, nor cruel and unusual punishments inflicted.

SEC. 10. That general warrants, whereby an officer or messenger may be commanded to search suspected places without evidence of a fact committed, or to seize any person or persons not named, or whose offence is not particularly described and supported by evidence, are grievous and oppressive, and ought not to be granted.

SEC. 11. That in controversies respecting property, and in suits between man and man, the ancient trial by jury is preferable to any other, and ought to be held sacred.

SEC. 12. That the freedom of the press is one of the great bulwarks of liberty, and can never be restrained but by despotic governments.

SEC. 13. That a well-regulated militia, composed of the body of the people, trained to arms, is the proper, natural, and safe defence of a free State; that standing armies, in time of peace, should be avoided, as dangerous to liberty; and that in all cases the military should be under strict subordination to, and governed by, the civil power.

SEC. 14. That the people have a right to uniform government; and, therefore, that no government separate from, or independent of the government of Virginia, ought to be erected or established within the limits thereof.

SEC. 15. That no free government, or the blessings of liberty, can be preserved to any people, but by a firm adherence to justice, moderation, temperance, frugality, and virtue, and by frequent recurrence to fundamental principles.

SEC. 16. That religion, or the duty which we owe to our Creator, and the manner of discharging it, can be directed only by reason and conviction, not by force or violence; and therefore all men are equally entitled to the free exercise of religion, according to the dictates of conscience; and that it is the mutual duty of all to practise Christian forbearance, love, and charity towards each other.

Appendix K

A Declaration of the Rights of the

Inhabitants of the Commonwealth of

Massachusetts (1780)[1]

ARTICLE I. All men are born free and equal, and have certain natural, essential, and unalienable rights; among which may be reckoned the right of enjoying and defending their lives and liberties; that of acquiring, possessing, and protecting property; in fine, that of seeking and obtaining their safety and happiness.

II. It is the right as well as the duty of all men in society, publicly, and at stated seasons, to worship the SUPREME BEING, the great Creator and Preserver of the universe. And no subject shall be hurt, molested, or restrained, in his person, liberty, or estate, for worshipping GOD in the manner and season most agreeable to the dictates of his own conscience; or for his religious profession of sentiments; provided he doth not disturb the public peace, or obstruct others in their religious worship.

III. As the happiness of a people, and the good order and preservation of civil government, essentially depend upon piety, religion, and morality; and as these cannot be generally diffused through a community but by the institution of the

[1] Francis Newton Thorpe, ed., *Federal and State Constitutions, Colonial Charters, and Other Organic Laws of the States, Territories, and Colonies Now or Heretofore Forming the United States of America* (Washington, D.C., 1909), III, 1889–93.

public worship of GOD, and of public instructions in piety, religion, and morality: Therefore, to promote their happiness, and to secure the good order and preservation of their government, the people of this commonwealth have a right to invest their legislature with power to authorize and require, and the legislature shall, from time to time, authorize and require, the several towns, parishes, precincts, and other bodies politic, or religious societies, to make suitable provision, at their own expense, for the institution of the public worship of GOD, and for the support and maintenance of public Protestant teachers of piety, religion, and morality, in all cases where such provision shall not be made voluntarily.

And the people of this commonwealth have also a right to, and do, invest their legislature with authority to enjoin upon all the subjects an attendance upon the instructions of the public teachers aforesaid, at stated times and seasons, if there be any on whose instructions they can conscientiously and conveniently attend.

Provided, notwithstanding, that the several towns, parishes, precincts, and other bodies politic, or religious societies, shall, at all times, have the exclusive right of electing their public teachers, and of contracting with them for their support and maintenance.

And all moneys paid by the subject to the support of public worship, and of the public teachers aforesaid, shall, if he require it, be uniformly applied to the support of the public teacher or teachers of his own religious sect or denomination, provided there be any on whose instructions he attends; otherwise it may be paid towards the support of the teacher or teachers of the parish or precinct in which the said moneys are raised.

And every denomination of Christians, demeaning themselves peaceably, and as good subjects of the commonwealth, shall be equally under the protection of the law: and no subordination of any one sect or denomination to another shall ever be established by law.

IV. The people of this commonwealth have the sole and exclusive right of governing themselves, as a free, sovereign, and independent state; and do, and forever hereafter shall, exercise and enjoy every power, jurisdiction, and right, which is not, or may not hereafter be, by them expressly delegated to the United States of America, in Congress assembled.

V. All power residing originally in the people, and being derived from them, the several magistrates and officers of government, vested with authority, whether legislative, executive, or judicial, are their substitutes and agents, and are at all times accountable to them.

VI. No man, nor corporation, or association of men, have any other title to obtain advantages, or particular and exclusive privileges, distinct from those of the community, than what arises from the consideration of services rendered to the public; and this title being in nature neither hereditary, nor transmissible to children, or descendants, or relations by blood, the idea of a man born a magistrate, lawgiver, or judge, is absurd and unnatural.

VII. Government is instituted for the common good; for the protection, safety, prosperity, and happiness of the people; and not for the profit, honor, or private interest of any one man, family, or class of men: Therefore the people alone have an incontestible unalienable, and indefeasible right to institute government; and to reform, alter, or totally change the same, when their protection, safety, prosperity, and happiness require it.

VIII. In order to prevent those who are vested with authority from becoming oppressors, the people have a right, at such periods and in such manner as they shall establish by their frame of government, to cause their public officers to return to private life; and to fill up vacant places by certain and regular elections and appointments.

IX. All elections ought to be free; and all the inhabitants of this commonwealth, having such qualifications as they shall establish by their frame of government, have an equal right to elect officers, and to be elected, for public employments.

X. Each individual of the society has a right to be protected by it in the enjoyment of his life, liberty, and property, according to standing laws. He is obliged, consequently, to contribute his share to the expense of this protection; to give his personal service, or an equivalent, when necessary: but no part of the property of any individual can, with justice, be taken from him, or applied to public uses, without his own consent, or that of the representative body of the people. In fine, the people of this commonwealth are not controllable by any other laws than those to which their constitutional representative body have given their consent. And whenever the public exigencies require that the property of any individual should be appropriated to public uses, he shall receive a reasonable compensation therefor.

XI. Every subject of the commonwealth ought to find a certain remedy, by having recourse to the laws, for all injuries or wrongs which he may receive in his person, property, or character. He ought to obtain right and justice freely, and without being obliged to purchase it; completely, and without any denial; promptly, and without delay; conformably to the laws.

XII. No subject shall be held to answer for any crimes or offence, until the same is fully and plainly, substantially, and formally, described to him; or be compelled to accuse, or furnish evidence against himself. And every subject shall have a right to produce all proofs that may be favorable to him; to meet the witnesses against him face to face, and to be fully heard in his defence by himself, or his counsel, at his election. And no subject shall be arrested, imprisoned, despoiled, or deprived of his property, immunities, or privileges, put out of the protection of the law, exiled, or deprived of his life, liberty, or estate, but by the judgment of his peers, or the law of the land.

And the legislature shall not make any law that shall subject any person to a capital or infamous punishment, excepting for the government of the army and navy, without trial by jury.

XIII. In criminal prosecutions, the verification of facts, in the vicinity where they happen, is one of the greatest securities of the life, liberty, and property of the citizen.

XIV. Every subject has a right to be secure from all unreasonable searches, and seizures, of his person, his houses, his papers, and all his possessions. All warrants, therefore, are contrary to this right, if the cause or foundation of them be not previously supported by oath or affirmation, and if the order in the warrant to a civil officer, to make search in suspected places, or to arrest one or more suspected persons, or to seize their property, be not accompanied with a special designation of the persons or objects of search, arrest, or seizure; and no warrant ought to be issued but in cases, and with the formalities prescribed by the laws.

XV. In all controversies concerning property, and in all suits between two or more persons, except in cases in which it has heretofore been otherways used and practised, the parties have a right to a trial by jury; and this method of procedure shall be held sacred, unless, in causes arising on the high seas, and such as relate to mariners' wages, the legislature shall hereafter find it necessary to alter it.

XVI. The liberty of the press is essential to the security of freedom in a state it ought not, therefore, to be restricted in this commonwealth.

XVII. The people have a right to keep and to bear arms for the common defence. And as, in time of peace, armies are dangerous to liberty, they ought not to be maintained without the consent of the legislature; and the military power shall always be held in an exact subordination to the civil authority, and be governed by it.

XVIII. A frequent recurrence to the fundamental principles of the constitution, and a constant adherence to those of piety, justice, moderation, temperance, industry, and frugality, are absolutely necessary to preserve the advantages of liberty, and to maintain a free government. The people ought, consequently, to have a particular attention to all those principles, in the choice of their officers and representatives: and they have a right to require of their lawgivers and magistrates an exact and constant observance of them, in the formation and execution of the laws necessary for the good administration of the commonwealth.

XIX. The people have a right, in an orderly and peaceable manner, to assemble to consult upon the common good; give instructions to their representatives, and to request of the legislative body, by the way of addresses, petitions, or re-monstrances, redress of the wrongs done them, and of the griev-ances they suffer.

XX. The power of suspending the laws, or the execution of the laws, ought never to be exercised but by the legislature, or by authority derived from it, to be exercised in such particular cases only as the legislature shall expressly provide for.

XXI. The freedom of deliberation, speech, and debate, in either house of the legislature, is so essential to the rights of the people, that it cannot be the foundation of any accusation or prosecution, action or complaint, in any other court or place whatsoever.

XXII. The legislature ought frequently to assemble for the redress of grievances, for correcting, strengthening, and con-firming the laws, and for making new laws, as the common good may require.

XXIII. No subsidy, charge, tax, impost, or duties ought to be established, fixed, laid, or levied, under any pretext what-soever, without the consent of the people or their representa-tives in the legislature.

XXIV. Laws made to punish for actions done before the existence of such laws, and which have not been declared crimes by preceding laws, are unjust, oppressive, and inconsist-ent with the fundamental principles of a free government.

XXV. No subject ought, in any case, or in any time, to be declared guilty of treason or felony by the legislature.

XXVI. No magistrate or court of law shall demand excessive bail or sureties, impose excessive fines, or inflict cruel or unu-sual punishments.

XXVII. In time of peace, no soldier ought to be quartered in any house without the consent of the owner; and in time of war, such quarters ought not to be made but by the civil magistrate, in a manner ordained by the legislature.

XXVIII. No person can in any case be subject to law-martial, or to any penalties or pains, by virtue of that law, except those employed in the army or navy, and except the militia in actual service, but by authority of the legislature.

XXIX. It is essential to the preservation of the rights of

every individual, his life, liberty, property, and character, that there be an impartial interpretation of the laws, and administration of justice. It is the right of every citizen to be tried by judges as free, impartial, and independent as the lot of humanity will admit. It is, therefore, not only the best policy, but for the security of the rights of the people, and of every citizen, that the judges of the supreme judicial court should hold their offices as long as they behave themselves well; and that they should have honorable salaries ascertained and established by standing laws.

XXX. In the government of this commonwealth, the legislative department shall never exercise the executive and judicial powers, or either of them: the executive shall never exercise the legislative and judicial powers, or either of them: the judicial shall never exercise the legislative and executive powers, or either of them: to the end it may be a government of laws and not of men.

Appendix L

Amendments to the Federal Constitution

Proposed by the Virginia Ratifying

Convention (1788)[1]

Friday, June 27, 1788

*A*nother *engrossed form of the ratification,* agreed to on Wednesday last, containing the proposed Constitution of government, as recommended by the federal Convention on the seventeenth day of September, one thousand seven hundred and eighty-seven, being prepared by the secretary, was read and signed by the president, in behalf of the Convention.

On motion, *Ordered,* That the said ratification be deposited by the secretary of this Convention in the archives of the General Assembly of this state.

Mr. WYTHE reported, from the committee appointed, such *amendments* to the proposed Constitution of government for the United States as were by them deemed necessary to be recommended to the consideration of the Congress which shall first assemble under the said Constitution, to be acted upon according to the mode prescribed in the 5th article thereof; and he read the same in his place, and afterwards delivered them in at the clerk's table, where the same were again read, and are as follows:—

"That there be a declaration or bill of rights asserting, and securing from encroachment, the essential and unalienable rights of the people, in some such manner as the following:—

[1] Jonathan Elliot, ed., *Debates in the Several State Conventions on the Adoption of the Federal Constitution* (2d ed.; Washington, D.C., 1836), III, 657–63.

"1st. That there are certain natural rights, of which men, when they form a social compact, cannot deprive or divest their posterity; among which are the enjoyment of life and liberty, with the means of acquiring, possessing, and protecting property, and pursuing and obtaining happiness and safety.

"2d. That all power is naturally invested in, and consequently derived from, the people; that magistrates therefore are their *trustees* and *agents,* at all times amenable to them.

"3d. That government ought to be instituted for the common benefit, protection, and security of the people; and that the doctrine of non-resistance against arbitrary power and oppression is absurd, slavish, and destructive to the good and happiness of mankind.

"4th. That no man or set of men are entitled to separate or exclusive public emoluments or privileges from the community, but in consideration of public services, which not being descendible, neither ought the offices of magistrate, legislator, or judge, or any other public office, to be hereditary.

"5th. That the legislative, executive, and judicial powers of government should be separate and distinct; and, that the members of the two first may be restrained from oppression by feeling and participating the public burdens, they should, at fixed periods, be reduced to a private station, return into the mass of the people, and the vacancies be supplied by certain and regular elections, in which all or any part of the former members to be eligible or ineligible, as the rules of the Constitution of government, and the laws, shall direct.

"6th. That the elections of representatives in the legislature ought to be free and frequent, and all men having sufficient evidence of permanent common interest with, and attachment to, the community, ought to have the right of suffrage; and no aid, charge, tax, or fee, can be set, rated, or levied, upon the people without their own consent, or that of their representatives, so elected; nor can they be bound by any law to which they have not, in like manner, assented, for the public good.

"7th. That all power of suspending laws, or the execution of laws, by any authority, without the consent of the representatives of the people in the legislature, is injurious to their rights, and ought not to be exercised.

"8th. That, in all criminal and capital prosecutions, a man hath a right to demand the cause and nature of his accusation, to be confronted with the accusers and witnesses, to call for evidence, and be allowed counsel in his favor, and to a fair and speedy trial by an impartial jury of his vicinage, without whose unanimous consent he cannot be found guilty, (except in the government of the land and naval forces;) nor can he be compelled to give evidence against himself.

"9th. That no freeman ought to be taken, imprisoned, or disseized of his freehold, liberties, privileges, or franchises, or outlawed, or exiled, or in any manner destroyed, or deprived of his life, liberty, or property, but by the law of the land.

"10th. That every freeman restrained of his liberty is entitled to a remedy, to inquire into the lawfulness thereof, and to remove the same, if unlawful, and that such remedy ought not to be denied nor delayed.

"11th. That, in controversies respecting property, and in suits between man and man, the ancient trial by jury is one of the greatest securities to the rights of the people, and to remain sacred and inviolable.

"12th. That every freeman ought to find a certain remedy, by recourse to the laws, for all injuries and wrongs he may receive in his person, property, or character. He ought to obtain right and justice freely, without sale, completely and without denial, promptly and without delay, and that all establishments or regulations contravening these rights are oppressive and unjust.

"13th. That excessive bail ought not to be required, nor excessive fines imposed, nor cruel and unusual punishments inflicted.

"14th. That every freeman has a right to be secure from all unreasonable searches and seizures of his person, his papers, and property; all warrants, therefore, to search suspected places, or seize any freeman, his papers, or property, without information on oath (or affirmation of a person religiously scrupulous of taking an oath) of legal and sufficient cause, are grievous and oppressive; and all general warrants to search suspected places, or to apprehend any suspected person, without specially naming or describing the place or person, are dangerous, and ought not to be granted.

"15th. That the people have a right peaceably to assemble together to consult for the common good, or to instruct their representatives; and that every freeman has a right to petition or apply to the legislature for redress of grievances.

"16th. That the people have a right to freedom of speech, and of writing and publishing their sentiments; that the freedom of the press is one of the greatest bulwarks of liberty, and ought not to be violated.

"17th. That the people have a right to keep and bear arms; that a well-regulated militia, composed of the body of the people trained to arms, is the proper, natural, and safe defence of a free state; that standing armies, in time of peace, are dangerous to liberty, and therefore ought to be avoided, as far as the circumstances and protection of the community will admit; and that, in all cases, the military should be under strict subordination to, and governed by, the civil power.

"18th. That no soldier in time of peace ought to be quartered in any house without the consent of the owner, and in time of war in such manner only as the law directs.

"19th. That any person religiously scrupulous of bearing arms ought to be exempted, upon payment of an equivalent to employ another to bear arms in his stead.

"20th. That religion, or the duty which we owe to our Creator, and the manner of discharging it, can be directed only by reason and conviction, not by force or violence; and therefore all men have an equal, natural, and unalienable right to the free exercise of religion, according to the dictates of conscience, and that no particular religious sect or society ought to be favored or established, by law, in preference to others."

Amendments to the Constitution

1st. That each state in the Union shall respectively retain every power, jurisdiction, and right, which is not by this Constitution delegated to the Congress of the United States, or to the departments of the federal government.

"2d. That there shall be one representative for every thirty thousand according to the enumeration or census mentioned in the Constitution until the whole number of representatives amounts to two hundred; after which, that number shall be continued or increased, as Congress shall direct, upon the principles fixed in the Constitution, by apportioning the representatives of each state to some greater number of people, from time to time, as population increases.

"3d. When the Congress shall lay direct taxes or excises, they shall immediately inform the executive power of each state, of the quota of such state, according to the census herein directed, which is proposed to be thereby raised; and if the legislature of any state shall pass a law which shall be effectual for raising such quota at the time required by Congress, the taxes and excises laid by Congress shall not be collected in such state.

"4th. That the members of the Senate and House of Representatives shall be ineligible to, and incapable of holding, any civil office under the authority of the United States, during the time for which they shall respectively be elected.

"5th. That the journals of the proceedings of the Senate and House of Representatives shall be published at least once in every year, except such parts thereof, relating to treaties, alliances, or military operations, as, in their judgment, require secrecy.

"6th. That a regular statement and account of the receipts and expenditures of public money shall be published at least once a year.

"7th. That no commercial treaty shall be ratified without the concurrence of two thirds of the whole number of the members of the Senate; and no treaty ceding, contracting, restraining, or suspending, the territorial rights or claims of the United States, or any of them, or their, or any of their rights or claims to fishing in the American seas, or navigating the American rivers, shall be made, but in cases of the most urgent and extreme necessity; nor shall any such treaty be ratified without the concurrence of three fourths of the whole number of the members of both houses respectively.

"8th. That no navigation law, or law regulating commerce,

shall be passed without the consent of two thirds of the members present, in both houses.

"9th. That no standing army, or regular troops, shall be raised, or kept up, in time of peace, without the consent of two thirds of the members present, in both houses.

"10th. That no soldier shall be enlisted for any longer term than four years, except in time of war, and then for no longer term than the continuance of the war.

"11th. That each state respectively shall have the power to provide for organizing, arming, and disciplining its own militia, whensoever Congress shall omit or neglect to provide for the same. That the militia shall not be subject to martial law, except when in actual service, in time of war, invasion, or rebellion; and when not in the actual service of the United States, shall be subject only to such fines, penalties, and punishments, as shall be directed or inflicted by the laws of its own state.

"12th. That the exclusive power of legislation given to Congress over the federal town and its adjacent district, and other places, purchased or to be purchased by Congress of any of the states, shall extend only to such regulations as respect the police and good government thereof.

"13th. That no person shall be capable of being President of the United States for more than eight years in any term of sixteen years.

"14th. That the judicial power of the United States shall be vested in one Supreme Court, and in such courts of admiralty as Congress may from time to time ordain and establish in any of the different states. The judicial power shall extend to all cases in law and equity arising under treaties made, or which shall be made, under the authority of the United States; to all cases affecting ambassadors, other foreign ministers, and consuls; to all cases of admiralty and maritime jurisdiction; to controversies to which the United States shall be a party; to controversies between two or more states, and between parties claiming lands under the grants of different states. In all cases affecting ambassadors, other foreign ministers, and consuls, and those in which a state shall be a party, the Supreme Court shall have original jurisdiction; in all other cases before mentioned, the Supreme Court shall have appellate jurisdiction, as to matters of law only, except in cases of equity, and of admiralty, and maritime jurisdiction, in which the Supreme Court shall have appellate jurisdiction both as to law and fact, with such exceptions and under such regulations as the Congress shall make; but the judicial power of the United States shall extend to no case where the cause of action shall have originated before the ratification of the Constitution, except in disputes between states about their territory, disputes between persons claiming lands under the grants of different states, and suits for debts due to the United States.

"15th. That, in criminal prosecutions, no man shall be restrained in the exercise of the usual and accustomed right of challenging or excepting to the jury.

"16th. That Congress shall not alter, modify, or interfere in the times, places, or manner of holding elections for senators and representatives, or either of them, except when the legislature of any state shall neglect, refuse, or be disabled, by invasion or rebellion, to prescribe the same.

"17th. That those clauses which declare that Congress shall not exercise certain powers, be not interpreted, in any manner whatsoever, to extend the powers of Congress; but that they be construed either as making exceptions to the specified powers where this shall be the case, or otherwise, as inserted merely for greater caution.

"18th. That the laws ascertaining the compensation of senators and representatives for their services, be postponed, in their operation, until after the election of representatives immediately succeeding the passing thereof; that excepted which shall first be passed on the subject.

"19th. That some tribunal other than the Senate be provided for trying impeachments of senators.

"20th. That the salary of a judge shall not be increased or diminished during his continuance in office, otherwise than by general regulations of salary, which may take place on a revision of the subject at stated periods of not less than seven years, to commence from the time such salaries shall be first ascertained by Congress."

———————

And the Convention do, in the name and behalf of the people of this commonwealth, enjoin it upon their representatives in Congress to exert all their influence, and use all reasonable and legal methods, to obtain a ratification of the foregoing alterations and provisions, in the manner provided by the 5th article of the said Constitution; and, in all congressional laws to be passed in the mean time, to conform to the spirit of these amendments, as far as the said Constitution will admit.

And so much of the said amendments as is contained in the first twenty articles, constituting the bill of rights, being read again, *Resolved,* That this Convention doth concur therein.

Appendix M

William Schley's Commentary

on Magna Carta (1826)[1]

HIS statute, which, by the English writers is called *"The great charter of English liberties,"* and which Sir Edward Coke declares to be, only a recognition and declaration of the ancient common law of the realm, is undoubtedly the foundation, and great corner stone of that system of civil and political liberty, which the English people enjoy in a greater degree, than any other nation, except the citizens of the United States of America. For, although on a cursory view of this charter, it would seem, that it was rather a matter of compromise between the King and the great Barons of the kingdom, whereby he was restrained from excess in many of the feodal exactions, and the Barons and great Lords secured in what they considered their rights, according to the feodal notions of the times; yet upon a critical view of this instrument, it will be seen, that many of its provisions are calculated to secure the subject in the enjoyment of the fundamental principles of rational liberty.

The fourteenth chapter ordains, "that no freeman shall be amerced, but after the manner of the fault, saving to him his contenement; and that by the oath of honest and lawful men of the vicinage." And the twenty-ninth chapter declares, "that no

[1] William Schley, *Digest of the English Statutes of Force in the State of Georgia* (Philadelphia, 1826), pp. 52–59.

freeman shall be taken, or imprisoned, or disseised of his free-hold, or liberties, or free customs, or be outlawed, or exiled, or any otherwise destroyed, &c. but by lawful judgment of his peers, or by the law of the land." These two chapters of them-selves, independently of many other valuable provisions in this statute, constitute a firm basis of freedom, and contain almost all the vital principles of liberty.

But, beautiful and salutary as these regulations may seem *on paper,* experience has proved to the English people, that the "artificial ties of parchment compact," without virtue and in-telligence in the people, are totally impotent and unavailing against the encroachments of power and ambition. And so repeated were the encroachments of the crown upon the char-tered liberties of the subject, that Magna Charta hath been confirmed above thirty times, and commanded to be put in execution from the first Edward to Henry the fifth. This fact however, serves to show that the principles of liberty were deeply interwoven in the character and feelings of the nation, and that although a powerful aristocracy, aided by an ambi-tious and tyrannical prince, did often disregard the rights of the people, and tread under foot their dearest privileges; yet as often did they procure a parliamentary declaration of their rights and liberties as contained in the great charter. But these declarations served very little to meliorate the condition of the subject; for, as often as they were made, they were violated and disregarded. The last confirming act was passed in the fourth year of Henry the fifth, A.D. 1416; and from this time to the reign of Charles the first, A.D. 1627, a period of 211 years, the people seem to have quietly submitted to the yoke of arbitrary power: for during the most of this time, the principles of the great charter were set at naught, and personal liberty borne down by unlawful prerogative.

From the time of Magna Charta, A.D. 1225, up to the third year of Charles the first, A.D. 1627, a period of more than four hundred years, the principles of English liberty, as contained in the twenty-ninth chapter of the great charter, seem never to have been properly understood and enforced. Nor indeed have we any reason to believe that the people of England ever were in the practical enjoyment of civil liberty, either before or after the grant of this charter, until the spirit of freedom imperfectly shone forth under the reign of Charles the first, when the oppressions of the times drew forth the *petition of right*. For the charter itself, was not a declaration of the rights and privileges of the people, by the people themselves, in whom alone all power and authority are, and of right ought to be vested: but it was a grant of privileges and immunities, proceeding from the sovereign, as matter of mere grace and favor, and for which he required and obtained in return, one fifteenth part of all the subjects' moveables.

The English people, during the whole of this time, from the ninth year of Henry the third, A.D. 1225; and indeed from long anterior to that period, up to the reign of Charles the first, were the subjects of arbitrary power, almost without a struggle to better their condition. This power was alternately exercised by the houses of York and Lancaster, as either happened to prevail, from the year 1399, when Henry the fourth raised in his own person, the house of Lancaster to the English Throne, by deposing and murdering Richard the second, until the year 1509, when these two houses were united in the person of Henry the eighth. But this union did not meliorate the condition of the English subject; for there was, not only a union of title to the crown, but a concentration of all the vices, profligacy, and tyranny of both the ruling factions, in this despotic prince. And, (excepting the short reign of his son, Edward the sixth) the succeeding reigns of Mary, Elizabeth, James the first, and Charles the first, were not more favorable to the enjoyment of personal rights, than that of Henry, or his predecessors.

We may, therefore, date the era of English liberty from the third year of Charles the first, A.D. 1627, when, for the first time, there was a formal declaration of liberty, in the shape of a petition of right made by the parliament, and the extorted assent of the King obtained. Magna Charta was made the foundation of this petition, the principles of which had lain dormant during the whole intermediate period: and the twenty-ninth chapter, which was intended to secure the subject from illegal arrest and confinement, had been totally disregarded until reiterated in this petition. Charles unwillingly granted it, although he subsequently made still more ample concessions, which perhaps were one cause of the fatal rupture between him and his parliament—brought him to the scaffold—and left the nation in a disturbed and unsettled condition, having by violent measures passed from one extreme to another. From oppressive monarchy to licentious liberty, or rather anarchy, a condition infinitely worse than that from which they had passed, as the worst government is better than none at all.

The commonwealth which succeeded the death of Charles, continued only twelve years; when in the year 1660, the monarchy was restored in the person of Charles the second, the son of Charles the first. The reign of this King, who was by no means a patron of civil liberty, was disgraced by the convictions of Russel and Sidney, and many others who were tried by packed juries, and before an unprincipled and time serving bench. Yet, averse as he was to liberal principles and personal liberty; still, during his reign, by a concurrence of fortunate circumstances, more perhaps was done to unfetter estates, and relieve the nation from the burthen of military tenures; and for the personal liberty and security of the subject, than ever had been done before. The statute of 12 Charles 2, chap. 24, for the abolition of military tenures, produced a change in the English law of real property much better suited to the spirit and genius of a commercial people, and more consonant to the feelings and principles of the age, than the feudal burthens of the old law. And the *Habeas Corpus* act, 31 Charles 2, chap. 2, which was produced by the confinement of an obscure individual, completely and effectually secured the subject against illegal and arbitrary imprisonment, and may well be called the great bulwark of the constitution, being a practical enforcement of the twenty-ninth chapter of the great charter. These two very important statutes, the one in relation to the property, and the other to the persons of individuals, formed a second Magna Charta, more effectual and beneficial even than the first, and may be called a new era in the history of English liberty.

To the wicked, sanguinary and turbulent reign of this King, succeeded that of his deluded brother, James the second, which was more intolerable even than that of Charles. James remained on the throne only about three years, during which time he attempted to enslave the nation; but the people had began to understand their rights, and resisting the undue and tyrannical exercise of royal prerogative, they forced him to abandon both his enterprise and his throne: and with him ended the reign of the house of Stewart.

The revolution of 1688, which ended by the abdication and flight of James the second, produced an entire new state of things, and may be considered as the consummation of that portion of civil liberty which Englishmen now enjoy. For the crown was then tendered to William, prince of Orange, and Mary his wife, the daughter of James the second, upon certain conditions which are particularly enumerated and set forth in the Bill of rights, and act of settlement, 1 Wm. and Ma. sess. 2, cha. 2, A.D. 1689; and which very materially restrain the royal prerogative, and extend and secure the rights and liberties of the subject. It is however to be lamented, that whilst the revolution abrogated the absurd doctine of *"the divine right of kings,"* and established the true and rational position, that the power of the crown flowed from no other source than that of a contract with the people, which is virtually declared in the bill of rights and act of settlement: and William and Mary ascended the throne in consequence of an express capitulation with them, that the parliament should have lost so favourable an opportunity of retrenching those prerogatives of the crown to which they imputed all the calamities of the kingdom. One of these is the power of the King to convoke, adjourn, prorogue, and dissolve the parliament at his pleasure, which in the hands of an aspiring and tyrannical prince, is a most dangerous enemy to the liberty and happiness of the people.

Much however was done towards perfecting the emancipation of the kingdom, which at that period enjoyed more of civil and political liberty than any other nation; the foundation and principles of which are to be found in *Magna Charta*—the *Petition of Right*—the *Abolition of Military Tenures*—the *Habeas Corpus act*—and the *Bill of Rights and Act of Settlement*. These taken together form what the English emphatically and exultingly call the ENGLISH CONSTITUTION.

Thus I have endeavored to give a concise history of the rise and progress of English liberty, with a view of showing the original foundation of our own. For, at this fortunate period, the first principles of our own free institutions were conveyed to this western hemisphere.

The colonies might with great propriety, be called *"a land of liberty,"*—having at their first emigration brought with them the principles of freedom as contained in the great charter, and successively improved in their political condition, in proportion as the principles of liberty were better understood and enforced in the mother country. The doctrines established by the revolution of 1688, were in accordance with the opinions and feelings of the colonies, who considered themselves entitled, as British subjects, to all the benefits flowing from them; and they were content to live under the English constitution, although it wanted a free, full, and equal representation of the people in the house of Commons. And nothing but an unwarrantable extension of royal prerogative, and a disposition in the English government to oppress the American people, in violation of the laws of England, and of the chartered rights of the colonies, produced that state of things, which finally eventuated in the independence of the United States.

When the colonies first opposed the aggressions of the crown and parliament, they had no idea of producing a separation between the two countries. Their object was merely to obtain a redress of their wrongs; and to this end, repeated petitions and remonstrances were made, all expressing the most loyal feelings, and claiming or asking only those rights and liberties to which they were entitled as British subjects. When, however, these were all disregarded, and new petitions produced only new violations of their rights—when the parliament assumed to itself the right to bind the colonies in all cases without their consent—and, when by repeated oppressions the burden became too heavy to be borne by a free people, they indignantly threw off the trammels of tyranny—declared themselves free and independent of the mother country, and by an appeal to arms, supported that declaration to the emancipation of thirteen states, from the oppressions of a weak and misguided king.

After the termination of the war, and, when by the treaty of

1783, England had acknowledged the independence of the states, it then became necessary that they should agree upon, and settle some form of government, and establish certain fundamental principles upon which it should be administered. This, at first view, would appear to have been no easy matter, when we reflect on the various and conflicting interests by which the different sections of the country were actuated. But a people who had been united in the cause of liberty against a common enemy, and had obtained their object by the combined exertions of all, were not disposed to endanger the union, by a pertinacious adherence to every right and benefit, which they would have been willing, under other circumstances, to have insisted upon. It was necessary in the formation of the federal government, that each state should give up a part of its sovereignty, delegating to this general government such powers as were necessary for its existence, and to enable it efficiently to sustain its own dignity, and to protect the individual states. This was accordingly done by the original framers of the constitution, and their acts were ratified by the states. But, neither the convention who formed, nor the states who ratified this constitution, had the most distant idea, that the doctrine of constructive powers would be carried to the alarming extent, contended for by some politicians of the present day; and which threatens the total destruction of state rights, and state sovereignty. If this doctrine be persisted in, and no remedy provided for the evil, the federal government, like Aaron's rod, will swallow up the state governments, and a final consolidation of the whole, will put an end to that beautiful system of liberty which is now the pride and boast of the free people of these states.

The idea of a written constitution, such as that of the United States, and of the individual states, is perhaps unprecedented in other countries, and was most probably suggested by the charters of the different colonies, which pointed out the tenures by which their political rights and immunities were holden, and were a recorded system of fundamental law, for the guidance both of the people themselves, and of the delegated holders of their authority. Our constitutions, however, differ widely from those charters in nature, the latter being mere grants of privileges from the crown, which could be repealed at the royal pleasure; whilst the former are voluntary limitations of their own privileges on the part of persons who recognise no political superior. And these constitutions are admirably adapted, not only to secure the liberty of the people, but to protect the independence of the states. For it is worthy of observation, that the government of the United States, has no other powers than those specially delegated to it by the constitution; whilst all other powers not given by that instrument, nor prohibited by it to the states, are reserved to the states respectively, or to the people. But the state governments possess the power to do all things that are not morally impossible, or prohibited by the constitution of the United States, or of the individual states.

In regard to the form of government which should be adopted, no difference of opinion seems to have existed among the members of the convention. All had in view a free republic, and equal representation, with a chief magistrate, who should be chosen by the people. They had suffered enough from hereditary monarchy and royal prerogative, and therefore took care to limit, within prescribed bounds, the powers of the President. And whilst the charters of the colonies which have been adverted to, were most probably the original cause of the prevalence of written constitutions amongst us; so also was the English constitution, or rather, Magna Charta—the Habeas Corpus act, and the Bill of Rights, the original foundation and basis of the liberty of the citizen, as contained in those constitutions. For, by a comparison of the two systems, it will be seen that, the former contains many of the valuable provisions incorporated in the latter. There is, however, this important difference between them: the one is the act of the sovereign conferring privileges on his subjects, and unwillingly consenting to an abridgment of his ancient prerogatives; whilst the other is the act of the people, forming a government of their own choice, and limiting the power of their rulers, whom also they create by their own free and unbiassed suffrages. "And the fact that such was the origin of our constitutions, will serve to explain the facility with which they were introduced, the ready acquiescence of the country in their establishment, and the immediate efficaciousness which they enjoyed when put in operation. For they were not, either in principle or in form, a radical innovation upon the social order, calculated to impress the people unfavorably by their strangeness, or to meet with obstacles to success on account of the novelty of their design. They were old and tried friends reappearing under more imposing auspices."

Appendix N

Due Process Provisions in

State Constitutions[1]

1. THE most common due process provision in state constitutions is that which is identical to the relevant part of the Fifth Amendment to the Federal Constitution. The typical state provision reads: "No person shall be deprived of life, liberty, or property, without due process of law." [2] (The comparable part of the Fifth Amendment reads: "No person shall . . . be deprived of life, liberty, or property, without due process of law. . . .") Twenty-five States have this provision.

Alaska (1959) : Art. I, §7.
Arizona (1912) : Art. II, §4.
Colorado (1876) : Art. II, §25.
Florida (1887) : Art. I, §12.
Georgia (1945) : Art. I, §1, para. 3.
Hawaii (1959) : Art. I, §4.
Illinois (1870) : Art. II, §2.
Iowa (1857) : Art. I, §9.
Louisiana (1921) : Art. I, §2.
Michigan (1964) : Art. I, §17.

Minnesota (1857 as amended 1904) : Art. I, §7.
Mississippi (1890) : Art. III, §14.
Missouri (1945) : Art. I, §10.
Montana (1889) : Art. III, §27.
Nebraska (1875) : Art. I, §3.
Nevada (1864) : Art. I, §8.
New Mexico (1912) : Art. II, §18.
New York (1939) : Art. I, §6.

---

[1] Dates are those of the effective dates of the respective constitutions.

[2] There are variations in the provisions of Florida, Georgia, Louisiana, Michigan, Minnesota, Mississippi, Nevada, South Carolina, and West Virginia which for present purposes are unimportant.

Oklahoma (1907) : Art. II, §7.
South Carolina (1895) : Art. I,
   §5.
South Dakota (1889) : Art. VI,
   §2.

Utah (1896) : Art. I, §7.
Washington (1889) : Art. I, §3.
West Virginia (1872) : Art. III,
   §10.
Wyoming (1890) : Art. I, §6.

2. Four States have substantially the same provision as (1) but appearing in the context of provisions dealing with criminal prosecutions although they are not in terms so restricted (that is, they read "no person") .

> California (1879) : Art. I, §13.
> Connecticut (1965) : Art. I, §8.
> Idaho (1890) : Art. I, §13.
> North Dakota (1889) : Art. I, §13.

3. Five States have substantially the same provision as (1) except that literally the provision is limited to the accused in criminal prosecutions: "In all criminal prosecutions, the accused has a right . . . nor shall he be deprived. . . ."

> Alabama (1901) : Art. I, §6.
> Delaware (1897) : Art. I, §7.
> Kentucky (1891) : Sect. 11.
> Pennyslvania (1874) : Art. I, §9.
> Rhode Island (1843) : Art. I, §10.

Of these five States, Alabama's provision uses the words "due process of law"; the other four use the language of chapter 39 of Magna Carta: "by the judgment of his peers or by the law of the land."

4. Maine's provision is like that of the last four States in (3) , except that it adds "or privileges" to "life, liberty, or property." Maine (1820) : Art. I, § 6.

5. Vermont's provision, also in a criminal context, is restricted to deprivation of "liberty": "Nor can any person be justly deprived of his liberty, except by the laws of the land, or the judgment of his peers." Vermont (1793) : Chap. I, Art. 10.

6. Two States provide that "No person shall be held to answer for a criminal offense without due process of law." In

Minnesota, this is in addition to the provision in (1). Minnesota (1857 as amended 1904): Art. I, § 7. In Wisconsin it is in lieu of (1). Wisconsin (1848): Art. I, § 8.

7. In seven States, in lieu of the more common provision noted in (1), the language extending the protection of the "law of the land" or the "due course of the law of the land" to life, liberty, and property is amplified by reference to "liberties or privileges," "privileges or immunities," etc. In some cases, such provisions come close to the language of chapter 39 of Magna Carta; Massachusetts (1780), for example, provides that no person shall be "arrested, imprisoned, despoiled, or deprived of his property, immunities, or privileges, put out of the protection of the law, exiled, or deprived of his life, liberty, or estate, but by the judgment of his peers, or the law of the land."

> Arkansas (1874): Art. II, §21.
> Maryland (1867): Decl. of Rights, Art. 23.
> Massachusetts (1780): Part I, Art. XII.
> New Hampshire (1784): Part I, Art. XV.
> North Carolina (1868): Art. I, §17.
> Tennessee (1870): Art. I, §8.
> Texas (1876): Art. I, §19.

8. Three States having the provision noted in (1) also prohibit disfranchisement or deprivation of rights or privileges secured to other citizens except by the law of the land.

> Hawaii (1959): Art. I, §6.
> New York (1939): Art. I, §1.
> Minnesota (1857): Art. I, §2.

9. In four States there is no due process provision other than that giving every man "remedy by due course of law" for injuries to his person, property, or reputation. (See Appendix O, *infra*.)

> Indiana (1851): Art. I, §12.
> Kansas (1861): Bill of Rights §18.
> Ohio (1851): Art. I, §16.
> Oregon (1859): Art. I, §10.

Note that of the States listed in (2) through (6) —States with due process provisions in one way or another more restricted than the typical provision noted in (1) —all except California have a provision giving every person a remedy for injuries, by due process or due course of law. (See Appendix O, *infra.*)

10. In the constitution of one State, New Jersey, there is no due process provision.

11. Oklahoma, in addition to the common due process provision (1), has another prohibiting transportation of any person out of the State without his consent, except by due process of law (but saving extradition laws, etc.). Oklahoma (1907) : Art II, § 29.

12. In two recent constitutions, the provision noted in (1) is followed by a provision which, while not using the language of due process, applies the concept to legislative and executive investigations by requiring "fair and just" treatment in the course of such investigations.

Alaska (1959) : Art. I, §7.
Michigan (1964) : Art. I, §17.

13. Virginia is the only State having separate provisions for criminal prosecutions and property. Together the effect is that of the common provision noted in (1). "That in criminal prosecutions a man . . . shall not be deprived of life or liberty, except by the law of the land or the judgment of his peers. . . ." Virginia (1902) : Art. I, § 8. "No person shall be deprived of his property without due process of law. . . ." *Ibid.,* Art. I, § 11.

Appendix O

State Constitutional Provisions Prohibiting the Sale, Denial, or Delay of Justice, Provisions That the Courts Shall Be Open, Provisions Guaranteeing Remedies by Due Course of Law, and Provisions for a Speedy Trial.

Sale, Denial, or Delay of Justice

1. FOURTEEN States have provisions which, drawing upon chapter 40 of Magna Carta, require that justice (or right and justice) shall be administered "without sale, denial, or delay."

Alabama (1901) : Art. I, §13.
Colorado (1876) : Art. II, §6.
Connecticut (1965) : Art. I, §10.
Florida (1887) : Art. I, §4.
Kentucky (1891) : Sect. 14.
Mississippi (1890) : Art. III, §24.
Missouri (1945) : Art. I, §14.
Montana (1889) : Art. III, §6.
North Carolina (1868) : Art. I, §35.
North Dakota (1889) : Art. I, §22.
Pennsylvania (1874) : Art. I, §11.
Tennessee (1870) : Art. I, §17.
West Virginia (1872) : Art. III, §17.
Wyoming (1890) : Art. I, §8.

2. Eleven States have the same provision in somewhat expanded form: "Freely and without purchase [or sale], completely [or fully], and without denial, promptly [or speedily], and without delay."

Arkansas (1874) : Art. II, §13.
Illinois (1870) : Art. II, §19.
Indiana (1851) : Art. I, §12.
Maine (1820) : Art. I, §19.
Maryland (1867) : Decl. of Rights, Art. 19.
Massachusetts (1780) : Part I, Art. XI.

Minnesota (1857) : Art. I, §8.
New Hampshire (1784) : Part I, Art. XIV.
Rhode Island (1843) : Art. I, §5.
Vermont (1793) : Chap. I, Art. 4.
Wisconsin (1848) : Art. I, §9.

3. Twelve States have essentially the same provision but vary in minor details, for example, by omitting mention of denial or of sale, by qualifying "delay" to read "unnecessary delay," by adding "prejudice," etc.

Arizona (1912) : Art. II, §11.
Delaware (1897) : Art. I, §9.
Idaho (1890) : Art. I, §18.
Kansas (1861) : Bill of Rights, §18.
Louisiana (1921) : Art. I, §6.
Nebraska (1875) : Art. I, §13.

Ohio (1851) : Art. I, §16.
Oklahoma (1907) : Art. II, §6.
Oregon (1859) : Art. I, §10.
South Dakota (1889) : Art. VI, §20.
Utah (1896) : Art. I, §11.
Washington (1889) : Art. I, §10.

Courts to Be Open

1. Nineteen States provide that "all courts shall be open":

Alabama (1901) : Art. I, §13.
Connecticut (1965) : Art. I, §10.
Delaware (1897) : Art. I, §9.
Florida (1887) : Art. I, §4.
Indiana (1851) : Art. I, §12.
Kentucky (1891) : Sect. 14.
Louisiana (1921) : Art. I, §6.
Mississippi (1890) : Art. III, §24.
Nebraska (1875) : Art. I, §13.
North Carolina (1868) : Art. I, §35.
North Dakota (1889) : Art. I, §22.

Ohio (1851) : Art. I, §16.
Pennsylvania (1874) : Art. I, §11.
South Dakota (1889) : Art. VI, §20.
Tennessee (1870) : Art. I, §17.
Texas (1876) : Art. I, §13.
Utah (1896) : Art. I, §11.
West Virginia (1872) : Art. III, §17.
Wyoming (1890) : Art. I, §8.

2. Five States provide that the courts shall be "open to every person":

Colorado (1876) : Art. II, §6.
Idaho (1890) : Art. I, §18.
Missouri (1945) : Art. I, §14.
Montana (1889) : Art. III, §6.
Oklahoma (1907) : Art. II, §6.

Remedies

1. Thirty-two States provide that every person is entitled to a remedy by due process of law, due course of law, in the laws, etc., for any injury to his person, property, or reputation (or character) :

Alabama (1901) : Art. I, §13.
Arkansas * (1874) : Art. II, §13.
Colorado (1876) : Art. II, §6.
Connecticut (1965) : Art. I, §10.
Delaware (1897) : Art. I, §9.
Florida (1887) : Art. I, §4.
Illinois * (1870) : Art. II, §19.
Indiana (1851) : Art. I, §12.
Kansas (1861) : Bill of Rights, §18.
Kentucky (1891) : Sect. 14.
Massachusetts * (1780) : Part I, Art. XI.
Minnesota * (1857) : Art. I, §8.
Mississippi (1890) : Art. III, §24.
Missouri * (1945) : Art. I, §14.
Montana (1889) : Art. III, §6.
Nebraska (1875) : Art. I, §13.
New Hampshire * (1784) : Part I, Art. XIV.
North Carolina (1868) : Art. I, §35.

North Dakota (1889) : Art. I, §22.
Ohio (1851) : Art. I, §16.
Oklahoma * (1907) : Art. II, §6.
Oregon (1859) : Art. I, §10.
Pennsylvania (1874) : Art. I, §11.
Rhode Island * (1843) : Art. I, §5.
South Dakota (1889) : Art. VI, §20.
Tennessee (1870) : Art. I, §17.
Texas (1876) : Art. I, §13.
Utah (1896) : Art. I, §11.
Vermont * (1793) : Chap. I, Art. IV.
West Virginia (1872) : Art. III, §17.
Wisconsin * (1848) : Art. I, §9.
Wyoming (1890) : Art. I, §8.

2. Five States have variants in the above provision:

Idaho (1890) : Art. I, §18 (speaks of injuries to person, property, or character but

does not speak of due process or its equivalent) .

* The ten States so marked specify a "certain" remedy.

Louisiana (1921): Art. I, §6 (speaks of injuries to "rights" as well as to person, property, or reputation; remedy to be "adequate").

Maine (1820): Art. I, §19 (speaks of injuries to "immunities" as well as to person etc.).

Maryland (1867): Decl. of Rights, Art. 19 (speaks of injuries only to person or property).

South Carolina (1895): Art. I, §15 (speaks of "wrongs sustained" without specifying).

Speedy and Public Trial

1. Forty States have provisions (which appear along with the provision for trial by jury) giving an accused the right to a speedy and public trial.

Alabama (1901): Art. I, §6.
Alaska (1959): Art. I, §11.
Arizona (1912): Art. II, §24.
Arkansas (1874): Art. II, §10.
California (1879): Art. I, §13.
Colorado (1876): Art. II, §16.
Connecticut (1965): Art. I, §8.
Delaware (1897): Art. I, §7.
Florida (1887): Art. I, §10.
Georgia (1945): Art. I, §1, para. 5.
Hawaii (1959): Art. I, §11.
Idaho (1890): Art. I, §13.
Illinois (1870): Art. II, §9.
Iowa (1857): Art. I, §10.
Kansas (1861): Bill of Rights, §10.
Kentucky (1891): Sect. 11.
Louisiana (1921): Art. I, §9.
Maine (1820): Art. I, §6.
Michigan (1964): Art. I, §20.
Minnesota (1857): Art. I, §6.
Mississippi (1890): Art. III, §26.
Missouri (1945): Art. I, §18 (a).
Montana (1889): Art. III, §16.

Nebraska (1875): Art. I, §11.
New Jersey (1948): Art. I, §10.
New Mexico (1912): Art. II, §14.
North Dakota (1889): Art. I, §13.
Ohio (1851): Art. I, §10.
Oklahoma (1907): Art. II, §20.
Pennsylvania (1874): Art. I, §9.
Rhode Island (1843): Art. I, §10.
South Carolina (1895): Art. I, §18.
South Dakota (1889): Art. VI, §7.
Tennessee (1870): Art. I, §9.
Texas (1876): Art. I, §10.
Utah (1896): Art. I, §12.
Vermont (1793): Chap. I, Art. §10.
Washington (1889): Art. I, §22.
West Virginia (1872): Art. III, §14.
Wisconsin (1848): Art. I, §7.

2. Three other States give simply the right to a speedy trial:

> Maryland (1867) : Decl. of Rights, Art. 21.
> Virginia (1902) : Art. I, §8.
> Wyoming (1890) : Art. I, §10.

3. Two others give simply the right to a public trial:

> Indiana (1851) : Art. I, §13.
> Oregon (1859) : Art. I, §11.

Appendix P

Statutory Compilations

Which Include the Text

of Magna Carta

THE following compilations of state laws include the text of Magna Carta:

California: *West's Ann. Calif. Codes,* volume containing Calif. Const., Arts, 12 to end, p. 759 (1954).

Connecticut: *Conn. Gen. Stats. Ann.,* Vol. 1, p. 685 (West, 1967).

Delaware: *Del. Code Ann.,* Vol. 1, p. 1 (Edward Thompson and West, 1953).

Florida: *Fla. Stats. Ann.,* Vol. 25, p. 1 (Harrison and West, 1944).

Illinois: *Smith-Hurd Ill. Ann. Stats.,* volume containing Ill. Const. Arts. VI to End and Organic Acts, p. 711 (1964).

Iowa: *Ia. Code Ann.,* Vol. 1, p. 33 (West, 1949).

Maine: *Maine Rev. Stats. Ann.,* Vol. 1, p. 513 (West, 1964).

Massachusetts: *Mass. Gen. Laws*

Ann., Vol. 1, p. 739 (West, 1958).

Michigan: *Mich. Stats. Ann.,* Vol. 1, p. 1 (Callaghan, 1965 rev.), and *Mich. Comp. Laws Ann.,* Vol. 1, p. 1 (West, 1967).

Minnesota: *Minn. Stats. Ann.,* Vol. 1, p. 109 (West, 1946).

Missouri: *Vernon's Ann. Mo. Stats.,* Vol. 2, p. 581 (1951).

Montana: *Rev. Codes of Mont. 1947,* Repl. Vol. 1, Pt. 1, p. 1 (Allen Smith, 1957).

New Jersey: *N.J. Stats. Ann.,* Constitution, p. 715 (West, 1954).

New York: *McKinney's Cons. Laws of N.Y. Ann.,* Bk. 2, Pt. 2, p. 493 (1954).

North Dakota: *N. Dak. Century*

Code, Vol. 13, p. 1 (Allen Smith, 1960).

Oklahoma: *Okla. Stats. Ann.,* volume containing Okla. Const. Arts. V to end, p. 937 (West, 1952).

South Dakota: *S. Dak. Code of 1939,* Vol. 2, p. 3 (State Pub. Co., n.d.).

Texas: *Vernon's Ann. Const. of the State of Texas,* Vol. 3, p. 675 (1955).

Wisconsin: *West's Wisconsin Stats. Ann.,* Vol. 1, p. 785 (1957).

Wyoming: *Wyoming Stats. 1957 Ann.,* Vol. 1, p. 1 (Michie, 1959).

Table of Cases

Index

Abridgement, by Bacon, 132n
Act of Settlement of 1701, 181, 182, 210, 214, 369
Acton, John E. E. D., 1st Baron, 224
Acts of Privileges to a Freeman (Pa.) , 92, 93-95, 98
Adams, John: and Massachusetts Constitution, 209-11, 370; and Otis' argument on writs of assistance, 133-36, 158, 211; and Stamp Act controversy, 150, 158-63, 426-29; compared with Samuel, 156, 163, 164-65, 167, 169; defense of British soldiers in Boston Massacre case, 161, 163, 164; defense of John Hancock, 161-63; description, education and career, 156-57, 158, 164, 217; intellectual approach, 163, 164-65, 167, 169, 193n; judiciary appointments by, 276-77; library of, 112, 124, 125, 211; on closing of Boston courts, 158, 159-60, 161; on common law as stating colo-nists' rights, 132; on English constitution, 159, 160, 163-64, 196-97; on factors making Revolution possible, 152; on legal education, 156; on right to jury trial, 162-63; on Samuel Adams, 165; on state constitutions, 164; use of Coke and Magna Carta by, 124

writings, 16, 146, 150, 158-61; *Autobiography,* 163; "Clarendon" letters, 160-61, 163; *A Defence of the Constitutions of Government of the United States,* 164; Diary, 158-59, 160-61, 165, 178, 186-87; *Dissertation on the Canon and Feudal Law,* 148-49, 158, 159
Adams, John Quincy, 267n
Adams, Peter, 157, 164
Adams, Randolph G., 130
Adams, Samuel, 164-69, 170; and Massachusetts Constitution of 1780, 209; and 1768 Massachusetts assembly address and peti-

The index was prepared by Miss Gwen Folsom. The author is much indebted to her for this work, as well as for her assistance in other aspects of preparing this book for publication.

Revolution, Russian, 203

Rhode Island:
  Colony, 20n, 105n, 140, 170; char-
    ters, 19, 20, 52, 96, 281-82
  State, 229, 231, 281-82, 286-87,
    289, 293-94

Richard I (the Lion-hearted), 6

Richard II, 15n

Richmond County, Va., 118-19

Rights of accused in criminal proceedings [*see also particular
  rights, such as* Notice and hearing, Due Process, Jury trial,
  etc.]: due process, 302, 339,
  348; in Massachusetts colonial
  law, 40, 43-44; indigents: court
  costs and expenses, 289-91, 313-
  14; indigents: furnishing counsel to (U.S. cases), 290-91;
  interrogation, 276; rights of accused to know basis of charges,
  68, 79, 83, 86-87, 91; sufficient
  time to appear and answer, 87

Rights of Englishmen: as reflected
  in American constitutionalism,
  272-73; and U.S. Constitution,
  221-31, 232-33, 240; asserted
  and defined in Continental
  Congress, 178-80, 199-200, 273;
  asserted by John Adams in
  Hancock's case, 162-63; asserted
  in colonial cases, 326-28; asserted in petition to Parliament
  on Boston Port Bill, 172; asserted in Stamp Act controversy, 145, 146-49, 166, 175,
  198-99, 273; attempts to legislate, in American colonies, 36,
  40, 54-55, 92-95, 98; based on
  compact theory, 101; basis of
  American statements of, after
  Revolution, 241; basis of colonial claims to, 34; Blackstone
  on Magna Carta and, 270-71;
  claimed by colonists, 30, 40, 61-
  63, 67, 72, 116, 118, 142, 166-67,
  174-78, 182-83, 251, 263-64, 320,
  343, 369, 372, 374; colonial
  lawyers' education respecting,

as affecting late prerevolutionary disputes, 12, 118, 125, 131-
32; George Mason on, 205-06;
guarantees in colonial charters,
11, 15-16, 18-20, 22-26, 41, 42,
50, 52n, 53-54, 57, 60, 63, 107,
140, 142, 151, 157, 271, 281-82,
369, 374; Henry Care on, 124,
125; in colonial sermons, 149,
157; in English colonies contrasted with those of other
countries, 18, 67, 151, 369; in
Maryland, 243; in Massachusetts, 37, 40, 41-42, 44, 96-97,
211, 372; in pamphlets and
resolutions, 128-29, 205-6; in
Pennsylvania, 90-92; in Virginia, 29, 140; James Otis on,
135-36; John Dickinson on,
144-45; Magna Carta as basis,
43-44, 106-7, 110-11, 112, 188-
202, 237, 270-71; New Hampshire assertion of Massachusetts
liberties, 51; of colonists, Board
of Trade counsel on, 103;
Penn on, 78-82, 83-85, 89, 370;
present status in England, 379-
81; Samuel Adams on, 165-69;
stated in early state constitutions, 164, 203, 206-7, 209-15;
William Henry Drayton on,
181-83

*Rights of the British Colonies As-
serted and Proved,* by Otis,
138, 146-47

Rights of the Colonists, by
S. Adams, 168

*Rights of the Commons of Eng-
land,* 118

*Rights of the Inhabitants of Mary-
land to the Benefit of the English Laws,* by Dulany the Elder,
61-63, 106, 129, 328

Roane, Spencer, 239

Roberts, Samuel, *Digest of Select
British Statutes,* 248-49, 253

Rochambeau, J. B. D. de Vimeur,
Comte de, 152

The Road from Runnymede

was composed, printed, and bound by
Kingsport Press, Inc., Kingsport, Tennessee.
The paper is Warren's 1854, and the
type is Baskerville with Bulmer initials.
Design is by Edward G. Foss.